THE OLD TRADITIONAL WAY OF LIFE

THE OLD TRADITIONAL WAY OF LIFE
Essays In Honor of Warren E. Roberts

Edited by

Robert E. Walls
and
George H. Schoemaker

with
Jennifer Livesay
Laura Dassow Walls

Guntis Šmidchens

Charles Frederick
Dee McEntire

Colleen Costello
Barbara Truesdell

TRICKSTER PRESS
Indiana University Folklore Institute
Bloomington, Indiana
1989

FRONTISPIECE: The Cover and frontispiece are courtesy of the Hohenberger Collection of the Lilly Library, Indiana University.

TITLE PAGE PHOTOGRAPH: Courtesy of Warren E. Roberts.

BACK COVER PHOTOGRAPH: Courtesy of Warren E. Roberts.

Library of Congress Cataloging-in-Publication Data

The Old traditional way of life : essays in honor of Warren E. Roberts
/ edited by Robert E. Walls, George Schoemaker,
with Jennifer Livesay, Laura Dassow Walls
    p. cm.
    Includes bibliographical references.
    ISBN 0-915305-02-X : $15.00
    1. Folklore--United States. 2. Material Culture--United States.
3. Vernacular architecture--United States. 4. Folk art--United States. 5. United
States--Social life and customs. I. Roberts, Warren E. (Warren Everett),
1924-   . II. Walls, Robert E. III. Schoemaker, George H.
GR105.053 1989
398'.0973--dc20   89-50952
                                                                         CIP

Printed in the U.S.A.

TRICKSTER PRESS
Indiana University Folklore Institute
504 North Fess
Bloomington, Indiana

Table of Contents

Preface

In his Afterword to *Viewpoints on Folklife: Looking at the Overlooked*, Warren Roberts noted that he felt his greatest contribution to folklife studies, and his "proudest boast," was his effect on the many graduate students in the Folklore Institute at Indiana University who had gone on to specialize in folklife research. Indeed, any quick glance at the field will immediately confirm his considerable impact on the landscape of folklife scholarship—as a teacher, researcher, and friend.

And Prof. Roberts continues to influence the careers of young folklorists, whether through formal instruction in the classroom, or informal discussions in the warmth of his home, or on a field trip somewhere in southern Indiana. What student can fail to remember the detailed demonstrations in his workshop of tool use common in the everyday world of "the old traditional way of life," complemented by the generous portions of cake and persimmon pudding provided by the always gracious Mrs. Barbara Roberts.

It is in appreciation of his 40 years of teaching at Indiana University, his scholarly contribution to the study of folklore in general, and in honor of his 65th birthday that we present to Prof. Roberts this festschrift.

This was essentially a student production, fueled by the energies of graduate students in the Folklore Institute. We truly appreciate the contributions, advice, and assistance of the scholars and students who helped bring this tribute to Professor Roberts' career to fruition. We are especially grateful to Profs. Henry Glassie and Edson Richmond who provided much needed counsel and encouragement throughout the

ix

entire process. We also greatly appreciate the generous financial support provided by Dean Roger Farr and the Office of Research and Graduate Development at Indiana University. Mrs. Barbara Roberts has been most helpful through the final stages of production, providing information, photographs, and encouragement for our "secret" endeavor. The cover and frontispiece photographs are reproduced from the Hohenberger Collection with the kind permission of the Lilly Library and the Indiana University Foundation.

We are greatly indebted to many other people for their advice and encouragement over the past year as this Festschrift took shape, including Ruth Aten, Richard Bauman, Velma Carmichael, Inta Carpenter, Bruce Carpenter, Syd Grant, Polly Grimshaw, Laura Harris, John Wm. Johnson, Cathy McAleer, Nancy Cassell McEntire, Dean Thomas Noblitt, Kenneth Pimple, Moira Smith, Mary Beth Stein, Beverly Stoeltje, and Dean Albert Wertheim.

Tabula Gratulatoria

Roger D. Abrahams
Dept. of Folklore and Folklife
University of Pennsylvania

Pauline Adema
Folklore Institute
Indiana University

Elizabeth Mosby Adler
Lexington, Kentucky

Thomas A. Adler
Lexington, Kentucky

Hessa Al-Rifai
Bloomington, Indiana

Richard W. Anderson
Royal Oak, Michigan

Rosemary Anderson
Columbus, Ohio

Museum of American Folk Art
New York, N.Y.

Dr. Kingkeo Attagara
Bangkok, Thailand

Jennifer Eastman Attebery
Pocatello, Idaho

Mac E. Barrick
Shippensburg University
Shippensburg, Pennsylvania

Richard Bauman
Folklore Institute
Indiana University

Dan Ben-Amos
Dept. of Folklore and Folklife
University of Pennsylvania

Donald Allport Bird
Dept. of Journalism
Long Island University

Inger and Olav Bø
Oslo University
Norway

Christopher Bobbitt
Folklore Institute
Indiana University

Lucy Breyer
Waterford, New York

Simon J. Bronner
American Studies Program
Pennsylvania State University
Harrisburg

Mary Ellen Brown
Folklore Institute
Indiana University

Jan Harold Brunvand
Dept. of English
University of Utah

Frank de Caro
Dept. of English
Louisiana State University

Inta and Bruce Carpenter
Folklore Institute
Indiana University

Thomas Carter
Graduate School of Architecture
University of Utah

Missouri Cultural Heritage Center
University of Missouri

William M. Clements
Arkansas State University

Center for the Study of
Comparative
Folklore and Mythology
University of California, Los
Angeles

Colleen Costello
Folklore Institute
Indiana University

Mary M. Dart
Folklore Institute
Indiana University

Linda Dégh
Folklore Institute
Indiana University

Elaine Caldwell Emmi
Salt Lake City, Utah

Tim Evans
American Studies Program
University of Wyoming

Doris Devine Fanelli
Glenside, Pennsylvania

Gary Alan Fine
Dept. of Sociology
Univ. of Minnesota

Institute of Folklore
Oslo University
Blindern, Norway

Folklore Institute
Indiana University

Charles R. Frederick
Cynthia J. Brubaker
Folklore Institute
Indiana University

Sean Galvin
Folklore Institute
Indiana University

Harry Gammerdinger
Center for Southern Folklore
Memphis, Tennessee

Robert Blair St. George
Dept. of Folklore and Folklife
University of Pennsylvania

Robert A. Georges
Folklore and Mythology Program
University of California,
Los Angeles

Helen D. Gilbert
Minneapolis, Minnesota

Angus K. Gillespie
American Studies
Rutgers University

Janet C. Gilmore
Mt. Horeb, Wisconsin

Henry Glassie
Folklore Institute
Indiana University

Christine Goldberg
Los Angeles, California

Kenneth S. Goldstein
Dept. of Folklore and Folklife
University of Pennsylvania

Hanna Griff
Folklore Institute
Indiana University

Herbert Halpert
Dept. of Folklore
Memorial University of
Newfoundland
Canada

William F. Hansen
Classical Studies
Indiana University

Phyllis A. Harrison
Institute of the
NorthAmerican West
Seattle, Washington

Elissa R. Henken
University of Georgia

Joseph C. Hickerson
Archive of Folk Culture
Library of Congress

Frank A. Hoffman
Dept. of English
State University College
Buffalo, New York

Bengt Holbek
Dept. of Folklore
Kobenhavns Universitet
Denmark

Dr. Hiroko Ikeda
Honolulu, Hawaii

Edward D. Ives
Dept. of Anthropology
University of Maine

Roger L. Janelli
Folklore Institute
Indiana University

Catherine Johnson
George Washington University

John William Johnson
Folklore Institute
Indiana University

Thomas Wayne Johnson
Chico Folklore Archive
California State University, Chico

Michael Owen Jones
Folklore and Mythology
Univ. of California, Los Angeles

Deborah Phillips King
Dept. of Geography
University of Akron

Ben Kroup
Waterford, New York

George E. Lankford
Arkansas College

James P. Leary
Mt. Horeb, Wisconsin

Dorothy Sara Lee
Archives of Traditional Music
Folklore Institute
Indiana University

William E. Lightfoot
English Department
Appalachian State University

Carolyn Lipson-Walker
Bloomington, Indiana

Jennifer Livesay
Folklore Institute
Indiana University

Dr. Betty Ritch Lombardi
Park Hill, Oklahoma

Eleanor R. Long
Folklore and Mythology
Univ. of California,
Los Angeles

Jens Lund
Washington State Folklife Council

Sabina Magliocco
Bloomington, Indiana

Kathleen E.B. Manley
Dept. of English
Univ. of Northern Colorado

Howard Wight Marshall
Cultural Heritage Center
University of Missouri

William Bernard McCarthy
Clarksville, Arkansas

Dee L. McEntire
Nancy Cassell McEntire
Folklore Institute
Indiana University

W.K. McNeil
Ozark Folk Center
Mountain View, Arkansas

Yvonne J. Milspaw
Middletown, Pennsylvania

Lynwood Montell
Folk Studies Program
Western Kentucky University

Willard B. Moore
Minneapolis, Minnesota

Alice Morrison Mordoh
Bloomington, Indiana

Peter Narváez
Dept. of Folklore
Memorial University of
Newfoundland
Canada

Venetia J. Newall
London, England

W.F.H. Nicolaisen
Dept. of English
State University of New York
Binghamton

Allen G. Noble
Dept. of Geography
University of Akron

Office of Research and Graduate
Development
Indiana University

Felix Oinas
Slavic Languages and Literatures
Indiana University

Mohamed Taib Bin Osman
University of Malaya
Malaysia

Thomas Passananti
Folklore Institute
Indiana University

Kenneth D. Pimple
Folklore Institute
Indiana University

Gerald L. Pocius
Centre for Material
Culture Studies
Memorial University of
Newfoundland, Canada

Betty and Edson Richmond
Folklore Institute
Indiana University

J. Sanford Rikoon
Dept. of Rural Sociology
University of Missouri

Neil V. Rosenberg
Dept. of Folklore
Memorial University of
Newfoundland
Canada

Anne H. Ross
Temple Terrace, Florida

Klaus Roth
Institut für Deutsche und
Vergleichende Volkskunde
Munich University
West Germany

Dr. Louise Russell
Northland Pioneer College
St. Johns, Arizona

Susan L. Scheiberg
Los Angeles, California

George H. Schoemaker
Folklore Institute
Indiana University

Gregory Schrempp
Folklore Institute
Indiana University

Henning K. Sehmsdorf
Scandinavian Department
University of Washington

Sherman W. Selden
Social Science Dept.
Plymouth State College

Wendy Ann Shay
Bethesda, Maryland

Catherine A. Shoupe
Sociology, Anthropology,
and Social Work
St. Mary's College

Guntis Šmidchens
Folklore Institute
Indiana University

Sandra Dolby Stahl
Folklore Institute
Indiana University

Gary Stanton
McKissick Museum
Univ. of South Carolina

Beverly J. Stoeltje
Folklore Institute
Indiana University

Kay F. Stone
University of Winnipeg
Canada

Scott H. Suter
George Washington University

Jan-Öjvind Swahn
Lund
Sweden

Greta E. Swenson
Lindsborg, Kansas

Thomas Tait
Kensington, Maryland

William Thatcher
Rehoboth, Massachusetts

Barbara Truesdell
Folklore Institute
Indiana University

Sue Tuohy
East Asian Studies Center
Indiana University

John Michael Vlach
Folklife Program
George Washington University

Thomas Walker
Brooklyn, New York

Robert E. Walls
Folklore Institute
Indiana University

Marie Walter
Irvine, California

Suzann M. Weekly
Piermont, New York

William H. Wiggins, Jr.
Afro-American Studies
Indiana University

D.K. Wilgus
Folklore and Mythology
Univ. of California, Los Angeles

Elva Van Winkle
Washington, D.C.

John and Mary Wolford
Folklore Institute
Indiana University

Hazel J. Wrigglesworth
Bukidnon, Philippines

Jonas Yeboa-Dankwa
Language Centre
University of Ghana

Don Yoder
Dept. of Folklore and Folklife
University of Pennsylvania

Introduction

W. EDSON RICHMOND

In the preface to his recently published book, *Viewpoints on Folklife: Looking at the Overlooked*, Warren E. Roberts says:

> I view my research which has been carried out over the years as an attempt–or a series of attempts–to throw light on a broad subject. This broad subject is folklife, a term I and others have used to refer to the way of life of the mass of humanity in Western Europe and the United States prior to the Industrial Revolution which instituted such drastic changes, as well as the ways in which that earlier way of life persisted in fragmented form after the Industrial Revolution.

In this same essay, he goes on to point out that the great mass of humanity is overlooked when most people write or talk about the past and that we know much about the urban elite and virtually nothing about the rural majority in any culture. Warren Roberts' academic, and much of his personal, life has been devoted to correcting this deficiency, and he has done so effectively, even brilliantly, for he has looked at the masses and their products from many different points of view.

First of all, he felt that he viewed mass culture as an insider, as one of its products. He was born in Norway, Maine, in 1924, certainly a rural area. His father was a saw-filer, employed in the lumber industry; obviously, therefore, Warren was not a member of the urban elite. In his middle youth, his family moved across the continent to the environs of Portland, Oregon, where his father continued his trade. Warren thus had an inborn, natural understanding of the way non-urban people thought and acted.

1

Secondly, he had a varied training: an undergraduate college degree from Reed College which, since he wrote his bachelor's thesis about traditional ballads, introduced him to folklore and to basic linguistics. At the same time, moreover, he became involved with music and his very fine voice led him to participate in many productions of Gilbert and Sullivan operettas. And finally, he was lured to Indiana University to study folklore by Stith Thompson whose reputation as a literary and folkloristic scholar was already giving Indiana University an international reputation. Under Thompson's direction, Warren Roberts wrote a dissertation that was a model historic-geographic folktale study and received the first Doctor of Philosophy degree in folklore ever granted in the United States.

Immediately upon receiving his degree, Warren was hired as a teacher of English literature, composition, and folklore by Indiana University. He remained as an employee of the Department of English until the Folklore Department was established, at which time he transferred into the new department. Upon the retirement of Professor Thompson a few years later, Warren took over Thompson's popular two-semester graduate seminar in the folktale and appeared to be on his way to following in his mentor's footsteps as the leading folktale scholar in the United States.

At this time, however, an avocational interest of Professor Roberts' asserted itself. He had always been interested in carpentry, and as a result he had developed sufficient skill to be truly called a first-class cabinetmaker. This skill was combined with a Fulbright grant to Oslo, Norway, in the academic year 1959-1960. In Norway he not only met the principal Scandinavian folklore scholars but also became acquainted with scholars involved in the study of material culture. He thus found a way to combine both his vocation and his avocation. When he returned to Indiana after his year in Norway, he was able to introduce into the curriculum of the Folklore Department a course entitled "Folk Art, Craft, and Architecture." Gradually, as he studied the artifacts themselves, he found it necessary to investigate both the people who produced them and the tools—many of which these people also made—employed in their creation. This led in turn to an investigation of the relationship of the artifacts to their producers, and to a realization that all of the folk were not necessarily the unlearned; instead, many could now be seen as a group of highly skilled artisans who existed outside of the mainstream studied by both conventional historians and folklorists, especially European folklorists who tended to look primarily at the unskilled peasantry. Thus it was that Warren

Roberts was to introduce into the folklore curriculum an interest in and a realization of the value of the study of material culture.

In addition to teaching courses in introductory folklore, the folktale, and material culture, immediately after his return from Norway Warren Roberts was to apply some of the information gained in Scandinavia to a very practical project which depended in large part upon his knowledge of verbal lore, architectural traditions, and crafts. He persuaded the administration of Indiana University to allow him to work on the development of an outdoor museum modelled in part upon those found in Norway and Sweden. For the next two decades, Warren was to wander the highways and byways of Indiana in search of early 19th-century buildings which reflected the folk culture of the day. Whenever possible, a number of these were purchased by the University, carefully taken down under the direction of Professor Roberts—who often participated in the actual dismantling himself—and moved to a storage spot on university property. All of this was done with an eye toward their reconstruction and the establishment of a living museum which would reflect Indiana's 19th-century heritage. Unfortunately, and despite the fact that he devoted most of his available research time to this project during the 1960s and 1970s, a change in the university administration and a restricted university budget left this project incomplete and the buildings await reconstruction still. But the project added greatly to Professor Roberts' understanding of the culture which produced these buildings and of the materials employed in their construction, and thus to the kind of information he has been able to pass on to his students.

In one of Warren's favorite operettas, *The Yeomen of the Guard*, there are some lines which possibly he has sung and he certainly would have sung had he followed a possible choice of careers when he left Reed to enter graduate school instead of joining a professional Gilbert and Sullivan company which he had been invited to do. These lines are sung by Jack Point, a strolling jester and a protagonist in the play:

> I've wisdom from the East and from the West
>   That's subject to no academic rule;
> You may find it in the jeering of a jest,
>   Or distil it from the folly of a fool.
> I can teach you with a quip, if I've a mind;
>   I can trick you into learning with a laugh;
> Oh, winnow all my folly and you'll find
>   A grain or two of truth among the chaff.

I can set a braggart quailing with a quip,
   The upstart I can wither with a whim;
He may wear a merry laugh upon his lip,
   But his laughter has an echo that is grim!
When they're offered to the world in merry guise,
   Unpleasant truths are swallowed with a will—
For he who'd make his fellow creatures wise
   Should always gild the philosophic pill.

Warren's teaching has become a part of his life, and like Jack Point's it's been subject to no academic rules except those he established himself. For a number of years it included leading field trips to investigate customs and material culture in southern Indiana, an unusual activity for one engaged in teaching the humanities. Even more unusual has been his involvement with the aforementioned outdoor museum and his direction of and participation in restoration work for houses in Bloomington. The result has been seminal for scholarship and it has developed a myriad of disciples ranging from townspeople whose enrolling in one of his undergraduate classes or attendance at one of his lectures has led them also to participate in restoration projects, to graduate students devoted to following in his footsteps. Some of the latter are now teaching at major universities; others work in the public sector on folk-arts' commissions and the like. Thus Professor Roberts' influence has spread far beyond academia and it continues to do so.

As evidence of Warren's popularity and influence as a teacher there is, among many other things, as well as his own writings, the present volume. It was conceived by a group of students and consists in large part of essays by one-time students, though colleagues contributed a number of items as well. Its organization into four principal parts ([1] *Folk Art, Craft, and Custom*; [2] *Folk Architecture*; [3] *History of Folklore Scholarship*; and [4] *Folk Narrative*) reflects the areas of research on which Professor Roberts has had a profound influence. Were this festschrift compiled for anyone else, one would, in fact, expect to find an essay by Warren Roberts in any one of the categories, each of which he has written about superlatively. It is safe to say, moreover, that were it not for his teaching, none of these essays would take the form it has taken. In fact, Warren is not only the kind of teacher who can "teach you with a quip if he's a mind," but also one who can say not only "do as I say" but also "do as I do!" By doing as he does and by learning from all that he has done, his students and colleagues have been able to produce this tribute for him.

The section devoted to "Folk Art, Craft, and Custom" begins with an essay about carved wooden figures found in rural districts in

Norway, written by a Norwegian friend and colleague, Professor Olav Bø, recently retired Professor of Folklore and Director of the Institute for Folklore Research at Oslo University in Norway. The article discusses the nature, origin, and significance of wooden images found in farmhouses in Setesdal and Telemark in the 19th century, images sometimes treated as idols or household gods by some farmers immediately after the reformation. "Fakses and the Remains of Churches" illustrates, as Warren Roberts has done in many of his writings, the importance of a painstaking investigation of both written records and oral traditions about material artifacts, as well as the appearance of the artifacts themselves, before drawing conclusions about them.

Closely related in theme to Professor Bø's article is that written by Lynwood Montell, Professor of Folk Studies at Western Kentucky University. Professor Montell has been both a student and colleague of Professor Roberts, and his paper reflects an interest that Warren has shown in gravestones as reflections of a culture. "Cemetery Decoration Customs in the American South," however, goes beyond the discussion of cemetery monuments and their decorations to discuss the importance of cemeteries and the formal and informal rituals related to them in the rural South. Like Professor Bø's article, it stresses the need for close investigation of the folk rationale for doing things if we are to understand the significance of artifacts and customs in a given culture.

John Michael Vlach, Director of the Folklore and Folklife Program at George Washington University, once a student of Warren Roberts, illustrates in his "Morality as a Folk Aesthetic" the fact that it is impossible to separate religion from any aspect of life in a truly religious culture. Thus even the artifacts which such people produce reflect their religious and moral aesthetic. A key to the whole article can be found in Professor Vlach's statement that "Any artifact if rendered with skill and care can convey both the enrichment of art and the enrichment of religion." It is this sort of insight which Warren Roberts has sought to instill in his students.

Four essays in this first section, all written by former students of Warren Roberts—"Spindles and Spoon Racks: Local Style in Nineteenth-Century Mormon Furniture," by Tom Carter; "'We Made 'Em to Fit Our Purpose': The Northern Lake Michigan Fishing Skiff Tradition," by Janet C. Gilmore; "The Reelfoot Stumpjumper: Traditional Boat Building in Tennessee," by Harry Gammerdinger; and "The Tradition of Geode Construction in Southern Indiana," by Alice Morrison Mordoh—all concentrate upon the relationship of form to function and to the ability of artisans to make the best use of their materials insofar as their culture allows them to do so. It is interesting to note that each of these papers is documented either by reference to a particular work by Professor Roberts or by reference to work done by one of his students.

Professor William H. Wiggins, Jr.—one of Warren Roberts' present colleagues and also a former student—describes a traditional festival in his paper "'Juneteenth': Afro-American Customs of the Emancipation." This informal festival, the Juneteenth Festival, celebrates the emancipation of slaves on June 19th, 1865, in east Texas and in portions of surrounding states. The festival activities are described along with an analysis of their evolution and the significance of these events.

The next paper in this initial section is, like the first, the product of Professor Roberts' colleagues, in this instance Beverly J. Stoeltje and Richard Bauman. "Community Festival and the Enactment of Modernity" indicates how widespread and enveloping the concept of folk has become by pointing out that a traditional festival, the Watermelon Thump of Luling, Texas, is supported by such professional groups as the Kiwanis and the Chamber of Commerce. Just as Professor Roberts has shown in other contexts, traditional activities are not limited to the unskilled and unlettered, and they can serve to draw communities together and to reflect their attitudes.

Though J. Sanford Rikoon's paper, "Grain Stacking in the Midwest, 1850-1920," does not refer in its documentation to anything written by Warren Roberts, it should be noted that it is closely related to the author's 1986 dissertation, "From Flail to Combine," which he directed. The essay draws attention to the process of change in the context of developing industrialization, and points out that "...traditional cultural practices continued through an ability to modify the use of new technologies within culturally familiar patterns."

The second section of this volume is devoted to "Folk Architecture," and all of the papers with the exception of one were written by former students of Professor Roberts: Jan Harold Brunvand, Howard Wight Marshall, Christopher Bobbitt, Jens Lund, and Phyllis Harrison.

In a note to his paper "Casă Frumoasă: An Introduction to the House Beautiful in Rural Romania," Professor Brunvand says "I studied the folktale at Indiana University with Professor Roberts in the pre-folklife days, but my subsequent work in material culture has been strongly influenced by Roberts' writings and talks on the subject." In accordance with this fact, Professor Brunvand's paper describes the style, construction methods, architectural peculiarities and ornamentation of village peasant homes in Romania in the context of their evolution and modern modifications.

Similarly, Howard Wight Marshall introduces his essay "The Sisters Leave Their Mark: Folk Architecture and Family History" with the comment "This paper offers in the spirit of Warren Roberts' way of closely studying cultural phenomena and traditional architecture in context through field research, a consideration of the story of the Cornetts and their Midwestern farm home." In accordance with these precepts, Professor Marshall examines an historic farm now in the care of the University of Missouri, with an eye to the relationship of its developers to its construction, evolution, and maintenance, pointing out how these things suited motivations, community social conditions, economic circumstances, and individual design sensitivities.

Christopher Bobbitt pays tribute to Professor Roberts by contributing an essay about the "Summer Kitchens of Harrison County, Indiana." After carefully describing the physical attributes of such kitchens, Mr. Bobbitt discusses their various reasons for being, their functions, and their demise.

In "Nomadic Architecture: The River Houseboat in the Ohio Valley," Jens Lund expands upon a section of the Ph.D. dissertation "Fishing as a Folk Occupation in the Lower Ohio Valley" which he wrote under the tutelage and direction of Warren Roberts. Here he describes in detail not only the architecture of the river houseboat and the manner in which it was built but also its effect upon a way of life and the relationship of that way of life to a land-bound culture.

Drawing upon the classes she once took from Warren Roberts, Phyllis Harrison describes the architecture and function of hop kilns in the Puyallup Valley of the State of Washington. She pays particular attention to the evolution of hop growing and curing and its effect upon the nature and structure of the kilns themselves. In addition, Dr. Harrison's paper points out the strong relationship between agricultural activities and social events, and how changes in agricultural production serve to change the nature of a culture.

In "Here Today, Gone Tomorrow," Allen G. Noble and Deborah Phillips King examine the disappearance rate of agricultural structures in Pike County, Ohio. The authors point out that obsolete but once essential structures for agricultural industry are also essential to our understanding of the culture which built them; however, they are rapidly disappearing. This paper demonstrates the necessity for examining such structures while they are still available for study, and gives factual evidence for the rate at which they are being destroyed.

The two essays in the section of this volume devoted to "The History of Folklore Scholarship" were contributed by Simon Bronner, presently Professor of Folklore and American Studies at the Pennsylvania State University at Harrisburg, and by W.K. McNeil, presently Folklorist at the Ozark Folk Center, Mountain View, Arkansas, both of whom are former students of Warren Roberts. In "Folklife Starts Here: The Background of Material Culture Scholarship in Pennsylvania," Simon Bronner points out the tremendous influence folklife scholarship in Pennsylvania had upon the development of Warren Roberts as a scholar. It points out the way in which the folklife approach in Pennsylvania differed from that of the British-inspired approach—the verbal lore approach—prevalent in the American Folklore Society until very recently, and concludes by noting that the activity in Pennsylvania supports Warren Roberts' own wish that the appreciation of America's craftsmen provides "an intellectual basis for democracy." W.K. McNeil's essay, "Charles Fletcher Lummis: The Man Who Lived the Life," on the other hand, is devoted to a scholarly biography of a Harvard drop-out who achieved renown as an expert on the American Southwest. Here is a man who, like Warren Roberts, could "teach you with a quip" if he'd a mind and who, also like Warren, could "always gild the philosophic pill!" Without formal training as a folklorist, Mr. Lummis became a forerunner of American folklife scholars, and his books are models for modern scholarship.

The final section of this festschrift is entitled "Folk Narrative," and is devoted to Warren Roberts' first love. Two of the articles in this section were contributed by Professor Roberts' one-time students, Robert A. Georges and Christine Goldberg, while the others are by his present colleagues at Indiana University, Linda Dégh, Mary Ellen Brown, John Wm. Johnson, and Sandra Dolby Stahl, the latter two who were also once students of Warren's.

The fascination with the works of Vladimir Propp did not prevail until Warren Roberts had shifted his sights to material folklore. In his analysis of folktales, Warren employed the historic-geographic method, and his works achieved international acclaim as models of this approach. As is apparent in Professor Robert A. Georges' essay entitled "Some Overlooked Aspects of Propp's *Morphology of the Folktale*: A Characterization and a Critique," scholars have been insufficiently critical of Propp's techniques and conclusions, and also insufficiently aware of his dependence upon the fruits of the labors of scholars such as Kaarle Krohn and Antti Aarne. In his article, Professor Georges points out a number of Propp's deficiencies and concludes that his major contributions to the study of the folktale could not have been made without the work of historic-geographic scholars.

It is with one of the principal students of the historic-geographic method that Christine Goldberg's contribution treats. Entitled "Antti Aarne's Tales with Magic Objects," this paper points out, after summarizing and analyzing his discussion of tales with magic objects and the conclusions which he drew, that Aarne's tale studies demonstrate that each tale is unique and that to say that tales follow laws or principles of composition or dissemination is simply a figure of speech indicating only that there are some regularities in the masses of data which have been compiled. Aarne's work is, however, as Warren Roberts illustrates in his *The Tale of the Kind and the Unkind Girls*, a part of a scholarly tradition that respects the vicissitudes and fluctuations of folktales and has made a permanent contribution to folktale studies, giving a comprehensive view of the whole tradition.

A prime example of what can be done by the application of the historic-geographic method to the study of a particular folktale type is seen in Professor Linda Dégh's article "The Ethnography of a Folktale," an article which examines AT570 (The Rabbit Herd) in the light of the aforementioned historic-geographic, or comparative, method. However, Professor Dégh's article also places the tale type in a Proppian and psychoanalytic context. Seen from these varying points of view, AT570 reveals much about the culture which produced it, and shows how the study of folktales is far more significant than simply the reconstruction of texts.

Just as Professor Dégh's article builds upon an extension of the historic-geographic analytic method of folk-narrative study, so does Professor John Wm. Johnson's contribution "Historicity and the Oral Epic: The Case of Sun-Jata Keita." This article analyzes an African oral-epic with a view toward understanding its relationship to history. Professor Johnson points out that factual history gives way to literary demands in the construction of the epic, and that ". . . events from the real life narrative of Sun-Jata as a person are not necessarily incorporated into the stereotyped plot of the contemporary epic."

An entirely different kind of tale and approach to it is discussed in Sandra Dolby Stahl's article "Family Settlement Stories and Personal Values." Here Professor Stahl examines the apparently unstructured but consistently traditional narrative usually passed on in a particular family, the sort of thing which often recurs in the same or very similar form under similar circumstances. Such stories, often inaccurate historically, are told as the truth, and the history is skewed to serve particular concerns and ideas; they are, in effect, parables more important for their moral than for their passing on of specific information. Professor Stahl concludes, as she begins, with the assertion that like the material culture so effectively described by Warren Roberts, stories change over time, but the change reflects not simply a change in collective culture but the assertion of individual values as well.

The final paper in this concluding section of the volume is entitled "Jamie Tamson's Legacy," and was contributed by Professor Mary Ellen Brown. Using as a springboard a Scottish poem composed by one James Thompson, "Willy Weir's Legacy," Professor Brown discusses the significance, function, and value of poems written by "local poets." The poem she focuses on is an inventory of the possessions left to his heirs by a typical Scottish farmer of the nineteenth century. This rhymed list of objects common to farmhouses is, of course, the sort of thing of especial interest to students of material culture. Professor Brown concludes by noting that few remember the poetry of James Thompson and his ilk because it was so tied to time and place, but she also goes on to emphasize the fact that these are qualities which make the work of Thompson and other local poets ideal sources for folklife specialists.

When Warren Roberts began his studies in folklore, such a diversity in the kinds of topics included in a festschrift for a folklorist would have been inconceivable. When Professor Roberts began his studies, he and his mentors centered their attention on the verbal arts—folktales, ballads and folksongs, proverbs, riddles, and the like—and they were concerned with the products for their own sake. In essence, Warren's teachers were interested in the lore in folklore; the producers of the lore were important solely as conduits. That the present generation of folklorists, many of whom were students of Warren's, focus their attention on the folk as they appear through their products is largely due to his efforts. This volume is evidence of how one man can help to shape the evolution of a discipline.

Skill

HENRY GLASSIE

In the fluid Introduction W. Edson Richmond provides to this volume, which we offer in affection to our teacher and colleague, our friend Warren Roberts, the word "skill" appears often enough to establish a theme for the whole. Skill unifies personal experience with collective wisdom. When skill is brought to bear upon a particular project, the artisan fuses completely a lifetime of practice with a technological tradition in which the tricks and techniques of uncountable others have been summarized. Neither idiosyncratic nor traditional, but both, the accomplished work, the old house in decay, the sturdy rocker, stands to draw the scholar in different directions: into the biographical or into the technological—in each realm to discover a massing of detail that conditioned the thing that we can see and touch, the thing we breathe back into life through explanations that require both a compassionate engagement with a particular artisan and a firm grip upon the fullness of a technical system. Warren Roberts has explored both of these directions in his scholarship. Writing wisely about technology in *Log Buildings of Southern Indiana*, he has illustrated the need for an exacting comprehension of technical detail; his consideration of tools and their uses in that book comprises the most significant breakthrough in the recent scholarship on the overvexed topic of the American log cabin. In his papers on Hoosier furniture makers he handles the biographical facts gracefully, and in his paper on the Turpin family in particular he brings the technological and biographical together, letting them reconnect in the crucial central concept of skill.

11

For the medieval doctors art meant skill, a merging of individual talent and traditional wisdom. As the word and idea of art became appropriated by the entrepreneurs of individualism, as art separated from craft, just as written literature separated from spoken, and class prejudice became frozen in academic formulations, the ideal of folklore was born. Delight though they will in new twists of diction, folklorists confronting the responsibility of definition will always present folklore as a version of a fundamental reality of human existence. All of us are individuals, alone, and all of us are members of social groups, families, teams, professions, clubs, clans, communities, nations, and folklore is the expression of that duality—a simultaneous unfolding of ourselves and our memberships, an expression of the individual and the collective, the personal and the traditional.

Our first doctor of folklore, the complete folklorist, Warren Roberts embodied our tradition so completely that when he shifted his focus from folktales to material culture, his motion was easy, natural, and he was able to argue smoothly that material as well as oral expressivity belonged to our field. Before him, Stith Thompson, his great teacher, had called for American folklorists to bring architecture, art and craft, into their discipline, but it was Warren Roberts who first answered the call and provided us with models and arguments for study. In the first session devoted to material culture at an annual meeting of the American Folklore Society, he compared a house type and a tale type to settle the matter. From that time to this, through his work and that of his students and colleagues, among whom Don Yoder deserves special mention, material culture has been an integral and expanding part of folklore scholarship. Houses like stories incarnate the personal and the collective; they rise out of the intense merger of individual experience with general—traditional—wisdom.

Within material culture, skill particularizes our old folkloristic philosophy. In opposition to those who would steal from art its traditional dimensions in order to isolate a tiny aristocracy of genius, and against those who would steal individuality from people by lumping then into masses for the benefit of historians or politicians, folklore preserves the power of both the individual and the tradition, the powers the artisan melds in the heat of skilled work. Warren Roberts was able to locate the center of material culture studies and hold himself there, creating a grand corpus of scholarship, because he is a fine folklorist, one in a long train of individuals committed to comprehending the world realistically, and because he is a fine craftsman. Turning lumps of truculent wood into gleaming works of art with flowing liquid lines, he has learned from his own endeavor.

The repetitive solution of concrete problems teaches both confidence in the self and an awareness of reliance upon the missing others who provided forms and tools, whose answers to enduring problems are bound within traditional technologies.

Through actions that test our skills, we find ourselves and position ourselves gratefully among our fellows. Splitting wood, blackening pages, rearranging nature, we put ourselves into things, become part of the world.

Others may wonder, Warren, at our fascination with the intricacies of the performance of a story or the making of a chair, at our concern with the little details of biography, context, and technology; but by centering our thought upon the skillful action of the singer and the potter, we have come near the heart of human experience. Old Walt will not mind the parody: with you, Warren, I have learned that there is wonder enough in a well-turned chair to stagger an army of academicians.

Fakses and the Remains of Churches

OLAV BØ

It is often convenient to make use of imprecise formulations when we come across something so ancient and unknown that we can neither decide upon its age nor compare it to familiar items or phenomena. In such cases, we often find the word "heathen" used, even in scientific works. The 17th and 18th centuries were a time rich in scientific speculations. To a great extent, religious conceptions dominated world view, and clergymen had positions which gave them an authority far beyond their real competence. It was a time of pietism. The century of the reformation was followed by an era of religious ardor, a reaction in favor of individual conversion and against institutionalized Christendom.

In the rural communities of Norway, many old traditions had survived the half-millennium of Catholicism and the later centuries of Lutheranism. Traditions are very often closely connected with specific customs and for that reason difficult to change. For a long time after the Reformation in 1536, clergymen were either met with direct opposition or what was said from the pulpit was ignored. Reliable historical sources even tell of ministers being murdered in the first decades of the Post-Reformation period. The situations changed slowly as time went on, and in the period of Pietism clergymen used every opportunity of accusing people of pageantry and secret idolatry. There may well be a connection with the numerous accusations of witchcraft in the same period. In communities, no one wanted to be known for keeping idols or "house gods," an expression commonly used in later descriptions.

The so-called "house gods" that I am going to discuss may be defined as wooden images. They were mostly discovered in remote districts in Telemark and Setesdal. These districts are known to folklorists as the best areas to document a wide variety of folk traditions. It is no mere coincidence that these districts also had taken care of different kinds of church remains.

One of the most zealous clergymen in 18th-century Denmark Norway was Erik Pontoppidan. Even before he was appointed bishop of Bergen he had published a book which aroused great interest: *Everriculum veteris fermenti* (1737). The title may be understood in these words: Broom to brush away old superstitions. Nothing less was his intention. In a chapter about "horrifying idolatry," Pontoppidan renders information given to him by an ex-minister of Western Telemark. The vicar had been dismissed from his position for neglecting his duties, so what he reported from his vicarage in Telemark was mainly a defense of his own behavior and his eagerness for service. Although very doubtful, his **narrationes** were accepted by Pontoppidan.

The ex-minister reported that on a farm in the parish of Vrådal there lived a man called Anund who had a wooden image, a roughly carved statue, in his possession. When the minister happened to see the figure, the farmer had to admit that it was a piece of heritage belonging to the farm. He himself had only taken care of the image, not sacrificed food or beer to it or venerated it in any way. The image was described as such: It was about two **alner** (i.e., 1.30 meter) high, roughly hewn and worm-eaten with age, and possessing a human face. The image was called Gudmund. The minister further explained that he himself had gripped an axe, split the image to pieces and thrown it into the fire. The description is very colorful, but most of it must, I think, be corrected. To do so, we can contrast this description with what other clergymen report later in the same century when the image was called Torbjørn and its appearance was described as such: It was big and broad at the bottom, had neither arms nor legs but a head like an ordinary human being. The eyes were filled with molten pewter. On top of the head was a kind of flat crown just large enough to hold a beer bowl. No idolatry was known about the image, and it was used as a stand for the wassail bowl on festive occasions, especially Christmas time. The image remained at the farm until the house burned down. A third minister, the well-known writer H.J. Wille, describes Torbjørn with almost the same words, but adds that every Saturday night the image was washed and placed in the owner's seat (høgsætet) like a holy thing. The most interesting point of

Wille's description is perhaps the mentioning of another image at the same place, which in his opinion was an image of a saint, the Icelander St. Gudmund.

Among the clergymen who have written about the image called Torbjørn is the first editor of Norwegian ballads (as well as other folk traditions from Telemark) M.B. Landstad. In his words, every guest took the wassail bowl from Torbjørn's head, drank, thanked him for the drink and replaced the bowl on his head. These descriptions may give reason to believe that there were two images on the same farm, but this assumption cannot be correct. Torbjørn was and still is a fairly common Norwegian Christian name, while Gudmund or St. Gudmund reminds us of Gudmund, bishop of Holar in Iceland from 1201 to 1237. His remembrance-day was the 16th of March, a day that was both an ecclesiastical and a popular day for rejoicing or feasting. Gudmund was, however, not the object of much veneration in Norway, although reliable historical sources report that in Romerike (not far from Oslo) a chapel was dedicated to him. There may well have been pictures of the saint in other churches too. Everything seems to indicate that the name Gudmund is the original name and Torbjørn a name that was adopted by tradition much later.

From the communities in the far western reaches of Telemark the distance is short to the valley of Setesdal. Throughout the centuries there was a lot of communication across the mountains. As might be expected, we find in Setesdal the richest and most characteristic tradition about images of a special kind, images that were called **faksar** (fakses).

In a vocabulary from the 1740's, a **fakse** is described in the following way: In the dialect of the Setesdal Valley in the bishopric of Kristiansand it is a carved image in the old farmhouses. They were called **røykstuer** because of the smoke from the open fireplace in the middle of the room rising up to an opening in the roof. The source of this piece of information was probably a former minister in Setesdal who, according to tradition, tried very hard to do away with all the old beliefs in the valley. The internationally-known sociologist Eilert Sundt visited Setesdal in the 1850's and during his stay in the valley he was told that peasants in the old days would place a wooden image in the high seat. They called the image Fakse and daubed it with butter. At about the same time, many artists, especially painters, discovered the valley of the Setesdal with its strong and old-fashioned traits and habits. Some of these pioneer painters heard about the fakses, and they have given vivid and colorful descriptions of the images, although it seems without ever actually having seen them.

Due to their various fantasies, great differences exist in the artistic reproductions of the tradition.

Not until Johannes Skar, the excellent collector of all kinds of folk tradition in Setesdal, published his books did folklorists procure reliable material. Skar was the last to describe the images and their context, but he was a very conscientious collector and had several reliable informants. According to his description, there were two images which bore the name of Fakse, named after the farms on which they were placed: Fakse Rygnestad and Fakse Brokke. Rygnestad is a farm with very old houses that today are the main part of the local folk museum. Among the houses is a large and very well-built **loft** (annex) from the last part of the 16th-century; it is said to have been built by a bailiff who in his younger days took part in the liberation war in the Netherlands.

Skar writes that Fakse Rygnestad looked like a human being. His head was flat on top. Through the lower part of the image there were three holes to fasten him to a wall. Most of the time he was kept in a small room beside the living room, but on Christmas Eve he was placed in the high seat, to the left of the farmer himself (the **husbond**). At the first drink of the Christmas beer, the farmer drank to Fakse before sending the wassail around. Skar received this information from an old woman on the farm. She added that the word about Fakse being an idol was not in any way reliable, and she appeared quite angry when mentioning this. When they rebuilt the house some years later, Fakse was removed from his usual place. A woman expressed deep regret over this action and said that luck would certainly leave the place. For many years Fakse was lying in the woodshed—until he was cut up for firewood.

Fakse Brokke was a timber log, carved into the likeness of a man, according to tradition. He was said to wear a hat and riding trousers. Through his head there was a hole. This Fakse had "sacrifices" made to him, of the same kind as were made to the **tussar**, i.e., guardian spirits belonging to the hidden people. The offerings were given to Fakse in order to receive good fortune with cattle and crop, and consisted mainly of butter and beer when brewing, but otherwise food in the cupboard on which he was standing. There was never peace and quiet in that cupboard, they said—and we can easily understand the reason for that. But when the neighbors began to call the mother's son Fakse, the image was removed from the house. In the end, he was lying by the wall on the backside of the house, until he was cut up for firewood. This is said to have happened a little before or around 1800. Several of the stories about the images from this late period appear rather journalistic and it is hard to decide what may have been true and what was added. More than once the descriptions border on the edge of sensationalism, and were introduced as a cultural sensation by, among others, a couple of professors at the University of Oslo. We shall leave their conceptions without any comment.

From Valle in Setesdal, the parish where the fakses were found, there are additional traditions about two other images. One of them is called "Ramnen" or "the raven of Tveitebø"; the other one "Herrnos." The second name is translated as a "likeness of a man," and it is told that an officer was allowed to take it with him from the farmhouse where it had had its place for a long, long time. "Ramnen" was standing in an annex (a loft) of unique construction, built in three stories, with a small room on the top floor. "Sacrifices" were made to the "raven."

From Romerike, only a short distance away from Oslo, there is a tradition about an old house where two wooden images had their place. The Old Norse name of this farm is "Skeiðihof," a name indicating an ancient cultplace, and during the Middle Ages there was a parish church on the farm. In all probability, the images came from this old and condemned church. From Valdres, in the central part of Norway, there is a tradition about an "idol" called St. Andreas which was placed on a nearby hill. This seems to have been an ordinary, much deteriorated image of a saint. The image of St. Nicolas from the parish of Eidsborg in Telemark is the artifact most naturally compared to the image of St. Andreas, as to some others; it can be seen in the collection of antiquities at the University of Oslo. There is much tradition associated with this image, particularly regarding medical practice on Midsummer-night. The image, however, most certainly came from a local stave-church in Eidsborg. It must have been removed from the church at the time of the Reformation, but was taken care of by the members of the community.

At this point, we can begin to appraise carefully the different sources in order to discern reliable information that can lead to plausible interpretations of such an unusual artifact. At the beginning, it seems obvious that tradition has preserved information about the images of saints coming adrift at the time of the Reformation. Names such as St. Andreas, St. Nicolas, and perhaps also St. Gudmund point clearly in this direction. But we still have to explain the reports about the images that obviously cannot be described as saints, and consequently must be judged from other points of view. To this group belong the "fakses" from Setesdal, the other images from the same district, and perhaps the image first mentioned, Gudmund or Torbjørn from Telemark. These specifically seem to have a background apart from the images of saints.

It is highly probable that the names in question are expressing a characteristic of the image itself, or of the place where it originally stood. Nevertheless, we cannot be sure whether or not the names are old in use, or whether or not they indicate medieval beliefs and denominations. The name Fakse must be a derivation of the Old Norse word **faks** (i.e. long hair), and therefore means "he with the long hair" or something along that line. In more recent tradition, we know of several persons who where called Fakse because of their long and stiff hair. This fact corresponds with a similar use of names known from the Old Norse literature. A **berserk** had been named Barek, but was called **Brenneyarfaxi** because of his long black hair. Likewise, horses might bear the name Fakse, **Freysfaxi** being the best known. Place names could in the same way have Fakse as the first part of the name, in order to explain certain traits of a particular place. In Norway, we have place names such as Faksefjell and Fakstind. Fakse in place names very often means a mountain with a glacier or eternal snow on top of it. Thus we can say with some certainty that there is a connection between hair and the shape of the head and the name of Fakse.

Obviously the name Ramnen has nothing to do with the bird name raven, but Skars' information about the upper part of the house being called **loftet** leads us in the right direction. It is defined as the upper room, under the ceiling, close to the short wall—and such rooms are sometimes called **ramloft** or **ramen**. During the repair of stave-churches, they often put up a new ceiling where the capitéls (the top of the wooden pillars) went through the floor of the new ceiling and into a dark loft. In a church that is being repaired or restored it is possible to stand in the loft and look at the images on top of the pillars or staves. In my opinion, this is a very plausible explanation for the image called Ramnen.

The word **Herrnos** is more difficult to explain. My interpretation is that it refers to the shape of the image's nose. The first part of the word (**Herr-**) might refer to a man of high rank, an official or an officer. Popular language has several expressions to point out the nose of men of rank, thought to be a rather large and often curved nose. It is possible that this image had a nose like that, as often is the case with carved figures, and the name herrnos could then be interpreted on the basis of a distinctive feature of the image, similar to the explanation offered for the name Fakse.

Outward appearances undoubtedly have influenced the naming of the images. Most important seem to be the shape of the head and of the body. Tradition varies concerning the height, with a range of 30 to 120 cm. (approximately one to four feet). All records but one report that the images were very simple. Most of the records tell about a beer bowl being placed on top of the figure, and all evidence points to a shape of the head where the outer frame, which evidently looked like hair, was standing upright, reminiscent of horse **faks**. We know of no other meaning of the word **faks**.

With this in mind, it seems logical to think about the pillar-heads of the inner staves in a stave-church: for example, those to be seen in the Gol stave-church at the Norsk Folkemuseum. There seems to be a very good correspondence between the images or masks on top of the staves and the information about the fakses and other similar images. The cross-piece or stave-beam had to rest on the pillar-head, and to this end the top was made flat. The upper part of the staves were, of course, not the same in all churches, because the wood-carver—we may well call him an artist—often wanted to vary his technique, as in other carvings.

This urge to vary and to compose something fantastic and grotesque is clearly shown in the shape of the faces. It is a remarkable fact that it is not the shape of the face but the eyes that have attracted the most attention. A couple of the images are said to have had eyes of lead or pewter and a fierce stare. People have wondered about this: What might be the basis of this impression?

It is unlikely that lead or pewter could have been cast into the face, but the paint, either gray or blue, may have led people to think of lead or tin. Probably, however, there is a better explanation. On the many medieval images for which we have information, whether church art or other types of wood carving, the eyes are unusually conspicuous. Frequently the artist has carved deeply around the edges so that the eyelids nearly vanish. Remaining, then, is the large round apple of the eye and the deep trenches around them, reflecting light and shadow. Thus, in their cruder versions, these images may portray a wild and fierce expression. Of course, we should keep in mind that the figures in question were not the best works artistically. They were carved to be seen from underneath, at a fair distance (six to eight meters), and in the dim daylight of the old stave-churches. The heads of the staves and similar carvings were usually simple and plain, although each artist was free to carry out his assignment as he wished. Descriptions such as "staring" and "frightening" remind us that the eyes can be such an effective means of characterization, especially when informed by popular belief where, as in wood carving, common concepts are the basis and inspiration.

From the information we have on Fakse Rygnestad we know that the image was triangular with three holes through it, so that it could be fastened to the wall with three nails. This never happened at Rygnestad, where the figure on certain occasions was placed beside the seat of honor (høgsætet). The holes, therefore, must have been made for some other purpose, and the staves of the church may again provide leads to a safer conclusion. In the Gol stave-church at Norsk Folkemuseum there are holes through the staves. According to architects, these holes might have several different functions in the construction of the church. Tradition tells us that the Herrnos image could be placed on top of a stake, such as a processional stick or pole (although this was not possible in the case of the large and heavy fakses). These poles were commonly carried in the Middle Ages on Procession days while walking around the fields in order to ensure a good harvest. The tradition has ancient roots and was accepted by the Catholic church, but only a few procession stakes remain today. In the old churches there were various kinds of fittings, and in the Norwegian stave-churches it is possible to divide these fittings into the permanent and the mobile parts of their interiors. The wooden images could have been either the actual images of saints or the upper part of the staves.

It does not seem unreasonable to assume that many sculptures of saints had gone adrift in the times following the Reformation in 1536. The Reformation was introduced to Norway on the command of the King and the administration, not on the people's desire. The reformists of the church saw it as their primary task to clear the churches of all reminders of Catholicism. They used the word "papistry" almost as an equivalent for paganism and the worshipping of idols. Contemporary clerical writings contain a wealth of information on the so-called "purification" of the churches, and the information is probably correct. People were suspicious of the new "religion," as they said, and reacted through indifference and even protest. All of the old furnishings had been precious to them, as to their forefathers, and therefore they felt obliged to care for whatever old equipment they might get hold of. Those who lived close to the churches which had been abandoned because of the Reformation were particularly keen on preserving the remains of the churches.

By the late Middle Ages some of the old stave-churches had been lost already, largely due to decay. At one time, there were an estimated number of 700-800 stave-churches in Norway. To give this some perspective, today only about 30 remain, most of which have been extensively restored. At the time of the Reformation, the state (i.e., the King) acquired all properties of the Catholic church, including churches which the state did not have sufficient means to maintain. In the 16th, 17th, 18th, and even the last century many churches were neglected to such an extent that they were either torn down or they simply collapsed. During the 18th-century, the Danish-Norwegian king was in particular need of money for warfare, and in this situation the selling of church buildings seemed necessary. In some cases local communities bought the churches, but usually wealthy individuals purchased them with the intent of leasing them to the congregation. These new owners had both a legal and a moral obligation to keep the buildings in order, but more than once neglected what had been prescribed. The maintenance of the churches did not improve until they were taken over by the local communities; by then, however, it was often too late.

It seems certain that all the churches in Setesdal but one were stave-churches, eight in number. One church was demolished at the time of the Reformation and six others were torn down in the 19th-century. Only the poor parish of Bykle in the northern part of the valley could not afford to build a new church, and had to be content with renovating the old church through rose-painting. Today, this is the only church in Setesdal of any particular interest. When a stave-church was torn down and a new church had to be built, materials that could not be used in the construction of the new church were usually distributed equally among the peasants of the parish. This served as a kind of compensation for the timber they had to contribute towards the construction of the church. In this fashion many pieces of ancient church furnishings went adrift.

Some of the finest examples of wood carving from medieval churches come from Setesdal, especially some unique church portals. On these portals are carved scenes from the myths of Sigurd Fåvnes-bane, a part of the cycle of myths in the Old German Niebelungen literature. Finding such motifs in a place of worship might seem amazing to us, though obviously not to people in the Middle Ages. To them it was no problem to unite tradition and folk belief on the one hand with church and worship on the other. Perhaps more astounding is the fact that the Catholic priests were so liberal as to accept the carvings with mythical motifs. When the stave-churches were torn down, the portals were lost until at last they were found by members of a newly established society for the preservation of antiquities. Legends tell of how images of saints were saved—until they were destroyed much later on the command of zealous clergymen. In Telemark and Setesdal the first Lutheran bishops had great difficulties persuading people to accept the new system, and it seems to be more than a coincidence that it is precisely in these districts that a large portion of the precious church furnishings has been preserved.

What then might we say about the remains of staves from the old churches? First, we must take into account the respect shown and the veneration offered to the images at certain times according to tradition. We know that there was a church in Valle (in tradition called the church of the Monks) that was deserted at the time of the Reformation. Remains from this church may well have been brought to one of the largest farms, Rygnestad, where a fakse found his dwelling, as we have discussed.

But why then venerate these images especially at Christmas time, a veneration reported to have included sacrifices of beer and butter? The information given in the body of tradition that tells us such images were placed in the high seat on Christmas Eve is so substantial that we must consider it reliable. Every part of that tradition indicates that at Christmas ancient customs were predominant. More recent elements gradually became stronger, but at the time in question the old customs and beliefs were still vivid. Characteristic of the beliefs is that Christmas was seen as the midwinter celebration, the midwinter solstice to which many ancient concepts and beliefs were attached, fertility ideas as well. It seems likely that a kind of sacrifice was included, though not directed to an idol. More likely, the sacrifices were offered to the spirits depicted in folk belief. A striking parallel to this can be found in the tradition of offering Christmas porridge to the old **jultomte** (not to be compared with Santa Claus in more recent customs).

This **tomte**, explained to be a spirit of the first settler on the farm, paid particular attention to the domestic animals and therefore, like all living creatures, was entitled to share in the material benefits of the Christmas celebration. The question remains of how long people have really believed in the tomte. It is quite possible that the strength of tradition itself has kept alive the old customs and behavior without being proof of a folk belief still in existence. This makes sense when we consider that later generations not familiar with the background of the old images, quite unaware that they were originally church equipment, showed religious veneration in the respect they still paid to these images. Again, we may compare this with the figures of St. Andreas and St. Nicolas, to which customs clearly derived from folk belief were attached.

We can now draw the conclusion that these images represent a tradition, and that originally they were old church relics from one of the many churches that were torn down in the course of time. People knew of this background for quite a while, but during a period of two centuries or more the function of the images changed into a protective one, related to but in many ways differing from supernatural beings. The supernatural beings were a kind of common property, whereas the wooden images were seldom found. On the few farms that were in possession of such images, the situation was as follows: The old images were inherited relics revered by their ancestors. Since these relics were not associated with the images of saints and other church furnishings, it became natural for people to venerate them in the same way as they had venerated the supernatural beings from ancient times. The images were thus integrated into the complex of folk belief, where there were many common characteristics as well as many distinguishing features. On certain occasions, sacrifices were offered to these images in accordance with other well-known sacrificial rituals.

This discussion is based on an analysis of various written sources and on folk tradition collected in the last century. The striking similarity with the upper part of the staves in the old stave-churches leads to a supposition that the wooden images were in all likelihood the remains of churches. But is it possible to find other evidence?

The former chief architect at Norsk Folkemuseum, Mr. Arne Berg, some years ago led an examination of the old farm buildings at Rygnestad. In the three-story annex building, he found that the round column at the corner of the gallery had in all probability come from a demolished church. This church could well be the one from the end of the Middle Ages that we previously mentioned. His conclusion ends with this statement: "It is most likely that the top of the column once had a covered hat. The basis for this assumption lies not only in the length and shape of the column, and in the fact that such columns were not ever (as far as we know) a feature of secular architecture, but also in the fact that many other features of the ground floor and first floor of the annex building have originally come from a stave-church." Mr. Berg further states that both the farmhouse and the annex in question most likely were built at the same time, i.e., in the 1590's. The statement from the architect corresponds very well, as it seems to me, with my folkloristic analysis of the written sources and the folk tradition from the 19th-century.[1]

NOTES

1   For further information see: Olav Bø/ Arne Berg: Faksar og ktrkjerestar, serleg på Rygnestad, Oslo 1959.

FIGURES

Figure 1.   Carved images at the top of staves in the Gol stave-church at Norsk Folkemuseum, Oslo. The church was removed from the parish Gol in Hallingdal to the king's farm near to the museum in the last part of the 19th century and later presented to the national folk museum by King Oscar II.

Figure 2.   Carved head from the Hegge stave-church in Valdres. The irregular shape of the right eye has led to the idea that the woodcarver might have had the chief god Odin in mind.

Figures 3 & 4. These carved heads are all from the Ål stave-church in Hallingdal. The woodcarver has varied his technique and composed different shapes for the faces.

Figure 2.

Figure 1.

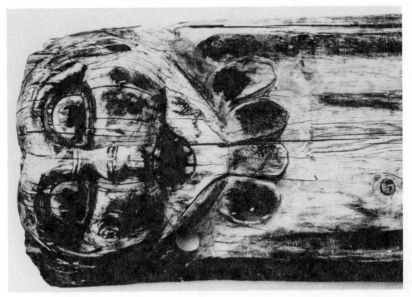

Figure 4.

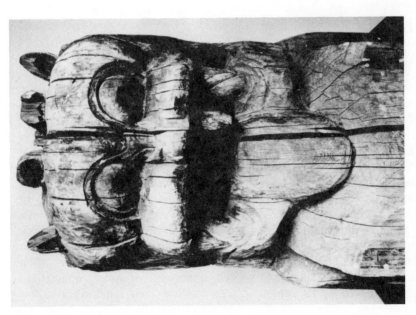

Figure 3.

Morality as Folk Aesthetic

JOHN MICHAEL VLACH

It is difficult to say where religion begins and ends in the life of any society. A religious person does not parcel out his or her devotion to use it on one occasion and hold it in reserve on another. To do so is in fact not to be religious but only to be seemingly religious. To behave in a sacred, moral manner only when it is advantageous is to be a religious opportunist and something of a hypocrite. Religious ideals, if they are indeed religious, are always in force, ever present, and constantly acted upon. This constancy allows us then to forge a link in our study of art and culture between social codes and moral codes, between art and religion. What we may perceive as distinct spheres of behavior are for many people combined into a single unified experience. This is why anthropologist and philosopher Robert Redfield (1947) characterized the little communities that he called folk societies as "sacred societies."[1] Following the lead of William Graham Sumner, Redfield noted that folkways were also mores, that is, ways of doing or thinking to which moral consequence was attached. Consequently, even the most menial task performed in a folk society might be freighted with sacred or religious implications. An act like plowing a field or cooking a meal which we might take to have nothing other than economic or nutritional significance might, in some societies, convey powerful religious or moral symbolism to its members. To understand the meaning of religion, then, in such societies we must be prepared to study not only their religious institutions and doctrines but all the contexts in which religious values might be displayed. On some occasions the influence of the moral code will be plainly or overtly manifest, but more often the code will be silent and hidden, although it is clearly understood and followed by its adherents. To consider only religion's manifest expressions is to miss much of the daily response to religion which remains latent.[2]

What all this means for the study of religious folk art should be clear. We cannot be content to collect and analyze only those works that overtly display religiosity. To do so is to overlook most of the experience of folk culture. Just as religion has both its manifest and latent expressions so too does art overtly and covertly serve religious functions. The manifest statement of religious doctrine found in a work like a saint's image or the cherub etched into a slate tombstone is a physical call to accept certain tenets of religious belief. Formed in part out of an artist's understanding of sacred teachings, these works provide symbols that encourage and inspire faith within the artist's community. While we may safely assume that at least the artist has thoughtfully pondered the religious values behind these symbols, we do not know how deeply the other faithful subscribe to those sacred ideals unless we can observe their responses. But then those responses are both a reaction to the talent of the artist as well as to the form and content of the image. Mere ownership of a religious object or attendance at the procession of a holy image is not a patent sign of devotion since participation can be motivated by social, political, and other factors. A greater proof of the fervor of a group, it seems to me, is to be found in the secular objects they make once they have been filled with the spirit of faith. More important than the question "How do the faithful use religious art?" is the question "How do the faithful perpetuate their religion day in and day out?" To answer this question we have to focus our attention on secular activities and objects used in nonreligious contexts. In this way we may learn how people internalize and personalize abstract religious concepts and convert their beliefs into a record of sacred actions and achievements. And furthermore, we may learn how the aesthetically appropriate is also the morally appropriate.

The Puritans of New England are one group whose history has been extensively studied. We know much about them as a people and much about certain persons among them. Their misssion in North America was to establish a new nation where they might freely practice their religion, and the "Bible Commonwealth" that resulted from their efforts is well-known.[3] Their church was a pervasive institution; there were few aspects of colonial life into which it did not intrude. Moreover, given their brand of Calvinist Protestantism, every act—human or natural—was interpreted as either a sign of God's grace or His wrath. While Puritans are generally thought of as an art-denying group, Alan Ludwig (1960) has shown that their gravestones carried a rich iconography. These graven images are, however, only a surface manifestation of the Puritan faith. In a society so given to religious feeling and a concurrent feeling for form, the passion for the sacred and the aesthetic could not be confined solely to markers for the deceased.

For the seventeenth-century English yeoman doing God's bidding and earning His grace meant that he commit himself completely to caring for and civilizing the "wastes" of New England. He used the terms "unbroken" and "broken" to identify progressive stages of development, hoping eventually to certify it "improved." Robert Blair St.George (1982:161) has written recently of the Puritan encounter with nature:

> The Puritans legitimized their mission as they symbolically broke open their landscape. As a result the yeoman would improve his lands, build miles upon miles of stone walls, and turn trees into towns, while still heeding the words of his minister as he urged the detailed study of nature.

Houses and towns, fields and fences are then to be regarded as important religious expressions. They were devices used to create a human order consistent with and parallel to God's plan for the order of the Universe. Their deliberate clearing of fields, hewing of timbers, laying out of gridded streets, and attentive husbanding of crops and beasts combined to form what one Puritan called "a little model of the Kingdom of Christ upon Earth" (160).

Although houses might be considered works of architecture rather than works of art, it is important to recognize that in design the winged skull or cherub on a tombstone and the facade of almost any saltbox or Cape Cod house are identical. Both house fronts and gravestone icons have symmetrical central sections flanked by symmetrically mirrored elements (Glassie 1972:269, 272-79). The sharing of this complex formula which simultaneously divides an object into two and three parts is not an accident but results from the fact that houses, gravestones, and many other Puritan artifacts share a single cultural underpinning: the desire for predictable, balanced order. A death's head overtly declares order; a house or a barn or a town plan covertly imposes the same tripartite order (Figure 1). If the functions —aesthetic and pragmatic—of both sets of objects are similar, there is little advantage to be gained in separating them. Art and architecture both demonstrate how seriously the Puritans considered the commands of their religion. Studying elements of the cultural landscape apart from art would only stunt our understanding of Puritan aesthetics by hiding the fact that designs for art are both literally and metaphorically also designs for living.   Because the Puritans lived their religion unceasingly, its moral prescriptions were never at rest.   Consequently, we are compelled to pursue all the forms and contexts in which their religious-formed aesthetic was displayed if we are truly interested in Puritan art.

While one can safely identify the latent dimensions of religious impulses in an overtly religious group like the Puritans or the Shakers, how does one determine whether a commonplace basket or quilt found in a more secularly-oriented society has any moral implications?   The answer lies in the object's maker.   If an artist is a religious person, every thoughtful, conscious act will bear some measure of religious significance.   Consider Vince, a chairmaker from Eastern Kentucky. Described by Michael Owen Jones (1975) as a stern, tight-lipped man, he is an adult convert to a fundamentalist version of Christianity.[4] His church, among other prohibitions, apparently considers secular music frivolous and as a consequence Vince gave up playing the banjo. Its aesthetic doctrine, which requires a denial of worldly pleasure in order to insure one's heavenly reward, has also had a marked influence on the chairs he makes.   Vince rejects the usual bands of lathe turnings or back posts with finials as "ugly;" he prefers "a decent, plain-made chair." The term "decent" here reveals that his chairs are not only sturdy pieces of sitting furniture but that they make a moral statement as well.   They extend the command to avoid wordly pleasure from the pulpit all the way to the front porch.   Vince has approached both his musical talent and his craft ability with the same moral map. Just as the fun-loving, quick tempo banjo tunes gave way to solid, respectable church hymns, so too was even the most modest of decorations replaced by plain round posts.   In this way both his chairs and his songs took on the basic contours of his religion.   We might also posit that other aspects of his life likewise assumed a similar profile, becoming plainer, more introverted, less ostentatious, more concerned with the repetition of correct form and less concerned with the possibility for variation.

The goodness of Vince's chairs, however, was not totally bound to their implicit morality.   Vince says that they are "good looking" because he tapers the arms of his chairs from the front end to the point where they enter the back posts. A chair with straight arms and "nubs" he considers "ugly." He avoids surface decoration or any embellishment that is superfluous to the function of the chair.   Thus a moral purpose dominates his rationale for production.   This point is underscored by his own evaluation: "people around here say I make the best chair of any one fella that's made 'em around here.   They don't say I make the *best-lookin'* chair—just the best one." The evident virtue of plainness is not lost on Vince's community. They register his chairs as: solid, decent, best, good. These are all adjectives rich with ambiguity since these terms refer equally to their moral code as much as to the aesthetics of chairmaking. Moral church-goers might be described with many of the same words.

If we might not expect to find religion in front porch chairs, perhaps we would be even less inclined to regard a field of corn as a sacred statement. This would be a serious mistake, however, for most agrarian peoples have rituals, some more magical than religious, which aid them in raising their crops. The German Catholics of Dubois County in Southern Indiana, for example, every Spring have their parish priest carry the Sacred Host, which they believe to be the body of Christ, through their fields in order to bless their efforts and to ensure the fertility of their plants.[5] The resulting stands of wheat, corn, and soybeans cannot be seen then as other than God's gift, and the fields become a holy landscape. They display the results of prayer and sacred devotion no matter what prices are guaranteed by the futures market. These farming people pray on Sunday when they attend Mass and they pray the rest of the week when they offer their work to their God, a God who has personally visited their fields.

A similar circumstance was reported among the Navajo by anthropologist W.W. Hill (1938:53). One of his informants explained to him that corn itself was sacred:

> My granduncle used to say to me "If you are walking along a trail and see a kernel of corn, pick it up. It is like a child lost and starving." According to the legends corn is just the same as a human being, only it is holier . . . When a man goes into a cornfield he feels he is in a holy place, that he is walking among Holy People . . . Agriculture is a holy occupation. Even before you plant you sing songs. You continue this during the whole time your crops are growing. You cannot help but feel you are in a holy place when you go through your fields and they are doing well.

Again we find no dividing line between worship and work. The Navajo Indian, like the German from Indiana, merges subsistence needs with spiritual needs so that a good harvest is simultaneously a sign of industry and of positive divine intervention. While we all might acknowledge that farming is a cultural act, some might question whether it is art. But if an artwork consists of natural material modified by man in order to give pleasure then surely a well-tilled field sprouting with endless furrows full of green plants must qualify (Glassie 1977:32-33). While the satisfactions provided to its maker might be tallied as economic, moral, and aesthetic, one category of response does not detract from the others. Rather the total impact is enhanced by the simultaneous service of different needs. Indeed, the interrelatedness of these needs serves to indicate how important the act of planting a field is, and further it demonstrates how a farmer is rewarded with a profound sense of accomplishment and well-being, for he has made money, created a pleasant scene, and served his God all at the same time.

Raising the possibility that entire folk societies may see themselves as built on hallowed ground captures all of their actions into the domain of religion. All behavior in such a society, and consequently all of its artistic statements, become then religious statements to some degree. But in order to avoid an oversimplified view of members of folk societies as people who blindly follow the dictates of faith, we must again closely study the behavior of individual artists. We must introduce into our analysis of art and religion some measure of will, the power of choice. People who do not choose to worship are not really believers, just as people who do not choose to create are only imitators. On this matter of personal will, Redfield (1947:300) has written:

> It must not be supposed that primitive man is a sort of automaton in which custom is the mainspring. . . . Within the limits set by custom there is an invitation to excel in performance. There is a lively competition, a sense of opportunity, and a feeling that what the culture moves one to do is well worth doing.

Applying this assessment to the members of folk groups, we should be prepared to allow folk artists to maintain their sense of ego even as they subscribe to the culturally-informed dictates of a moral agenda.

Philip Simmons, a blacksmith and ornamental ironworker from Charleston, South Carolina, who began his career in 1925 has since the late 1930s served the decorative needs of that city (Vlach 1983).[6] Many of the homes in the famous Battery District as well as those in the working class sections are graced with his gates and fences (Figure 2). The designs that he uses derive mainly from the early works done by English and German blacksmiths that can be found throughout the city, and yet for Simmons what is most important is that all his work should be "good" work. Even while he acknowledges the importance of observing local artistic patterns, he asserts a higher set of standards derived from his religious beliefs:

> All work by man is the hand of God. Edison made the light but everything he used was made by God. Same for my work, I look at nature a lot. The greatest history is "In the beginning God created heaven and earth." Nothing before that; all comes from that, isn't it?

Thus the fanciest palmette or animal sculpture which he might place in the screen section of a gate or in a window grill is but a weak echo of God's initial creation. With each work that Simmons makes, he is sure to reinforce his personal feeling of humility for God's work which is not only prior to his but also perfect unlike his own approximations of nature. Yet humility does not eliminate or override his sense of self for he notes "I take a lot of pride in my work. I do a good job." One feels good, asserts Simmons, when one observes certain standards of excellence, standards that derive from what is morally correct as well as what is demanded by the customary codes of the local iron working traditions. Speaking directly about these two sets of rules he notes:

> I know how long wrought iron supposed to last. I build a gate, I build it to last two hundred years. If it looks good, you feel good. I build a gate and I just be thinking about two hundred years. If you don't, you're not an honest craftsman.

His traditional apprenticeship and his membership in the Reformed Episcopal Church have taught him how to work. His blacksmith teacher and his ministers both instilled in him the same sense of ethics—work well and you will be honest, be honest and you will work well.

What is important here is that the moral virtue of honesty is not simply bestowed but earned. The gate is honest, the craftsman is honest, only if the work is done in compliance with tough local standards for durability and beauty. In Simmons's mind the success of his creativity is to be measured in pragmatic, aesthetic, *and* moral terms. Ironically, his success is in part attained by overcoming the challenge posed by one of the requirements of good work—pride. As a master of his art, Simmons is often called upon to design unique works, works in which he is expected to show off. He is quite frank about the pleasure he derives from such requests saying: "I enjoy doing the work . . . but I enjoy the one when they come and say 'I don't know what I want.'" In such circumstances he is free to let his imagination roam the entire span of his creative potential. When he is free to explore his options in an open-ended manner the level of ego in the design process is significantly raised. This is certainly evident in the following statement:

> Sometime I draw the whole thing and don't like it myself, not the customer. What that comes from (is) you think you like it to start, (but) it isn't always you like something you can visualize. But one thing, you can visualize, it give you a background like this drawing here. I may not like these scroll when I start, but still I see it that way after puttin' it in and I see where I can improve it.

Personal initiative is definitely required to become a successful artist. In contemporary mainstream American society, when a person solves his or her problems on their own, they are usually praised and rewarded for their ingenuity. In a folk society, however, one has to be careful not to seek such acclaim too aggressively or too directly.[7] Drawing excessive attention to one's self is generally regarded as immodest and is bad form if not immoral. Thus we find that Simmons often deflects attention away from himself and assigns the bulk of the credit for his work to his community, saying "I owe all my career to the people of Charleston. Without they giving me a chance, I couldn't have anything." By so doing, he is able to sidestep the dangers of being too full of pride.

Honors come to him as his clients express their thanks and grant him esteem for his modesty. Simmons thus does not have to demand prestige or fame, it is bestowed upon him. He attains greatness while honoring the moral charge to remain humble. Hence, we see that the moral or ethical standards that intertwine with the aesthetic require- ments for folk art can make life very complicated. The artist must learn to balance carefully between what is possible and what is allowable, between what looks good and what is good. If he wants to be successful, he must find a way to place his own vision within the limits of the vision of the community in which he lives. Their aesthetic becomes his, their morality becomes his. His prime challenge then is to blend these two sometimes-conflicting sets of standards not only with each other but with his own personal desires. In Simmon's case, pride in one's craft is matched against the communal dues of required honesty and modesty, while he simultaneously tries to enjoy his work. Thus, if he is a good man, it is because he works hard to maintain a balance among these requirements so that he might be judged as honest, moral, and good. The command to work in this manner comes from two sources: it is imposed from outside of the artistic process by his religion and it emerges from within the artistic process itself.[8] Consequently, the moral issue can never be effectively escaped or avoided.

In this paper I have attempted to make only two points: that folk art is often also religious art and, conversely, that moral tenets are often the rules for folk art. These are not unique or novel hypotheses; Robert Redfield said as much over forty years ago. While it may be convenient for us to discuss different social domains like kinship, law, politics, art, economics, technology, religion, and so forth as if they were bounded by precise limits, it is crucial for us to recognize that life does not admit to such a neat scheme of verbal pigeonholes. Consider how quick we are to draw the chaos of reality's swirling experiences into order by assigning and compounding labels. Note how we attempt to reduce our confusions regarding the domain of things by separating things that are art from things that are craft, and then art that is folk from art that is fine, and then folk art that is religious from folk art that is secular. I hope that I have been able to demonstrate some of the shortcomings of such a strategy. All craft is partly art, a lot of fine art is influenced by folk art, and much that is secular is also religious. The actual experiences of the numerous faithful will not permit us to remake their view of the world for the convenience of our categories. We have to recognize that not only are images of saints, grave crosses, fraktur certificates, and Bible pictures religious folk art but so are chairs, quilts, baskets, houses, fields, gardens, and countless other utilitarian objects when the spirit of belief fills their makers. Any artifact, if rendered with skill and care, can convey both the enrichment of art and the enrichment of religion. We should then be wary of the simplicity of generic conventions regarding religious folk art and look instead beyond them into the realm of folk values as lived. Should we begin our inquiry with a group's thoughts and feelings about religion, we are more likely to end up understanding their expressions of faith in their terms and through their chosen forms. Viewing the art and culture of folk society from the inside looking out is certainly much more desirable than considering it from the outside looking in.

NOTES

[1]   See Redfield (1947:293, n.2; 303-04). A similar interpretation of a folk community was suggested by Henry Glassie in his *Passing the Time in Ballymenone.* See especially p.758, note 13, where he identifies rural Ireland as a "culture founded upon religion."

[2]   See Robert K. Merton's essay "Manifest and Latent Functions," in *On Theoretical Sociology* (1967:114-15).

[3]   There is a copious bibliography on colonial New England. Particularly significant to the shaping of the viewpoint presented here, however, is the work of John Demos (1970).

[4]   All quotations from Vince are taken from Michael Owen Jones' *The Handmade Object and Its Maker* (1975, Chapter 6). See also Jones (1972).

[5]   This information is derived from a field study done by Michael Simmons of Indiana University in 1972 and conveyed to the author in a personal communication.

[6]   All quotations from Philip Simmons are taken from Vlach (1983).

[7]   See, for example, George M. Foster (1965).

[8]   See also James Fernandez (1973).

REFERENCES CITED

Demos, John
   1970 *A Little Commonwealth: Family Life in Plymouth Colony.* New York: Oxford
       University Press.
Fernandez, James
   1973 The Exposition and Imposition of Order: Artistic Expression in Fang Culture.
       in *The Traditional Artist in African Societies.* Warren L. d'Azevedo, ed.
       Bloomington: Indiana University Press, pp.194-220.
Foster, George M.
   1965 Peasant Society and the Image of Limited Good. *American Anthropologist*
       67:293-315.
Glassie, Henry
   1972 Folk Art. in *Folklore and Folklife.* Richard M. Dorson, ed. Chicago:
       University of Chicago Press, pp.253-80.
   1977 Meaningful Things and Appropriate Myths: The Artifact's Place in American
       Studies. *Prospects* 3:1-49.
   1982 *Passing the Time in Ballymenone: Culture and History of an Ulster Community.*
       Philadelphia: University of Pennsylvania Press.
Hill, W.W.
   1938 *The Agricultural and Hunting Methods of the Navajo Indians.* (Yale University
       Publications in Anthropology, No. 18) New Haven: Yale University Press.
Jones, Michael Owen
   1972 'For Myself I Like a Decent, Plain-Made Chair': The Concept of Taste and
       the Traditional Arts in America. *Western Folklore* 31:27-52.
   1975 *The Handmade Object and Its Maker.* Berkeley: University of California Press.
Merton, Robert K.
   1967 *On Theoretical Sociology: Five Essays, Old and New.* New York: The Free
       Press.
Redfield, Robert
   1947 The Folk Society. *The American Journal of Sociology* 52:292-308.
St. George, Robert Blair
   1982 'Set Thine House in Order': The Domestication of the Yeomanry of
       Seventeenth-Century New England. In *New England Begins: The Seventeenth-
       Century.* Boston: Museum of Fine Arts, pp.159-88.
Vlach, John Michael
   1983 *Charleston Blacksmith: The Work of Philip Simmons.* Athens: University of
       Georgia Press.

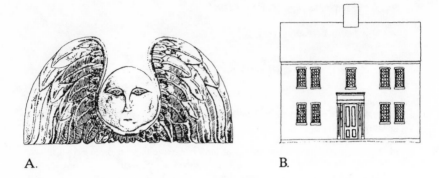

A.

B.

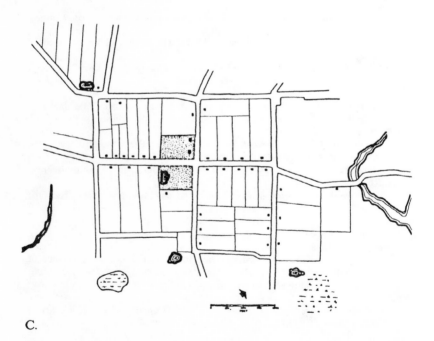

C.

Figure 1. Three examples of the Puritan Order in New England: A. Gravestone of
Rebeckah James of Newport, Rhode Island, who died in 1730. B. Facade of
a saltbox house from Hampden, Massachusetts. C. Symmetrical gridiron plan
of Fairfield, Connecticut. (Artwork for A and B by Henry Glassie (1972),
reproduced with permission of Henry Glassie. Town plan by John Reps from
his book *Town Planning in Frontier America* [Princeton: Princeton University
Press, 1969], reproduced with the permission of John Reps.)

Figure 2. Detail of a wrought iron gate insert by Philip Simmons. Made and installed in Charleston, South Carolina, in 1972. (Photo by John Michael Vlach)

Spindles and Spoon Racks: Local Style in Nineteenth-Century Mormon Furniture

THOMAS CARTER

In contrast to the substantial research accomplished on Utah and Mormon folklife generally, furniture produced in the West by Mormon cabinetmakers has received only passing attention. It has been treated in several regional catalogs (Morningstar 1976; Richards 1980) and briefly in the vernacular sections of American furniture surveys (Fairbanks 1975:179-84; Bates and Fairbanks 1981:438-42), but thorough investigation of the topic remains negligible. One reason for such disregard may lie in the historical community's abiding distrust of the artifact as reliable evidence (Berkhofer 1969:17). Another may be the elusive nature of the objects themselves. Pieces of furniture—like old chairs, for example—have often been moved many times and as a result it is often difficult to know when and where and by whom they were made, and who used them and how. Stripped of what archaeologist James Deetz calls a "behavioral context," furniture lacks connection with "the larger material culture system" that makes analysis practical (Deetz 1976:121). Folklorists therefore have generally backed away from furniture studies in the West, and the extensive fieldwork characteristic of most material culture research in the region has not yet been accomplished or even attempted.[1]

This essay has the objective of beginning such an effort by reporting on a small group of pine cupboards discovered during the course of a larger architectural study of Utah's Sanpete Valley (Carter 1984).[2] In doing so it modestly continues the tradition of intensely local folklife investigation established by Warren Roberts at Indiana University (Roberts 1981, 1988). The cupboards were produced between 1860 and 1880 and are distinguished by their decorative applied turnings, mostly split spindles, and by the presence in the upper case of a notched spoon rack for the display of silver flatware (Fig. 1). Fieldwork was initially directed toward finding out what furnishings people in the area—the people who built and lived in the old houses under investigation—had in the past. But as more cupboards surfaced, so did the questions. Who was responsible for these appealing objects? Where did the cupboard designs come from? Most importantly, what did they mean? During the winter and spring of 1979-80, I did further fieldwork, recording in all over 150 pieces of early Sanpete Valley furniture, of which 26 were cupboards. All were photographed and measured, approximate dates were assigned on the basis of paint color—red mahogany typified the 1850s and 60s, while golden oak and dark brown walnut predominated in the 1870s and 80s—and a basic provenance was established through a series of oral interviews. Taken as a whole, the 26 cupboards provided a small but tightly controlled body of artifactual data.

Central to the study's main purpose was an understanding of the importance of *style* in folk furniture. And by suggesting that folk objects have style I do not mean that they necessarily aspire to high art ideals—though they often do exactly that—but simply that they may be studied for their own intrinsic artistic value, for their own style (Kubler 1962:1-2). Style itself is not an easy concept to pin down, but generally it refers to a set of shared aesthetic conventions that unite a particular group of objects (Shapiro 1953). More specifically, art historian Jules Prown contends that the unstated cultural principles and values of a society are "most clearly perceivable, not in what a society says it is doing in its histories, literature, or public and private documents, but rather in the way it does things." He concludes that "the way in which something is done, produced, or expressed is its style." (Prown 1980:198). Implicit in Prown's definition is the idea that the behavioral consistency within a certain context that we call style results from a system of common assumptions, an underlying "aesthetic philosophy," to quote Henry Glassie, "that governs the selection, production, treatment, and use of forms" (Glassie 1972:253-54). The historian of things must therefore look at an object for signs of the "internal logic" (Trent 1977:10) or "psychological reality" (St. George 1979a:29) that led to its creation. Composition, decoration, materials, techniques—in essence, style—these are the things explanation is built upon.

A logical extension of this thinking was the idea that there should be a *Mormon style* in material culture. If, as historian Mary Lynn Ray asserts, the furniture of the Shakers can be viewed as an "abstraction of their convictions" (Ray 1977:108), it seemed right to assume that the utopian vision and communitarian spirit of early Mormonism would have found expression in the decorative arts as well. Was there a distinctive Mormon furniture style in the West, one built upon such Saintly virtues as simplicity and practicality? Surprisingly, no study has developed such a thesis because Mormon furniture has been discussed only in relation to contemporary Eastern styles rather than scrutinized for its own stylistic qualities (Richards 1980:72). Furthermore, the Sanpete cupboards—highly embellished objects designed to display worldly possessions—tend to undermine the rather simplistic notion of a highly functional Mormon style, yet the fundamental question of what constitutes Mormon style in material culture remains and becomes the principal focus of this essay.

The Sanpete Valley was settled during the fall of 1849 by members of the Church of Jesus Christ of Latter-day Saints, the Mormons, as part of their larger occupation of the Great Basin during the second half of the nineteenth century (Arrington 1966; Antrei and Scow 1984). Located about 120 miles south of Salt Lake City, the Sanpete colony was intended as a bulwark against non-Mormon intrusion as well as an agricultural colony for the increasing number of converts flowing into the parent community. The valley's population was diverse from the beginning, with sizeable contingents of Scandinavian and British converts joining settlers from the eastern and midwestern United States (Carter 1984:78-80, May 1985). By 1860, eleven towns had been established, of which Manti, Ephraim, and Mount Pleasant were the largest. The valley grew steadily and by 1880 had a population of about 12,000.

Most Mormon immigrants made the western journey with only a few prized possessions and arrived in the West needing tools, implements, and furnishings almost immediately. It is not surprising, therefore, that furniture production commenced in all Sanpete Valley communities soon after the initial settlement, replacing the homemade, the makeshift, and the temporary, as described in the reminiscences of Oluf Larsen, a Norwegian convert: "We commenced with two tin cups, two tin plates, a coffeepot, a three quart pan, a kettle we had used across the plains and a baking skillet which a friend lent us. Our furniture consisted of two slab benches and a table made by knocking two sticks into the wall and putting a couple of narrow boards on them" (Larsen 1898:38).

The skilled cabinetmakers among the convert population quickly responded to the strong local market for superior furniture. One writer noted that "Edwin Whiting's shelter must have been crowded for besides his family of three wives and eight children, he set up a foot lathe and went to work making chairs" (Christensen 1979:201). Another craftsman was Samuel Gifford, a chairmaker from Barnstable, Massachusetts, who had earlier plied his trade in the Mormon settlement of Nauvoo, Illinois. Gifford came to Manti in the first wave of settlement and in addition to making chairs for local use had enough left over for export, noting in an 1853 diary entry that he "took about 150 chairs to Salt Lake City and sold some of them for the money" (Gifford n.d.:9).

Census documents bear out the importance of the Sanpete Valley furniture industry: between 1860 and 1880 over sixty-one different cabinetmakers were working in the area. These craftsmen reflected the healthy ethnic mixture of the Latter-day Saint population as a whole. Of the total number, forty-two, or about sixty-nine percent, were of Scandinavian origin: twenty-six Danes, three Norwegians, and eight Swedes. The next largest group, numbering seven, had emigrated from England; the rest were from all over the United States, including several from Massachusetts and New York, two were from Ohio, and one each from Kentucky and North Carolina.

Even though many of the cabinetmakers can be identified by name and country of origin, little is known of their actual operations. No account books or journals have surfaced that describe cabinetmaking activities in detail and few pieces are signed, making it difficult to document the contributions of individual craftsmen or shops. Generally speaking, however, it appears that small operations were the rule, with a single cabinetmaker working alone, perhaps assisted by a solitary apprentice or helper. The largest private operation was in Ephraim, where the Norwegian Carl Uckerman ran a water-powered factory employing four turners and joiners. Ephraim also had a church-sponsored cooperative furniture factory that in 1869, according to a local newspaper correspondent, was "doing a good business, some specimens of work, especially several centre [sic] tables, being elegant in design and finish" (Antrei and Scow 1984:63). But the documentary evidence is fragmentary and inconclusive and we must turn to the furniture itself if we are to construct a collective portrait of the local cabinetmaking tradition. The china cupboards are of particular interest because being the most complex pieces they also yield the most cultural information (Glassie 1983:377).

Sanpete Valley cupboards are in form very typical of this large category of furniture. They are conceptually composed of two cases, upper and lower, both roughly square in shape. Doors are typically found on both upper and lower cases; the upper doors are glazed, the lower ones paneled. The cupboards measure 74-90 inches tall and 45-54 inches wide. The lower cases are 16-20 inches deep and were used primarily for linen storage. The upper cases are only 8-12 inches deep, a difference that leaves a small counter or shelf at the front of the cupboard just about waist height. Two or three shelves with plate rails span the upper case and at the very top there is a notched spoon rack (Fig. 2). Here the best dishes and silver were kept.

Although apparently two separate cases, the cupboards were invariably constructed in one piece. The long vertical side boards are uninterrupted and are generally dovetailed into the top and bottom boards. The back boards are nailed in place, while the shelves in both upper and lower cases are rabbeted into the side boards. The front rails, or facing boards, are butted against the frame and nailed.

The wood used is almost universally the Douglas fir (*pseudotsuga taxifola*), called locally "red pine," that was hauled out of the nearby canyons. Occasionally, packing crates were recycled for drawer bottoms and door panels, but this practice was not common. The earliest cupboards, those dating to the mid-1860s when local furniture production was in its infancy are often hand-planed throughout, but by the 1870s such handwork had generally been replaced by water-powered planing, turning, and milling.

Symmetry is the driving force in the cupboard design. Within the formal constraints of the symmetrical model, however, great variation occurred, suggesting either that individual shops produced a large number of different designs, or, more likely, that many different cabinetmakers were producing cupboards in the same basic style. The most important structural option is a narrow row of drawers placed in either or both of the cases that added six to fourteen inches to the height of the cupboard. These drawers may have been used for storing candles, napkins, and other small household items. The location of the drawer row is a simple diagonistic feature that is useful in forming a typology of the Sanpete cupboards. *Type 1* cupboards (Fig. 3a) contain no drawers and may lack doors, especially on the upper case. The *Type 2* group—quite rare—(Fig. 3b) has drawers in the bottom case only. The most common form is the *Type 3* variety (Fig. 3c) which has a row of drawers in the upper case. *Type 4* (Fig. 3d), with drawers in both cases, is also rare.

All the cupboard types are highly decorative. The standard embellishment has cresting at the top above a small and rather simple cornice. Most crests are doweled into the top board and are invariably symmetrical and tripartite, the larger middle element emphasizing the center point of the design and reiterating the symmetry of the cupboard below. The base is often treated similarly; many pieces have a scroll-cut, symmetrical, tripartite apron running across the bottom.

The finest touches were reserved for the cases themselves. Ornamentation here occurred exclusively in the form of applied turnings. Round medallions are occasionally found on the lower doors, crests, and aprons, but such devices were much more common on beds and lounges. The preferred decorative detail on the cupboards were split spindles. The spindles were formed by ripping a board in half and then gluing it back together. The reconstituted whole was then turned on a lathe, either in an urn or spool pattern, and then re-split along the seam. The halves were then applied to opposite sides of the case and nailed. Generally the spindles were applied vertically to the outside rails. Although several Ephraim pieces have lighter, more delicate spindles on the upper case offsetting heavier ones on the bottom, most examples show little difference between the upper and lower turnings. Several cupboards are even fancier. In addition to spindles on their side rails, they have one on the center rail and others applied horizontally to the crest and apron (Fig. 4).

The cabinetmaker's last step was the finish. In the Sanpete Valley of the nineteenth century this meant painting the local "red pine" to resemble exotic hardwoods such as mahogany and walnut. The process was designed to hide the wood's knotty grain and often entailed what was locally called "killing" the knots by desiccating them with lye. The open knot holes were then covered with plaster before the white, smooth surface was painted. In the 1860s, a dark red mahogany was the favored wood to imitate, but by the late 1870s dark brown walnut had achieved considerable appeal. Oak graining did not gain currency in the valley until the early 1880s.

Split-spindled cupboards with spoon racks are the most commonly encountered Sanpete Valley cupboard form, but they are not found in other parts of the Mormon-settled West (Thatcher 1988; Morningstar 1976:77,79; Richards 1980:70-71), nor are they easily traceable to a particular tradition originating in the American Midwest or East (Garvin 1979; Weidman 1984; Waters 1984; Sikes 1976; Churchill 1983; Winters 1977; Melchor, Lohr, Melchor 1982; Dudrow 1983; Taylor and Warren 1975; Atlanta Historical Society 1983; Western

Reserve Historical Society 1972; Reed 1987). Given the predominantly Scandinavian background of the local cabinetmakers, northern Europe might appear a likely source for the cupboard's design, particularly Denmark, which accounted for a disproportionate number of craftsmen in the area. Yet the spindled cupboard form is not Scandinavian; it has neither Danish (Steensberg 1977; Friis 1976) nor Swedish (Erixon 1938; Frelund 1977) antecedents.[3] In clear rebuttal to the power of diffusionist theory, the Sanpete Valley spindled cupboards have their origin, not in Denmark or in Illinois, but in the Sanpete Valley itself. The form is not an imported one; it is, rather, a product of the western frontier. The Sanpete cupboards represent the creative synthesis of several streams of influence, both folk and popular.

Four basic ingredients were combined to produce the distinctive identity of the Sanpete Valley cupboard: the free-standing cupboard form, the simulated-wood painting, the applied spindled ornamentation, and the inclusion of the spoon rack. Each had its own history before converging in Sanpete Valley workshops. The first two—the cupboard form and the painting— are widely distributed and of relatively recent origin. Before the nineteenth century, Scandinavians customarily stored precious possessions and fancy dinnerware in built-in architectural furniture (Michelsen 1973; Friis 1976:113). By the early nineteenth century, however, free-standing, detached furniture was becoming increasingly fashionable and cupboards, both the flat-wall and corner varieties, began to appear (Michelsen 1973; Friis 1976:109-18). In the English tradition the cupboard form dates to at least the fourteenth century and acquired its joint storage and presentation function early (Lyon 1977:34; Ward 1987:68-69). During the eighteenth century, cupboards in both England and English America lost their low, chest-like medieval form, gradually assuming a taller rectangular shape (Lyon 1977:68-69). Such pieces enjoyed widespread popularity in rural America during the nineteenth century (Churchill 1983:68-69; Taylor and Ward 1975:241-56; Melchor, Lohr, Melchor 1982:61-69; Muller 1984:18-32; van Ravenswaay 1977:333-47; Madden 1974:110) and became important fixtures in Mormon households throughout the West.

The graining of furniture was another popular nineteenth-century tradition that migrated westward with the Latter-day Saints. The essential idea in such practice was to transform—with a veneer of paint—plain, non-prestigious woods like pine and poplar into more exotic and fashionable varieties like mahogany, walnut, and oak. The painting of furniture in colors is an old one throughout Scandinavia, but the nineteenth century witnessed a significant change as older preferences for bright colors (usually blues and greens) and floral designs were replaced by the new simulated wood grains (Franzen 1970). And while Danish, Swedish, and Norwegian cabinetmakers emigrating to Utah would have been well-versed in the new style, their Anglo-American counterparts would also have been comfortable with it, since painted furniture was enjoying a similar vogue in the United States (Fales 1972; Herman 1977). Thus, painted furniture is not unique to the Sanpete Valley or to the Mormon culture region; instead it constitutes an important element in nineteenth-century furniture style generally.

The history of the applied spindles also involves an understanding of nineteenth-century popular culture. Originally, split spindles were features of the Mannerist style that was popular in sixteenth- and seventeenth-century England and became the predominant style in colonial New England (Lyon 1977; Trent 1982; St. George 1979a, 1979b). Mannerist ideals eventually passed out of fashion and spindles as decorative devices lay dormant until they were resurrected by furniture designers of the mid-nineteenth century and incorporated into what was then called the new Elizabethan style. Also called "cottage furniture," furniture in the Elizabethan style was generally mass-produced and inexpensive. The pieces were characterized by "spiral or spool turned legs and stiles" (Dubrow 1983:161) and "spool and ball turnings, easily and cheaply turned out on lathes" (Fitzgerald 1982:213). The use of applied decorative turnings, especially spindles, was emblematic of the Elizabethan style (Naeve 1981:33) and apparently quite widespread on factory-produced pieces. One writer has noted that "with split halves glued or nailed on so many cased pieces, these turnings grew in usage until by 1840 some factories more profitably retired from general furniture making and only supplied such turnings to other makers" (McNerney 1981:18).

The national media helped disseminate the new furniture styles. Architectural stylebooks such as Andrew Jackson Downing's *Architecture of Country Houses* discussed appropriate interior settings and contained plates showing spindled furniture in the "Elizabethan style" (Downing 1969:448-60). Tradebooks and catalogs also carried examples of spindled and painted furniture (Fig. 5) and undoubtedly helped bring the new ideas and techniques to cabinetmakers throughout the country (Foster and Lee 1858; McKinstry 1984). Examples of locally produced spindled cupboards are found in Ohio (Muller 1984:28-29; Hageman 1984:66), Iowa (Nelson 1979:110-14; Viel 1983:69,85,88), and Newfoundland (Peddle 1983:103-15), but nowhere have they been found in the quantity exhibited in the Sanpete Valley.

The final defining element, the spoon rack, has its origins in the folk traditions of Scandinavia. Notched shelves or racks for the storage and display of pewter or silver spoons are rare in the Anglo-American tradition, but occur frequently in Denmark in built-in cupboards, hanging shelves, and nineteenth century case pieces (Friis 1976:111-13). The general presence of the spoon rack in northern European tradition is further illustrated by the fact that in the United States this element is found only among the Pennsylvania Germans (Shea 1980:78-79; Forman 1983:152).

The question of origins, then, is complex and multifaceted. The concepts behind the Sanpete cupboard form were carried unified and intact into the valley. None of the four major elements that define the form, however, were particularly original. The cupboard form and the technique of wood-grained painting were ubiquitous, the spindles were prominent in the popular literature of the day, and the spoon rack was well known to Scandinavian craftsmen. What is significant is the innovative way these elements were combined to produce a distinctive local form, instead of simply a copy of an older or a contemporary popular one. The Sanpete cupboard style—the "way they were made," to paraphrase Prown—is based upon a mixture of imported ideas. Each cupboard is different, but they all share a common vision that is at once imaginative in breaking with the past, resourceful in using materials and ideas that were locally available, and practical in their functionality. Such principles are the wellspring of style, and through their style the Sanpete cupboards articulate values and attitudes that are valuable to the historian of the Mormon West.

At a very basic level the cupboards speak of frontier life. The attention and care that went into their production belies the difficult living conditions of their makers and owners. These are not simply expedient and incompetent copies of Eastern prototypes. To the contrary, the cupboards maintain through their symmetrical composition and smoothly finished exteriors a strong formal link with established art conventions, suggesting a continuation of civilization rather than its demise or devolution. The cupboards also reveal a healthy appreciation for older aesthetic values and contemporary fashion. Fancy painted veneers and modish spindling are clues to an underlying vanity—a concern for material things—that must be recognized in the Mormon psyche (Carter 1981).

The cupboards also speak to the complex myth of Mormon homogeneity. Certainly there was in the Mormon West a regional furniture—a furniture, that is, built by and for Mormons that appears different from the furniture traditions of the Midwest and East. To some extent this regional furniture results from the exigencies of the frontier, but it would be wrong to think that all early Mormon furniture is the same. Sanpete cupboards, for instance, do not closely resemble those of the Cache Valley—the only other location where there is reliable comparative data—nor do they ape styles common in the provincial capital at Salt Lake City. To understand the enigma that is Mormon culture, then, we must begin not by assuming that there is a single Mormon identity, but by looking carefully at different subregional expressions, the building blocks upon which a complex regional whole may be understood.

The style of the Sanpete cupboards also suggests some other conclusions about Mormon culture, a subject that has proved elusive over the years (Sorensen 1973). Recent studies have demonstrated the correlation between social structure and art (Fischer 1971; Glassie 1975:181-82; Pocius 1979:281-82) and suggest that a spectrum may be constructed with egalitarian societies on one end and differentiated, hierarchical, bourgeois societies on the other. Art styles in egalitarian societies are marked by the repetition of simple, symmetrical elements, while hierarchical societies create styles characterized by complexity, non-repetitiveness, and asymmetry.

Along this spectrum, Sanpete cupboards fall somewhere in the middle. Adhering to a basic symmetrical form and stylistically unified from an early date, they are repetitious. But at the same time they are neither plain nor visually simple; they are complex, ornamental, and individualized. Also, by functioning to display the family's best personal belongings—plates and silver—the cupboards served as vehicles of differentiation themselves. Although precise locations of these cupboards in the houses cannot be readily determined (there are no room-by-room inventories from the area), oral histories and recollections verify that they occupied places of prominence within the household. Generally the cupboard was placed in the living room or—when there was one—the dining room, places where visitors would not be likely to miss them or their symbolic significance.

From the perspective of the bipolar model introduced above, the Sanpete Valley cupboards suggest a society simultaneously egalitarian and hierarchical. A study by Henry Glassie of folk housing in eighteenth-century Virginia casts light on this apparent paradox. Glassie found a similar contradiction in house design; there was a strong degree of repetition, yet the buildings remained complex in appearance and highly differentiated in terms of their size and ornamentation. Glassie concluded that the aesthetic conflict visible in the Virginia houses reflected deeper cultural confusions between

American egalitarian ideals and the realities of a competitive capitalistic society (Glassie 1975:181-82). The Mormon colonists in the Sanpete Valley perhaps were not so different. Confronting the task of building a new Kingdom of God, they faced life with a mixture of ideas about how that vision would be translated into reality. On the one hand, there were communitarian objectives that recognized the need to bring the people together in the spirit of cooperation and unity (Arrington, Fox, and May 1976). On the other hand, they maintained the traditional American ideals of individualism and the goal of success, social, spiritual, and economic. Historians have often viewed this duality in Mormon culture as a sign of discontinuity, conflict, and weakness in the social fabric, in opposition to the scholarly ideal of a single Mormon mindset. For the Sanpete Valley Saints, however, those who built and bought cupboards and placed them in their houses, such a duality was seemingly comfortable, reflecting both their cultural heritage and their current aspiration. And it was probably just the way life was.

NOTES

Earlier versions of this paper were read at the American Folklore Society meeting in Cincinnati in 1985 and at the Mormon History Association meeting in Salt Lake City in 1986. The research was partially funded by a grant from the American-Scandinavian Foundation and a Benno C. Forman Fellowship at the Winterthur Museum. Nancy Richards Clark, now of the Princeton Historical Society, participated in the initial field research. The author would like to thank Warren Roberts for kindling an interest in material culture studies, and Ken Ames, Gary Stanton, and David Stanley for their advice concerning the manuscript.

[1]   The notable exception is the work of Elaine Thatcher in northern Utah's Cache County (Thatcher 1983). Thatcher's research, however, was largely confined to pieces available in local museums or through the largess of collectors and was not based on a systematic town-by-town survey.

[2]   Examples of early furniture were observed and recorded while documenting over two hundred of the older houses in the valley. Most of the cupboards were found in attics, basements, and outbuildings where they had been moved in the early 1900s to make room for newly purchased oak chests and sideboards.

[3]   Extensive research was conducted in the furniture collection of the Danish National Museum in Copenhagen. Access to the collection was generously provided by curator Birget Vorre.

REFERENCES CITED

Antrei, Albert and Ruth Scow
  1982 *The Other Forty Niners: A Topical History of Sanpete County, Utah.* Salt Lake
     City: Western Epics.
Arrington, Leonard J.
  1966 *Great Basin Kingdom: Economic History of the Latter-day Saints.* Reprint from
     1958. Lincoln: University of Nebraska Press.
---------, Feramorz Y. Fox, and Dean L. May
  1976 *Building the City of God: Community and Cooperation Among the Mormons.*
     Salt Lake City: Deseret Book.
Atlanta Historical Society
  1983 *Neat Pieces: The Plain Style Furniture of 19th Century Georgia.* Atlanta: Atlanta
     Historical Society.
Bates, Elizabeth Bidwell and Jonathan L. Fairbanks
  1981 *American Furniture: 1620 to the Present.* New York: Richard Marek.
Berkhofer, Robert, Jr.
  1969 *A Behavioral Approach to Historical Analysis.* New York: The Free Press.
Carter, Thomas
  1981 Cultural Veneer: Decorative Plastering in Utah's Sanpete Valley. *Utah
     Historical Quarterly* 49: 68-77.
  1984 Building Zion: Folk Architecture in the Mormon Settlements of Utah's
     Sanpete Valley, 1849-1890. Ph.D. Dissertation, Indiana University.
Christensen, Clare B.
  1979 *Before and After Mount Pisgah.* Salt Lake City: Christensen.
Churchill, Edwin A.
  1983 *Simple Forms and Vivid Colors: An Exhibition of Maine Painted Furniture,
     1800-1850.* Augusta: Maine State Museum.
Deetz, James
  1977 *In Small Things Forgotten: The Archaeology of Early American Life.* Garden
     City,N.Y: Anchor Press.
Downing, Andrew Jackson
  1969 *Architecture of Country Houses.* Reprint from 1850. New York: Dover.
Dubrow, Eileen and Richard Dubrow
  1983 *American Furniture of the Nineteenth Century.* Exton,Pa: Schiffer Publishing.
Erixon, Sigurd
  1938 *Folklig Möbelkultur i Svenska Bygder.* Stockholm.
Fairbanks, Jonathan L.
  1975 *Frontier America: The Far West.* Boston: Museum of Fine Arts.
Fales, Dean A., Jr.
  1972 *American Painted Furniture, 1660-1880.* New York: Bonanza Books.
Fischer, John L.
  1971 Art Styles as Cultural Cognitive Maps. In *Art and Aesthetics in Primitive
     Societies.* Pp. 171-92. New York: E.P. Dutton.
Fitzgerald, Oscar P.
  1982 *Three Centuries of American Furniture.* Englewood Cliffs, N.J: Prentice-Hall.
Forman, Benno C.
  1983 German Influences in Pennsylvania Furniture. In *Arts of the Pennsylvania
     Germans.* Pp. 102-70. New York: W.W. Norton.
Foster and Lee
  1858 *Furniture Dealers.* New York: J. Higgins.

Franzén, Anne Marie
1970 *Målade Kistor och Skåp: Om det Folkliga Möblelmaleriet in Skåne under 1700-och 1800-talen.* Lund: Bokforlaget.
Friis, Lars
1976 *Gemmemøbler: Kister, Skabe, Skuffemøbler, og Chatoller på Frilandsmuseet.* København: Nationalmuseet.
Fredlund, Jane
1977 *Allmogemöbler.* Vasteras: ICA Bokforlag.
Garvin, James L.
1979 *Plain and Elegant, Rich and Common: Documented New Hampshire Furniture, 1750-1850.* Concord: New Hampshire Historical Society.
Gifford, Samuel Kendall
n.d. Journal (1821-1857). Historical Department of the Church of Jesus Christ of Latter-day Saints, Salt Lake City, Utah.
Glassie, Henry
1972 Folk Art. In *Folklore And Folklife: An Introduction.* Ed. Richard M. Dorson. Pp.253-80. Chicago: University of Chicago Press.
1975 *Folk Housing in Middle Virginia.* Knoxville: University of Tennessee Press.
1983 Folkloristic Study of the American Artifact: Objects and Objectives. In *Handbook of American Folklore.* Ed. Richard M. Dorson. Pp. 376-83. Bloomington: Indiana University Press.
Hageman, Jane Sikes
1984 *Ohio Furniture Makers.* Cincinnati: Janes Sikes Hageman.
Herman, Lloyd E.
1977 *Paint on Wood: Decorated American Furniture Since the 17th Century.* Washington, D.C: Smithsonian Institution Press.
Kubler, George
1962 *The Shape of Time: Remarks on a History of Things.* New Haven: Yale University Press.
Larson, Oluf Christian
n.d. Autobiography. Historical Department of the Church of Jesus Christ of Latter-day Saints, Salt Lake City, Utah.
Lyon, Irving W.
1977 *The Colonial Furniture of New Enland.* Reprint from 1891. New York: E.P. Dutton.
Madden, Betty I.
1974 *Arts, Crafts, and Architecture in Early Illinois.* Urbana: University of Illinois Press.
May, Dean L.
1983 A Demographic Portrait of the Mormons, 1830-1980. In *After 150 Years: The Latter-Day Saints in Sesquicentennial Perspective.* Pp. 37-70. Brigham Young University, Charles Redd Monographs in Western History, No. 13. Provo, Utah.
McNerney, Kathryn
1981 *Victorian Furniture: Our American Heritage.* Paducah, Ky: Collector Books.
Melchor, James R., N. Gordon Lohir, and Marilyn Melchor
1982 *Raised Panel Furniture, 1730-1830: Eastern Shore, Virginia.* Norfolk, Virginia: The Chrysler Museum.
Michelsen, Peter
1973 *Frilandsmuseet: The Danish Museum Village at Sorgenfri.* Copenhagen: The National Museum of Denmark.
Morningstar, Connie
1976 *Early Utah Furniture.* Logan: Utah State University Press.

Muller, Charles R.
1984 *Made in Ohio: Furniture, 1788-1888.* Columbus, Ohio: Columbus Museum of Art.

Naeve, Milo M.
1981 *Identifying American Furniture.* Nashville, Tenn: The American Association for State and Local History.

Nelson, Marion J.
1980 The Material Culture and Folk Arts of the Norwegians in America. In *Perspectives in American Folk Art.* Ed. Ian M.G.Quimby and Scott T. Swank. Pp. 79-133. New York: W.W. Norton.

Peddle, Walter W.
1983 *The Traditional Furniture of Outport Newfoundland.* St. John's, Newfoundland: Harry Cuff.

Pocius, Gerald L.
1979 Hooked Rugs in Newfoundland: The Representation of Social Structure in Design. *Journal of American Folklore* 92:273-84.

Prown, Jules David
1980 Style as Evidence. *Winterthur Portfolio* 15:197-210.

Ravenswaay, Charles van
1977 *The Arts and Architecture of German Settlements in Missouri.* Columbia: University of Missouri Press.

Ray, Mary Lynn
1973 A Reappraisal of Shaker Furniture and Society. *Winterthur Portfolio* 8:107-32.

Reed, Henry M.
1987 *Decorated Furniture of the Mahantongo Valley.* Lewisburg, Pa: Center Gallery of Bucknell University.

Richards, Nancy
1980 Mormon Craftsmen in Utah. In *Utah Folk Art: A Catalog of Material Culture.* Pp. 61-90. Provo, Utah: Brigham Young University Press.

Roberts, Warren E.
1981 Turpin Chairs and the Turpin Family: Chairmaking in Southern Indiana. *Midwestern Journal of Language and Folklore* 7:57-106.

1988 *Viewpoints on Folklife: Looking at the Overlooked.* Ann Arbor: UMI Research Press.

St. George, Robert Blair
1979a Style and Structure in the Joinery of Dedham and Medfield, Massachusetts, 1635-1685. *Winterthur Portfolio* 13:1-46.

1979b *The Wrought Dovenant: Source Material for the Study of Craftsmen and Community in Southeast New England, 1620-1720.* Brockton, Mass: Brockton Art Center.

Shapiro, Meyer
1953 Style. In *Anthropology Today: An Encyclopedic Inventory.* Pp. 287-312. Chicago: University of Chicago Press.

Shea, John G.
1980 *The Pennsylvania Dutch and Their Furniture.* New York: Van Nostrand Reinhold.

Sikes, Jane E.
1976 *The Furniture Makers of Cincinnati, 1790-1849.* Cincinnati: Jane E. Sikes.

Sorensen, John
1973 Mormon Worldview and American Culture. *Dialogue* 8:17-29.

Steensberg, Axel
  1973 *Danske Bondemøbler.* København: Arnold Busck.
Taylor, Lonn, and David B. Warren
  1975 *Texas Furniture: The Cabinetmakers and Their Work, 1840-1880.* Austin: University of Texas Press.
Thatcher, Elaine
  1983 Nineteenth-Century Cache Valley Folk Furniture: A Study in Form and Function. Masters Thesis, Utah State University.
  1988 'Some Chairs For My Family': Furniture in Nineteenth-Century Cache Valley. *Utah Historical Quarterly* 56: 331-351.
Trent, Robert E.
  1979 *Hearts and Crowns: Folk Chairs of the Connecticut Coast, 1770-1880.* New Haven: New Haven Colony Historical Society.
  1982 The Concept of Mannerism. In *New England Begins: The Seventeenth Century.* Vol.3, Pp. 368-412. Boston: Museum of Fine Arts.
Viel, Lyndon C.
  1983 *Antique Ethnic Furniture.* Des Moines, Iowa: Wallace-Homestead.
Ward, Gerald W.R.
  1987 Some Thoughts on Connecticut Cupboards and Other Case Furniture. *Old Time New England* 72: 66-87.
Waters, Deborah Dependahl
  1984 *Plain and Ornamental: Delaware Furniture, 1740-1890.* Wilmington: Historical Society of Delaware.
Weidman, Gregory R.
  1984 *Furniture in Maryland, 1740-1940.* Baltimore: Maryland Historical Society.
Western Reserve Historical Society
  1972 *American Furniture in the Western Reserve, 1680-1830.* Cleveland: Western Reserve Historical Society.
Winters, Robert E. Jr.
  1977 *North Carolina Furniture, 1700-1900.* Raleigh: The North Carolina Museum of History.

Figure 1: Iver Petersen cupboard with spoon rack, ca. 1865-70, Spring City, Utah. The exterior of this cupboard was originally painted a dark red mahogany, while the interior was a rich blue. For many years it stood in the larger room of a small hall-parlor type house built by the Danish immigrant, Iver Petersen (photograph by Thomas Carter).

Figure 2: Detail of the Petersen cupboard showing the notched shelf, or spoon rack (photograph by Thomas Carter).

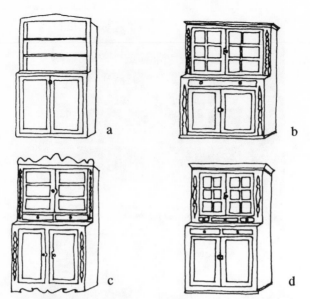

Figure 3: (3a) Type I: Tuttle-Folsom cupboard, ca. 1875, Manti, Utah; (3b) Type II: Peter Monson cupboard, ca. 1880, Spring City, Utah; (3c) Type III: F.C. Sorensen cupboard, ca. 1865-70, Ephraim, Utah; (3d) Type IV: George Bradley cupboard, ca. 1865-70, Moroni, Utah (drawing by Thomas Carter).

Figure 4: Swensen cupboard, ca. 1875, Manti, Utah. This cupboard retains its original red mahogany painted exterior and off-white interior (photography by Nancy Richards).

Figure 5: Spindled decoration on a chest of drawers from the nineteenth-century trade catalog *Miami Valley Furniture (1865-1870)*. (Courtesy, The Winterthur Library: The Joseph Downs Collection of Manuscripts and Printed Ephemera. No. 68 x 84.)

"We Made 'Em To Fit Our Purpose": The Northern Lake Michigan Fishing Skiff Tradition

JANET C. GILMORE

Commercial fishing is an occupation fraught with change. Experienced fishers know that the abundance of fish ebbs and flows cyclically, but they cannot predict the exact amounts they will be able to catch each year. Likewise they know that fish do not return at precisely the same times nor to exactly the same fishing spots year after year. When the fish are plentiful, they may not be worth much on a glutted market; when scarcer but more valuable, the weather can unexpectedly undo that rare good day of fishing by swamping the boat, dumping the catch, and perhaps destroying the fishing boat and gear as well.

Because of the unpredictability of the business, most commercial fishers follow several kinds of fish and employ different varieties of equipment. If one kind of fish is not plentiful, perhaps another will be; if one kind of gear is not working, perhaps another will; and if one location is not productive at the moment, perhaps another is. Before the days of state-mandated fishing districts, Great Lakes fishermen, like nomads, went where the fish were, over the lakes and across state lines. Louis Ruleau of Cedar River, Michigan, recalls Lake Erie pound-netters coming to the northern Lake Michigan shore in the 1940s to try their luck (Interview 1988). Northern Lake Michigan fishermen like the late "Pep" Nylund fished out of Oscoda on Lake Huron, as well as along the Wisconsin, Illinois, and lower Michigan shores of Lake Michigan (Interview 1986). (See Fig. 1) Tom Ruleau of Bark River, Michigan, formerly migrated over the upper peninsula in the fall with his father and uncles to fish herring and whitefish at Big Bay on Lake Superior (Interview 1988). His cousins, Louis and

58

Bob Ruleau of Cedar River, built their first steel pound-net skiff in 1958 in order to pack a boat in their semi and bounce it down the highway to Two Rivers, Wisconsin, where they could take good advantage of the earlier arrival and higher prices of smelt in that area; their wooden skiff would not have endured the trip (Louis Ruleau interview 1988).

Wherever they went, fishers encountered other fishers from other Great Lakes locations, observed their equipment and working methods, and picked up ideas. Because of the questing nature of commercial fishermen, pound nets and accompanying pound-net boats spread with and among fishermen from New England to Lake Erie, and by the 1850s, to upper Lake Michigan (Smith and Snell 1891:26,72). At one time they were one of the most prevalent types of fishing gear used throughout the Great Lakes, and Green Bay was "the center of the pound-net fishery" on Lake Michigan during the late 1800s (Smith and Snell 1891:72-73). Subsequently the gill net and the more complicated but less labor-intensive trap net have overshadowed the pound net in popularity for capturing whitefish, the commercial fisher's chief quarry. Yet over the years, fishers in the Green Bay area of Lake Michigan have persisted in making and employing pound nets, most often to capture prolific and low-valued species such as alewives, smelt, and suckers. Some few Wisconsin Lake Superior and Lake Michigan fishers, like Dennis Hickey of Bailey's Harbor, Wisconsin, remain dedicated to using the gear to entrap whitefish, claiming that it injures the fish less and thus produces a better quality catch than the other types of nets do (Hickey interview 1986).

In spite of the flux and experimentation traditional in the fishing business, and despite radical changes in equipment and the character of the fisheries wrought by machines, materials of the industrial era, and legislation during the past century, pound-net fishing equipment has remained remarkably constant. A semi-permanent fish-impounding device, the northern Lake Michigan pound net (pronounced "pond net") consists of three main components—"pot," "hearts," and "lead" —staked in place by wooden poles imbedded in the lake bottom (see Fig. 2).[1] The vertical sections of the net are positioned additionally by floats on the top lines and lead weights on the bottom lines. Composed of netting on the bottom and all four sides, the giant rectangular "pot" is open at the top. It measures ten to sixty feet deep, twenty to forty feet wide, and thirty to forty feet long. A long 1,000 to 1,200 foot fence-like "lead" of netting stretches from the pot shoreward to lead the fish to the pot and into it through a tunnel. In case the fish turn away from the pot, additional fences of netting, called "hearts," extend from the tunnel opening to confuse the fish and send them back toward the pot. Fishers tailor the dimensions and mesh-sizes of the nets according to the type of fish they seek, the depth and character of the fishing location, and the lengths of their boats.

The related trap net operates on the same principle and is similar in configuration and size. However, the tunnel and hearts are more intricately fashioned; the "trap," the equivalent of the pound-net pot, is entirely enclosed in mesh, top, bottom, and sides; the hearts are also covered and floored with netting; and the entire construction is held taut with lines and anchors instead of wooden stakes. While trickier in design, the trap net has several advantages over the pound net: it can be set on rocky lake bottoms where stakes can not be implanted; it can be pulled up by machine instead of by hand; the prey is protected from predators (birds); and the gear is hidden better in the water from competitors and poachers. As its use has expanded in the past two decades for catching the major commercial species of fish, fishers and specialized net-builders have rapidly refined its design.[2]

For both kinds of net, fishermen employ two boats, generally a larger one with greater power and carrying capacity to get to the nets and carry the catch, and a smaller one with much less power, which can be paddled or rowed, to tend the lines. To work the pound net, fishers generally place the smaller boat, but sometimes the larger one instead,[3] inside the pot; they lift the bottom of the pot up by hand as they move the boat along, "bag" the fish in one end, and scoop the fish out of the net into the larger boat (cf. Hornell 1950:86; von Brandt 1984:190). With the trap net, fishers use the larger boat to lift the trap up over the boat so they can open up the trap and scoop or dump out the fish into the big boat.

A hundred years ago, the two pound-net boats were built of wood, simply and economically (Chapelle 1951:50), "by both boat-builders and fishermen, without plans or models" (Chapelle 1951:128). In the Green Bay area, according to pound-netter Richard Grabowski of Menominee, Michigan:

> Most of the fishermen made their own boats, years ago. Most all the old timers, they always made their own boats. . . . The ones that had money had the carpenters come in and help them . . . just plain carpenters . . . anybody that fished could get ahold of any carpenter that would. . . . A carpenter, he can cut better fits, you know, if he's used to it, and do a lot nicer work, than a guy that isn't used to it. [Interview 1988]

Both the larger "pound boat" and the smaller pound-net dinghy were constructed in roughly the same shape as their New England sharpie relatives (Collins 1891:25-26; Chapelle 1951:104-33, 352-54). They were open boats with a sharp bow, slight flare to the sides, a square stern with a raked transom which was quite wide in the larger boat and proportionately narrower in the dinghy, and a flat bottom which had "a good deal of camber to the after part" (Collins 1891:26). (See Figs. 3-5) The larger boat was built to sail, and averaged twenty to thirty-four feet in length, seven to twelve feet in beam, and two-and-a-half to four feet in depth on Lakes Erie, Michigan, and Superior (Collins 1891:26; cf. Chapelle 1951:126-31, 354; and Chapelle 1960:302-03). Fish Commission field worker Mr. L. Kumlien reported in 1880 that the pound boats along the northern Lake Michigan shore from the Peshtigo River to the Cedar River (Menominee area) averaged twenty-two feet by seven feet and were steered by a long oar (Collins 1891:26). The dinghy averaged sixteen to eighteen feet long and five feet wide at the fullest part (Collins 1891:28); it was built to be rowed or, according to Richard Grabowski, sculled with one oar that passed through the transom (Interview 1988). (See Fig. 5)

Contemporary Menominee-area fishermen, David Behrend, Richard Grabowski, and Louis Ruleau, now in their fifties, recall working with the smaller wooden boats into the 1950s and '60s (Interviews 1988). Independently, each described a procedure for building the "skiffs" that is virtually identical to the one Howard Chapelle outlined for the sailing sharpie/flat-bottomed skiff class of the American bateau model (Chapelle 1951:46-48). They were built upside down around a jig-like frame. First the side planking was bent around the frame and nailed to the bow stem and stern transom; softwood planking would not be steamed first, whereas hardwood planking would. Each side and the stern consisted of two or three wide (12"), usually pine or cedar planks placed edge to edge lengthwise (cf. Chapelle 1951:128). Side planking was generally 5/8" to 1" thick (1-1/8" planed down to 1" according to Grabowski), while the stern was composed of thicker 1-1/2" to 2" boards. The straight, raked bow stem, carved of a single piece of white oak, was rabbeted so that the butt-ends of the side planks fit into the grooves on each side.[4] Louis Ruleau recalls that:

> . . . they whittled the bow stems out, you know, they were a vee-shaped piece of wood, and notched. They cut in there, I remember them chiseling that out. And then they fit the boards in that so that was a smooth piece. . . . so that this here bow stem took the, if you hit anything, you know I mean that was the whole bow, that was one solid chunk of usually oak. [Interview 1988]

After the side and stern planking had been installed, white oak ribs were inserted every twelve inches to hold the planks together. A strip of white oak was steamed, fitted, and nailed lengthwise to the ribs inside the "gunnels" (gunwales), the uppermost part of each side (see Figure 6). Another strip, which Grabowski called the "bilge keelson" and Chapelle terms the "chine log," was similarly installed along the ribs inside the bottom of each side. The bottom planking, also of pine or cedar but sometimes 2" thick (and usually no more than 6" wide), was laid crosswise, not lengthwise, and nailed to the sides, the two "bilge keelsons," and additional blocks of oak that had been inserted between the ribs and keelsons at the bottom. The bottom planking was sometimes further secured lengthwise, down the center, with a 4" wide, 1" thick plank inside, and a 4" x 1" to 2" plank outside, which was sometimes rabbeted to the bow stem.[5] According to Louis Ruleau, the outer "center board" additionally acted as a keel and kept the caulking in the bottom seams. Seats placed at the stern, in the bow, and across the center for rowing, supplied additional stiffening; Grabowski called the seats "thwarts," pronouncing the term like "thoughts." All seams were generally caulked except sometimes not between the bottom planks where the swelling of the wood as it soaked up water often sufficed to close up the gaps. Louis Ruleau remembers forged iron square nails as the earliest fastenings, and in later years builders switched to galvanized steel—galvanized screw nails according to Behrend, galvanized eight-penny nails according to Grabowski.

As engines became available, fishermen abandoned sail power and installed inboards in the pound boats and, eventually, outboards in the skiffs. The inboard took up space, added weight, and strained the flat-bottomed build, but it provided the opportunity to fish deeper waters farther from shore more safely. Fishermen began preferring features more characteristic of the bigger, sturdier gill-net tugs; they installed decking and cabins and adopted hulls with slight vee-bottoms and longer, beamier, deeper dimensions. Few pound-net fishermen continued to fish with the open pound boat, but all retained the open skiff. When non-tribal Michigan fishermen were required to switch from gill-netting to trap-netting gear during the 1970s (Kuchenberg 1978: 88-94), many purchased existing pound-netting, trap-netting, and gill-netting "rigs"—mostly steel vessels built after World War II, often obtained from the lower lakes—and subsequently modified them. Many of today's trap-net boats are modified pound-net rigs, and the same kind of big boat is often used for both kinds of fishing. As in current pound-netting, an open skiff remains an integral part of the rig.

Fishermen embraced steel construction and began replacing first the larger wooden boats after World War II, and later the smaller wooden skiffs, with steel versions. Compared to wood, the steel was "much more durable, didn't need all this maintenance," exclaimed Louis Ruleau (Interview 1988). The non-specialized builders and self-taught welders found the material more forgiving to work, and the "shell" construction even easier to execute in steel.[6] Welder and occasional boat-builder Curtis Folstad of Menominee explained:

> I could cut these pieces out and put them together and shape it up, and if I didn't like it I could change it real easy, you know, taper a little bit more here. . . . If I didn't like it, then I'd just cut a few tacks of weld and lay it down and cut it out a little different. It was easy to change the shape if you didn't like it, or if you didn't have what you wanted. I could change it easy. [Interview 1988]

Whereas the wooden boats "had to be absolutely perfect," according to Richard Grabowski, in order to resist the abuses of work and water, the steel ones would work well even when their shapes and joinery were not true (Interview 1988). Concluded Louis Ruleau, "they weren't real sharp-looking, but they were usable" (Interview 1988).

In order to repair, modify, and build the steel vessels, most northern Lake Michigan fishermen began to acquire "electric" or "stick" welding equipment and skills, often in that order, during the 1940s and 1950s—shortly after electrical service was extended into the area (Louis Ruleau interviews 1986 and 1988). In recent years a few have graduated to more modern "wire-feed" equipment. Richard Grabowski, who picked up the rudiments of welding from a co-worker while temporarily working at the local shipyard, Marinette Marine, in 1950, justifies his acquisition of the equipment this way:

> I bought that welder and that acetylene torch . . . in the fishing business you pr't' near got to have, you got to have that stuff, because you couldn't afford to have it hired all the time. And if you break down right on the job, you got your own stuff to do it with, you know. So you couldn't think of calling a welder out here to weld a patch on a boat, you know, it'd cost you too much. [Interview 1988]

And farther up the shore at Fairport, "Junior" Vetter echoes this sentiment:

> You just buy a machine. You have to. You can't afford to go to town every time you want something welded or something breaks, you know. [Interview 1988]

For the same reasons of economy, speed, and self-sufficiency that they had often built their own wooden skiffs, many fishermen in turn began building their own steel skiffs, basing them directly on wooden forerunners. Similarly today, fishermen base new steel skiffs on existing ones. As in building the wooden skiffs and in acquiring welding skills and equipment, they continue to build steel skiffs because it is cheaper to do the work themselves than to hire someone else to do it. Richard Grabowski re-used two sheets of steel formerly engaged in making press board at a local plant to build his skiff for well under $100 (Interview 1988). Bob and Louis Ruleau built their first skiff of two new 8' x 4' sheets of steel for a total of $130 (Interview 1988). The same amount of steel purchased new today would cost around $500, but a custom-built steel skiff might run well over $1,000, and there are few custom welders in the region who will readily take on a boatbuilding project for just any commercial fisherman.

The procedure is also perceived to be relatively simple, as Fairport trap-netter Wayne Seaman says, "Nothing to build a boat, 'cause all you got to do is get some idea what you want, then with welding and a steel torch, you can do anything. . ." (Interview 1988). Armed with basic welding skills and equipment, and steel plates easily obtained and custom cut at a local steel supply house, machine shop, or boilerworks, a fisherman—usually with a helper to lift and position the steel plates—takes about three to five days to build a skiff from scratch. Working alone at a less intense pace, some spread the job over ten days to two weeks.

Fishermen also build the small boats because each wants something a little different and, accordingly, they do not make the best clients. Menominee-area pound-netter David Behrend reasoned:

> . . . each individual fisherman will have his own idea what he wants, and if you built it for him it would be nothing but a giant headache because he'd be standing over your shoulder telling you, "I want this, I want that, I don't want what you're doing." Best thing to do is to let him build his own boat. [Interview 1988]

They know what they want in a skiff from their own experiences, observations, and trial and error. Trap-netter Ben Peterson of Fairport states his capability to design and build the skiffs this way:

> I kept watching and looking around, and I watched other guys's boats and I seen how they were holding up, and then we got in their boats and seen how tippy they were and whatnot, and finally, one day, I said, "Well, I think I can build a boat." [Interview 1988]

Pound- and trap-netter Tom Ruleau of Bark River, ". . . more or less went by the ones my uncle had and that stuff there, we kind of got an idea from them there and kind of made them similar to them" (Interview 1988). Basically, says Richard Grabowski, "If you know what a boat looks like, and you've done any welding at all, you just got to, you got to shape it like you got in your mind, whatever you want, the way you want it. You cut it accordingly" (Interview 1988).

With all the differences in opinion and experiences among their builders, naturally modern-day skiffs vary quite a bit in construction details—materials, building method, exact dimensions and shapes—just as the wooden ones of days past did.[7] Fishermen have variously tried ten-, twelve-, fourteen-, and sixteen-gauge steel, but most are leaning toward the heavier gauges, ten gauge especially.[8] As with the wooden skiffs, some have used heavier gauge material for the stern piece and bottom (ten gauge, for example) than for the sides (twelve gauge, for example).

Fishermen also do not follow the same methods of replicating existing skiffs. David Behrend simply encased his wooden pound boat in steel, later extracting the wooden planks when he decided to enlarge the vessel (Interview 1988). Some make a full-scale pattern from an existing boat, placing cardboard against each plate (side, stern, [bow], bottom) and trimming it to the proper shape. In Fairport, Bill Seaman built his skiff (Fig. 8) from a pattern he made in this manner from a Folstad skiff owned by fellow fisherman Peter Hermess (Interview 1988); in turn Jeff Harvey and "Junior" Vetter made a pattern from Seaman's skiff in order to build theirs (Interview 1988). Richard Grabowski (Fig. 7), however, took key dimensions off a wooden pound boat by placing steel rods on the boat at appropriate intervals along the bottom and sides, and cutting each rod a few inches longer; he first lofted the rods into a skeleton of the boat before cutting the steel plates according to the shapes he had defined (Interview 1988).[9] Still others, like Ben Peterson, figure measurements from internalized models:

> I bought all the steel that I figured I needed. I just kind of drew a plan up in my head and decided what I needed and wrote down dimensions. And I got the steel home and I drew up a pattern on the floor of my dad's garage, on what I had wanted. . . . I had the measurements in my mind, what I wanted, how I wanted it. [Interview 1988]

Most commonly, as in the wooden skiff building tradition, fishermen build the boat upside down, shaping the sides around a jig-like wooden frame. Welder and occasional boat-builder Lyle Thill of the Fairport area explains:

> First of all you make a form out of wood, you know, especially for the center of it and for the stern so you will know that when you get your two sides made, how to pull it into shape, what shape you want. [Interview 1988]

Says Tom Ruleau of the process:

> . . . the shape it more or less falls right into place when you kind of bend it and that stuff there, and bring it in, they pretty much shape theirself. . . . You got an idea what it's going to be like, you know, and you pretty much know. [Interview 1988]

As in the wooden skiff building tradition, they install ribbing or stiffening after the side plates have been shaped and tacked together. Thill continues:

> . . . then you put in the framework afterwards, for your ribs inside and your vee-bottom. You build these upside down, you know. Tack-weld it all together first, get the whole boat tack-welded, and then you start your welding . . . .[Interview 1988]

Richard Grabowski, however, invoked the larger gill-net tug-building tradition by first shaping a skeleton of steel rods, upside down, and then welding the side, stern, and bottom plates onto this framework (Interview 1988). Similarly Ben Peterson reports that he set up his steel ribbing first, upside down, then put on the bottom, sides, stern and bow pieces (Interview 1988). And Jeff Harvey and "Junior" Vetter built their vee-bottom skiff upright, tacking the four bottom plates together and bending the entire structure with a hand-operated winch called a "come-along" "until it shapes how you want it." They then added on the sides and inserted the ribbing later (Interview 1988).

The actual dimensions and shapes of the skiffs vary widely according to the individual's preferences and work habits, just as Richard Grabowski explained of the wooden boats:

> Everybody had a little different idea, they maybe, Williams wanted his built this way, a little longer, a little narrower. See, these boats were all built for what you wanted to use them for, you know. [Interview 1988]

Indeed, increasingly the variations fall into one of two categories of use: pound-netting or trap-netting.

Skiffs built for pound-netting (Fig. 7) bear the strongest resemblance in size and shape to the earlier wooden pound dinghies. Some pound-netters have even kept to the sixteen-by-five-foot average recorded for Green Bay skiffs in the 1880s. Most, however, have modified or built the boats wider, as wide as six to seven feet, proportionately increasing their beam slightly. As Louis Ruleau explains:

> We made 'em to fit our purpose, for lifting these pound nets in. It was a lot nicer lifting in a larger—sixteen foot they were by six foot—and they were real stable, you

know, you could get three, four guys on one side and they didn't lean down very much . . . .[Interview 1988]

With changes in licensing procedures for tenders, most Michigan pound-netters have also lengthened the skiffs beyond the former sixteen-foot limit to as long as nineteen to twenty feet;[10] the greater lengths ease the use of wider pots that can capture more fish (cf. Taylor 1982:67).

The flat bottom has remained particularly well-suited for the typical pound-net operation, which is worked just off the beach for smelt or in the mouths of shallow rivers for redhorse suckers. The shape rides high even when loaded and thus allows working in the shallow shoal waters; it also gives the vessel good carrying capacity for the typically large loads of fish (cf. Taylor 1982:67). "It carries a big load, and for smelts, that's what we need," confirms Louis Ruleau (Interview 1988). Coupled with adequate beam, the flat bottom additionally affords a measure of stability for working from the boat (cf. Taylor 1982:67).

While pound-netters have also retained the sharp—"peak-ed" they say—bow of the wooden boats, some have curved the forefoot of the bow stem so that the boat will tow more easily (ride up instead of dive) and move more effortlessly over the lines into the pound-net pot. Also to improve the shape's towing performance, some have added one to three keels to the bottom. Finally, in addition to enlarging the boat, widening it proportionately, and making small adjustments for improved performance, most pound-net fishermen have omitted all or most ribbing. They have found that a top rail of 1" diameter steel pipe provides the necessary stiffening; an inner rail that some position for pinning netting while working the net gives additional support.

At the same time in the 1950s, '60s, and '70s that fishermen were building their own steel skiffs, some preferred to purchase them custom-made. In particular, Curtis Folstad of Menominee and his chief welder, Bernie Barker, turned out dozens—some custom built, some stock built—for fishermen all over the Great Lakes (Interview 1988). As a youngster, Folstad had also built wooden skiffs of roughly the pound-net dinghy shape and size, but he applied the bottom planking lengthwise and fitted the boat with ribs that extended across the bottom from side to side—a construction that some area fishermen disliked because the planks tended to splinter when they hit the beach, and their replacement took more work (Louis Ruleau 1988). Later, similarly, Folstad built full ribs across the bottoms of his steel skiffs, applied a keel, and eventually gave the bottom a slight "V" toward the bow, mimicking features of both sportfishing boats and the bigger

wooden vee- and round-bottomed fishing tugs used in the area. Partly
in response to his customers, many of whom were trap-netters, he also
created more work space in the bow, lessening its sharpness.

When non-tribal Michigan gill-netters suddenly needed trap-netting
skiffs in the 1970s, they employed existing ones, the flat-bottomed
pound-net variety or Folstad's slight-vee and ribbed type. Over the
past decade or two, they have used, modified, and worn out these
skiffs, and built new ones incorporating features that work best for
their purposes. Elements of the Folstad design have proven particularly workable. Trap-netters have retained roughly the same length to
beam ratio for their boats (Figs. 8 and 9) as in the pound-net skiffs,
but they prefer slightly shorter lengths, twelve to sixteen feet, with a
four- to five-foot beam. With the heavy-gauge steel, the smaller shape
guarantees a sturdy build that can take more abuse than the pound-
net skiff, but that remains comparatively light enough for two men to
lift on board the bigger boat when necessary. Lyle Thill reasons:

> . . . these boats got to be pretty seaworthy out there . . . they use them for setting
> anchors all the time, for the trap net anchors, and there's two guys in the boat all
> the time, they use them in the fall of the year for pulling trap net anchors. And if
> they're not sturdy little boats—and they got to be built light—you know, it could mean
> somebody's life, if they weren't built sufficient. [Interview 1988]

Because the trap-net skiffs are towed behind the bigger boat for
greater distances and at much higher speeds than the pound-net skiffs
are, they take a real beating, pounding in the waves from the big
boat's wake. Trap-netters insist on plenty of well-braced ribbing, that
extends down the sides and across the bottom, to keep the bottom
well secured. To keep the boat from pounding and darting back and
forth over the waves, they also favor a keel and a slight vee-bottom.
Explains "Junior" Vetter, "it breaks the sea, you don't bam all the time
with it, throws the waves off to the side. When you're towing it, it
follows you straight down the line" (Interview 1988). Finally, because
trap-netters often work out of the bow of the boat instead of the side
as in pound-netting, they have lessened the sharpness of the bow, and
some have built skiffs with pram-like square noses narrower than the
stern (Fig. 9).[11]   Ben Peterson explains:

> . . . I decided that I'd put a pug nose on it, because we do a lot of the work right
> in the bow of the boat, and I figured if it was a pug nose, then it would have a little
> bit more room up there, you know, sometimes two of us have to get in the bow, like
> when you check over a net . . . .[Interview 1988]

Today, northern Lake Michigan fishermen are building two different kinds of steel fishing skiff depending on "what you wanted to use them for." Fishers mainly in the Menominee area—the "ancient" seat of the pound-net fishery, where pound-netting remains active—articulate a broad, flat-bottomed, "peaked" boat (Fig. 7) for working in shallow, calm waters and bearing large loads of fish, mirroring the wooden pound boats of days past. Fairporters, "converts" from gill-netting to trap-netting, are rapidly evolving a smaller, sturdier, boxier, vee-bottomed skiff (Figs. 8 and 9) for traveling at higher speeds in turbulent offshore water, integrating ideas from pound-net and Folstad skiffs especially.

While the differences between these two builds appear to be increasing, both still share the most basic characteristics and bear the kernel of the older wooden pound-net boat idea. In building either style, fisher-builders adhere roughly to the rule that "one-third the length would be the width" (Folstad interview 1988). They keep within a fairly narrow range of lengths (12' to 20'), widths (4' to 7'), and depths (of the sides; 2' to 2-1/2'). They flare the bow—even a square-nosed one—and the sides to turn water away from the boat. They keep the transom flat and "taper" it (rake it outward), nowadays mostly to accommodate the outboard instead of to row the boat (see Fig. 5).

There still are a few fishermen who like rowing capability, so in addition to retaining the taper of the stern, they "cut up" the bottom (see Fig. 5) and place a seat usually just back of the center and fullest beam so that when rowing the bow will not dive and the stern will ride the water properly. Most fishermen do not care to row the skiffs, however, so they flatten out the after part of the bottom and omit the center rowing seat. Indeed, since the steel build does not require thwarts and because the open work space is most desirable, there is a tendency to eliminate all seats. But many retain some seats anyway: in the stern for convenience while operating the outboard, and in the bow and stern for safety, to double as flotation chambers. Relieved of the need for rowing capability or rowing-seat stiffening, but perhaps frustrated by the resistance of heavy-gauge steel to produce the fairest of lines, builders rarely articulate the graceful continuous curve of the sides from the stem around a midships bulge to the stern. Now they usually make a boxier boat, placing the fullest beam at the stern or keeping the beam constant from the stern to well forward of amidships (at the point where the bow begins to taper into a peak or pug).

For northern Lake Michigan's fisher-builders, the pound-net skiff remains a powerful idea. They see its essence confirmed in the existing pound-net and trap-net tenders of their peers; they recall it in past generations of skiffs logged now only in memory; and when they begin to build a new skiff, they use it as their point of departure. Conceivably there are other boat shapes with different proportions that might serve as well (cf. Taylor 1982:66-67). But until there is a major upheaval in their fishing methods, these fisher-builders will maintain their legacy, perhaps because the familiar shape and the easy build lend themselves so well to an attitude that appears to have been as current among fishermen a century ago as it is today. David Behrend articulates this stance:

> Most of these boats were built just to serve a purpose, and they weren't supposed to be beautiful or anything else, they just did a job and that was it. I mean it wasn't something you went riding in on Sunday, it was to use. . . . And generally you didn't monkey around with it too much because you needed a boat and you needed it just as quickly and cheaply as you could get it, and hurry up. Get at it and build it, because it's going to have to go in the water. [Interview 1988]

Now over a century old, the fishing skiff building tradition on the northern Lake Michigan shore will likely remain healthy as long as commercial fishermen see a reason for "making them to fit their purpose."

NOTES

I dedicate this very descriptive first step in the analysis of Lake Michigan fishing skiffs to Warren E. Roberts in recognition of his love for the fit of form to function and the legacy of "the old traditional way of life." A shorter, even rougher version of this paper, and the fieldwork upon which it was based, were commissioned by the Michigan Traditional Arts Program of the Michigan State University Museum in East Lansing. The first paper, published in the 1988 Festival of Michigan Folklife program booklet, benefitted from readings by Yvonne H. Lockwood, James P. Leary, and especially David A. Taylor. The opportunity to rework the paper allowed me to act upon many of Taylor's "boatological" suggestions, to improve the accuracy of the description, and most importantly, to bring to the public more of the fisher-builders's wonderful observations about their skiffs, in their own words. I thank all of the victims of my quick fieldwork forays into the U. P. for their graciousness and help in taking me in and answering my peculiar questions. Particularly I am grateful to Richard Grabowski, Louis Ruleau, and David and Eileen Behrend for their patience, kindliness, and helpfulness in talking about those common little skiffs. Hopefully the dialogues will continue and the data will take yet more and better shapes.

[1] Cf. Hornell 1950:153-157 and von Brandt 1984:191-192; also Smith and Snell 1891:108-109 for descriptions and measurements of the nets as used in the area during the 1880s. The description of this type of net and its operation, as well as of the trap net, are based especially on interviews conducted in August 1986 with pound-netter Richard Grabowski, pound- and trap-netter Louis Ruleau, trap-netter Ben Peterson (and his crew, Rod Gierke and Rich Lynts), and net-builders Alvin Champion and Otis Smith. Richard Grabowski and Charlie Nylund additionally instructed me in the workings and

set-up of the nets at the Festival of American Folklife in Washington, D.C., in June-July 1987.

2   According to the testimony of contemporary fishermen, the trap net appears to have as long, but not as wide, a use as the pound net on the Great Lakes and adjacent smaller, primarily sportfishing lakes such as Lake Winnebago in eastern Wisconsin.

3   Richard Grabowski's larger boat, for example, is a boxy 18' x 35' powerless "scow" which he uses inside his pound-net pots.

4   In contrast, Chapelle (1951:48) claims that the stem was usually not rabbeted but "built up" of an inner and outer piece instead. The side planks were thus nailed to the inner piece and sawn off flush with its outer edge, and the outer piece then covered the inner piece and sawn edges of the planks.

5   Louis Ruleau claims that the inner "center board" was sometimes used in the early stages of construction as part of the initial framework of bow stem, transom, and "form."

6   Shell construction, where the ribbing is inserted after the skin of the boat has been shaped, is distinguished from skeleton construction where the ribbing is set up first to define the skin. See Greenhill 1976:287-292.

7   Chapelle (1951:128) noted the concomitance of variation in skiff construction details with the variety of specialized and non-specialized builders who used neither plans nor models in building the boats.

8   The gauge of a sheet of steel pertains to its thickness; a ten-gauge sheet is one-tenth of an inch thick, twelve-gauge one-twelfth of an inch, and so on. The higher the gauge number, the thinner the steel.

9   He thus bypassed the step of translating the measure into a numerical equivalent and using the numbers in turn to mark the proper measure on each rod.

10   With the massive changes in Michigan's fisheries legislation enacted in the late 1960s and mostly in the 1970s, came changes in the registration of boats. Fishers could no longer avoid a registration fee on their smaller boat by claiming it on the larger boat's registration as a powerless tender under sixteen feet.

11   The square nose is not an anomaly in the area. Peterson's fellow Fairporter, Wayne Seaman, also decided to try out a square nose in his latest skiff, recalling that when he was around eight years old (c. 1942), his father built the family a twelve-foot square-nosed flat-bottomed wooden row boat. Seaman referred to the boat as having a "scow-type" shape, and Peterson calls his skiff a "scow," a name that locals usually apply to large, boxy vessels that some area fishermen, like Richard Grabowski and his partner Kurt Williams, use in pound-netting to carry the large catches. Over the past one hundred years, scows appear to have been used to complement other pound-netting boats in one capacity or another. The pile-driving equipment used through the 1940s to hammer pound-net stakes into the lake bottom was generally borne on a scow; Collins describes such a "stake-boat" in Smith and Snell's 1885 fisheries report (1891:29).

REFERENCES CITED

Brandt, Anders von
  1984 *Fish Catching Methods of the World.* Third Edition. Surrey, England: Fishing News (Books) Ltd.
Chapelle, Howard I.
  1951 *American Small Sailing Craft: Their Design, Development, and Construction.* New York: W.W. Norton and Company.
  1976 *The National Watercraft Collection.* Second edition. Washington, D.C., and Camden, ME: Smithsonian Institution and International Marine Publishing Co.
Coberly, Catherine E. and Ross M. Horrall
  1980 *Fish Spawning Grounds in Wisconsin Waters of the Great Lakes.* Madison: University of Wisconsin Sea Grant Institute.
Collins, J.W.
  1891 Vessels and Boats Employed in the Fisheries of the Great Lakes. In *Review of the Fisheries of the Great Lakes in 1885.* Edited by Hugh M. Smith and Merwin-Marie Snell, pp. 19-29. In Report of the Commissioner for 1887. *U.S. Fish Commission Report,* Vol.15, Appendix I. Washington, D.C.: Government Printing Office.
Gilmore, Janet C.
  1987 Fishing for a Living on the Great Lakes. In *Festival of American Folklife Program Book,* pp. 60-64. Washington, D.C.: Smithsonian Institution.
  1988 'We Made 'Em to Fit Our Purpose': The Upper Lake Michigan Fishing Skiff Tradition. In *1988 Festival of Michigan Folklife,* pp. 32-39. East Lansing, MI: Michigan State University Press.
Greenhill, Basil
  1976 *Archaeology of the Boat: A New Introductory Study.* Middletown, CT: Wesleyan University Press.
Halverson, Lynn H.
  1955 The Commercial Fisheries of the Michigan Waters of Lake Superior. *Michigan History* 39: 1-17.
Hornell, James
  1950 *Fishing in Many Waters.* Cambridge: The University Press.
Kuchenberg, Tom
  1978 *Reflections in a Tarnished Mirror: The Use and Abuse of the Great Lakes.* Sturgeon Bay, WI: Golden Glow Publishing.
Smith, Hugh M. and Merwin-Marie Snell
  1891 Review of the Fisheries of the Great Lakes in 1885. In Report of the Commissioner for 1887. *U.S. Fish Commission Report,* Vol.15, Appendix I. Washington, D.C.: Government Printing Office.
Taylor, David A.
  1982 *Boatbuilding in Winterton, Trinity Bay, Newfoundland.* Canadian Center for Folk Culture Studies Paper, No. 41. Ottawa: National Museums of Canada.

AUTHOR'S INTERVIEWS

Behrend, David and Eileen (Kleinke)
  1988 (March 29). Menominee, MI. For the Michigan Traditional Arts Program, MSU Museum, East Lansing.

Champion, Alvin and Steven
  1986 (August 24). Marinette, WI. For the Office of Folklife Programs, Smithsonian Institution, Washington, D.C.
Folstad, Curtis
  1988 (March 28). Menominee, MI. For the Michigan Traditional Arts Program, MSU Museum, East Lansing.
Grabowski, Richard
  1988 (March 28). Menominee, MI. For the Michigan Traditional Arts Program, MSU Museum, East Lansing.
  1986 (August 26). Menominee, MI. For the Office of Folklife Programs, Smithsonian Institution, Washington, D.C.
Hermess, Peter
  1986 (August 25). Garden, MI. For the Office of Folklife Programs, Smithsonian Institution, Washington, D.C.
Hickey, Dennis
  1986 (August 16). Bailey's Harbor, WI. For the John Michael Kohler Arts Center, Sheboygan, WI.
Nylund, Charlie
  1988 (March 27). Menominee, MI. For the Michigan Traditional Arts Program, MSU Museum, East Lansing.
  1986 (August 26). Marinette, WI. For the Office of Folklife Programs, Smithsonian Institution, Washington, D.C.
Nylund, Wilbert "Pep"
  1986 (August 26). Marinette, WI. For the Office of Folklife Programs, Smithsonian Institution, Washington, D.C.
Peterson, Benjamin
  1988 (March 31). Fairport, MI. For the Michigan Traditional Arts Program, MSU Museum, East Lansing.
  1986 (August 25). Fairport, MI. For the Office of Folklife Programs, Smithsonian Institution, Washington, D.C.
Ruleau, Louis
  1988 (March 29). Cedar River, MI. For the Michigan Traditional Arts Program, MSU Museum, East Lansing.
  1986 (August 24). Cedar River, MI. For the Office of Folklife Programs, Smithsonian Institution, Washington, D.C.
Ruleau, Tom
  1988 (April 1). Bark River, MI. For the Michigan Traditional Arts Program, MSU Museum, East Lansing.
Seaman, "Bill"
  1988 (March 31). Fairport, MI. For the Michigan Traditional Arts Program, MSU Museum, East Lansing.
Smith, Otis
  1986 (August 25). Fayette, MI. For the Office of Folklife Programs, Smithsonian Institution, Washington, D.C.
Thill, Lyle L.
  1988 (March 31). Garden, MI. For the Michigan Traditional Arts Program, MSU Museum, East Lansing.
Vetter, Emil "Junior" and Jeffrey P. Harvey
  1988 (March 30). Fairport, MI. For the Michigan Traditional Arts Program, MSU Museum, East Lansing.
Weborg, Jeff
  1986 (August 16). Gill's Rock, WI. For the John Michael Kohler Arts Center, Sheboygan, WI.

Figure 1. The western Great Lakes region.

Figure 2. Pound net typical in the Green Bay area of Lake Michigan in the 1880s. Drawing by L. Kumlien reprinted from Smith and Snell 1891: Plate XXI.

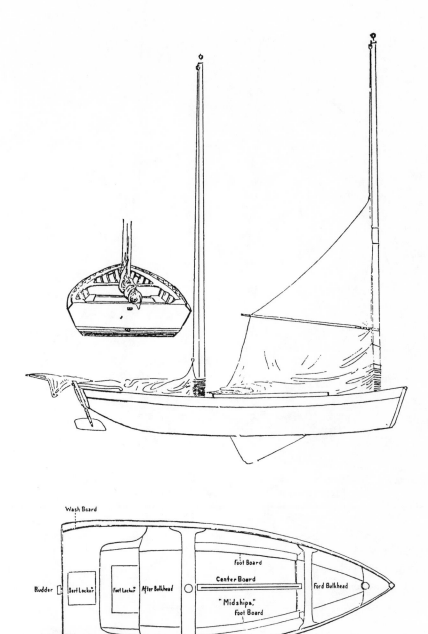

Figure 3. Plans of an 1880s pound-net boat probably more typical of the lower lakes than of northern Lake Michigan. Drawing by Henry W. Elliott reprinted from Smith and Snell 1891: Plate VI.

Figure 4. Pound-net boat under sail on Lake Erie in the 1880s. Drawing by Henry W. Elliott reprinted from Smith and Snell 1891: Plate VII.

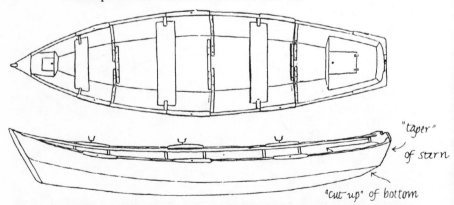

"taper"
of stern

"cut up" of bottom

Figure 5. Plans of an 1880s pound-net dinghy drawn by Henry W. Elliott and reprinted from Smith and Snell 1891: Plate VIII. The Green Bay area dinghies were roughly the same shape, but the positioning of the thwarts (seats) appears to have been somewhat different and the interior framing substantially different, more like that in the pound boats shown in Figs. 3 and 4.

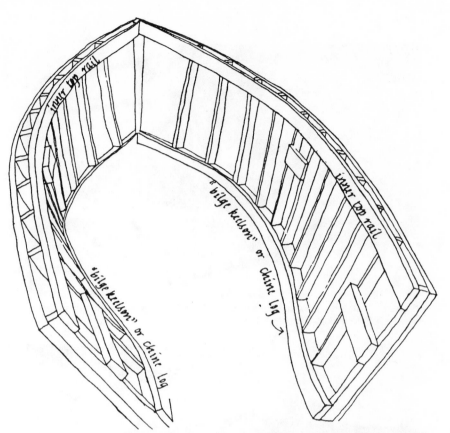

Figure 6. Interior framework of wooden pound-net skiff built and used in the Menominee, Michigan, area. The illustration was drawn from a slide of a skiff deteriorating on the shore of Lake Michigan's Green Bay. The stern transom had disappeared, leaving the side planking and attached frames to open out; the bottom was covered inside with a dense mat of leaves; and the bow framework was obscured inside with a heavy piece of driftwood. In other words, the drawing is not exact.

Figure 7. Richard Grabowski's steel pound-net skiff which he fashioned directly after a wooden pound boat. Menominee, MI.

Figure 8. "Bill" Seaman's steel trap-net skiff which he built from a pattern he made of a Folstad skiff. Fairport, MI.

Figure 9. Wayne Seaman's square-nosed vee-bottomed steel trap-net skiff. Fairport, MI.

The Reelfoot Stumpjumper: Traditional Boat Building in Tennessee

HARRY GAMMERDINGER

For a century or more Reelfoot has been a magic word. It described in the minds of men a most unusual bit of the earth's surface.

For a century most persons interested in Reelfoot have been intensively interested. They have fought and they have killed because of their interests in Reelfoot. [Tennessee 1958:i]

Fortunately, there have been other responses to Reelfoot Lake besides the intensively interested murders recognized by the executive director of the Tennessee State Planning Commission. The rich fishing found at Reelfoot did cause bitter disputes over fishing rights, but the lake has also generated interest because of its unusual creation and geography. Reelfoot's distinctive features prompted early residents to develop a unique boat design adapted to the lake's particular conditions.

By the turn of the century an active boat building tradition had become established on Reelfoot Lake. The most active craftsman working in this tradition today is Dale Calhoun, a fourth-generation boat builder who continues to build boats on Reelfoot Lake. His work is remarkable not only because of its traditionality but by its demonstration of adaptation to changing environment, technology, and consumer needs.

Reelfoot Lake

Reelfoot Lake is located in the northwest corner of Tennessee, lying only three miles east of the Mississippi River and immediately south of the Kentucky border. This shallow lake surrounded by bald cypress swamps is situated on the floodplain between the Mississippi River and the bluffs to the east. Reelfoot is unlike conventional freshwater lakes because of its sudden creation during a series of earthquakes in 1811 and 1812.

A succession of severe earthquakes, known as the New Madrid earthquakes, began on 16 December 1811. There were major quakes on 16 December, 23 January, and 7 February and hundreds of smaller ones. These quakes, centered near the village of New Madrid, Missouri, were some of the most powerful ever to occur in North America. Although they were felt as far away as Canada and rattled windows in Washington, D.C., few lives were lost because of the sparse settlement near the earthquakes' center. But the natural damage was tremendous; entire forests were uprooted and craters were formed by gases erupting from the earth. Settlers' accounts describe the air filled with sulfurous gases, the formation of waterfalls on the Mississippi, and boats sunk by tidal waves caused by the collapse of riverbanks and trees falling into the river.

These earthquakes created Reelfoot Lake through a combination of topographic changes. Some 50,000 acres of low-lying marsh east of the river fell 5 to 20 feet (Tennessee 1958:5) and the underlying channel clay soils were compacted, making a more impervious basin for retaining water. The land south of the lake rose, damming the depression by impeding drainage from the area, and Reelfoot Lake was formed as the basin filled with water. Reelfoot has an unusual shape because it lies in old channels cut by the Mississippi as the river's course has changed over the centuries. It actually consists of several bodies of water largely surrounded by marsh and connected by channels and bayous (Tennessee 1958:11). Although Reelfoot is roughly 5 by 14 miles and encompasses a total area of 19,000 acres, the average depth of the water is only 5 feet and is nowhere deeper than 18 feet (Tennessee 1958:1 and Middleton 1986:130). The shallowness of the lake, combined with the fact that its bottom is flooded forest, created a lake filled with standing trees, stumps, and other snags. Boating was so difficult that the Tennessee Supreme Court pronounced the lake unnavigable when ruling on a land claims case in 1902 (Vanderwood 1969:11).

But Reelfoot is a rich area for fish, waterfowl, and other game because this shallow, calm lake with a fertile bottom is excellent for fish propagation. In the late 1800s extensive commercial fishing developed on the lake when it became possible to ship catches to distant markets, including New York City. Many residents made their living off the lake through a combination of fishing, hunting, trapping turtles and gigging frogs. In 1894 more fish were caught in Reelfoot Lake than were taken in the entire Tennessee River system (Comeaux 1978:91), and turn-of-the-century newspaper accounts report five hundred commercial fishermen operating on the lake (Smith 1988). It is estimated that in 1925 fishermen were running 200 miles of trotline in the lake with 500 hooks per mile (Smith 1988). Sport fishing and hunting became an important part of the local economy in the 1920s. Many residents began guiding visiting fishermen and waterfowl hunters on the lake, renting boats and earning income through other tourist businesses. Tourism dwindled during the 1930s and 40s but resurged during the 1950s (Smith 1988) and continues to be an important part of the region's economy.

Besides fishing, residents also commercially hunted other wildlife on Reelfoot Lake. During the 1920s and 30s as many as 1000 ducks a day were killed on the lake and shipped by train to distant markets including Chicago and New York. Commercial fishermen also often supplemented their income by turtling. In 1949 a biologist estimated that 20,000 turtles were taken between the first week of April and the end of August of the previous year, making a total of 62,000 pounds marketed during the season. This combination of fishing and turtling supported many of the families living on the lake (Schoffman 1949).

Commercial fishing and hunting have greatly declined from these peak figures. There are now only about twenty-five commercial fishermen operating on the lake, most of whom work another job, and only a few residents trap turtles to supplement their income. But catfish and crappie continue to be fished commercially and Reelfoot currently yields the largest fish poundage per acre of any Tennessee Lake (Middleton 1986:130).

These livelihoods created the need for a dependable, affordable craft that could navigate on the snag-filled Reelfoot Lake. The difficulty of boating on Reelfoot was attested to by a government-sponsored plan for development which observed that, "The hazard of using conventional type boats on the lake probably reduces fishing pressure below what it might otherwise be . . ." (Tennessee 1958:70). While this danger did apply to conventional boats, craftsmen at Reelfoot had for a long time solved this problem with their own boat design.

Origin of the Stumpjumper

The answer to these needs was the Reelfoot stumpjumper, so called because of its ability to ride over submerged stumps. This unique wooden boat with its flat bottom and double bow resembles a wide canoe, and is generally referred to simply as a "lake boat" by residents. The exact origin of the stumpjumper is the stuff of local legend. Boat builders and commercial fishermen credit the original design to a man named Herman B. "Con" Young. Very little is know about Herman Young except that he is said to have lived in the late nineteenth century and built boats.[1] William Calhoun, a 76-year-old retired boat builder, reports that the first stumpjumpers were made by Herman Young, but he admits that, "I never seen him or seen nobody that seen him. That was way back."[2]

Ralph Burrus, the superintendent of Reelfoot Lake State Park when it was established in 1956, and widely recognized for his knowledge of local history, was interviewed concerning the origin of Reelfoot boats.

> A cabinet maker came in here to fish and hunt a little bit and never went back to his work. He started building Reelfoot Boats, that was Con Young. He designed this round-ribbed (?) boat that we use here now because when he came in we were using bateaus. Before that we were using dugouts. Then they got a sawmill in here and it slabbed up some of the cypress and we put it together and caulked it, and made a bateau. But this man came in and the idea of getting on that stump and staying so long without getting off and the wood wasn't protected. Sometime the stump would have a point and you really got hung. So he designed this that you could rock the boat without tilting it without dipping water. . . .
>
> The first Reelfoot Boat was built around night rider time. [1907-08] That's when it started and he had two or three people working with him and each one left and built boats on his own. But each one changed it enough and these fishermen like Lex's father can identify a Cap Lye (?) boat or a Milligan boat or a Con Young boat, Sam Morgan boat. They originally were from the same pattern. [Smith and Pardue 1985:117]

Young was not working in a total vacuum. There is a pervasive tradition of boat building in the region from which he no doubt drew upon for construction techniques and designs. Large scale commercial fishing, which would have required boats, began along the Mississippi probably about the time of the Civil War (Comeaux 1978:75) and the availability of Southern cypress and Pacific redwood after the 1880s made skiff-building an important industry in many river towns (Lund 1983:690). While I have not found any references to boats entirely like the Reelfoot stumpjumper being independently developed elsewhere, many of its characteristics can be found in other traditional boat building designs. Although establishing a precise history of boat design is difficult because of the wide variation in names used for specific boat types, it is clear that the stumpjumper utilizes many traditional construction techniques and design elements. The stumpjumper appears to be most closely related to the pirogue, a term which has been used for a dugout canoe or plank boat built to the dimensions of a dugout canoe (Lund 1983:680). Although the pirogue is generally associated with Francophone Louisiana, it is found in many parts of the Mississippi Valley, particularly on shallow, swampy water. Jens Lund believes that most of the canoes used during the settlement of the Ohio Valley were probably similar to this type and notes that in the lower Ohio Valley pirogues are still occasionally used by duck hunters in tree-filled swamps (1983:682). Malcolm Comeaux has described the use of canoes by hunters and fishermen for navigating swamps and overflowed land and characterized the Reelfoot stumpjumper as a type of canoe (1978:88). In east Tennessee there is a tradition of building flat-bottomed, plank boats for negotiating the swift, rocky streams found there. These boats resemble Reelfoot stumpjumpers in length, width, and rib structure, but they are blunt at both ends (Kear, Stout and Ross 1978). These boats sometimes have a rudder, but its dimensions and function are very different from the rudder found on Reelfoot stumpjumpers.

Calhoun Boat Builders

By far the most recognized builder of Reelfoot stumpjumpers today is Dale Calhoun. Although he works full-time as a shift captain at a local prison, he still manages to build on the average a boat each week. When asked how he learned the trade Dale usually explains that, "It's a hand-me-down generation thing." He proudly describes himself as a fourth generation Reelfoot boat builder and cites the Calhoun lineage of boat builders: his father, William Calhoun, grandfather, Boone Calhoun, and great-grandfather, Joseph Marion Calhoun.

Although now retired, William Calhoun remembers well his boat building days and family boat building history. William was told that Joseph Marion, the first acknowledged Calhoun boat builder, lived in Dyer, Tennessee, a small town thirty miles southeast of Reelfoot Lake, where he worked as a brick mason and also did some carpentry work.[3] While Joseph Marion was living in Dyer his eldest child, Boone, was born in January 1889.

Between 1900 and 1910 Joseph Marion and his family moved to Obion County on the eastern shore of Reelfoot Lake. He bought a farm in the hills near Shawtown, a small community about four miles by road east of Reelfoot Lake. Joseph Marion started farming, erected a brick kiln, and built chimneys and other brickwork in the area. William recalls that Joseph Marion made a few john boats (plain, flat-bottomed boats with blunt ends) but he did not make any stumpjumpers. Joseph Marion died in 1926 or 1927 when he was 75 years old.

William's father, Boone Calhoun, had a blacksmith shop in Shawtown. Besides doing blacksmith work Boone also worked as a farrier, carpenter, automobile mechanic, and boat builder. Boone hired John Milligan, a migratory laborer, because he needed someone to help him build boats. Milligan had learned boat building from Herman Young (Andrews 1973:5 and Smith and Pardue 1985:117) and passed some of these techniques on to Boone. William was born on 6 February 1913 and began working with his father and Milligan when an adolescent.

William estimates that his father began making the stumpjumpers around 1927.[4] He believes that Boone refined his own design but drew upon the stumpjumpers that he saw on the lake. His stumpjumper resembled those built by Herman Young, but Boone's was generally larger and had a wider bottom. William describes this design as the perfect adaptation for Reelfoot Lake, "just like it was supposed to be," and Dale Calhoun continues to build stumpjumpers using essentially the same design.

William built his first boat when he was fourteen and soon became a full-time boat builder, along with his brother, in their father's shop. Around 1940 they moved the shop from Shawtown to the south shore of Reelfoot Lake. William worked in a Michigan factory during World War Two because of a lack of demand for boats during that time, but he returned after the war and continued to build boats. Shortly after the war, Boone moved to Michigan where he worked in a factory until his death in August 1965.

William estimates that he built 100 to 150 boats per year on Reelfoot Lake for 35 years (Andrews 1973:5). Most of these boats were stumpjumpers, but he also occasionally built boats for other purposes. He built two or three skiffs for commercial fishermen, a few john boats, and some custom boats designed to the specifications of the buyer. William built boats out of many woods but principally he used cypress, sassafras, and catalpa obtained from local sawmills. Although he stopped building boats thirty years ago he proudly observes that some of his boats are still on the lake.

William's son Dale was born on 24 July 1935. William notes that, "Dale's got my dad's mind," and quickly showed an aptitude for building boats. He enjoys telling the story of returning from vacation to find a boat in the shop built by fourteen-year-old Dale. Dale credits learning most of his boat building skills by working with his father. Dale's earliest responsibilities were making the chairs that go in the boats and nailing the tin covering onto the boats.

The busiest time for the Calhouns was during the late 1940s and 50s when Dale and William hired two helpers but still had difficulty keeping up with the demand for stumpjumpers. Even though they were finishing three boats each day they often had twenty to fifty boats on order.

But the demand for the Calhoun stumpjumpers declined around 1960, probably due to the growing popularity of fiberglass and aluminum boats and a decrease in guide trips. William felt that there was not enough business to support both Dale and himself so he left to do carpentry work in Michigan and Memphis.

At about this time Dale tore down the original shop and built a larger one at the same location. He continued to build boats but sometimes worked other jobs as well. He opened a store that sold boats, motors, and trailers and operated a boat dock (Pomeroy 1974). In the early seventies there were busy periods and slow times but Dale still produced 150 to 200 boats per year (Andrews 1973 and Tennessee Department 1974:20). About ten years ago Dale decided to begin working full-time at the nearby Lake County Regional Prison because, "its a lot easier and I make more money."

But Dale remains a very committed boat builder, and he manages to average forty hours a week building boats. He finds no need to advertise because word-of-mouth and his reputation creates a sufficient demand for his boats.   There have been several newspaper and magazine stories about Dale published during the 1970s and 80s, and he has also begun demonstrating at festivals, including the 1982 World's Fair in Knoxville and the 1986 Smithsonian Festival of American Folklife in Washington, D.C.

Changes in the Stumpjumper
Although Dale uses essentially the same design as Boone Calhoun, the stumpjumper has undergone some changes over the last sixty years due to changing technology and the availability of materials. Originally the stumpjumpers were made entirely of caulked wood, but Boone began covering the boats with metal strips, and later tin, to help protect them from snags. William continued covering the sides and bottoms of the boats with tin. Before nailing on the tin, both Boone and William covered the boats with canvas which they saturated with paint to make it waterproof.   William covered the boats with aluminum for awhile, but he went back to tin when aluminum became

too expensive. In the 1950s William began covering the boats with fiberglass instead of tin.

The Reelfoot stumpjumpers were originally propelled with paddles or oars. Fred Allen, a sport fisherman from Monmouth, Illinois, often visited Reelfoot Lake and used stumpjumpers. While home in 1884 he invented an articulated oar which allowed boaters to face the direction in which they were rowing. Generally called "bow-facing oars," they caught on immediately because of their usefulness in the tree-filled waters of Reelfoot. In 1959 Dale bought the company that manufactured these oars from Allen's heir and continues to market them. Dale assembles the components, which are cast in an Iowa foundry, and then outfits his own boats with them and sells the oars separately.

The advent of small, gasoline-powered motors allowed boat builders to motorize the stumpjumper about fifty years ago. Boone began mounting one-third horsepower, kick-start motors from Maytag washing machines in the rear of his boats. At the time such power seemed adequate but as more powerful engines became light enough they were put in the boats. Today Dale installs engines ranging from three to sixteen horsepower, according to the customer's request. The stumpjumpers that are built today are generally wider than those built at the turn of the century. Dale still builds the boats with the same length, about fifteen and one-half feet, but he has increased the width from a three foot beam to a four or five foot beam. Dale increased the width because the addition of motors made streamlining less important and sport fishermen today generally want to take more equipment with them.

Current Building Technique

Although Dale has built boats out of almost every wood except hickory and oak, most of the boats he builds are made of air-dried cypress planks nailed to a white oak frame. He prefers cypress because of its durability in a maritime environment and generally obtains it from local sawmills.

Dale begins construction by laying out the bottom, made of two 3/4" planks which run the full length of the boat, and then attaching the ribs. There are generally nine ribs, laid about 15" apart. The bottom ribs (1" x 1 1/2") cross the flat bottom of the boat and to the ends of these are attached the side ribs (1" x 1"). Bow and stern stems are nailed to the ends of the bottom.

Dale then places the bottom and ribs upside down in a jig to hold the work. William built this jig in the early 1940s, patterning it after a similar jig used by Boone.

Dale steams the 16 foot, 3/8" side planks and then quickly bends them to the curve by nailing two planks to the ribs on each side. The planks are steamed by immersing them in a vat of boiling water behind the shop. Boone used to steam the wood by laying it out in the sun wet but found that he could get better results by using a steamer. Dale has also steamed the wood by laying it in the sun during hot weather but finds steaming a more dependable technique. After nailing on the sides Dale turns the boat upright and nails a wood strip or "whaling" on top of the gunwales. A spray rail is added on top of the whaling from the bow to amidships and a small section of decking is added to the bow and stern. If the boat will have a motor he adds a shelf at the stern for the battery. Cypress chairs are generally included, the height of which are designed to fit the customer. A hinged mount for a trolling motor is sometimes added to the side of the boat near the bow.

Dale covers the outside of the boat with fiberglass to make it waterproof and then sands and paints the boat. Dale says that customers may choose any color but they generally want gray or green because these colors are better camouflage. Dale will still occasionally tin a boat instead of coating it with fiberglass because the tin makes a heavier boat which sits deeper in the water and is consequently more stable.

Dale builds the stumpjumpers with essentially the same shape that his grandfather used but works without plans. Dale uses templates to cut parts of the boat but he only uses the two entire bottom templates built by Boone which hang in the shop to measure for pieces when repairing boats. The planks Dale uses are 16' long when they come from the sawmill, but he explains that this is not the reason why the stumpjumper is 15 1/2' long. He feels that, "It just balances out better that way. It has to be that long to have the room in it." But Dale does note that he would have to splice boards together to make a longer boat. Other typical dimensions for the stumpjumper are 2'3" at the widest part of the bottom, 4'1" wide at the gunwales and 1'4" tall at the sides, but the width and height can vary according to the customer's request.

Most of the stumpjumpers Dale builds today have motors mounted to the floor in the stern. Dale buys these general purpose industrial motors, which are installed in such equipment as concrete mixers, hay balers and pumps, direct from their manufacturers. These gas motors range from three to sixteen horsepower but the most popular size is the eight horsepower which can propel the boat at about fifteen miles per hour. Dale recalls that a three horsepower motor used to be considered sufficient power for winding through the trees standing in Reelfoot Lake, but now that there are fewer trees standing bigger motors have become popular (Tuberville 1987:5).

The addition of motors required modifications in the design to accommodate a propeller and rudder. The shaft and bronze propeller are protected from snags by a steel plate extending beneath it. Dale cuts this protecting plate, called a "log" or "shoe" locally, from 3/16" steel plate and bolts it to an oak wedge on the bottom of the boat. Dale also cuts the rudder from 3/16" steel. The rudder, typically 13 1/2" long by 11" tall, is hinged so that it will kick up and not be damaged if it strikes a submerged obstruction. The steering mechanism consists of a 6 1/2' steel rod, which extends from a lever attached to the rudder post forward to a wooden stick hinged to the boat floor. The rudder is turned by pushing the stick forward and backward. Dale is fond of the simple design because of its dependability and economy.

Customers still often ask Dale to build an "oar boat," a stumpjumper without an engine. Oar boats are virtually identical to motorized stumpjumpers except that they are more narrow, generally three feet wide, and do not need a rudder. An oar boat typically weighs 185 pounds while a motorized stumpjumper weighs 250 pounds.

Dale occasionally makes other kinds of boats besides the stumpjumper. He sometimes makes skiffs for commercial fishermen on Reelfoot, and the particular design is referred to locally as a "D-line skiff." These skiffs have a pointed or "model" bow, flat stern, and sides which flare out. The design is especially suitable for commercial fishing because the fishermen can walk along the flared side while handling nets and haul nets in and out of the water at the stern. These skiffs are powered by outboard motors which are taken off once fishing begins and then oars are used to move the boat. Their longer length of twenty feet also provides more room and allows the skiff to carry a heavy load. Dale explains that one of his skiffs can haul, "two men, a wet net and a ton of fish." There is little demand for skiffs today because of the decline in commercial fishing but at one time Dale and his father made so many skiffs that, "We used to make them until we'd get so sick and tired seeing them we'd like to scream."

On rare occasions Dale makes custom designed boats to a client's specifications. In these cases people bring in a photograph or design for the boat and ask him to construct one like it. Dale and William have made inboard cruisers and once an inboard boat designed for ice breaking. They also made a tug for a farmer to pull his ferry of farm equipment to an island in the Mississippi River that he farmed. This tug was about twenty-two feet long with a powerful engine and enclosed cabin. Dale also sometimes builds john boats for sport fishermen.

Current Market for Stumpjumpers

Dale finds that he gets all the orders for stumpjumpers that he can fill working forty hours per week. These boats remain in demand because of their adaptation to Reelfoot Lake and the local boating clientele. The boats are used for a wide variety of purposes including pleasure boating, hunting, fishing, and transportation by government agencies. Dale sells most of his boats to local individuals and rental businesses on Reelfoot, but his boats are also used on neighboring lakes and are occasionally shipped far away. The most often recognized advantage of these boats is their adaptation to shallow, snag-filled water. The flat bottom of these boats gives them a shallow draft so they can generally navigate in six to eight inches of water. The boat is protected from snags by having the shoe beneath the propeller and the kick-up rudder. The stumpjumper's flat bottom and flaring sides also make it a more stable platform than round-bottomed boats.

The stumpjumper is designed to be an economical boat. Dale uses a relatively simple design and general purpose hardware and motors in order to keep the boat competitively priced for local boaters. He is able to sell the oar boats for 700 dollars and the lowest-priced motor boat for 975 dollars. While a comparably-sized aluminum boat can be bought for less, it will tear more easily on a snag and be more expensive to repair.

The stumpjumper is a very durable boat. Dale proudly explains that a stumpjumper will last you the rest of your life if you take care of it. Dale points out that there are stumpjumpers afloat on the lake that are fifty years old. The motors that Dale installs are very durable, some continue to run after thirty to forty years, and he uses galvanized or coated box nails which resist corrosion.

A major attraction for fishermen is that a wood boat is quieter. Alvin Gooch, a commercial fisherman on Reelfoot Lake, explains that the noise made by net leads hitting the sides of an aluminum boat will scare away fish. He prefers the quiet operation of a wood boat and rowing so that the fish will not scatter. Although there are fewer commercial fishermen on Reelfoot now, they generally prefer to use the D-line skiffs and commercial guides often use the stumpjumper.

Reelfoot Lake Boat-Building Tradition

While the Calhoun family has received the most attention in newspapers and magazines, there have been other boat builders working on Reelfoot Lake. Photographs of Reelfoot Lake from the 1920s through 40s show a wide variety of boats on the lake (Nelson 1924 and Smith 1988). Along with a range of stumpjumpers there are also john boats, D-line skiffs, larger inboard motor boats with cockpits, and boats used for towing strings of stumpjumpers.

Besides the occasional john boat builder, knowledgeable older residents remember several craftsmen who used to build stumpjumpers on Reelfoot, although none of these individuals appear to be making boats today. Along with these full-time boat builders, there were individuals who would occasionally make a stumpjumper. An example of such a boat builder is Grady Taylor. Now deceased, Taylor was an amateur woodworker and made several stumpjumpers in the 1960s. Taylor knew Dale Calhoun and used the Calhoun pattern for his boats (Smith 1988).

Bob Kelly, Sr. of Lawrenceville, Illinois, built a stumpjumper after seeing them on Reelfoot Lake (Lund 1983:683-684). During the 1950s and 60s he had built many boats, mostly john boats, at his band-sawmill on the Embarras River, but he also built a stumpjumper like those he had used while on hunting trips to Reelfoot. Kelly's stumpjumper closely resembles those on Reelfoot although he inserted the ribs after assembling the boat's planking. After viewing a photograph of Kelly's boat, Dale remarked that it was a lot like his boats but it had fewer ribs, no whaling on the gunwales, and the steering mechanism used a rope and pulley system. Dale remembered that such a steering system was sometimes used in stumpjumpers so that the hunters could steer with their feet.

Probably the only other boat builder currently making stumpjumpers is Thomas Alexander of Samburg, on the eastern shore of Reelfoot. Alexander has been fascinated by boats since he was a child and promised himself that he would build one when he grew up.[5] Alexander was raised in a woodworking family and his uncle was an active boat builder during the 1920s through 40s. Now 42 years old, Alexander has built about twenty-five stumpjumpers and six skiffs. Alexander is largely self-taught but he also learned some from Lewis "Booster" Walden, a recently deceased boatbuilder who was an uncle to Dale Calhoun. Alexander got his stumpjumper pattern from Walden but Walden never built a skiff. Alexander's stumpjumper resembles Dale's and is generally equipped with a eight horsepower

Briggs engine. Alexander is a commercial fisherman himself and enjoys going out on the lake when not working at the nearby Goodyear plant.

Declining Demand

Despite the fact that Dale is kept busy turning out one stumpjumper per week, the overall demand for stumpjumpers appears to be declining, judging from the number of full-time boat builders who once made their living at Reelfoot. The primary reason for the declining demand is the advent of fiberglass and aluminum boats which are now often used in the place of wooden boats. Many of the boats now in use on Reelfoot are aluminum john boats.

Another technological change that has reduced the demand for stumpjumpers is the development of the outboard motor. Outboard motors came into widespread use after World War Two as they became more sturdy and reliable. With these improvements in outboards the disadvantages of the stumpjumper engines became less tolerable. The stumpjumper engines have only one gear because of their direct drive to the prop and some boaters find them more difficult to operate than an outboard.

The stumpjumper is also losing its environmental niche. When the stumpjumper was developed Reelfoot was filled with standing trees and snags, but over the decades these obstacles have been greatly reduced. The number of trees and snags in Reelfoot has decreased because they have been gathered for firewood and during the winter they are worn down by ice. It has also been reported that fishermen would burn standing trees to serve as beacons while fishing at night (Smith 1988). With this reduction in obstacles, standard aluminum boats have become a less treacherous means of boating.

A final cause for the decline in the demand for stumpjumpers is the fact that most tourists today bring their own boats when visiting Reelfoot. In earlier times visitors would rent stumpjumpers for their fishing and hunting activities, but the increased number of private boats and their portability make renting a rarer occurrence. Today many pleasure boaters find the stumpjumper too small for their needs.

Despite these reasons for the declining demand for stumpjumpers from their peak production, probably during the 1920s and 30s, there continues to be a market for the boat. Part of this steady demand can be credited to the stumpjumper's adaptation to Reelfoot Lake and local needs, but the aesthetic preference for hand-built wooden boats with a local heritage also contributes to supporting this boat building tradition.

NOTES

I wish to thank Dale Calhoun, William Calhoun, Thomas Alexander, and Alvin Gooch for the information they generously shared through interviews. I also wish to thank Jens Lund and Robert Cogswell for identifying several useful references, Jack Tuberville for contributing a photograph and Wintfred Smith for providing very helpful historical information. I am indebted to Jens Lund and Wintfred Smith for reviewing a draft of this essay. Most of all I wish to recognize Warren E. Roberts with this article, which is grounded on the training in material folk culture studies I received from him while a graduate student at Indiana University.

[1] A Herman Young appears in the 1910 Census of Obion County, the county which borders the eastern shore of Reelfoot Lake. He is identified as a 50-year-old carpenter born in New York State.

[2] The description of Calhoun family history and boat building is based upon interviews with William and Dale Calhoun conducted by the author during October through December of 1988.

[3] Joseph Marion is listed in the 1900 Census of Gibson County, which contains Dyer. He is identified as being a farmer born in November of 1851 in Tennessee, and with a wife Emma and four children including a son Boone born in January of 1889. The same family appears in the 1910 Census of Obion County. All the information in the later census is the same except that his birthplace is listed as Alabama.

[4] Most publications on the Calhoun boat building tradition assert that they began making stumpjumpers around 1860, but census records appear to make this early date virtually impossible. The only reasonable date to appear in print is, "Three generations of Calhouns have been handmaking wooden boats at the lake since 1914" (Tennessee Department 1974:20).

[5] Interview with the author, 22 December 1988.

REFERENCES CITED

Andrews, James G.
  1973 The Reelfoot Boat-Builders. *The Commercial Appeal Mid-South Magazine*
    30 December, pp.4-6.
Carter, John Ray
  1958 Life and Lore of Reelfoot Lake. M.A. Thesis, George Peabody College for
    Teachers.
Comeaux, Malcolm L.
  1978 Origin and Evolution of Mississippi River Fishing Craft. *Pioneer America* 10:
    72-97.
Humphreys, Cecil C.
  1938 *The History of Reelfoot Lake.* n.p:n.p.
Kear, Steve R., David C. Stout, and Robert H. Ross
  1978 Fishing Folk Culture in East Tennessee. In *Glimpses of Southern Appalachian
    Folk Culture: Papers in Memory of Norbert F. Riedl.* Tennessee Anthropological

Association Miscellaneous Paper, No. 3. Ed. by Charles H. Faulkner and Carol K. Buckles. Pp. 97-107. Chattanooga, Tenn: Tribute Press.

Leeper, John H.
1978 Trammeling on Reelfoot Lake. *The Commercial Appeal Mid-South Magazine* 12 November, pp. 6-18.

Lund, Jens
1983 Fishing as a Folk Occupation in the Lower Ohio Valley. 2 Vols. Ph.D. Dissertation, Indiana University.

Marshall, E.H.
1941 *History of Obion County: Towns and Communities, Churches, Schools, Farming, Factories, Social and Political.* Union City, Tenn: The Daily Messenger.

Middleton, Harry
1986 Reelfoot: Tennessee's Earthquake Lake. *Southern Living* 21 (February): 126-31.

Nelson, Wilbur A.
1924 Reelfoot—An Earthquake Lake. *The National Geographic Magazine* 45 (January): 95-114.

Pomeroy, Maurice
1974 The Stump Jumper of Reelfoot Lake. *The Tennessee Conservationist* 40 (September): 18-20.

Schoffman, Robert J.
1949 Turtling for the Market at Reelfoot Lake. *Journal of the Tennessee Academy of Science* 24 (April): 143-45.

Smith, Wintfred L.
1988 Interview with the Author. Martin, Tennessee, 3 December.
-----------and Steve Pardue
1985 Interpretive Research Document for the Reelfoot Interpretive Center. Unpublished report which will be deposited in the Tennessee State Archives.

Tennessee Department of Economic and Community Development
1974 Reelfoot Lake: Vacation Paradise. *Tennessee Thrusts* 2 (Spring): 18-21.

Tennessee State Planning Commission
1958 *Reelfoot: Plan for Comprehensive Development.* Prepared by Otis M. Timble and Walter L. Criley.

Tuberville, Jack
1987 The Reelfoot Lake Boat: A Tennessee Original. *The Tennessee Conservationist* 53 (Nov./Dec.): 3-5.
1988 A Well-Used Boat: The Reelfoot Lake Stumpjumper. *Wooden Boat* 82 (May/June): 19-25.

Vanderwood, Paul J.
1969 *Night Riders of Reelfoot Lake.* Memphis: Memphis State University Press.

Viitanen, W.J.
1972 The Winter the Mississippi Ran Backwards: The Impact of the New Madrid, Missouri Earthquake of 1811-1812 on the Life and Letters in the Mississippi Valley. Ph.D. Dissertation, Southern Illinois University.

Figure 1. William and Dale Calhoun in an oar stumpjumper on Reelfoot Lake. (Photograph by Jack Tuberville)

Figure 2. Dale Calhoun working at the band saw in his shop. The boat-building jig is in the foreground.

Figure 3. Stern of stumpjumper which will be motorized. Note articulated oars and steering mechanism.

Figure 4. The propeller, protecting plate and kick-up rudder of a stumpjumper.

The Tradition of Geode Construction
in Southern Indiana

ALICE MORRISON MORDOH

The Indiana Geode Belt runs directly through the south-central part of the state (see Fig. 1), and corresponds to the geographical parameters of my fieldwork on the subject of geode construction. Geodes are essentially nodules of rock with a silicon rind, often hollow inside and containing crystals, usually quartz but also often a large variety of other minerals, including semi-precious amethyst (in Kentucky) and iron pyrite. Some are solid inside, and one can generally tell whether or not a geode is worth cracking open by its weight. The name "geode" comes from two Greek words meaning earth-like, because of the globular shape of these formations. They range in size from less than one inch to several feet in diameter, and the largest known geode from the midwestern United States is 347 pounds and 26 inches in diameter, currently on display at the Indiana Geological Survey at Indiana University, on loan from the farmer in Salem, Washington County, Indiana, who found it. Geodes are often collected along stream beds or plowed up by farmers in their fields.

In this area geodes are used as a decorative element in the construction of homes and landscaping, and apparently have served this function since at least the nineteenth century. A 1945 article entitled "Hunting Geodes in Indiana" describes the author's excursions in the same area that I traversed. He tells of one isolated area southeast of Bedford, Lawrence County, called the Devil's Backbone, a high knife-ridge of land, where he found abandoned old farmhouses. "Here, behind the house, in the deep grass and bushes, can be seen rows of geodes that marked the border of old flower beds, and we know that some early pioneer wondered at their strange symmetry and loved their color and crystals just as we do today" (Eisele 1945:112). Likewise, a collector in 1947 noted that "the people around Bedford and vicinity use the geodes around flower beds, to outline walks, and even in concrete work" (Riley 1947:818).

People in this area today use geodes in quite a variety of ways to decorate their homes, yards and gardens: geodes are often placed, piled or lined on patios, porches, steps, walks, or in front of the foundations of houses; they are embedded in the earth to help bank up a sloping section of lawn or as accentuation around other objects such as mailboxes, electric or telephone poles, trees, fish ponds; flower beds and large gardens are made entirely from geodes, and they are incorporated into elaborate lawn sculptures made from wood, figurines and other objects; geodes are mortared together to build planters, birdbaths, wishing wells, gateposts, fence posts, lampposts, mailbox stands, and shrines; geodes are pressed into cement to help form walls around houses and walls of houses (external and internal), foundations and chimneys. The geodes are usually left whole, although in a few cases they are all cracked open.

There is no doubt that these geode creations constitute a type of folk art. They are, like most gardens in general, as E. N. Anderson, Jr. notes in "On the Folk Art of Landscaping," "the product of traditional rules transmitted by word of mouth, observation, or such ephemeral literature as the 'home' sections of Sunday newspapers." (Anderson 1972:180). The familiar conservatism/dynamism duality within folk art is immediately apparent in these artifacts. The makers use identical or similar construction materials, techniques, forms, and subjects, but inject their own individual styles, thus demonstrating the "variation within tradition" dictum of folklore. There is no identifiable original inventor of the technique of working with geodes in this way—one of my informants claimed to have "just thought it up" when asked what gave him the idea of building geode constructions, while others were even more vague about their inspiration: "Oh, I don't know. I've just always done it" (Nethery).

These geode artifacts, moreover, conform to two major laws operative in most of Western folk art: the dominance of form and the desire for repetition (Glassie 1972:271-72). By dominance of form is meant that the basic form of the folk artifact is never obscured by ornamentation; rather, ornament serves frequently to reinforce the visual effect of form. Folk ornament also often consists of the continual repetition of the same motif. The ideal frequently is to form a symmetrical whole through the repetition of individually symmetrical units. The geode constructions which I observed demonstrate exactly such repetition and symmetry. The geodes are initially carefully selected as to uniformity of size and then placed in rows or groups, sometimes with a gradation from smaller to larger incorporated into the overall design.

Geodes are commonly found throughout this area in what might be termed "minimal artistic expression": heaped in piles or placed singly on patios, porches, steps, walks, or lining house or trailer fronts. The next stage of artistry involves deliberately embedding the geodes in the ground along some utilitarian object, such as front steps, as an added decorative element, or to form a border for a flower bed, or to bank a sloping section of yard. In one elaborate example in a working-class neighborhood of Bloomington, Monroe County, fieldstone was used for banking a large section of sloping lawn alongside a driveway and geodes trimmed the fieldstone. A carved limestone nameplate lay in the center of the banking, with another trimming of geodes above it. Geodes are often placed around the bases of trees as a decorative touch, and around electric and telephone poles, lamp posts and mailboxes. In front of a mobile home just inside the city limits of Bloomington is a more elaborate than usual example of such decoration: large geodes are piled at the base of a mailbox leaving a small circular area in the center where a small planter sits. The planter is built of very small geodes mortared together into a cylindrical shape and holds a large cactus.

Round geode flower beds are very common in all of the counties surveyed, either simply piled or mortared, in both back and front lawns, or surrounding shrubs. A very singular and skillfully executed flower bed in a working-class neighborhood of Bedford, Lawrence County, consists of a ring of piled geodes mortared in such a way that no concrete is visible. In the center of the flower bed is a small geode sculpture consisting of a cylindrical base embedded with very small geodes, topped by one huge geode, which is in turn topped by a small wood disk on which sits a clump of white balls. In one Bloomington example in an upper-middle-class neighborhood, nine very uniform geodes embedded in the ground surround each of two evergreen bushes planted on either side of the base of a long gravel driveway. An early twentieth-century stone city house in the center of Bloomington, now a neglected rental property in the university district, has an elaborate series of three round, mortared geode flower beds within a stone patio. One brand-new home in a middle-class subdivision of Bloomington has a large round flower bed in the front lawn made of bricks with geodes mortared on top. The owner explained that the "niggerheads" had been unearthed during construction of the house and he thought they were "real pretty," so he built the bed. Several of my informants used the term "niggerhead" but qualified it by stating that the geodes were called that in the past, while others used the term without hesitation. Other examples of the folk terminology for geodes in this area include "muttonheads" (one woman using this word was unaware of the technical term "geode") "bullheads," "rattlers" (hollow geodes which rattle when shaken), and "thunderballs" ("They said the Indians, ther'd come a big rain and water would wash 'em down the hill, they'd come rollin' down the hill, they'd call 'em thunderballs. . . . That is the original name for 'em" [Brandt 1984:20].)

Occasionally one will see roadside stands where geodes are for sale. One such stand, in Jackson County near the border of Lawrence County, consists of four huge piles of geodes, sorted by size, lining the front lawn of the seller's trailer home. They were available for "from a dime to a dollar apiece." I asked the owner where he had found them all and he was reluctant to answer (evidently a trade secret) until I specified that I meant in general terms. He then stated that he collected them all over, in the past from streambeds now covered by Lake Monroe (built in the early 1960s), and today he still plows them up in fields. All of the creators of the geode objects I photographed in the surrounding areas, however, had gathered their geodes by themselves or with friends and relatives.

The category of objects which I call lawn sculptures consists of a wide variety of combinations of elements, usually placed in a prominent position in the front yard or within a flower bed. In this type of ornament, individual creativity is displayed in the often asymmetrical, fanciful use of various commonly used objects, including geodes and other things such as pieces of interestingly shaped wood, driftwood, branches, bricks, flowers, fieldstone and other rocks, old tires, buckets, metal rims, animal and dwarf figurines, plastic flowers, carved birds, placed together in widely varying combinations, but usually clustered around a central, larger object. For example, one such lawn sculpture from rural Monroe County consists of a tree stump with an eagle perched on top and several geodes seemingly randomly strewn around the base of the eagle. Another example, from a working-class neighborhood in Bloomington, includes a branched tree stump with geodes placed on different levels of branches along with flower pots and bird feeders, a plastic yellow daisy and a hand-made wooden cardinal, and geodes and gnome figurines piled at the base of the stump. The artisan, Mr. Phil Taylor, was unfamiliar with the term "geode." This sculpture stands in a driveway-parking lot which takes the place of a front lawn, and a geode flower bed borders the small house. In a side yard, beside the detached garage, is a wishing well of geodes constructed by Mr. Taylor, and stainless steel coffee pots hang from nearby bushes.

I encountered many other examples of such elaborate yard decoration, always in working-class or lower-middle-class neighborhoods or rural areas and never in the more affluent subdivisions. This finding corresponds with Anderson's observation that "One of the important things communicated by gardens is social class" (Anderson 1972:185). Anderson describes the differences between lower-class, middle-class, and upper-class yards and gardens, citing such factors as lawn versus ground cover, symmetry of the placement of bushes, and the shapes of lawns, and he notes the tendency of lower-middle-class gardens to be ornamented with concrete statues. Likewise, a 1978 study of the folk art of mailbox decoration demonstrates that while decorated mailboxes are a facet of the folk culture of the American middle class, "the character of a particular neighborhood influences the style of decorated mailboxes located there, and . . . there is a tendency for folk mailboxes to be replaced by popularized versions of folk styles in developments that are in a higher socio-economic class" (Jarrett 1978:20).

While Anderson's conclusion that gardens and landscaping are a mode of communication, "a paralanguage" (Anderson 1972:182), sending a message about the social class of a home's or neighborhood's occupants (among other possible messages) seems to apply as well to these lawn sculptures, there is a great deal of variety between individual works. One retired truck driver in Bloomington, who collected geodes during his drives, has many geode decorations around his house and yards: he mounted two very large geodes singly, one each in his front and side yards. He decorated his side yard with a loose pile of geodes, mounted on top by a particularly large one, which covers a pipe sticking out of the ground. Next to this pile is an old gasoline pump. At the base of his mailbox is a large rock painted white, with his name lettered in black. Lining one side of the driveway is one long row of rocks of all sorts, each of varying shapes and sizes and placed with spaces between them. In summer, flowers are planted between these stones, while in winter their stark shapes against snow make a striking effect. Mr. Grubb has a definite personal opinion on the aesthetics of working with geodes. "You know they don't make a purty wall. . . . I don't think so . . . no, I, I think the purtiest thing is just one big rock, but I don't think they're purty in a wall" (Brandt 1984:11). This sentiment may be shared by the creator of another lawn "sculpture" just outside of Bloomington consisting of a single geode placed atop a huge granite stone embedded close to the road in a front lawn. It is evident that individual artistic self expression is as dominant a force as neighborhood influence in the creation of these lawn decorations.

When constructing free-standing objects out of geodes, most of the artists employed a similar technique, using cement as mortar and often affixing the geodes onto a frame or base such as cement blocks (in the case of a mailbox stand, for example), a barrel (wishing well), a large pipe (birdbath), or a metal tub (fountain or pond). Wishing wells are usually cylindrical while birdbaths are usually hourglass shaped, as in mass-produced examples. There is much variation in the amount of mortar allowed to show between geodes, in the size of the geodes used in construction, and whether or not they are left intact or cracked open. In most cases the geodes are placed symmetrically, in horizontal or vertical rows. In many cases, only geodes of the same size are used in the formation of one object, though sometimes there will be a gradation from rows of smaller to larger geodes. Less often, though occasionally, one finds a mixture of sizes scattered throughout one object, just as one only occasionally finds a mixture of intact and broken geodes within one object. The tendency is towards symmetry of form instead of asymmetry.

Functions for these completed objects vary. One wishing well in Lawrence County is used as a planter, and birdbaths and planters are sometimes used interchangeably. One wishing well was later hooked up with a tap and hose, almost as though its status as solely a decoration were somehow an affront. I spoke with the creator of this well at length, but the only explanation I could draw from him as to why he built the well was "I wanted one." The well sits in the small front yard of a single-pen house in rural Monroe County, accompanied by the ubiquitous broken children's toys, non-functional washing machine, dozens of canning jars, and other odds and ends. The creator of this well also mortared geodes onto the top of his front porch rail. The well was formed by pressing geodes of various sizes into cement spread onto an old barrel, leaving large spaces of concrete visible in the end. A high pitched, tin roof was then placed on top. These objects represent this man's first and last attempts at such artistry, and they display less craftmanship than most of the other creations I observed. However, apparently a woman driving by on this typical Indiana secondary road stopped and asked the artisan if he would make one for her, but he refused: "I weren't interested—too much aggravation."

One commonly shaped, cylindrical geode and mortar planter displayed a unusual added detail—an old automobile luggage rack placed above so that a rose would grow up onto it. The rose later died and was not replanted, so that at first glance the planter appears to be an odd sculpture. The creator of this and two other geode objects on his front lawn, Virgil Frye of rural Monroe County, was entirely noncommittal about his work, which was completed in the 1970s. One of the objects is an unusual and striking birdbath of the common hourglass shape, but constructed of four large geodes mortared together as a base with a dish on top decorated with uniform, smaller geodes. Most birdbaths are built by mortaring smaller geodes onto a frame in the same manner as Mr. Frye's planter. The third geode construction on his front lawn is a very large, oblong planter completely encrusted with geodes. Virgil Frye demonstrates a high degree of artistry and craftsmanship in his geode creations, but dismisses them as a meaningless hobby abandoned years ago.

As Katherine Jan Jarrett noted in her 1978 article, rural delivery mailboxes "are a lively element of our continuing tradition of material folk culture in the late 20th Century" (Jarrett 1978:19). Floyd Hawkins, in rural Monroe County near Bloomington, built his mailbox post in 1983 with a great deal of skill and resultant pride. His wife, Darla, proclaimed her husband's ability and desire to create: "He's all the time makin' things, thinkin' things up like that" (Hawkins). The initial impetus for building the mailbox post had been functional—the old one had gotten knocked down and Mr. Hawkins said that he was going to "build one the kids couldn't tear down." The post has concrete blocks as a base, completely mortared over with intact geodes. The largest geodes are at the base of the post and the smallest ones towards the top. Another mailbox post on a secondary road outside Bloomington has an oval shape similar to that of Mr. Hawkins' stand, but the mailbox on top is enclosed by a row of geodes. This post also has the largest row of geodes at the bottom, and tapers in slightly towards the top, as does Mr. Hawkins' work. However, the second mailbox post consists of broken as well as intact geodes. The latter post sitting in front of a mobile home, was erected because cars on the very curved road kept running into the occupant's mailbox. The initial motivation for building this piece of folk art was again utilitarian. However, after the builder put geodes around the concrete block mailbox post to prevent it from being knocked down, he decided that the mailbox looked so nice, he would build geode posts all along the road, which he linked with a chain (Brandt 1984:13). More geodes are banked around trees in the front yard.

Gateposts and lampposts are other examples of geode objects constructed initially or primarily with a functional purpose, but eventually exhibiting an equal decorative component, as is the case with much folk art. One pair of large, elaborate gateposts in rural Monroe County was built in the 1940s by a jack-of-all-trades, Scott Richards, according to his son (Richards). The six-foot tall posts are cylindrically shaped and made with uniform sized, intact geodes placed in even rows, and each post is topped by one very large geode. A similar pair of five-foot tall lampposts sits at the base of the house walk. This craftsman's brother had been a stonemason. According to his son, Mr. Richards liked his property "kept up real nice," and had many other hobbies, one of which was cabinetmaking.

I discovered another gatepost in an isolated area of Brown County, still attached to a dilapidated rail fence. It is about two feet high, rectangular in shape, and topped with a square limestone slab. It is mortared with even rows of small, intact geodes, with more mortar visible than in the Richards' gateposts.

A modern use of geodes on gateposts, in an affluent suburb of Bloomington, uses only one very large geode atop each post. The two-foot tall gateposts are made of manufactured limestone veneer covering concrete forms. This home also has factory-made lampposts—directly behind the gateposts at the foot of the asphalt driveway—which are decorated with replicas of birds and squirrels.

Most of the objects I observed were made from geodes which were left intact, with some exceptions as noted in the above descriptions. One very unusual planter which I found in the small town of North Vernon, Jennings County, is in the shape of a large basket and built from very small geodes, all of which have been cracked open to reveal the sparkling quartz centers. While I was not able to locate the creator of this object, one of my informants in Brown County expressed a decided preference for geodes which were cracked open; this was his sole technique in his many constructions. He told me almost with disbelief that many people preferred the geodes left whole (Hartley). Virgil Hartley is the creator of a large, impressive shrine on his front lawn. Every geode has been cracked open and embedded in cement, except for the unusual, pointed geodes bordering the top edge of the shrine. A white Virgin Mary statue stands inside the shell of the common upturned bathtub, but this tub is encrusted with cracked geodes. On either side of her there are symmetrical geode walls, each one formed by three rows of identical large squares composed of geodes, tapering down on each end. Thus each of the top two rows is formed by two squares and one triangle, the middle rows by three squares and one triangle, and the bottom rows by four squares and one triangle.

Virgil Hartley is a retired industrial electrician for General Motors from Anderson, Indiana, who also builds birdhouses and dollhouses as a hobby. I asked him if he were Catholic, because it is unusual to find Virgin Mary shrines in the Monroe and Brown County area, and he emphasized that he and his wife were not Catholic. His "wife's parents" are Catholic, but he just built the shrine because "it seemed like a pretty idea." The shrine sits on the front lawn facing the road. This subject seemed sensitive; perhaps there had been problems commonly associated with such religious intermarriage in the 1940s, as his wife had evidently left her faith upon their marriage. This subsequent building of a classic shrine to the Virgin Mary (folk "bathtub" style) forty years later seems to be an intriguing act, probably with more underlying it psychologically than the reasoning "it seemed like a pretty idea." Such a shrine is not usually found on the lawn of a non-Catholic. That Mr. Hartley is capable of choosing other subjects for his geode constructions is evident in the fact that he has also built two interior walls in his house completely out of cracked-open geodes, one in his kitchen and one surrounding a stone fireplace in the living room.

I photographed one other example of geodes used in the creation of objects with a religious theme, a truly spectacular construction filling a lot one block west of the huge, sandstone Catholic church in the center of Jasper, Dubois County. Dubois County is an area of nineteenth-century German Catholic settlement and is quite a bit west of the Indiana Geode Belt. This huge grotto of geode shrines and planters was built by the members of a home for the mentally retarded which is located adjacent to the grotto. The geodes were bussed in from other areas. The shrines are largely composed of intact geodes, but also have intermittent sections using only broken ones. The elaborate shrines are composed of strictly symmetrical units: on the largest, central shrine, for example, a circular base built from uniform geodes is topped with several groups of identical geode pillars, grouped in even rows or clusters, all topped by another, smaller base of geodes. This second base of geodes is decorated on the perimeter of the shrine with single geodes lined in a row. At the center of the shrine, however, it is topped with another row of geode pillars, which has another base on top of it, then a row of single stones, then a bathtub type shrine (encrusted with geodes) with a Virgin Mary in the center. Surrounding the bathtub is another row of geode pillars, topped by another base of geodes, topped by single geodes.

Geodes are also used decoratively in the building of house foundations, chimneys, and walls, and porch, carport, and house lot walls, both as actual construction material and as veneer, though their use in this way is less common. One self-designated "rock lover" in rural Jennings County—a woman whose small house inside is a museum of labeled semi-precious stones and fossils—has used geodes extensively outside her home. Two huge rock gardens in her front and side lawns consist largely of whole geodes of all sizes (Kahrs). Her carport wall and house foundation are embedded with intact geodes, and piles of unbroken geodes line her house, front walk and steps.

In the town of Mitchell, Lawrence County, a striking geode wall, about two feet high and made with even rows of uniform geodes, runs along the sidewalk in front of a white clapboard cottage in a working-class neighborhood. Very large geodes are placed on top of the wall all along it, evenly spaced and about a large geode size apart. Taller gateposts (about three feet high) flank each opening in the wall, and each is topped by an extra-large geode. There are several such openings—two or three for walks and as many opening onto lawn.

In Bloomington, the base of a screened porch was embedded with geodes in the 1960s by Mr. Beyer, who collected them during the construction of the Lake Monroe Dam. Mr. Beyer felt that he had been original in using geodes to decorate in this manner, though he acknowledged seeing geodes used in other ways (Brandt 1984:19).

A unique, modified bungalow in Bloomington, designed and built around the turn of the century by "Bloomington's first architect" (Craig 1980), makes extensive use of geodes in the construction of the foundation, front porch (which is adorned with Greek Revival pillars and a wide front gable), and side garden. Originally there were also rows of huge geodes, mortared together, lining the driveway and the sidewalk in front of the house.

There is a unique example of a whole house constructed of geodes, an enormous two-story Victorian known locally as "the Rock House," in Morgantown, Morgan County. It was built in 1896 by a local man, James Knight, as a home for his more than twenty children. Mr. Knight worked at various times as a U.S. postmaster, and sawmill, livery stable, and general store owner. The home is made of home-made concrete blocks, poured in forms, and before completely dry embedded with rocks, primarily geodes. Some forms were also embedded with items such as shells, pottery pieces, jewelry, marbles, dice, and animal skeletons. Knight's name appears in coal over the east front door and his wife's name (Isabelle) over the east window on the first floor (Rock House 1984).

The tradition of using geodes in landscaping, house decoration, mailbox ornamentation and gate, fence, and lamppost construction falls within the realm of folk art. As Michael Owen Jones has noted, folk practices are "generated spontaneously among people with shared identities and values (Jones 1972:47). Like most landscaping, such geode creations are the product of traditional rules transmitted informally, such as by word of mouth or imitation, in most cases among members of the working-class or lower-middle class in the area observed. While these artists conform as to materials used, techniques of construction, forms and subjects, there is a great deal of variety exhibited in individual styles. This finding confirms Jarrett's observation with regard to folk mailbox art that "trends vary from neighborhood to neighborhood and run along a continuum from a random variety of folk styles along rural roads, through more conformity of style in some suburban developments, to nearly totally conforming popular styles in the more exclusive developments" (Jarrett 1978:20). The few geode constructions observed in upper-middle-class neighborhoods were very simple, utilizing only a few, large, uniform geodes.

This semi-public folk art, the landscaping and decorative objects, is communicating more than just social class or the norms and values inherent within it, or, in some cases, religious beliefs. Each object represents a need for creative self-expression on the part of its maker, demonstrated by the variety exhibited. What is the source of this need, and why does it seem to be less prevalent in the middle- and upper-middle-class neighborhoods? What controls the dynamics between conformity and individuality in these material expressions of the self, one's home and land? Obviously, there are neither simple nor single answers to these queries, only the acknowledgment that there is much room for more research on the topic.

INTERVIEWS CITED

Frye, Virgil, Monroe County, Indiana, September 15, 1984.
Hartley, Virgil, Brown County, Indiana, August, 1984.
Hawkins, Darla, Bloomington, Indiana, July 17, 1984.
Kahrs, Mrs., Jennings County, Indiana, September 15, 1984.
Nethery, Mary, Monroe County, Indiana, July 17, 1984.
Richards, Bob, Bloomington, Indiana, September, 1984.

REFERENCES CITED

Anderson, E.N. Jr.
1972 On the Folk Art of Landscaping. *Western Folklore* 31(3): 179-88.
Brandt, Amanda
1984 Geode Art. Unpublished manuscript. Indiana University Folklore Archives.
Craig, Karen S. and Diana M. Hawes
1980 *Bloomington Discovered.* Bloomington: Discovery Press.
Eisele, Walter F.
1945 Hunting Geodes in Indiana. *Rocks and Minerals* 20(3): 112-13.
Glassie, Henry
1972 Folk Art. in *Folklore and Folklife.* Richard M. Dorson, ed. Pp. 253-80.
Chicago: University of Chicago Press.
Jarrett, Katherine Jan
1978 Neighborhood Influence on Mailbox Style. *Pennsylvania Folklife* 27(3): 19-
24.
Jones, Michael Owen
1972 'There's gotta be New Designs Once in a While': Culture Change and the
Folk Arts. *Southern Folklore Quarterly* 36:43-60.
Riley, Marie S.
1947 Indiana Geodes. *Rocks and Minerals* 22(9): 818-19.
The Rock House Restaurant
1984 Menu for the Rock House Restaurant. Morgantown, Morgan County, Indiana.

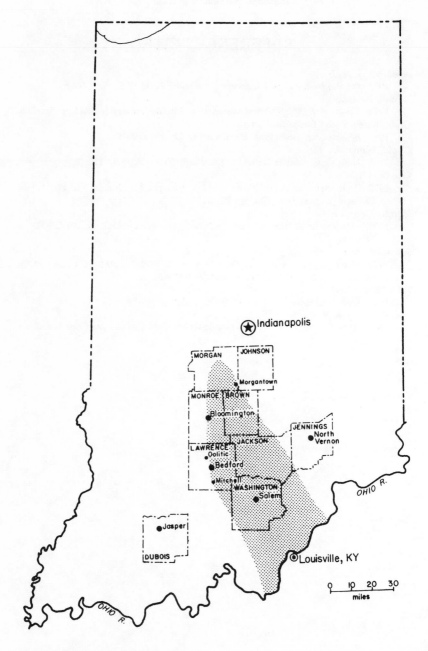

Figure 1. The Indiana Geode Belt.

Figure 2. Fieldstone and geode banking, Bloomington, Monroe County, Indiana.

Figure 3. A striking geode birdbath or planter, Bloomington, Monroe County, Indiana. Artist unknown.

Figure 4. Front lawn shrine built of cracked-open geodes with whole, oval shaped geodes mounted on top. Note the repetitive three pattern. Brown County, Indiana. Virgil Hartley.

Figure 5. Geode foundation, built around the turn of the century by Bloomington's first architect, John Nichols.

Cemetery Decoration Customs in the American South

LYNWOOD MONTELL

This paper looks at southern cemetery decoration customs practiced across the years, how these customs have changed, and what remains the same about them. While this study is limited to the American South, certain examples from other parts of the world will be included for comparative purposes. Many of the older southern traditional practices surrounding death and burial, such as preparing the corpse, sitting up with the dead, and carrying the corpse to the grave, have been absorbed in recent years by funeral professionals. And while there may be other viable folk customs and practices associated with death and burial, I am concentrating only on social interactions associated with decorating graves and cemeteries. These represent customs and unifying group activities that have continued to the present day.

Here I will describe two basic kinds of folk activities associated with cemetery decoration: one-time activities and those that are on-going or repeated year after year. One-time customary activities consist of choosing and erecting gravestones, and of building structures such as gravehouses, walls, or fences, all of which are intended to be permanent, on or around the graves. The matter of choosing and erecting relatively permanent gravestones affords an excellent opportunity to study community levels of technology and human thought and emotion in historical perspective. Gravestone types and materials have, after all, evolved from the simple to the complex—from the days of fieldstones and hand-hewn, hand-lettered stones to the era of standardized marble and granite stones, which exhibit both standardized sizes, forms, and machine chiseled lettering.

The older custom of erecting nondescript fieldstones or shale is still practiced in some areas of the South by less affluent members of society such as tenants and sharecroppers. While these fieldstones, when whitewashed, may reflect a local aesthetic for tidiness, there is little about them to cause others to pick up on the custom and perpetuate it, especially since the identity of the deceased is not preserved on the stone except when roughly carved initials are used for this purpose.   Less enduring even than fieldstones and, perhaps consequently, less widely used, are gravemarkers made of wooden slabs or planks (Ball 1977:167-70),[1] wooden crosses (Ibid),[2] and clay pots (Smith and Rogers 1979:142-43).[3]

The practice of using hand-hewn hand-lettered stones as grave markers was introduced into most southern communities at an early date. The custom grew up alongside that of using fieldstones to mark graves, and was practiced until the early years of the twentieth century. Rock used for making hand-hewn gravestones was generally obtained from nearby limestone and sandstone quarries, although many gravestones, like chimney rocks, came from creek beds where sedimentary rock was found in relatively thick layers. Quarried and creek-bed stones were hewn into appropriate shapes and lettered by community craftsmen who worked closely with representatives of the bereaved families. While the shape of the stones, the amount of lettering, and the motif choices were dictated by the family of the deceased, the final appearance of the stone was distinctly and unmistakably that of the mason, and his products can be spotted in different cemeteries within the geographical area where he worked (Taylor & Weldy 1976:15-33). In addition to the stones executed by local masons, some grave markers were hewn and lettered by amateurs, possibly by members of the family. This may have been the origin of such stones as the one in Monroe County, Kentucky, bearing the epitaph "Dear Papa" and having a heart carved in raised relief on the reverse side.

While a limited number of granite and marble gravestones were utilized during the earliest days of settlement in most southern communities, monuments made from these stones did not win wide acceptance until after the Civil War, when they became more accessible due to a gradually improving economy and more efficient rail transportation. The standardized sizes and forms of these granite and marble stones may be attributed to silent conformity to community standards; that is, it was customary to purchase a gravestone about the same size as others in the cemetery. The community norm was not to outdo one's neighbor on the one hand, nor to be outdone on the other. Tall obelisks and boulder-like stones, though present, are even today the exception rather than the rule, and occur more frequently in town and city rather than rural settlement or community.[4]

All types of stone markers, save fieldstones and shale, contain motifs (pictorial or symbolic representations carved into the stone) and epitaphs (word messages carved into the stone) that, while expressing the individuality of the deceased, are often national or international in popularity. One example of an epitaph popular in England and throughout the United States reads as follows:

> Remember friend as you pass by,
> As you are now so once was I;
> As I am now so ye shall be,
> Prepare in death to follow me.

Southern uniqueness in cemetery customs is not as likely to be found in motifs and epitaphs, or in rock types and forms, as in other practices associated with cemeteries and graves. One such predominantly southern folk custom is that of mounting a photograph of the deceased on the face of the gravestone near the top center. This custom, which apparently originated about 1890, knows no age limitations. I have viewed the photographs of people of all ages, from infancy to one hundred years, mounted in the stones. Like the practice of photographing corpses in their coffins, this one filled the human need for visible, tangible reminders of those who had died. Although it is not utilized as frequently as it once was, the custom of mounting photographs on gravestones is still practiced (Jeane 1966:41).

Here and there across the rural South, clusters of small gabled buildings were once built in profusion to shelter in-ground interments. Referred to variously as gravesheds, graveshelters, shelter houses, spirit houses, and gravehouses (Ball 1977:30), these rapidly vanishing structures may still be found in Euro-American cemeteries in the South within a line drawn from eastern Texas, northern Louisiana, and the Arkansas Ozarks on the west, to western West Virginia, western Virginia, western North Carolina, and northeastern Georgia on the east. According to data compiled by cultural geographers, archaeologists, and folklorists, it appears that middle and east Tennessee, south-central Kentucky, and east Texas contain the greatest number of them (Jordan 1980:252; Ball 1977:30; Fielder 1980). Verla Parrish, a resident of Floyd County, Kentucky, noted that these structures were numerous in that county until they were all torn down in the 1960s by Job Corps employees who were paid to clean up the cemeteries (Anderson 1980). Gravehouses are also part of Native American heritage in the South; John Lawson observed many of these tiny structures among the Indians of the Carolinas in the late eighteenth century (Jeane 1966:39).

The gravehouse, a rather distinctive form of grave decoration, may be defined as a shelter used to cover the graves of those whose corpses were buried in the earth. Most of these tiny houses are of wood, but brick, brick and wood, and metal examples have also been observed (Price 1973:9; Ball 1977:29). In rural southern cemeteries, these little houses usually consist of four posts supporting a gabled roof. While a few are open on the sides, most are enclosed with plain picket or stylized picket walls, or with weatherboards covering the bottom half of the walls (Coleman 1971:188). Gravehouses have a front door and sometimes one or more windows, making it possible to read the gravestone inscription without entering the tiny house. Most of these rather unique structures cover only one grave; some cover two. In two discoveries (in Monroe County, Kentucky, and Overton County, Tennessee), I found houses that covered from four to six graves, thus enclosing and sheltering entire families.

Some of these houses contain only grave markers, with the enclosed graves periodically decorated with flowers by survivors of the deceased. Some structures are more fully decorated with personal mementos of the deceased, however, or decorations placed there by bereaved survivors (Garrity and Wyss 1976:216). On Upper Devil's Creek in Wolfe County, Kentucky, for example, the grave of a nineteen-year-old girl, who drowned in 1939, is covered by a little white weatherboarded house, complete with a door, a double-hung window containing two sashes with six panes each, interior walls neatly papered, and a picture of the dead girl hanging on the wall above the headstone. Flowers adorn the grave itself (Treadway 1964). In another instance, this one from Claiborne County, Tennessee, the grave inside the gravehouse is decorated with plaster-of-Paris bulldogs, a framed picture of Christ, and other religious symbols (Corn 1977:34-37).[5]

The contemporary function of gravehouses appears to be one of keeping pigs, dogs, and other scavenging animals away from the corpse, or of sheltering the grave from rain. These two reasons are reported from New Guinea (Bendann 1930:110), and from Anglo-Americans in the Upland South (Ball 1977:53). I personally talked with a man in Pickett County, Tennessee, whose teenage brother accidentally shot himself in the 1920s. The parents erected a gravehouse over the son's grave in order to keep water from reaching his body.

Gravehouses may have served early people's presumed needs to control the spirit of the deceased. The desire to appease the spirit influenced what they did with their dead or, in the case of gravehouses, what people did for their dead. Egyptians made mummies as lasting bodies for spirits to dwell in, and the Etruscans placed the corpses of the dead in house-like tombs, believing that the dead lived in these structures (Bendann 1930:xi). The Greeks believed that the ghosts of the deceased came out of their tombs and sepulchers and wandered about the spot where their remains lay buried (Brand 1913:474), thus explaining in part why many cemeteries and church buildings are replete with reported ghosts. The same belief about wandering spirits seems to have persisted in the European folk mind across the centuries. We may conjecture that those early people who built coverings over graves wanted the spirits to come back and be close to the living, or that they were providing an abode for the spirits as a means of appeasing them and thus preventing them from inflicting harm upon the living.

Unlikely archetypes of southern gravehouses have been reported at various times in history in Sweden, Bosnia, Russia (Oinas 1964-:77-86), Indonesia, Melanesia, New South Wales (Bendann 1930:110), England (where cruck roof dwellings introduced during or before the Danish invasion bear resemblance to stone slab "hogback" graves), West Africa, and among some Native American groups. Further library research and fieldwork should be conducted before claims regarding the origins of southern gravehouses are made.

Other types of gravecovers, perhaps related to gravehouses, need to be dealt with here. Graves covered with sandstones, hand-hewn and placed together to look like small houses with gable roofs, are found in Cumberland and Wolfe counties, Kentucky (Treadway 1964)[6] and in portions of Tennessee (Fielder 1980). Such stone grave structures, referred to as cairns by one writer (Fielder 1980), are perhaps closely related to the Anglo-Danish hogback tombstones. These rather rare and archaic stone edifices are older than all other southern gravehouse forms. Unlike the roofs of the Anglo-Danish hogback tombstones, which are almost invariably slightly arched lengthwise and have tegular surfaces, the roofs of the stone cairns in Kentucky and Tennessee are entirely parallel with the ground lengthwise, and the gabled slope of the roof is achieved by hewing stones in the shape of a triangle and by exposing the hypotenuse (Walton 1954:68).

Another stone gravecover, prismatic in shape, is formed lengthwise over the grave by using two thinly sawn or hand-hewn sandstones, spaced about two and a half feet apart at the ground and tilted together at the top to form a gable roof. Triangular-shaped stones are generally set in the gable ends to provide a house-like appearance. Their distribution in the South is yet unknown; however, fieldwork has uncovered numerous examples in central Tennessee, with scattered occurrences in east-central Alabama, and the Arkansas Ozarks.

Another ancient activity associated with covering graves is that of placing flat stone slabs (hewn or unhewn), or concrete slabs, over graves to protect them not only from animal scavengers, but also from early medical students in need of cadavers (Coffin 1976:151). This form of grave covering, known across the southland, is mentioned by Cicero and by various English and Welsh writers as well (Brand 1913:481). The custom was common in England by 1775 (Puckle 1968:147), with some of the stones being whitewashed with lime at Christmas, Easter, and Whitsuntide (Brand 1913:481). The inscriptions on such stones are at the head.

In the early Middle Colonies and New England, these table stones stood free above the ground on four stone legs (Coffin 1976:154). In the South, stone walls were built around individual graves and topped with the large, flat stones so that the physical appearance is not unlike a mausoleum. Many family and community cemeteries of the Upland South with burials predating 1850 have one or more of these three-dimensional rectangular rock gravecovers.

Finally, there are occurrences of coffin-shaped, coffin-size stones used as gravecovers reported in Boyd (Cann 1969) and Mercer counties, Kentucky, and in Fentress and Lincoln counties, Tennessee. More common, although still rare in the Upland South, is the practice of carving a half-inch profile of a coffin into the top surface of the flat table stones that are used to cap the rock fences described in the previous paragraph.

Most southern cemeteries began as single family graveyards, then grew to include extended members of the family. Because virtually no one was denied burial privileges in a family's burial plot, such spots often evolved into community burial grounds. Cemeteries of this variety are at times identified with certain religious denominations and with nearby church houses, although most burial grounds in the South are truly communal in nature and predate the construction of churches.

Even in contemporary community cemeteries, the identities of families within them are retained by various means of demarcation. Family plots, usually consisting of six burial sites, are fenced, walled, staked out, or marked with quarried marble or granite corner posts.[7] The original function of fences and walls around family grave plots or even entire cemeteries probably served no aesthetic impulse. However, individual, family, and community pride has generally kept these enclosures in good repair and uniquely suited to the aesthetics of cemetery landscapes.

The older community cemeteries have no business manager; thus the grave plots are available at no cost on a first come, first served basis. Since burial plots are free, however, most of the cemeteries have no endowments for perpetual care and must be cared for on a volunteer basis by the people of the community. For this reason many of the rural people of the South still come together on a community basis once or twice each year to clean and decorate the cemetery, and to share in fellowship around the graves of their deceased family members and friends. Even in those instances where cemetery labor is hired by means of interest-income derived from endowment bonds, members of the community annually contribute funds for cemetery upkeep, or raise money by selling refreshments, chances on calves, quilts, cars, and other commodities, and by holding bingo games and cakewalks (Ball 1975:93).

Rituals associated with cemetery decoration in the South often involve community celebrations variously referred to as "decorating the burial grounds," "decorating the graves," or simply "Decoration Day" or "Memorial Day," two terms in common and widespread usage. Since the celebration is generally observed on May 30, some southern people refer to the day when graves are decorated as "the thirtieth." The event may actually be celebrated on any date convenient for the community. While a day on or near May 30 is commonly observed as Decoration Day, there are numerous exceptions to the rule. To avoid possible conflict with a nearby community (a body of people with common ties to a particular cemetery), a given community may elect to celebrate Decoration Day a week or so on either side of the date chosen by its neighbor. Dates even further removed from May 30 are not uncommon. Barbara Allen and I observed a Decoration Day homecoming near East Lynn Lake in western West Virginia on July 6, 1980, and the fourth Saturday in August is the traditional day set aside by a church community in western Hardin County, Kentucky (Hoskinson 1959:117-19). The date for these later-in-the-year celebrations originated during pre-World War I times when social interaction was dependent on a "stabilized and orderly sequence of agricultural events," that is, the period between cultivating and harvesting crops (Ball 1975:93).

Decoration Day, as it is known and practiced today, began in the South, a fact that helps to explain its continued popularity there. Regarding the origin of the "official" Decoration Day, I quote from a note written by a resident of Slippery Rock, Pennsylvania, and published in an 1894 issue of the *Confederate Veteran:*

> To the South belongs the credit of having established one of the most touching customs that has ever arisen out of war—namely, that of decorating soldiers' graves.
>
> During the time the war lasted, the people of the South suffered bitterly, and thousands of her bravest men and most promising youths fell in battle or died in prison. It was a long night in which the death angel flew over the land and when at last dawn appeared it was found he had touched the firstborn of nearly every household in the land.
>
> The brave men of the South, however, left behind them wives, mothers, and sisters whose devotion was imperishable.
>
> These devoted women, in order to show that they cherished the memory of loved ones, established the custom of strewing flowers on the graves of their dead sons and heroes, and since the war have devoted one day each year to honoring their dead by placing chaplets of laurel and flowers on their graves. [Murphy 1894:267]

Some scholars feel, however, that the real origins of Decoration Day lie not in Civil War times, but in Protestant modifications of All Saint's Day (November 1) and All Soul's Day (November 2), and ultimately, perhaps, in the pre-Christian Celtic celebration of Samain (Ball 1975:95-96; Rees and Rees 1961:89-92).

Just prior to Decoration Day each year, usually one to seven days in advance, present and former members of the community assemble to repair cemetery fences, clean individual and family burial plots, right overturned stones, repair broken stones, trim hedges and shrubs, and cut and rake the grass. When the physical landscape and/or cultural preference dictates a grassless, barren cemetery surface, people scrape and sweep the cemetery and reshape the graves by piling up dirt into tall mounds (Kniffen 1967:427). In many cemeteries, a pile of dirt, usually that which is left over from burials, is kept adjacent to the burial area for use by persons who desire to fill in or mound family graves in this traditional manner. "Cemetery cleanings," as these events are usually called, have taken on aspects of group or family ritual behavior; for in addition to bringing shovels, hoes, rakes, moving blades, and brooms, the group often brings basket lunches, and there is a communal sharing of food, which is prepared by the women, some of whom are present at the cemetery and take active parts in raking or sweeping the grounds. Reminiscing about former times is the order of the day. Thus, cemetery cleanings serve not only as a means of preserving and maintaining the physical appearance of the cemetery, but also as a social gathering for the area or as a family reunion, drawing relatives together again (Jeane 1966:39).

If the cemetery is adjacent to a church or chapel, there may be interdenominational religious services inside during late morning hours on Decoration Day; most people remain outside, however, to meet friends and former acquaintances and to talk over old times.   When the religious service is concluded, all present indulge in a bountiful meal on the premises and continue with their visiting.

An Ozark writer describes the festive meal and accompanying human interactions as follows:

> Long wooden tables have been nailed to trees to hold the loads of fried chicken, ham, baked hens, potato salad and other garden vegetables, roasting ears and deviled eggs, dozens of pies and cakes. . . .
>
> Since the motor companies no longer provide running boards for vehicles, the men will back against a tree, slip down to their heels and balance well-filled plates on their knees. Others will use the hood or trunk of a car or truck. The coffee will be black.
>
> There will be much visiting and jollying, eye-balling of relatives never before seen. There will be group singing, gospel songs, and quartets. Decoration Day is THE day in the Ozarks. They would not trade it for Christmas or all the days in between. [McConnel 1980:67]

Permanent tables like those described by the Ozark writer have been built in numerous burial grounds across the South, from the larger, more elaborate community cemeteries to the small family graveyards in out-of-the-way places.   The tables, themselves of folk derivation and construction, have virtually replaced the older tradition of "dinner on the ground."

The events taking place on Decoration Day are as much for the living as for the dead, as we have demonstrated.   However, the first order of business on Decoration Day is grave decorating. The chief difference between these decorations and those described in the earlier part of this paper is that the objects used in the annual ritual on Decoration Day are not meant, for the most part, to remain as permanent fixtures.

The usual form of annual grave decoration is a floral arrangement. Flowers brought to the cemeteries in early years were seasonal. Home-grown varieties of flowers and roses, as well as wildflowers such as daisies and dandelions, were used for decoration.   There was a time in the rural South when flowers for Decoration Day were handcrafted from crepe paper, using scissors, wire, needles, and thread.   Entire families often spent many evenings before Decoration Day cutting, pulling, and fluting crepe paper into roses of various colors, which were then made more durable and weather resistant by being dipped in melted paraffin or wax (Stacy 1971). This art form declined rapidly with the introduction of plastic flowers following World War II, and is now virtually nonexistent.

Flowers, both real and artificial, are placed on graves in every conceivable type of container and manner, from cut-glass vases, tin cans (Bettis 1978:113), and plastic bottles, to metal frames clipped over the grave markers. The general practice is to locate the flowers somewhere between the chest area and the headstone, unless cemetery rules stipulate that all floral offerings be placed on headstones themselves (Ibid).

Decorating graves with flowers was practiced among ancient Christians (Brand 1913:485), and pollen analyses of grave sites reveal that Neanderthal people may have made similar use of flowers (Ball 1980). It is said that sweet-scented flowers were historically used to fill the bed, room, and coffin of the deceased. Such practices represented efforts to conceal the progress of bodily decay (Brand 1913:485). It was standard practice in South Wales in 1804 to cover the grave of the deceased with flowers for a week or two after the funeral. Common among the smaller villages and poorer folk of South Wales at the same time was the practice of planting flowers on graves as a more enduring tribute (Ibid). Some southerners likewise decorate graves by means of rose bushes, evergreens, and even trees. One person from east Tennessee claimed that some people there were buried with acorns in their hands. The acorns germinated in a year or so and grew into trees (Bettis 1978:113).

As a general rule in the American South, the choice of grave decorations is a family matter; thus, the variety of decorations above and beyond floral arrangements is extensive. Most of the decorations, such as the ubiquitous flowers, serve an aesthetic function for the living; but other decorative items, such as telephone line insulators, American flags, children's marbles, dolls, toy cars, toy airplanes, toy images of animals, light bulbs, and metal-tipped vacuum tubes from radio and television sets, had particular meaning to the deceased (Jeane 1966:4; Puckett 1926:105). Other items used to decorate graves serve ritualistic, symbolic functions. Black people in Mississippi, North Carolina, and South Carolina have been known to place the cup and saucer used in the last illness on the grave to keep the dead from coming back again as a spirit. Medicine bottles are placed there also, turned upside down with corks loosened so that medicine will soak into the grave (Puckett 1926:104; White 1952:259; Bronner 1987:167-68). Throughout the southern Cotton Belt, broken crockery, broken glassware, broken pitchers, soap dishes, lamp chimneys, coffee cups, bits of stucco, and countless other items, generally from the kitchen, have been used to decorate the graves of black people (Bolton 1891:214; Ingersoll 1892:68-69; Bronner 1987:168). Most glass and pottery items used to decorate graves are broken. There are divergent views as to why this is so. Most southern blacks feel that the broken bits symbolize the family that has been broken by death (Puckett 1926:106). African people, on the other hand, intentionally break the pottery and glass containers to release the spirits from them so as to let them go to the next world to serve the owner (106). Such a belief is likely to be a survival of animism, even though the persons practicing it are not conscious of the fact (White 1952:260).

In addition to the many broken decorative items, lamps in a solid, unbroken state are frequently placed on graves. According to a 1925 report, one small black cemetery in Lee County, Alabama, contained at least twenty-three lamps at one time, some complete with oil and chimneys. Some said the lamps were there because they were aesthetically pleasing; others said their function was to light the darkness; still others believed the lights led the deceased person on to glory (Puckett 1926:106; White 1952:260).

One researcher found a grave with a drinking glass and pitcher of water neatly perched on a nearby flat stone, while another grave in the cemetery was covered with dishes (Jeane 1966:41). From Alabama's Black Belt comes the report that on a young murdered girl's grave, relatives placed the fan she had carried to a dance, along with the razor dropped by the presumed murderer (Sisk 1959:169-71). Again from Alabama black tradition, we read that lightning rods are placed on the graves of those persons who are restless in the grave (Lee 1960:120-21).

Large, white flint stones, as well as various unclassified fieldstones, are used by some southerners, both blacks and whites, not only to beautify graves, but also to define their limits clearly and thus safeguard the occupant against encroachment (White 1952:259,122). The most striking natural ornamental objects used on graves, however, are shells of both ocean and freshwater varieties. The custom has been practiced since early times by blacks on the Sea Islands and in the historic Cotton Belt, where it appears to be a continuation of an African custom (Toplovich 1980; Vlach 1978:139-47).

While the shell tradition is typically carried out as a means of decorating graves, some people feel that the shells have various supernatural qualities, such as insuring the peaceful rest of the dead (Ibid); others claim that the sounds of death can be heard to whistle through them.

Much attention has been given to the widespread use of shells among southern blacks, but it is seldom acknowledged that shell-decorated graves are found in scattered occurrences among Euro-Americans in the southeastern United States, from the coast of Florida to the interior of Texas, and northward through northern Arkansas into west Tennessee and west Kentucky. Southern whites likely borrowed the custom from black neighbors, but the possibility of an inheritance from Scotland exists (Ibid; White 1952:259; Kniffen 1967:427; Wilson 1966:31-40).

Two Tennessee archaeologists, Ann Toplovich and Vic Hood, have determined that shells used on the graves in Tennessee are freshwater mussels, generally collected from the Tennessee River or its tributaries (Toplovich 1980). Freshwater mussels are also present in western Kentucky streams, a fact that likely explains the use of shells on graves as far eastward in the state as Logan, Butler, and Edmonson counties, located in and adjacent to the Mammoth Cave area.

A former resident of northern Logan County responded to my direct line of questioning regarding the use of shells in Logan County in the following manner:

> Now, you may not believe this. When my sister was a little thing, she burned her hand something awful. My mother didn't know what to do about it; was really worried about what to do. This old lady there in the community told her to get some sea shells and burn them, then put the powder on the burn.
>
> Well, Mother wanted to know where in the world she could get some shells. The old woman said, "Go up here to the graveyard at Gupton's Grove near Bald Rock and there's some shells there on some of the graves."
>
> Well, Mother went and got some shells off the graves. And you know, it must have helped, for my sister's hand got all right. [Campbell 1980]

The cemetery customs and social activities discussed in this paper represent a variety of practices that had and still have a rather wide distribution in much of the American South. Certain of the older, one-time-only folk practices, such as the choice of grave-marker forms and types, erecting tiny houses, house-like forms, or other permanent covers over graves, placing photographs of the deceased on the gravestones, and building fences and walls around entire cemeteries and/or individual graves, are radically on the decrease, and their complete demise will likely occur with the passing from the cultural landscape of the extant examples.

Social gatherings and other on-going activities, in evidence at cemetery-cleaning events and on Decoration Day, represent tenacious folk customs and indicate a continuing cohesiveness and sense of identification with a particular hallowed spot by the persons involved in these social activities. Even these "never-say-die" customs are subject to change, however, as modern funeral technology makes deeper and deeper inroads into regional folkways. Southern cemeteries are already changing, as grassless, scraped cemeteries with mounded graves are yielding to grass-covered grounds replete with flat, ground-level grave markers. Patrons of those cemeteries that possessed grass covers all along find themselves, like patrons of the older, barren-earth cemeteries, compelled to place floral offerings on top of the grave markers or have the ground-level arrangements removed by caretakers in a week or so to make way for power lawn mowers. "Indeed," one person writes, "in a few years the old folk graveyard may be only a memory" (Jeane 1966:41). We must bear in mind, however, that customs and traditions seldom die out altogether, and that evolving human activities are understood only as we understand societal change and the factors that attend upon change.

In conclusion, I wish to make three additional observations: first, in order to obtain a broader data base on cemetery customs, it is imperative that we do adequate and proper fieldwork while there are extant artifacts and older living persons who can direct us to and describe for us the already diminishing or nonexistent customs and practices once commonly in vogue; second, the person researching cemetery customs and practices should exercise caution in making sweeping claims regarding origin and dissemination until more data are in; and third, even if the origins of cemetery decoration customs are never determined, and if we are never able to ascertain the motivations behind older practices, we can, by observing and talking with people, get at the folk rationale for doing things as they are done today. After all, for the people this is the most important consideration. To borrow the words of one investigator, "To observe only the outward form of any activity is to negate its function in the eyes of the participants and render fieldwork meaningless" (Ball 1975:98).

NOTES

[1]   Stuart Downs, a former student of mine, sent color slides of examples of plank markers from the Virginia Tidewater.

[2]   I have observed additional examples in Arkansas, Kentucky, Tennessee, and Virginia.

[3]   I have personally observed clay pot examples in Georgia and South Carolina.

[4]   I have intentionally avoided consideration of lawn-type cemeteries and ground-level gravestones that came into vogue, in the main, following World War II and bear every imprint of modern funeral technology.

[5]   While picket/slat/paling walls are most common, latticed wooden walls were photographed by John C. Campbell, *The Southern Highlander and His Homeland* (1921; rpt.,

Lexington: University of Kentucky Press, 1969), p.146, and Jack Corn, "Covered Graves," *Kentucky Folklore Record* 23 (January-March 1977):34-37.

⁶ I discovered and photographed the one in Cumberland County.

⁷ The custom of constructing walls around cemeteries stems from ancient Britain, possibly originating with early Celtic Christianity (Jordan 1980:254). In A.D. 752 the Pope issued a special decree to move church-related cemeteries inside the city limits; thus came the idea of consecrating a definite tract of land for burial purposes, isolated by walls or other means. Care was to be exercised so that the enclosed ground should not be neglected (Puckle 1968:141). An English bishop moved to strengthen the old decree in 1229 by requiring all cemeteries to be walled and by forbidding the grazing of livestock in the cemetery (Jordan 1980:141).

REFERENCES CITED

Anderson, Linda (Kentucky Historical Society)
    1980 Letter to the author. 4 September.
Ball, Donald B.
    1975 Social Activities Associated with Two Rural Cemeteries in Coffee County, Tennessee. *Tennessee Folklore Society Bulletin* 42:93-98.
    1977 Observations on the Form and Functions of Middle Tennessee Gravehouses. *Tennessee Anthropologist* 8:29-62.
    1977 Wooden Gravemarkers: Neglected Items of Material Culture. *Tennessee Folklore Society Bulletin* 43:167-70.
    1980 Letter to the author. 19 October.
Bendann, Effie
    1930 *Death Customs.* London: Kegan Paul, Trench and Trubner.
Bettis, Myra et al.
    1978 The Care of the East Tennessee Dead. In *Glimpses of Southern Appalachian Folk Culture: Papers in Memory of Norbert F. Riedl.* Charles H. Faulkner and Carol K. Buckles, eds. Knoxville: Tennessee Anthropological Association. (Miscellaneous Paper No. 3) Pp. 108-20.
Bolton, H. Carrington
    1891 Decoration of Graves of Negroes in South Carolina. *Journal of American Folklore* 4:214.
Brand, John
    1913 *Observations on Popular Antiquities Chiefly Illustrating the Origin of Our Vulgar Customs, Ceremonies and Superstitions.* (Reprint of 1813 edition) London: Chatto and Windus.
Bronner, Simon J., Ed.
    1987 *Folklife Studies from the Gilded Age: Object, Rite and Custom in Victorian America.* Ann Arbor, Mich: UMI Research Press.
Campbell, Kermit
    1980 Interview. Bowling Green, Kentucky. 11 September.
Cann, Norine
    1969 Letter to Anne McDonell of the Kentucky Historical Society. 29 November.
Coffin, Margaret M.
    1976 *Death in Early America.* Nashville: Nelson Publishing.
Coleman, J. Winston
    1971 *Kentucky: A Pictorial History.* Lexington: University Press of Kentucky.

Fielder, Nick (Historical Archaeologist, Tennessee Department of Conservation)
    1980 Letter to the author. 3 September.
Garrity, Thomas F. and James Wyss
    1976 Death, Funeral and Bereavement Practices in Appalachian and Non-Ap-
       palachian Kentucky. *Omega: Journal of Death and Dying* 7:216.
Hoskinson, Philip E.
    1959 Decoration Day at Pleasant Grove. *Kentucky Folklore Record* 5:117-19.
Ingersoll, Ernest
    1892 Decoration on Negro Graves. *Journal of American Folklore* 5:68-69.
Jeane, Donald G.
    1969 The Traditional Upland South Cemetery. *Landscape* 18(2):39-41.
Jordan, Terry G.
    1980 The Roses So Red and Lilies So Fair: Southern Folk Cemeteries in Texas.
       Southwestern Historical Quarterly 83:227-58.
Kniffen, Fred
    1967 Necrogeography in the United States. *Geographical Review* 57:426-27.
Lee, Harper
    1960 *To Kill a Mockingbird.* Philadelphia: J.P. Lippincott.
McConnel, Lloyd
    1980 Decoration Day Traditions in the Ozarks. *Ozarks Mountaineer* 28:67.
Murphy, D.C.
    1894 Memorial Day. *Confederate Veteran* 2:267.
Oinas, Felix J.
    1964 Russian Golubec 'Grave Marker, Etc.' and Some Notions of the Soul.
       International Journal of Slavic Linguistics and Poetics 8:77-86.
Price, Beulah M.
    1973 The Custom of Providing Shelter for Graves. *Mississippi Folklore Register* 7:9-
       10.
Puckett, Newbell Niles
    1926 *Folk Beliefs of the Southern Negro.* Chapel Hill: University of North Carolina
       Press.
Puckle, Bertram S.
    1968 *Funeral Customs, Their Origin and Development.* (Reprint of 1926 edition)
       Detroit: Singing Tree Press.
Rees, Alwyn and Brinley Rees
    1961 *Celtic Heritage: Ancient Tradition in Ireland and Wales.* London: Thames and
       Hudson.
Sisk, Glenn
    1959 Funeral Customs in the Alabama Black Belt, 1870-1910. *Southern Folklore
       Quarterly* 23:169-71.
Smith, Samuel D. and Stephen T. Rogers
    1979 *A Survey of Historic Pottery Making in Tennessee.* (Tennessee Division of
       Archaeology Research Series, No. 3) Nashville: Tennessee Department of
       Conservation, Division of Archaeology.
Stacy, Helen Price
    1971 Forms of Art in Country Graveyards. *Frankfort (KY) State Journal* 2 May.
Taylor, David and Mary Helen Weldy
    1976 Gone But Not Forgotten: The Life and Work of a Traditional Tombstone
       Carver. *Keystone Folklore Quarterly* 21:15-33.
Toplovich, Ann (Cultural Resource Surveyor, Tennessee Department of Conservation)
    1980 Letter to the author. 8 September.

Treadway, C.M.
  1964 Unique Grave Sites Found in Wolfe. *Lexington Kentucky Leader* 25 August.
Vlach, John M.
  1978 *The Afro-American Tradition in Decorative Arts.* Cleveland: Cleveland Museum of Art.
Walton, James
  1954 Hogback Tombstones and the Anglo-Danish House. *Antiquity* 28:68-77.
White, Newman I., Ed.
  1952 *The Frank C. Brown Collection of North Carolina Folklore* (Vol. 1) *Games and Rhymes, Beliefs and Customs, Riddles, Proverbs, Speech, Tales and Legends.* Durham, NC: Duke University Press.
Wilson, Gordon
  1966 Studying Folklore in a Small Region, IX: Folk Beliefs About People. *Tennessee Folklore Society Bulletin* 32:31-40.

Figure 1.   Gravehouse, Overton County, Tennessee, 1976. Photo by Lynwood Montell.

Figure 2.   Stone grave covering, Cumberland County, Kentucky, 1974. Photo by Lynwood Montell.

Figure 3.   Prismatic gravecover, Tuscaloosa County, Alabama, 1980. Photo by Lynwood Montell.

Figure 4.   Mausoleum-like gravecover, Clinton County, Kentucky, 1972. Photo by Lynwood Montell.

Figure 5.   Grassless cemetery, Tuscaloosa County, Alabama, 1980. Photo by Lynwood Montell.

Figure 6.   Sharecroppers' graves, Mississippi, 1935. Photo courtesy of the Library of Congress.

The Shift From Artist to Consumer: Changes in Mormon Tombstone Art in Utah

GEORGE H. SCHOEMAKER

"... that pretense of art, to wit, which is done with machines, though sometimes the machines are called men, and doubtless are so out of working hours: nevertheless long before it was quite dead it had fallen so low that the whole subject was usually treated with the utmost contempt by everyone who had any pretense of being a sensible man, and in short the whole civilized world had forgotten that there had everbeen an art made by the people for the people, as a joy for the maker and the user." William Morris, HOPES AND FEARS FOR ART

The study of tombstone art is one way of approximating attitudes, values, and beliefs of a particular culture. Of this idea, James Deetz says, "Material culture, it is often correctly said, is not culture but its product. Culture is socially transmitted rules for behavior, ways of thinking about doing things" (1977:24). Henry Glassie echoes this notion by saying, "Artifacts are worth studying because they yield information about the ideas in the minds of people long dead" (1975:17). While it may be that tombstones are only the product of social beings from within their culture, they speak different things to different people. They reflect world views of individuals in addition to those of the society from which individuals emerge.[1]

Research in the area of gravestone studies has examined funerary art from numerous perspectives since the beginning of the century. Fieldwork and scholarship focusing on tombstone art of particular culture groups have dealt with the Puritans of New England (Benes 1953, Deetz 1977, Forbes 1927, Ludwig 1966, Tashjian 1974), and the Amish of Pennsylvania (Barba 1953, McDonald 1975). Studies dealing with African-American communities and their influences have been done in the Southeast (Vlach 1977, 1978) and as far north as Rhode Island (Tashjian 1989). Richard Meyer has pointed out, however, that the geographical emphasis has been predominantly on New England and Pennsylvania material while other regions have been more or less neglected or overlooked (1989:4). The Mormons of the Great Basin region represent one such group.

The pioneering work of Austin and Alta Fife surveyed the rich decorative art tradition of the Intermountain West (1988). The recent treatment of Mormon tombstone art has been sparse and of a relatively descriptive nature in comparison to studies done on other groups. Studies of a descriptive type have been done by Hal Cannon (1980a, 1980b), and Carol Edison (1983). Edison also weaves biographical accounts of stonecutters and their craft into some of her writing (1989), while in other studies she writes about the influence of popular cultural forms on tombstone art in southern Idaho (1985). Keith Cunningham's work has dealt perceptively with cross-cultural comparisons between Navajo, Zuni, and Mormon funerary ritual in the Southwest (1989:197). Finally, Richard Poulsen deals in some depth with tombstone art and what he terms as the fluctuating symbolic process (1982).

Using these works as a catalyst, I will maintain that nineteenth-century tombstone art in Utah underwent changes of considerable significance with the introduction of advanced technology and new materials in the early twentieth century. These changes were marked by a shift in power from the traditional competence of the artist in handcrafting tombstone art of the nineteenth century, to the consumer demand for mechanically reproduced, sandblasted personalized images in the twentieth century.

My research and fieldwork concentrate on tombstones of Weber, Cache, Salt Lake, Utah, Sanpete, and Tooele counties, in northern and central Utah dating from 1850 to 1920. This time period was chosen because of the distinct changes in materials and technology that I observed in stonecutting. These changes were marked initially by the use of hand tools in working with sandstone and marble, to using pneumatic tools in working with marble and granite, to sandblasting in working exclusively with granite. My conclusions are also based on an interview with Arthur Child, whose Springville, Utah, family has been involved with stonecutting during the past four generations.

When the Mormons began to settle in the Great Basin area of Utah, Brigham Young—spiritual, political, and social leader of the Mormon Church—directed many of the Saints to establish settlements in other parts of Utah, Idaho, Montana, Arizona, and Alberta, Canada

(Allen 1976:263-65). Thomas Child (1825-1910) came to America from England and followed the Mormon pioneers westward with his family. His great grandson, Arthur Child, recalls that Thomas borrowed $250.00 from the Mormon Church in order to make the trip and join the Saints in Utah.

Thomas settled in Springville, Utah, and became its first schoolmaster. This occupation was permanently interrupted, however, by his call by Church officials to work on the construction of the Salt Lake Temple (1853-1893). Thomas was assigned to work the teams of horses transporting the granite from Parley's Canyon to the Salt Lake Temple site.

Thomas Child also began working in the quarry and developed a keen interest in stonecutting. Arthur Child, in his description of stonecutting materials, shared with me a similar interest, especially the importance of the grain and the personality of the rock.

> The grain become a big deal. . . . it wasn't long 'till you learnt that the grain was a lot like . . . have you ever watched . . . I doubt it, you're . . . maybe you're too young even for this, but when I was a young man they used to have ice boxes not fridges not electric refrigerators, and I used to, (pause) it intrigued me to watch the iceman go out there and break up the ice, 'cause when he hit it in certain areas, he could break very square blocks, very neat sizes. And granite, I noticed and not sandstone incidentally, but granite and marble both had this same, ah, consistency that you could control the way it was going to break, by very careful planning. They (early stonecutters) must have learnt this, (because) they come back and proceeded to use the trade they had used in building the temple to start the monument business. [Child]

In 1858 Thomas Child began the monument business which served towns in all parts of Utah, including Salt Lake City, Springville, Provo, American Fork, Spanish Fork, Payson, and as far south as Saint George (Fig. 1). After the death of Thomas Child, his son, Alma H. Child, took over the business and it became known as A. H. Child and Sons. After Alma's death it was turned over to Ivan Child, Alma's son.

When Arthur Child began working for A. H. Child & Sons as a young teenager, his father Ivan started him off on traditional hand tools, the heritage of his family. When I asked Arthur why his father might have started him on hand tools, he responded:

> He was very much, he was just in favor of equal understanding of the rock, understanding the personality, the characteristics of rock and stone, and you couldn't do that with sandblasting stuff, you could only do that when you were working with a chisel and a mallet or a hammer or whatever . . . . you had to become personally involved with (it) to understand the personality of the different rocks, and the things we were working with. And I'm sure that's why he did it. [Child]

The perpetuation of traditional knowledge and methods in the Child family business made it possible for Arthur to understand the craftsmanship involved in stonecutting and also gave the artist an affinity for the different types of stone.

During the nineteenth century, tombstones were made primarily of sandstone and marble. Sandstone was quite easy to obtain in Utah, but marble was usually imported into the state from Vermont, Missouri, and as far away as Italy. Because marble was used as ballast on ships and arrived freight free, it was relatively inexpensive to import the marble from Italy to Utah via New Orleans.

Sandstone and marble were fairly durable in nature as long as they remained moist, but in Utah's arid climate sandstone tended to erode after many years. Hand tools, chisels, and mallets were used on sandstone and marble. But as the technology began to change, so did the materials, and soon consumers were demanding granite instead of marble because of its enduring qualities, and the Childs found it necessary to change with the times.

Pneumatic tools were introduced during the mid-1920's and essentially replaced the mallet. Pneumatic tools provided an alternative means of carving the stone; however, the stonecutter still needed a strong, steady hand in order to accomplish his work without making errors and incurring great expense through wasted materials. During this time it was found that pneumatic tools could be used more effectively on granite than with marble. Finally during the mid-1930's, sandblasting became a more efficient way of working with granite. Carol Edison explains the effectiveness of sandblasting:

> Sandblasting eliminated the chisel, replacing it with a stream of fine silica directed and controlled, not manually, but through the use of a latex stencil. Stones are incised by scouring away those areas that are exposed while leaving intact those surfaces covered by the stencil. [1985:185]

Sandblasting became a more efficient and economical means of reproducing tombstone designs and inscriptions because the stonecutter had complete control over even the most complicated designs by using the latex stencils. Ultimately, however, changes in both materials and technology brought about a new era in stonecutting.

During the nineteenth century, the monument business depended on the stonecutter for its success or failure. The stonecutter was an artist, and as such, often signed his work, partly out of pride, partly as a means of advertising. The stonecutter crafted each stone with a personal touch, something called style. Consumers were able to distinguish between the styles of different tombstones done by different stonecutters. Thomas Child had a style which was clearly recognizable. In examining closely the signed tombstones of Thomas Child, I was able to identify at least eight characteristics of his particular style, and as a result, I was able to recognize other stones which were done by Child, but which were unsigned. These eight characteristics were: 1) S-marks in the canopy area, 2) convex and concave bands separating the body from the medallion and base, 3) Christian and/or surname in bas-relief, 4) B-mark in relief area of name, 5) cutter mark separating base from body, 6) backward slant in the inscription of the epitaph, 7) proportionate utilization of space, and 8) distinct tripartite plan clearly delineated (Fig. 2 and 3).

The personal touch of the artist, so apparent in nineteenth-century tombstones, is lacking in sandblasted tombstones of the twentieth century. Sandblasting requires very little artistic skill compared to tombstones that are handmade. Reflecting on the changes in attitudes toward stonecutting, Arthur Child commented:

> Well now, as a matter of fact, the last ones I seen when I was able to get around, it isn't an art or a craft anymore, it's machine done. The machine cuts the letters, the machine . . . there's no . . . personal work anymore. . . . They get their stencils, they put them in, they stamp them, they stamp out the letters, they sandblast them they take out the letters that they do, . . . All you do is be fast like a mailman sorting mail and you could be a good monument craftsman today. [Child]

Arthur raises several issues in this interview. What had become of the tombstone as an artifact? What meaning did it impart once the technology had changed? Were consumers concerned about the craftsmanship of the artist? Did the fact that these stones became mechanically reproducible diminish the importance of the artist and the aesthetic authenticity of the artifact?

Walter Benjamin addresses similar questions in his seminal work *The Work of Art in the Age of Mechanical Reproduction* (1968). He states that throughout human history most works of art have been subject to reproduction in the form of imitations and replicas, studies done by students of their Master's work, or by third parties in pursuit of some kind of remuneration (1968:220). He is quick to point out, however, that "Even the most perfect reproduction of a work of art is lacking in one element: its presence in time and space, its unique existence at the place where it happens to be. . . . The presence of the original is the prerequisite to the concept of authenticity" (Ibid:222). In the case of hand-carved tombstone art, the fact that many of the stones were man-made reproductions does not diminish the authenticity and the presence of that particular work of art. Each stone still possesses a history, the unique style and technique of the artist/stone-cutter and, importantly, the potential for human error.

On the other hand, some folklorists believe that the advancement of technology opened up the way for a more individualized aesthetic (Edison 1985). The prevailing notion is that repetition of images is mundane and commonplace in nineteenth-century folk artifacts. While this notion may be true for certain artifacts, it is not the case for the majority of them. Writing about the idea of repetition in folk architecture structures and artifacts, Richard Poulsen contends that "the further an art form moves from the ritual repetition, the more abstract and limited in meaning it becomes" (1982:112). Repetition in folk architecture was not a reflection of a lack of innovation or style, it was a conscious decision to employ it. For example, the facades of many traditional folk architecture are simple and repetitious. Of this feature Poulsen continues, "the repetition itself becomes one of the fundamental, aesthetic traits for the culture as a whole. Such repetition is meaning that is reiterated and retrievable, meaning that is always part of the present simply because it can be re-made, re-used" (Ibid:113). The idea of repetition in nineteenth-century tombstones reflects this fundamental aesthetic trait of the culture, something which underwent changes during the early twentieth century with the advent of sandblasting.

Of the product of mechanical reproduction, Benjamin writes that the "quality of its presence is always depreciated. . . . its authen-ticity—is interfered with . . ." (1968:223). But what does Benjamin mean by the term *authenticity*? He says that, "The authenticity of a thing is the essence of all that is transmissible from its beginning, ranging from its substantive duration to its testimony to the history which it has experienced", or in other words *aura*. Benjamin conti-nues, ". . . that which withers in the age of mechanical reproduction is the aura of a work of art" (Ibid:223). While *aura* diminishes with the introduction of sandblasting in the twentieth century, it is substituted by a superficial aesthetic. According to Arthur Child, consumers of mechanically reproduced stones were mostly concerned with cosmetically attractive work. Child suggests a reason for the shift in consumer attitude:

> I think the economy had a lot to do with it, and an influx of people. . . . It was obvious that people become more interested in the cosmetic than the personal. That was prior to the end of World War II, but during World War II the economy started to change, people started to get money, and more people started to come in, course U.S. Steel come in and other industries started to work and ah, I'm not saying it's wrong or right, it's just that cosmetics become more important then. So a lot of things were done for cosmetic reasons. As a matter of fact, if you were

selling, (laughs) it got so you weren't very happy with your day sometimes, because you found yourself selling cosmetically. . . . and it wasn't fun, it was a little bit degrading sometimes. [Child]

At the beginning of the twentieth century, the Mormon church began taking measures to enter American mainstream culture.[2] The sudden flood of industry entering into the Great Basin region brought about economic changes giving the consumer more power, more freedom of choice. The demand to reproduce in quantity diminished the role and power of the artist. It also produced an alienation between the artist and his work, an alienation which Child felt when he would sell his work. This alienation is explained by Benjamin in this way: "the technique of reproduction detaches the reproduced object from the domain of tradition. By making many reproductions it substitutes a plurality of copies for a unique existence. . . . The uniqueness of a work of art is inseparable from being imbedded in the fabric of tradition" (1968:223, 225).

The economic factor gave power to the consumer, a power which contributed to the elimination of what Henry Glassie might call traditional or local competence. In determining which vernacular dwellings he might study, Glassie chose to focus on houses whose construction was based upon local or traditional competence and not those houses built according to purchased plans (1975:57). He says, "The break was abrupt. It was not only a break in a tradition, but a break in the responsibilities and capabilities of the house carpenter. He lost his designing role and became solely a builder" (1975:57). Similarly, the stonecutters role as artist had become one of a sand-blaster, the power of creativity had shifted towards the consumer. Consumers could now choose many different types of images and lettering styles from catalogues, and as a consequence, the tombstones became more personalized in terms of imagery, but less personal in terms of *aura*.

This transformational shift, however, is not exclusive to aesthetic concerns. The expression of meanings must have some kind of form to be understood by people of the community. Language provides one means of communication, but symbols provide a culture with a language which is replete with meaning. Clifford Geertz comments:

Meanings can only be stored in symbols: a cross, a crescent, or a feathered serpent. Such religious symbols, dramatized in rituals or related in myths, are felt somehow to sum up, for those for whom they are resonant, what is known about the way the world is, the quality of the emotional life it supports, and the way one ought to behave while in it. [1973:127]

If Geertz is correct in saying that symbols are repositories of meaning and sum up the ethos and world view of a culture, then symbols are dependant upon a culture for their use and disuse. The central argument of Mary Douglas' book, *Natural Symbols*, reflects a similar idea:

> Systems of symbols, though based on bodily processes, get their meaning from social experience. They are coded by a community with a shared history. Because of their hidden origins and community background, many such symbols seem to be more natural than language, but they are culturally learned and culturally transmitted. [1982:ix]

In doing fieldwork in Utah, I was especially intrigued by the preponderance of handclasp symbols used on nineteenth-century tombstones (Fig. 4). While this is a common motif found in cemeteries across the United States and in Canada (see Huber 1982, Lindahl 1986), nevertheless, during the nineteenth century it had been acculturated into the Mormon world view and was endowed with a meaning which reflected certain sacred religious temple rites (Schoemaker 1989; see also Poulsen 1982). The handclasp motif seems to eventually disappear around 1915 or 1920 depending on the region. What became of this communal symbol? Why is it no longer used by stonecutters of the Mormon culture in twentieth-century decorative arts? I asked my informant, Arthur Child, what his thoughts were on the disappearance of the handclasps in tombstone art:

> I'm not sure so I'll speculate. And I've thought the same thing you did. But there become a time when there weren't just LDS (Latter Day Saints) people here, like I said at first there were just Mormons around here. And there become other people and I think then the LDS church began fighting to keep these things a certain secrecy about these things. And some of these headstones were getting pretty close to giving the message. And so perhaps—I was never told, because they disappeared before I worked on them. But I'm sure that at one point the Church give the boys a message. The Church was never bashful about telling you when you got out of line. . . . I think that the Church started to become . . . got to a point where they could start worrying about those things. I'm sure one of the first things they would say later is, "Look! These things are not supposed to be discussed or talked about, let alone carved in stone outside of the temple." [Child]

Writing of a similar situation, Richard Poulsen presents what he calls the fluctuating symbolic process. He discusses an item of material culture found in central Utah—namely the Old Rock Schoolhouse built in 1870 in Spring City. Poulsen states that the Schoolhouse could possibly have been used as a religious edifice because of the carved symbols in the facade (Fig. 5):

These symbols, from left to right, were the square, the beehive, and the compass, symbols of transcendent importance in Mormonism as well as Masonry. The beehive symbolized industry to early Mormon settlers. However, the compass and square are significant not only as marks in the Mormon Temple Garment, worn by faithful Mormons, but as symbols in the Mormon Temple ceremony, representing truth, moral accuracy, and unbending obeisance to the Lord and His Gospel. [1982:71-72]

He then discusses the erasure of the square and compass from the facade, while the beehive remained intact (Fig. 6). One reason he gives for the erasure of the symbols is the fact that these symbols were perceived as extremely sacred and an important part of the Mormon Temple Ceremony while the beehive was not (1982:73). In other words, it is quite possible that there was a kind of suppression of symbols by the official church, or as Poulsen calls it, vernacular regression (Ibid:75), and that handclasps and other sacred symbols were eventually phased out.

But the question arises as to why these symbols were shown openly during the nineteenth century and suppressed during the twentieth century? Mark Leone provides us with a possible answer: "Artifacts from the past symbolize attitudes and behavior of the past, symbols motivate behavior. Therefore, the artifacts (symbols) of the past may conflict and even impede new and different behavior" (1973:31). This statement illustrates that handclasps in Utah might have been phased out during the early part of the twentieth century because the concepts they represented were outdated and served a completely different function in the Mormon world view.

Writing about the explosive proliferation of personalized images on twentieth-century sandblasted gravestones in Idaho, Carol Edison states, "These new symbols, which are more specific and personal in nature, are both relevant and understandable to twentieth-century Idahoans and consequently have gained acceptance and ever-growing use" (1985:186). While I agree that with the shift from artist to consumer personalized images have become dominant during the twentieth century, I question whether motorcycles, guitars, temples, and wilderness scenes express shared knowledge and communal identity in the same way as earlier symbols did? In the following example, the twentieth-century sandblasted image of a Mormon Temple is equated with the nineteenth-century handmade handclasp motif:

The representation of a Mormon temple, the holy place where members of the Church . . . are married . . . symbolizes the reunion of the family after death in the same way the clasped hands of the nineteenth century symbolized reunion for earlier Mormons. [1985:187]

Too often folklorists attempt to understand nineteenth-century symbols in terms of twentieth century attitudes and perspectives. While it may be possible to interpret symbols in this manner because of the relatively short time frame, twentieth-century temple images cannot and do not parallel the symbolic significance of nineteenth-century handclasps. By virtue of the fact that nineteenth-century Mormonism had undergone cultural transformations upon becoming integrated into American culture at the turn of the century, it cannot be said with much validity that the new symbols retained old meanings. Meaning is the arbitrary relationship between the signifier (form) and the potential signified (concept). A symbol requires an arbitrary form, "the relation to the signified object of which arises from social convention of limited validity in time and space" (Thom 1985:275). The new symbols have new meanings which are based upon a shared history, a shared world view, but also the infusion of extra-cultural influences. The temple design can be a personal expression by living relatives to the fact that the deceased was probably married in the particular temple. It can also be a direct reference to something or some event. It can also be an indirect allusion to something else as were handclasps or other communal symbols. But they will never mean exactly what nineteenth-century handclasps meant.

Consequently, with the emphasis shifting from the artist in the nineteenth century towards the consumer during the twentieth century, tombstone art has undergone changes of aesthetic and symbolic significance. What the gravestone gains in personalized images and statements in the twentieth century, it loses in symbolic and aesthetic features from the nineteenth century because of the changes in materials, technology, economics, the integration of Mormonism into mainstream American culture, and ultimately the hegemonic influence of the church on aspects of everyday life. Perhaps Arthur Child is correct in his assessment of the situation when he says, ". . . once they were monuments, now they're just markers" (Child).

NOTES

I would like to thank Warren Roberts for his interest and confidence in my research, for his instructional seminars, and for the enjoyable fieldtrips to southern Indiana. I would also like to thank Robert E. Walls and Phillip H. McArthur for reading and discussing earlier versions of this chapter. Finally, I would like to recognize the influence of Richard C. Poulsen and Pamela A.R. Blakely on my interest in material culture of the West and of Utah in particular.

[1]   An earlier version of this essay appears in *Material Culture* 20:(1988)2/3, 19-26.

[2]   Most Mormon scholars agree that such an attempt at cultural integration began at
      the turn of the century and as early as the Nauvoo, Illinois, period. The reasons for
      the integration, however, are diverse. (See Allen and Leonard 1976, Shipps 1985,
      Alexander 1986, and Poulsen 1988).

REFERENCES CITED

Alexander, Thomas G.
    1986   *Mormonism in Transition: a History of the Latter-Day Saints 1890-1930*.
           Urbana: University of Illinois Press.
Allen, James B. and Glen M. Leonard
    1976   *The Story of the Latter-Day Saints*. Pp. 435-514. Salt Lake City: Deseret Book.
Barba, Preston A. and Eleanor Barba
    1953   *Tombstones: A Study in Folk Art*. Allentown: Schlecter's for the Pennsylvania
           German Folklore Society.
Benes, Peter
    1977   *The Masks of Orthodoxy: Folk Gravestone Carving in Plymouth County,
           Massachusetts, 1689-1805*. Amherst: University of Massachusetts Press.
Benjamin, Walter
    1968   The Work of Art in the Age of Mechanical Reproduction. In *Illuminations*.
           Translated by Harry Zohn. Pp. 219-53. New York: Harcourt, Brace and World,
           Inc.
Cannon, Hal
    1980a *The Grand Beehive*. Salt Lake City: University of Utah Press.
    1980b *Utah Folk Art*. Ed. by Hal Cannon. Provo, Utah: Brigham Young University
           Press.
Child, Arthur
    1987   *Interview: 24 Mar. 1987*. Springville, UT. by George H. Schoemaker.
Cunningham, Keith
    1989   Navajo, Mormon, Zuni Graves: Navajo, Mormon, Zuni Ways. In *Cemeteries
           and Gravemarkers: Voices of American Culture*. Ed. by Richard E. Meyer. Pp.
           197-215. Ann Arbor, Michigan: UMI Research Press.
Deetz, James
    1977   *In Small Things Forgotten*. Garden City: Anchor Press.
Douglas, Mary
    1982   *Natural Symbols: Explorations in Cosmology*. New York: Pantheon Books.
Edison, Carol
    1983   The Gravestones of Parowan. *Folklore Society of Utah Newsletter* 17:(1).
    1985   Motorcycles, Guitars, and Bucking Broncs: Twentieth-Century Gravestones
           in Southeastern Idaho. In *Idaho Folklife: Homesteads to Headstones*. Ed. by Louie
           W. Attebery. Pp. 184-89. Salt Lake City: University of Utah Press.
    1989   Custom-Made Gravestones in Early Salt Lake City. *Utah Historical Quarterly*
           56:310-30.
Fife, Austin E.
    1988   Western Gravestones. In *Exploring Western Americana* Ed. by Alta Fife. Pp.
           195-213. Ann Arbor, Michigan: UMI Research Press.
Forbes, Harriett Merrifield
    1927   *Gravestones of Early New England and the Men Who Made Them*. Boston:
           Houghton Mifflin.

Geertz, Clifford
  1973 Ethos, World-view and the Analysis of Sacred Symbols. In *The Interpretation of Cultures*. Pp. 126-141. New York: Basic Books, Inc.
Glassie, Henry
  1975 *Folk Housing in Middle Virginia: A Structural Analysis of Historic Artifacts*. Knoxville: University of Tennessee Press.
Huber, Leonard V.
  1982 *Clasped Hands: Symbolism in New Orleans Cemeteries*. Lafayette, Louisiana: Center for Louisiana Studies.
Leone, Mark
  1973 Why the Coalville Tabernacle Had to be Razed. *Dialogue* 8:31.
Lindahl, Carl
  1986 Transition Symbolism on Tombstones. *Western Folklore* 45:165-85.
Ludwig, Allen I.
  1966 *Graven Images: New England Stonecarving and Its Symbols, 1650-1815*. Middletown, Connecticut: Wesleyan University Press.
McDonald, Frank E.
  1975 Pennsylvania German Tombstone Art of Lebanon County, Pennsylvania. *Pennsylvania Folklife* 35:2-19.
Meyer, Richard E.
  1989 *Cemeteries and Gravemarkers: Voices of American Culture*. Ann Arbor, Michigan: UMI Research Press.
Poulsen, Richard C.
  1982 *The Pure Experience of Order: Essays on the Symbolic in the Folk Material Culture of Western America*. Albuquerque: University of New Mexico Press.
  1988 The Fracture of Mormonism: Science as Religion, or Religion as Science. In *Misbegotten Muses: History and Anti-History*. Pp. 117-24. New York: Peter Lang.
Schoemaker, George H.
  1988 Symbolic Considerations in Nineteenth-Century Tombstone Art in Utah. *Material Culture* 20:19-26.
  1989 Acculturation and Transformation of Salt Lake Temple Symbols in Nineteenth Century Tombstone Art in Utah. Paper presented to the Cemeteries and Gravestones Section of the American Culture Association in St. Louis, MO. April 1989.
Shipps, Jan
  1985 *Mormonism, The Story of a New Religious Tradition* Pp. 109-29. Urbana: University of Illinois Press.
Tashjian, Ann and Dickran Tashjian
  1989 The Afro-American Section of Newport, Rhode Island's Common Burying Ground. In *Cemeteries and Gravemarkers: Voices of American Culture* Ed. by Richard E. Meyer. Pp. 163-96. Ann Arbor, Michigan: UMI Research Press.
Tashjian, Dickran and Ann Tashjian
  1974 *Memorials for Children of Change: The Art of New England Stonecarving*. Middletown, Connecticut: Wesleyan University Press.
Thom, René
  1985 From the Icon to the Symbol. In *Semiotics: An Introductory Anthology* Ed. by Robert E. Innis. Pp. 272-291. Bloomington, Indiana: Indiana University Press.
Vlach, John Michael
  1977 Graveyards and Afro-American Art. In *Long Journey Home: Folklife in the South*. Pp. 161-65. Chapel Hill, North Carolina: Southern Exposure.
  1978 *The Afro-American Tradition in Decorative Arts*. Cleveland, Ohio: Cleveland Museum of Art.

Figure 1. Wheeler & Child's Undertakers and Marble Works. Walter Wheeler and Thomas Child of Springville, Utah, 1888. (Photograph: Taken by G.E. Anderson, produced by Rell G. Francis, Heritage Prints, Springville, Utah)

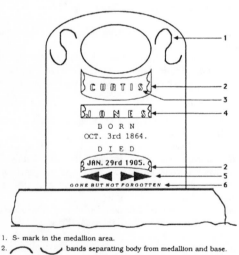

1. S- mark in the medallion area.
2. ⌒ ⌣ bands separating body from medallion and base.
3. Christian/Surname are in bas relief.
4. B-mark.
5. ◀▶ mark separating base from body.
6. Backward slant in the inscription of the epitaph.
7. Proportionate utilization of space.
8. Distinct tri-partite plan is clearly delineated.

Figure 2. Stylistic characteristics of Thomas Child tombstones.

Figure 3. Two Thomas Child stones. (A) Abigail Lucinda Badham stone, Payson, Utah, c.1889; (B) Lydia Clisbee stone, Tooele, Utah, c. 1879. (Photograph by George H. Schoemaker)

Figure 4. Provo Marble Works. Addie M. Swensen stone, Moroni, Utah, c.1891. Very stylized script, handclasp motif with draping veil. (Photograph by George H. Schoemaker)

Figure 5. Old rock schoolhouse facade. Spring City, Utah, 1876, before the erasure of square and compass. (Utah State Historical Society, Salt Lake City).

Figure 6. Old rock schoolhouse. Spring City, Utah, 1876, after the erasure of square and compass. (Photograph by Matthew K. Heiss)

'Juneteenth': Afro-American Customs
of the Emancipation

WILLIAM H. WIGGINS, JR.

Juneteenth is the major Afro-American secular celebration in the region encompassing eastern Texas, western Louisiana, southwestern Arkansas, and southern Oklahoma. A 1923 Juneteenth handbill promised the celebrants an "occasion with fitting ceremonies, feasting, games of merriment and joy making."[1] (See Figure 1) An informant confirmed the fact that celebrants perpetuated this secular tradition through the 1950s:

> . . . most [celebrants] looked on the nineteenth of June as having a good time, eating and all of that. . . . The nineteenth of June you didn't have no hymn singing, if you want to put it like that, or prayer and all like that [chuckles]. He didn't care a thing about the thanksgiving prayer and that type thing. All he wanted to do was get to the ball game and get him some booze, corn likker. Whatever I may use [chuckles]. That's what they were looking for. Goodtimes![2]

And Juneteenth celebrations of the last three decades often feature such good-time events as blues concerts[3] and social dances.[4]

Historically, June 19, 1865, was freedom day for slaves in East Texas and portions of the surrounding states. It was on this day that General Gordon Granger landed with federal troops in Galveston, Texas, with the express mission of forcing the slave owners to release their slaves.[5] Many of these slaves had been brought to East Texas from other southern states, such as Tennessee, Georgia, Virginia, and "all over the South," by slave owners "because the abolitionists had talked freedom for the Negroes and they were afraid that their slaves would be freed and all that investment that they had [made]. . . ."[6]

146

Three legends have arisen to explain the genesis of the celebration: first, the news was withheld to make one last crop; second, the news was delayed because travel was by mule; and third, the news was delayed by the murder of the messenger.[7] The most frequently collected legend is the one that explains the date in light of the master's need to make one more crop. Versions of it have been used to explain the observance in East Texas and southwestern Arkansas.

The mule legend is not so popular. One informant said that he had heard it, but confessed, "I don't know the whole story."[8] Another simply said, "It is celebrated on this day because of the story of a man riding on a horse to Texas to tell the slaves that they were free."[9] And a third fragmentary account was given by an informant who had "heard" that a mule was ridden from Washington "through the South" and that the messenger "rode a horse and buggy and wore out two horses or something."[10]

This legend gives a fairly accurate account of Juneteenth's geographical spread. The tradition is strongest in East Texas. It is observed in southeastern cities of the state, such as Galveston and Orange, up to the northeastern section in towns such as Texarkana and Sherman. Juneteenth celebrations have been reported in cities as far west as San Antonio, but these are most likely celebrations that have been transplanted from the rich slave culture of East Texas. Big Juneteenth celebrations are also held in the twin cities of Fort Worth and Dallas. But all in all, the Juneteenth celebration in Texas is limited primarily to East Texas, the original area of the state into which the slaves were brought.

Juneteeth was also originally celebrated in Louisiana. Rupert Secrett, retired barber and former sponsor of the celebration in Brenham, Texas, mentioned friendly "hurrahing" among blacks of Louisiana and Texas as to which state was the first to celebrate emancipation. Louisiana blacks often said, "The people in Texas didn't know they was free until the people from Louisiana came over and told 'em [chuckles]."[11] David Johnson, Dean of Students at Texas College, Tyler, Texas, and a native of Louisiana, recalls the celebration being observed "all over the state of Louisiana."[12] He specifically recalled the celebration being strong around New Orleans, the city from which General Granger began his historic voyage to Galveston.[13] And U.T.D. Williams of Tyler, Texas, attended Juneteenth celebrations in the northwestern town of Grand Bayou, Louisiana, where "the white folks" furnished all the food.[14]

Southwestern Arkansas was another area of an adjoining state into which the Juneteenth celebration spilled over. This part of Arkansas, like adjoining East Texas, is heavily populated with blacks. Mrs. E.B. Tollette, who lived in the all-Negro town of Tollette in this rural southwestern section of the state, described it as being "a large community" of "farmers" and "home owners," which had its own post office.[15] She also remembered that black farmers in Blevins, Paraloma, Nashville, Tollette, and similar towns had "great big picnics on the nineteenth of June."[16]

In the 1880s many ex-slaves began to migrate out of this tri-state area into the territory that was soon to become the state of Oklahoma. Louisiana, Arkansas, and Texas were among the states in which the promise of Reconstruction had been crushed and replaced with a new political and economic oppression of blacks. Hence, many ex-slaves gave up on the land of their enslavement; they joined the wagon trains led by such black wagonmasters as "Pap" Singleton and headed west for the promise of freedom in the new territories of Oklahoma and Kansas.[17] According to Marzee Douglass, high school teacher of black history and native of Ardmore, Oklahoma, blacks from these three states often mingled with the ex-slaves brought into the territory by the five "civilized Indian tribes," namely, the Seminoles, Cherokees, Creeks, Chickasaws, and Choctaws, to form all-black towns like Boley, Oklahoma.[18]

Juneteenth celebrations reflect the rugged individualism of this frontier area and follow no certain pattern. Even in East Texas, the area in which the celebration's tradition is strongest, the observances may be a completely secular celebration of picnics and baseball games, or cultural activities like speeches and pageants may be added to extol the richness of black culture and the advancements made by the race against great odds. For example, Onion Creek, Texas, had a diverse cultural/secular celebration where blacks played baseball, met "old friends," and heard "a history speech" that recalled "what they had accomplished and . . . the role they had to play to keep it changing and doing better. . . ."[19]

The most common type of Juneteenth celebration was an all-day secular affair that began around ten o'clock in the morning with a parade and ended around one o'clock the next morning with the break-up of the dances or "suppers." In the afternoon there were various activities, the biggest being the baseball game, "tie downs," individual games, and eating. One of the largest parades was held annually in Brenham, Texas. These marchers were routed through the heart of the downtown area and witnessed by very large mixed crowds. One informant recalled that it was so crowded "you couldn't walk on the streets."[20]

The parade was composed of blacks from the surrounding communities who prepared their own floats. Mrs. Eloise Holmes, a retired school teacher who grew up in Brenham, recalled that "each community would decorate floats and they would select children from the community to ride on these floats."[21] Accompanying these ten or twelve floats were men on horseback and a brass band.

The parade had a king and queen. The queen wore the title "The Goddess of Liberty" and was selected by a money-raising contest, in which several "nice looking girls" solicited donations. Each one carried shoeboxes for this purpose and raised sums that ranged from $600 to $1,000.[22] The king was selected by the queen.

On one occasion there were two parades. Around 1927 or 1928 Chancey Williamson and Ed Henderson vied for the right to stage the celebration. These two men, like Jacob and Esau, were worlds apart in terms of lifestyles. Chancey was "tight and Ed was a sport."[23] Chancey owned a store and a farm, but Ed was a "sport" who made his money through gambling and prostitution. And he looked the part with his "gambler clothes . . . slow walking . . . and gold teeth in front."[24] But their parades "met up" in downtown Brenham, with "one going one way, one going the other."[25] This was their only confrontation. Chancey did not have any more parades and Ed's celebration began to surpass Chancey's.[26]

All of Brenham's Juneteenth parades ended at the park. One informant recalled the crowded scene at Henderson Park:

> People would be everywhere. [muffled] Yeah, it used to be some people down to that park! I declare. If you would go down there with somebody and they got away from you, you never find 'em back no more. And they wouldn't find you back no more. You had to push and squeeze and pull to get through people. That's a fact.[27]

Baseball games and "tie downs" were the big spectator sports played at the park. The "tie downs" consisted of such events as calf tying and cowboy tournaments.[28] But these celebrants were Americans, and it was the "national pastime," baseball, that was played at almost every Juneteenth celebration. In many East Texas towns, these hotly contested games closed the downtown businesses and attracted large numbers of whites.[29]

Many baseball anecdotes were told on these occasions. Judson Henry, owner of the Chatterbox Cafe in Hawkins, Texas, grew up in Daingerfield, Texas, and had the once-in-a-lifetime thrill of hitting the game-winning home run in a Juneteenth game with arch rival Jefferson, Texas. He recalled that this mighty blow came with two outs, two strikes on him, and the score tied two-to-two. The fans carried him around the park on their shoulders and gave him sixteen dollars for his heroics, an event in his life that he "never willllllllll forget."[30] However, Floyd "Skeet" Martin, retired outfielder of the Rockdale Tigers was not so fortunate. He made a once-in-a-lifetime defensive play that saved a Juneteenth baseball game for Rockdale over Georgetown, Texas. With two outs, the ball was hit to him with such force that "two strings broke" on his glove, but he held on to the ball to preserve a three-to-two victory. Even though "four girls come out of the stands and grabbed [him]," however, Skeet's exploits did not earn him "a piece of pussy."[31]

After the local cowboys and baseball players had entertained the crowds, Juneteenth celebrants settled down to large picnic meals of "special food, barbecue beef, mutton, pork."[32]   Other Juneteenth menus have included "chitlings, greens, potato salad, corn bread and red beans and homemade cakes and bread."[33] Red (strawberry) soda water, also known as "June Nineteenth soda," was the most popular celebration drink. Watermelon and homemade ice cream were among the more popular desserts.

In Bastrop, Texas, these free dinners were served on "long, long tables." The young adults acted as waiters and waitresses, serving "crew" after "crew" of hungry celebrants who had to pay only for their soft drinks and ice cream.[34] Whites often attended these dinners, and in some instances a special table was set up for them.[35]

After the meal, the late afternoon and evening were given over to the carnival and dancing.[36] Carnivals were not held so widely as dances; however, they could be found in cities like Dallas, Texas, where the state fairgrounds were used,[37] and towns like Brenham.[38] One informant noted that the Brenham celebrations "would have something like a carnival for the children to ride, like on a Ferris wheel and hobby horses."[39]

There was great variety in the dances held on the night of June nineteenth. In smaller communities such as Ballenger, Texas, the celebrants hoedowned to fiddle music, while the larger cities like Abilene had "little four- or five-piece bands" who played the blues.[40] White citizens often attended these dances, but rarely joined the black celebrants on the dance floor.[41] However, there were Juneteenth dances at which neither whites nor the Christian segment of the local black community were to be found. These "suppers" catered only to the local "Frankies and Johnnies." They were held on the Saturday night nearest the nineteenth of June. The atmosphere was enhanced by the soft glow of "bottle lights," coal-oil lamps fashioned from pop bottles and rag wicks.[42]   During the evening the dancers consumed large draughts of "bootleg whiskey," "home-brew," and "Sister-get-you-ready" in fruit jar tumblers. This heavy drinking often led to the expected Saturday-night type of violence, such as ice-pick stabbing or a knifing with a "Dallas Special."

Juneteenth celebrations were financed in different ways. The Juneteenth committees were usually comprised of outstanding black citizens, "maybe a couple of deacons and a minister and maybe the high school principal,"[43] who were motivated primarily by the desire to keep the tradition alive. They were men like Louis Brown of Temple, Texas, who was so dedicated to this task he was given the nickname "Celebration Daddy" by fellow members of "The Red Shirts," the original sponsoring group of the celebration in Brenham.[44]

In later years the profile of these committees changed radically, with men dedicated to honoring freedom being replaced by entrepreneurs who were interested in Juneteenth only as a means of financial gain. Mr. Multree was a member of one such committee whose members put up $15.00 and "cleared $35.00 a piece in profit." But avarice is a poor replacement for racial pride, and in the end it caused the destruction of the committee. Multree recalled that on two separate occasions men ran away with the total Juneteenth funds of $200 and $75.[45]

In addition to a group of individuals pooling their money to sponsor Juneteenth celebrations for profit, there were two types of nonprofit financial canvasses made by other Juneteenth committees. One method was to ask donations from the local white population.[46] A more common practice was to solicit annual dues of two to five dollars from each member of the local black community.[47] In both instances the food was free; the celebrant paid only for his red soda water and store-bought ice cream.

Many of these Juneteenth committees were informally organized each year about a month before the celebration date. Normally they met in the local Baptist or Methodist church, forming committees to buy meat, barbecue it, and haul water, among other things.[48] At this time the year's officers were elected by popular vote. Usually there would be just one accounting meeting after the Juneteenth celebration. In the case of the syndicate group it would be called to divide the profits into equal shares, but with the community-based Juneteenth committee "they would have one more meeting to distribute out and pay off all the bills and whatever it was [with] . . . the rest of it stay[ing] in the treasure until next year."[49]

Many Juneteenth committees raised money by selling booths. The Brenham committee sold "stand" space and charged admission to the park. They operated the beer stand but leased space for barbecue, hamburger, confectionery, and various other stands on the grounds.[50]

The Juneteenth committee was also responsible for generating publicity. The most popular means, after word of mouth, was the leaflet, which one informant described as being a "great looooooong paper with everything [celebration information] on there."[51] One flyer I collected listed these "feature attractions": "shetland pony races—bicycle races—tow sack race—shoe scramble race—barefoot race—softball games (boys and girls) . . . carnival attractions" and a "big dance."[52] (See Figure 3) It also announced that a "prize will be given to the oldest colored citizen in Rockdale," and that "prizes will be awarded to winners of each race."[53] Another flyer lists these "amusements": softball game, croquet, mule race (bareback), and bicycle race.[54] (See Figure 2) These eye-catching handbills featured "different colors, green, red, [with] black print."[55] Recently, sponsors have paid for radio spots. They have also run stories in local newspapers.[56]

The patriotism of World War II caused a temporary decline in the popularity of Juneteenth. Many younger and educated blacks shunned the traditional Juneteenth celebration and replaced it with the Fourth of July. As one informant aptly explained, they "have been taught that they're a part of this country and that the Fourth of July is the day for them."[57] This conflict of celebration dates was resolved partially by some committees transferring the Juneteenth program to the Fourth of July.[58] But this compromise did not satisfy either the older traditionalists or the young radicals. The older members of one community that tried moving the June 19 program to July 4 "didn't participate . . . they just didn't want it. They wanted the nineteenth of June."[59] The younger blacks have failed to keep the Fourth of July tradition alive.

The civil rights movement of the 1950s marked a resurgence in the celebration of Juneteenth among blacks. Once again it has become a symbol of racial pride. On June 17, 1972, the black artist Burford Evans opened a one-man show in Houston's New American Folk Gallery entitled "I Remember Juneteenth," which is "a suite of 19 paintings [that] . . . capture the mood . . . of the day Texas blacks honor the Emancipation Proclamation of 1863."[60]

Finally, this renewed interest in Juneteenth has generated efforts to make the day an official state holiday. In 1972, Zan Holmes of Dallas and Curtis Graves of Houston, two black congressmen, introduced a Juneteenth resolution that recognized "Juneteenth as an annual, though unofficial, 'holiday of significance to all Texans and, particularly, to the blacks of Texas, for whom this date symbolizes freedom from slavery.'"[61] This unanimously passed resolution helped pave the way for the efforts of black state representative Al Edwards, who in 1979 introduced a successful bill in the Texas legislature to make Juneteenth an official Texas holiday.[62] The June 19, 1980, observance of emancipation, 115 years after General Gordon Granger landed at Galveston Bay, marked the elevation of this celebration from being merely an informal Afro-American secular celebration of the American Southwest to its present status as an official Texas holiday. From now on the Lone Star State's official calendars will recognize June 19 as the date of Afro-American emancipation. And this achievement would not have happened without the annual barbecues, "tie downs," "suppers," dances, parades, and baseball games of past Juneteenth celebrations.

NOTES

[1] Daingerfield, Texas, Juneteenth handbill, June 19, 1923.

[2] Willie Hygh, interview, Karnack, Texas, June 16, 1972.

[3] "Live Blues: Juneteenth Blues Spectacular Miler Outdoor Theatre, Houston," *Living Blues* no. 39, (July-August, 1978):44.

[4] Wanda Pryor, "Juneteenth Celebration: A Flavor of the 1890's" *Austin* (Texas) *American-Statesman*, June 20, 1976.

[5] "Juneteenth: Texas Carries On Tradition of Emancipation Holiday with Amusement Park Celebration," *Ebony* 6, no.8, (June 1951):30.

[6] Uriah Weisner, interview, Karnack, Texas, June 16, 1972.

[7] "Juneteenth," *Ebony*, p.30.

[8] Artis Lovelady, interview, Rockdale, Texas, June 19, 1972.

[9] Shelia Marshall, questionnaire, Austin, Texas, November 15, 1972.

[10] William H. Ammons, interview, Tyler, Texas, November 12, 1972.

[11] Rupert Secrett, interview, Brenham, Texas, November 14, 1972.

[12] David Johnson, interview, Tyler, Texas, November 13, 1972.

[13] Ibid.

[14] U.T.D. Williams, interview, Tyler, Texas, November 13, 1972.

[15] Mrs. E.B. Tollette, interview, Little Rock, Arkansas, September 19, 1973.

[16] Ibid.

[17] John Hope Franklin, *From Slavery to Freedom: A History of Negro Americans* (New York: Alfred A. Knopf, 1969), p. 399.

[18] Marzee Douglass, interview, Ardmore, Oklahoma, June 21, 1972.

[19] Paul Darby, interview, Austin, Texas, November 15, 1972.

[20] Holsey Johnson, interview, Brenham, Texas, November 14, 1972.

[21] Eloise Holmes, interview, Hawkins, Texas, November 14, 1972.

[22] Booker T. Washington Hogan, interview, Brenham, Texas, November 15, 1972.

[23] Ibid.

[24] Ibid.

[25] Ibid.

[26] Ibid.

[27] Holsey Johnson, interview.

[28] Smith Overton, interview, Austin, Texas, November 15, 1972.

[29] J.L. Donaldson, interview, Hawkins, Texas, November 14, 1972.

[30] Judson Henry, interview, Hawkins, Texas, November 14, 1972.

[31] Floyd "Skeet" Martin, interview, Rockdale, Texas, June 19, 1972.

[32] Darby interview.

[33] Pryor, "Juneteenth Celebration."

[34] Florence Hygh, interview, Karnack, Texas, June 16, 1972.

[35] Almond Multree, interview, Rockdale, Texas, June 19, 1972.

[36] "Juneteenth," *Ebony*, p.30.

[37] Secrett interview.

[38] Ibid.

[39] Katherine Burton, interview, Hawkins, Texas, November 14, 1972.

[40]   Ammons interview.

[41]   Henry interview.

[42]   Eva S. Riggs, Los Angeles, California, to William H. Wiggins, Jr., no date.

[43]   Ammons interview.

[44]   Secrett interview.

[45]   Multree interview.

[46]   Washington interview.

[47]   Darby interview.

[48]   Multree interview.

[49]   Darby interview.

[50]   Secrett interview.

[51]   Mrs. A.T. Lewis, interview, Milano, Texas, June 19, 1972.

[52]   Rockdale, Texas, Juneteenth handbill, June 19, 1972.

[53]   Ibid.

[54]   Karnack, Texas, Juneteenth handbill, June 19, 1947.

[55]   Mrs. C.A. Nelson, interview, Milano, Texas, June 19, 1972.

[56]   "Juneteenth Events Slated," *Rockdale Reporter and Messenger*, June 15, 1972.

[57]   Ammons interview.

[58]   Darby interview.

[59]   Ibid.

[60]   "Notebook: Evans Show Set at Adept Gallery," *Houston Chronicle*, June 16, 1972.

[61]   "Austin Wire: Juneteenth Recognized by House," *Dallas Morning News*, June 20, 1972.

[62]   "'Juneteenth' Day Becomes State Holiday in Texas," *Jet* 56, no. 18 (July 19, 1979): 8.

FIGURES

Figure 1.   Juneteenth handbill from Daingerfield, Texas, 1923.

-58th Anniversary-

Emancipation Celebration

June 19, 1923

At Suedon Park, Daingerfield, Texas

The colored citizens of this and adjoining communities in memory of the famous Emancipation Proclamation issued Jan. 1, 1863, and later made effective by order of Gen. Granger in Texas June 19, 1865, will celebrate the above occasion with fitting ceremonies, feasting, games of merriment and joy making.

Program

1:30 P.M.

Song, "America."
Invocation, Rev. C. Davenport.
Song.
Introduction of speaker.
Address, Prof. T.W. Pratt of Dallas, Texas.

2:30 P.M.

DINNER - Everybody requested to bring well filled baskets.

4:00 P.M.

BALL GAME - Daingerfield White Socks vs. Jefferson Black Cats.

Plenty of refreshments of all kinds, cool shade, free [illegible], an ideal place for enjoyment. Come everybody and let's make merry the occasion which gave us this freedom.

Committees

On Program: Rev. A. Austin, Jr., J.T. Heath, Jas. M. Henry.
On Grounds: H.P. Wallick, Chas. W. Williams, E.B. Edwards.
On Arrangement: M.Gilstrap, M.Austin, Julius Hodge, Robert Austin.
On Baskets: Mesdames Clara Henry, Shella Gilstrap, Mattie Wallick, Donie Whitmore, Texana Easley, Ilsie Wilkerson.

Figure 2.   Juneteenth handbill from Karnack, Texas, 1947.

Nineteenth June Celebration

Leigh Community Center

1947

----

12 noon	Picnic Starts
3 pm	Public Program
Song	
Invocation	
Remarks	Mr. U.R. Weisner
Quartet	
Why celebrate June 19th	Taylor Vocational
	Agri., G.W. Carver High
Solo	Mrs. Lucile Buchanan
Address	Guest Speaker
Financial Reports:	
1. Anne Glade	Mr. Charley Richardson
2. Antioch	Mr. Kahn Whiten
3. Carver	Mr. Henry Hygh
4. High Ridge	Mr. J.L. Strange
5. Lake Chapel	Mr. Tom Taylor
6. Pleasant Hill	Mr. Willie Roberson
7. Smithonia	Mr. Henry Price

4:30 pm Announcements

5:00 pm Amusements   Sponsored by Mr. A.I. Coleman

  1. Soft Ball Game

  2. Croquet

  3. Mule Race (bare back)

  4. Bicycle Race

Come One! Come All!

TO ROCKDALE FAIR PARK

JUNE 19, 1972

To Help Celebrate the 105th Anniversary
of the Emancipation Proclamation

GUEST SPEAKER FOR THE DAY WILL BE
MRS. FRANKIE McDONALD

Feature Attractions Will Be

SHETLAND PONY RACES — BICYCLE RACES
TOW SACK RACE — SHOE SCRAMBLE RACE
BAREFOOT RACE — SOFTBALL GAMES
(BOYS AND GIRLS)

Prizes will be awarded to winners of each race.

PRIZE WILL BE GIVEN TO THE
OLDEST COLORED CITIZEN IN ROCKDALE

ALL KINDS OF REFRESHMENTS
PLENTY BARBECUE — CARNIVAL ATTRACTIONS

BIG DANCE

Music by

T. D. BELL AND HIS CADILLAC BOYS
OF AUSTIN, TEXAS

Artis Lovelady, manager; Dennis Brooks, secretary; Mrs. Lucy M. Brooks, treasurer; the Clarks and others.

Figure 3. Juneteenth handbill from Rockdale, Texas, 1972.

Community Festival and the Enactment
of Modernity

BEVERLY J. STOELTJE
RICHARD BAUMAN

The more we explore the genesis and development of the core concepts of our field in the late eighteenth and early nineteenth centuries, the more abundantly clear it becomes that the very idea of folklore itself was born of the epochal social transformation represented by the advent of modernity—the rise of mercantile and industrial capitalism, the growth of modern urban centers and the nation state, the emergence of a naturalistic and secular world view, and all the other political, economic, social, and intellectual concomitants of what we call the modern era (Bauman 1989). The strains of adjustment to modernity and the omnipresence of marked contrasts between the old and the new demanded comprehension, and folklore was one of the symbolic constructions of this intellectual effort. As social thought turned increasingly to the great enterprise of explaining the modernization of traditional societies (Habermas 1984:5-6), folklore took up the task of comprehending traditional, preindustrial society, while sociology, economics, and political science concentrated their efforts on modern social forms.

Warren Roberts, in his essay on "Folklife and Traditional Material Culture: A Credo" (1988), has argued cogently and effectively for the productiveness of defining the purview of our field of study as "the traditional society of the pre-industrial era" (1988:18). As the social and cultural forms of the pre-industrial era persist into the industrial age, however, Roberts affirms the need to examine the conditions of persistence—and presumably transformation—by which they continue to be a part of our lives. In the spirit of that charter, we undertake in this paper to explore a traditional cultural form, the community festival, in its modern guise as an enactment of modernity. As Milton Singer has noted (1959:145), "cultural performances" such as festivals, fairs, dramas, and spectacles, in which the central meanings and values of a group are embodied, acted out, and laid open to examination and interpretation in symbolic form, are especially well suited to the investigation of the dynamics of persistence and change in modern society.

Before proceeding further, let us specify what we mean by modernity. The subject is a complex one, and we cannot hope to do it full justice within the scope of this brief paper. For present purposes, we will concentrate on two tendencies that are prominent in all discussions of the forces of modernity, namely, social differentiation and centralization. By *differentiation* we mean the process by which "social life constantly subdivides and reorganizes itself in ever-increasing complexity" (MacCannell 1976:11), the range of categorical distinctions used to differentiate among members of society increases, and social relationships become more and more functionally specific, less and less functionally diffuse (Peacock 1975:9). *Centralization* refers to the process by which levels of social interdependency and integration grow successively deeper, and local structures are progressively incorporated into more and more centralized ones. The problem we will explore in this paper, then, is how differentiation and centralization are enacted in a community festival, the Luling Watermelon Thump, within the larger compass of the traditional event. The Watermelon Thump is not of great antiquity—it was first celebrated in 1954—but it is rooted in community and the seasonal cycle. It is, in fact, a first-fruits celebration, held on the last weekend in June when the first watermelons come in, and it is fashioned out of the same set of universal festival building blocks and transformations that people everywhere have used to construct their festivals: feasting, drinking, music, dance, noise, costume, display, play, performance, symbolic condensation, and so on (Stoeltje 1983, 1989).

Luling, Texas, is a small town of approximately 4,700 people, located in Caldwell County about forty-five miles south of Austin. It is primarily an oil town, the center of a large oil-producing area. Oil was discovered there in 1922 by Edgar B. Davis, a Massachusetts man who went on to develop the field in the years that followed. In 1926, Davis sold his oil interests for $12,100,000, using one million dollars of his fortune the following year to establish the Luling Farm Foundation, devoted to agricultural research. One result of the Foundation's efforts was the discovery that soil conditions around Luling were ideally suited to the growing of watermelons, which soon became established as an important crop in the area. At its height, in the 1940s and '50s, there were close to 150 growers in the vicinity of Luling. In 1954, Mr. Herman Allen, then principal of the Luling Elementary School and President of the Luling Lions Club, conceived the idea of organizing a "celebration to honor the growers and promote the Luling watermelon market," and with the aid of various civic organizations and other interested parties the Watermelon Thump was founded.

In recent years, the watermelon industry has declined, largely because the cheap labor on which it depended has been drawn away by the higher wages and better opportunities of the oil fields. Now, there are only about twenty-five growers left, many of whom do it only part-time or as a hobby. But the Watermelon Thump is very firmly established and going strong; it has become a valued community tradition with its own momentum. Indeed, there are beginning to be some indications that some of the growers continue to raise melons in order to help sustain the festival and their participation in it. The Watermelon Thump is a—perhaps *the*—major element of Luling's public identity, a link with an agrarian tradition, however recent, and the major event for the people of Luling to look forward to and back upon throughout the year (Abrahams 1977). For the three days of the festival, Luling is the center of the universe for its people. But this is not to say that for the purposes of the festival Luling draws in upon itself—quite the contrary. While much of the festival represents a series of symbolic statements by which the people of the community act out their social structure and social relations for themselves, among those themes most prominently displayed and enacted in the Watermelon Thump is Luling's place within a full range of levels of integration in the modern world. We propose to look briefly at two of the constituent events of the Watermelon Thump to suggest how aspects of modernity are addressed and played out within them.

The Queen Contest

The processes of differentiation and centralization of interest to us as features of modernity operate as basic organizing principles of the Watermelon Queen contest in constructing a model of gender relations (cf. Stoeltje 1988). Like other concepts displayed in festivals originating in modern social life, concepts relating to gender are not labeled or displayed as such, but are communicated through enactment. Interpretation must take into consideration, therefore, the purposes served by differentiation and centralization as they shape the Queen contest. Expressed at every level of the event, and the source of its attraction, is the social power manifested in these relations linking female and male.

Like initiation rituals in some cultures, the Watermelon Queen contest selects young, nubile women as its subject, and rewards the participants with public recognition if they complete the ritual. When the contest finishes and the participants play their roles in the Queen's coronation, they are completing the American female rite of passage. Transforming selected high school girls into young women and presenting them formally to the community, the ritual is disguised as a competition for a fantasy position of royalty. Those selected to participate learn the ideal role of the female as the community defines it through the intensity of the experience. While this role varies from one ethnic group to another or one nation to another, the meaning of gender enacted in a specific Queen contest derives from the two segments of the contest: (1) the selection process; and (2) the final performance of the Queen. It is through these that differentiation and centralization function to define the goals of the competition, who controls them, and how one competes for them. When men control the selection process and the competition, and the final performance presents the Queen as a passive object on display, the processes of differentiation and centralization have defined the ideal young woman as an object of display, subservient to males in spite of the fantasy position of power, as dependent upon male institutional power for identity, status, and recognition.

We will, then, consider first the process of selecting the Watermelon Queen. The formal eligibility criteria for this honored position are few: a girl must be of high school age, have lived in Luling for at least one year prior to the election, and be nominated by one of the voluntary organizations of the community. For most of the history of the festival, nominees have been put forward by the prestigious businessmen's civic clubs—the Kiwanis Club, the Evening Lions, the Noon Lions, the Chamber of Commerce, the Fire Department and the like. Within the last few years—a sign of significant social change within the community—minority group organizations like the Excelsior Social Club (a Black group) and LULAC (a Mexican-American civic and political group) have sponsored candidates as well.

Not just any girl will do—a candidate must be "appropriate," meaning that she must be physically attractive and an active participant in extracurricular high school activities. A record of academic achievement, while not essential, helps also. Here, for example, are the credentials of the girl who became Queen of a recent Watermelon Thump:

> Terry is a member of the Luling Eagle Band and has been selected as head twirler for the upcoming school year. She is a band officer and received Division One on solos and ensembles. Terry has served as manager of the High School Baseball team and was an active member and officer in the Future Teachers of America. She was selected for Who's Who Among American High School Students and the Society of Distinguished American High School Students. . . . Her hobbies include playing the piano, twirling, cooking, dancing and reading books.

The actual election of the Queen is a two part process. First, the candidates and their supporters compete in selling tickets (priced at one dollar each) to the Coronation ceremony. Each girl must sell a minimum of 200 tickets, but that is easy—indeed, total ticket sales reach nearly 10,000 although the Evening Lions Building where the Coronation is held only has a capacity of a few hundred. Each ticket counts as one vote for the candidate on whose behalf it was sold; the totals are added up on a specified Friday evening several weeks before the festival. On Saturday, the so-called "popular vote" is held throughout the day at a designated place. Here, every person who has purchased one or more tickets is eligible to vote, but on a one person-one vote basis, no matter how many tickets an individual has. The two sets of votes are then totaled and the girl with the most votes is elected Queen, while the runner-up is the Princess. All the other nominees become the Queen's in-town court. (There is also an out-of-town court, to be discussed later.)

The Queen's Coronation is held on the second evening of the Thump, a Friday, at the Evening Lions Building. The huge ticket sales notwithstanding, the Coronation attracts an enthusiastic crowd, primarily the girls' families and friends, reporters and photographers. In fact, no one even checks or collects tickets at the door any more—the tickets are important only as votes. We cannot describe the entire ceremony here, and so will restrict ourselves to a few of its salient features. Framed as a coronation, in the main it consists of the presentation and display of the young women who qualify as the most attractive to the men of the community and those whose fathers have influence. One after another, the members of the Queen's court, made up and dressed up in formals (white for the Luling girls, different colors for the girls representing other towns), walk down the elevated runway to the front platform, where they are met by their young male consorts, also in formal dress, and arrange themselves around the stage. First comes the Queen whose reign is ending, then the Visiting Royalty, who are the Queens of the festivals in their own respective towns in the surrounding region but reduced to Duchesses in Luling, then the in-town court, and finally the new Queen attended by her train bearers, a scepter bearer, and a crown bearer—all young children. As each girl walks down the runway, the announcer recites her praises, until finally:

> Presenting the Luling Watermelon Thump Queen, her most gracious majesty Queen Susan of the house of Crawford. Susan is the daughter of Mr. and Mrs. F.A. Crawford. She is a member of the drill team, F.H.A. All State, F.F.A. Miss Personality first runner-up, F.F.A. Sweetheart. Her hobbies include swimming. Train Bearers: Kelly Crawford, Julie Crawford; Crown Bearer: Fred Richards; Scepter Bearer: Bill Kent. Queen Susan is escorted by Prince Consort Joe Phillips.

The new Queen, resplendent in her white gown and white train decorated with watermelon wedges made of red and green sequins, is crowned by the City Manager, the retiring Queen steps down from the throne at the center of the assembled royalty, and the new Queen ascends to her rightful place. The rest of the ceremony consists of interminable entertainment provided by local performers which we won't go into here.

Now, what does all this mean? A great many things, we believe, but let us just suggest a few of them. Clearly, the Queen competition represents an expressive mechanism for the creation and display of hierarchy (see Stoeltje 1983). This is especially interesting in view of the American ideology of egalitarianism, still strongly professed in Luling as in so many small towns reported in the community-study literature. This is the "just plain folks" and "we're all equal" public ethos of Springdale, for instance, reported by Vidich and Bensman in their classic *Small Town in Mass Society* (1968). It leads, among other things, to strongly negative feelings and sanctions against flaunting one's wealth, demanding deference because of it, or acting in public as if it makes a difference. But of course no observer of the American character has failed also to note the vigorous impulse toward economic achievement and the deep competitive spirit that makes American people run. Now, many analysts have addressed the problem of how the contradictions between the egalitarian ideology and the competition for status are worked out and expressed in American life. As folklorists, we are especially interested in expressive adaptations, and the Luling Queen competition is a case par excellence. How does it work?

First of all, the Queen selection process is publicly framed as a competition among young girls. Clearly, though, the girls are just the public surrogates of other elements in the community. Each contestant is sponsored by a voluntary association of *men*, prosperous middle-class and wealthy men. A girl can be elected Queen only with strong support, manifested by the money that goes for the purchase of tickets, from the organization that sponsors her, and from the personal network of family and friends for whom she stands. The more money and people in a contestant's support network, the more likely she is to win. Moreover, a girl's sponsors and backers can share in her status elevation: the girls at the Coronation ceremony are presented as nominees of a club and as representatives of "the house of" their families; the Queen's younger relatives are often recruited as her train-, scepter-, and crown-bearers; the girls' parents—especially the Queen's—are highly visible at the event; their boyfriends serve as their consorts, and so on.

Now, under ordinary, everyday conditions, men, families, and voluntary civic associations in Luling, as elsewhere, are not supposed to compete openly and publicly, especially in terms of how much money they can mobilize. But the Queen contest makes it all legitimate by framing it in a number of ways that establish it as "not real." Festivals, of course, have always been privileged mechanisms for this kind of transformative operation, and the Watermelon Thump is no exception. Additionally, by enacting this differential process in terms of the metaphor of royalty, it is framed as playful pretense—these are, after all, not "real" Queens, Princesses, or Duchesses; we don't have royalty in our democratic country, let alone in our town. But the metaphor is an effective one, insofar as it does signal clear status elevation, and the play of the Queen competition is very susceptible to becoming deep play, for some men have been known to spend several thousand dollars in support of their claimant to the throne. And finally, of course, it is all legitimized as being for the good of the community as a whole, for all of the proceeds from the competition go to the Watermelon Thump Association for the support of the *community's* festival, and the Queen becomes one of the principal signs of the festival and the community, to be displayed and employed in a variety of festive and ceremonial contexts. Not only does the context allow for the "play" of pretense that permits male competition through the Queen candidates, but simultaneous with the community competition a domestic model of gender relations is enacted in which the males of the community create their ideal female and exercise their authority over her.

In this female rite of passage the young women learn that the public construction of the ideal female rests on male competition. The several organizations of men who select candidates reflect the process of differentiation, allowing competing males to select candidates and to do so according to their own criteria. As the competition proceeds, the men continue to exercise control over the choices through the purchase of tickets. Finally, the winner's performance as Queen at the Coronation, her public ritual, requires of her only that she appear in her virginal white watermelon dress to be gazed upon as she sits upon her throne. Thus, as the competition moves toward the selection of the winner, the Queen, the process of centralization dissolves differentiation into community integration, and the power of ritual has been employed by the collective Pygmalion to transform high school girls into women, informed about the nature of power and skilled in the "appropriate" performance of their gender.

The Watermelon Thump Parade

Up to this point, in treating the Queen Contest we have emphasized the operation of expressive mechanisms of differentiation within the festival. There are elements of centralization at work in this event as well: for example, the regional structures of reciprocity whereby the Queens of the various community celebrations in the region serve in turn as supporting members of the enactments in other communities. However, the core dynamic of the Queen Contest has to do with structures of differentiation within Luling, implicating families, sex roles, voluntary associations, businesses, etc. We turn now to a consideration of a second constituent event of the Watermelon Thump in which the centralizing dynamic is more clearly played out, namely the Watermelon Thump Parade, held on Saturday morning, opening the main day of festival activity.

A parade is a display form par excellence, in which a succession of carefully selected signs is presented to an audience. Each of the entries in a parade stands for an element of the social structure, culture, or history of the social unit by and for whom it is enacted. The sign relations may be multifarious and complex: parades present us with iconic signs, such as floats in the shape of watermelons; indexical signs, such as the presentation of members of a voluntary association who stand for that association and its activities; or symbolic signs, such as the display of flags. Moreover, each of the signs is itself presented in a particular metacommunicative frame or combination of frames: esthetic, ludic, performative, display, etc. In addition, the parade as a whole may be seen as a unitary message with its own syntagmatic structure and meaning, and its overall movement may be seen as a message as well, often about the expressive laying of claims to a territory and endowing it with special significance by the act of physically encompassing it, marching over it, or displaying special signs upon it. Unfortunately, the scope of this paper does not allow for a full analysis of the Watermelon Thump Parade. Rather, we will concentrate on a special order of meaning within the parade, focusing on the way in which the parade entries stand for particular elements of social structure and their interrelationships. Every entry in the Watermelon Thump Parade indexes a social unit or level of integration, not an individual or group of individuals. This is the dimension we propose to consider.

As might be expected in a community-based celebration, a substantial number of the entries in the Watermelon Thump Parade represent the social order of Luling itself. Examination of these entries, in fact, reveals a significant cross-section of the social categories and group organizing principles that give shape to community life. At or near the front of the parade, we find representatives of the civil government of the town: the Chief of Police, the City Manager, the Fire Department, and other civic officials. Here too are the officers of the Thump Association, one of many voluntary associations in the community, but for this occasion singled out for special pride of place. Voluntary associations have long been noted as a major feature of American social life, and they are well-represented in Luling and in the parade. These range from businessmen's associations (Chamber of Commerce, Lions, Kiwanis, etc.), to veterans' organizations (Veterans of Foreign Wars), to hobby clubs (Luling CB [Citizens Band] Club), to recreational groups (Luling Saddle Club). Some of them reflect additional categorizing criteria: ethnicity (LULAC [Mexican-American], Excelsior Social Club [Black]), age (Cub Scouts, Little League), or gender (Beta Sigma Phi women's group). The town's institutions are also on display in the parade, in the form of entries from the schools, churches, and the local convalescent home. The final major category of entry we would mention is economic, namely the town's business firms, including automobile and farm implement dealers, oilfield service companies, and so on. Together, all these entries in the parade give one a pretty comprehensive overview of the ways that Luling is structured institutionally and organizationally, and most of the salient social categorizing principles by which the people of Luling sort each other out. To this point, then, we are still dealing with differentiation, but in terms of expressive indexes of acknowledged everyday organizing and sorting principles, rather than expressive mechanisms for the creation and display of hierarchical differentiation that can only be done publicly during the framed interval of the festival.

Beyond the scope of the community, however, the parade reveals to us lines of centralization at successively higher levels of integration. To begin with, the Caldwell County Commissioners and other county officials index the next highest level of government above the town, while the float of the Caldwell County Fair Association shows that the voluntary association that organizes the Watermelon Thump is also a part of a county-wide association of associations. Both in turn are part of the South Texas Fair Association, also represented in the parade.

As a community, Luling also maintains relations of various kinds with other communities in the region. While the reciprocal appearances of community celebration Queens has already been mentioned, we can also see representations of business ties (through Chambers of Commerce and individual businesses from other surrounding towns), organizational relationships (brother or sister chapters of national voluntary associations like the VFW), and links of institutional cooperation (e.g., the Lockhart Fire Department, which joins forces with the Luling Fire Department to fight especially big fires). But small towns do not just exist in a network of small towns and county structures. They are also connected by a variety of linkages—though chiefly economic ones—to the larger urban centers where economic institutions and power are concentrated. In the case of Luling, this means Austin, San Antonio and Corpus Christi. These links are not manifested by overtly economic signs, but at one remove, through representations of large-scale urban celebrations centered in those cities which are organized and sustained by their respective Chambers of Commerce.

Moving up still further through the levels of integration, we find the signs of Luling's participation in state and national government, in the persons of the State Representative, State Senator, and United States Congressman who represent Luling in the Texas Legislature and in Congress. In each case, we might note, Luling is only part of a legislative district, and the districts get successively larger as we move from State Representative, to State Senator, to United States Congressman, thus tying Luling into a series of progressively larger governmental units. Other signs of state and national links are manifested by National Guard, Army, and Air Force performing groups from various bases in San Antonio and Austin.

Finally, we find one lone sign, albeit a prominently featured one, that Luling is part of a larger international order. Riding on one of the floats is Ulla Kekkonen, a high school exchange student from Finland.

This is a very rough and ad hoc summary, but sufficient, we hope, to convey that part of the energy devoted to one of the major events of the festival is given over to a display and enactment of Luling's place in a range of higher and higher structural levels (including county, region, political district, state, nation, and world), and that the range of relations implicated in these structures is functionally and organizationally complex: political, economic, and expressive; institutional and associational; reciprocal and hierarchical.

Now, the existence of these various levels and mechanisms of centralization and the fact that local communities in the modern world are enmeshed in level upon level of centralized structures are not news. There is a long sociological tradition that has been devoted to the exploration of these phenomena of modern life, including the seminal work of Tönnies, Durkheim, Redfield, Parsons, and others. And certainly, the ways that these forces affect and are played out in Luling, as in any other small, rural community, are far more ramified and complex than we have been able to discuss here. But let us suggest at least one important fresh perspective that can be brought to these considerations by an examination of festivals like the Watermelon Thump, a contribution that folklorists are especially well-qualified to make.

There is a persistent tendency in the study of centralization and small communities to treat the phenomenon from the top down, viewing the local rural community as progressively invaded and dominated by more and more centralized structures, surrendering more and more of its local autonomy to higher level forces. This is the perspective, for instance, that dominates Vidich and Bensman's influential study, *Small Town in Mass Society* (1968). We do not propose to debate the reality or productiveness of this viewpoint; in certain terms, its validity is undeniable. As folklorists, though, our interest is in how people give expressive form to their social and material experience (cf. Hebdige 1979:80), how they create, recreate, transform and enact their experience and values on the vernacular level by expressive means, in the various symbolic discourses by which they explore and communicate the meaning of their lives to themselves and others. Hence, in this case, our interest in a community festival like the Watermelon Thump.

From the vantage point of this community-based symbolic enactment, a very distinctive dynamic is revealed. As viewed through the lens of the festival, what we see is a force that runs counter to the invasion-from-above-and-without view of the forces of centralization. In the Watermelon Thump, the people of Luling present *themselves* at the center of the macro-system, not on its periphery. In constructing their festival, especially the parade but other events as well, it is *they* who incorporate and assimilate the higher level structures, bringing them right onto the main street of Luling to be displayed and enacted as part of a Luling-eye view of the world. This is centralization in reverse. By combining the signs of extra-community structures and relations with those of their own community structure and culture into one comprehensive statement, they reaffirm each year their own capacity to comprehend the order of existence in the modern world in their own terms. This is at least as powerful a conception of reality as the alternative view of centralization.

What we hope to have suggested in this brief examination of a contemporary community festival is that the forces of modernity, specifically differentiation and centralization, are played out in complex and revealing ways in these public enactments of community. These forces certainly represent powerful factors in the everyday life of the community, but the festival events give them a concreteness and immediacy that they do not have in daily life by making them into enactments and framing them as public displays. Display heightens the process of objectification by setting things off in special contexts, marking them with special intensity as being on view, available for examination, contemplation, reflection, whether the object is woman, flag, agricultural product, or association.

The first of the events we have considered, the Queen Contest, represents an expressive mechanism for the playing out of hierarchical differentiations and gender relations in symbolically transformed guise. Framed in special ways, the festival allows the expression of otherwise suppressed but strongly felt impulses. The Watermelon Thump Parade, on the other hand, displays more regularly acknowledged and openly employed principles of differentiation within the community, but then incorporates them as well into an enactment of the ties of centralization in which Luling is enmeshed. But, as we have emphasized, this is centralization in reverse—not a matter of outside, extra-community centers drawing Luling into their own structures, but Luling incorporating *them* into its own, by marching them down its main street.

These, then, are some of the ways that the people of Luling deal expressively with the forces of modernity within the traditional framework of their community festival. As such, they offer us, as folklorists, the opportunity to come to terms with these large-scale social processes ourselves.

ACKNOWLEDGEMENTS

Much of the data on which this paper is based was collected by students in Stoeltje's 1975 and 1976 classes on Festival, at the University of Texas, and we would like to acknowledge their contributions.

REFERENCES CITED

Abrahams, Roger D.
  1977 Toward an Enactment-Centered Theory of Folklore. In *Frontiers of Folklore.*
    Ed. by William R. Bascom. Pp. 79-120. Boulder: Westview Press.
Bauman, Richard
  1989 Folklore. In *International Encyclopedia of Communications.* Ed. by Erik
    Barnouw. Pp. 177-81. Oxford: Oxford University Press.
Habermas, Jürgen
  1984 *The Theory of Communicative Action, Vol. I: Reason and the Rationalization
    of Society.* Transl. by Thomas McCarthy. Boston: Beacon Press.
Hebdige, Dick
  1979 *Subculture: The Meaning of Style.* New York: Methuen.
MacCannell, Dean
  1976 *The Tourist: A New Theory of the Leisure Class.* New York: Schocken Books.
Peacock, James
  1975 *Consciousness and Change: Symbolic Anthropology in Evolutionary Perspective.*
    New York: John Wiley.
Roberts, Warren E.
  1988 Folklife and Traditional Material Culture: A Credo. In *Viewpoints on Folklife:
    Looking at the Overlooked.* Pp. 15-19. Ann Arbor: UMI Research Press.
Singer, Milton
  1959 The Great Tradition in a Metropolitan Center: Madras. In *Traditional India:
    Structure and Change.* Ed. by Milton Singer. Austin: University of Texas Press.
Stoeltje, Beverly J.
  1983 Festival in America. In *Handbook of American Folklore.* Ed. by Richard
    M. Dorson. Pp. 239-46. Bloomington: Indiana University Press.
  1988 Gender Representations in Performance: The Cowgirl and the Hostess.
    Journal of Folklore Research 25(3):219-41.
  1989 Festival. In *International Encyclopedia of Communications.* Ed. by Erik
    Barnouw. Pp. 161-66. Oxford: Oxford University Press.
Vidich, Arthur J. and Joseph Bensman
  1968 *Small Town in Mass Society: Class, Power, and Religion in a Rural Community.*
    Rev. Ed. Princeton: Princeton University Press.

Grain Stacking in the Midwest, 1850-1920

J. SANFORD RIKOON

The evolution of traditional agricultural practices in the American Midwest is largely the result of interplay between an individual cultural heritage, local social contexts, the natural environment, and available technologies. Folklorists who document the tools, techniques, and products of the rural nineteenth century Midwest generally focus on relevant cultural, social, and environmental influences. Scholars devote less attention, however, to the impact of technology, particularly the results of changes motivated by the mechanization of agricultural processes. Perhaps some of our discipline's avoidance of cultural contexts in which mechanization is a crucial influence results from continued acceptance of an early-developed assumption about cultural determinism. This view holds that traditional cultural processes are hopelessly powerless in situations including machines and other forms of complex technology. Forecasts of "disorganization" or "disintegration" of folk culture in competition with industrial or popular culture, respectively made by Robert Redfield and Iowerthe Peate, are only two examples of this still-dominant idea.

In this short essay, I will focus on grain stacking patterns in the Midwest in order to demonstrate that farmers experience the ripple effect of technological development in work spheres related to the use of that technology. Farmers have never had mechanical devices to actually assist in the stacking and shocking of small grains. Their adoption of new technologies in the reaping and threshing of these crops, however, required producers to reconsider overall grain harvest patterns in order to make most efficient use of local resources. In essence, we can assume that the employment of complex machinery in one or more spheres of agricultural activity is not socially or culturally deterministic. The use of particular devices may limit the scope of local response, but people must adapt as well as adopt. They may modify their use of nonindigenous technologies to fit local conditions, for example, or extend existing sociocultural patterns to incorporate the use of new tools or processes.

Prior to the adoption of combined harvester-threshers in the Midwest during the second quarter of the twentieth century, farmers needed a system to handle their crops between the first steps of the harvest—reaping and binding—and the threshing of the grain from the straw and chaff. The major requirements of this middle phase were to protect the crop from inclement weather and to promote drying, and to carry on this process in a manner most appropriate to the anticipated plan for threshing. Three primary techniques were used by Midwestern farmers around 1860: piling the bundles by tiers into large structures or "stacks" at the site where the threshing would later take place; constructing small formations, normally called shocks, of ten to fifteen sheaves in the fields where the bundles were formed; and, transporting the sheaves to storage in barn mows, a system often termed "mowing." Of these systems, stacking was favored by the majority of grain producers until the last decades of the nineteenth century.

Mid-nineteenth century Midwestern farm diaries reveal that most farmers allowed their wheat, oats, and barley to mature on the stalk, so that stacking took place only a short time after reaping. Most operators allowed their grain to dry in shocks for ten days or more before they stacked; others simply cut and bound the grain and allowed the crop to lie in rough windrows for a few anxious days before hauling it in to the stackyard (Dorringh 1853; Downer 1863). The primary characteristics of a good stack were that it hold as much grain as possible, protect the crop from foul weather and vermin, and provide maximum drying and air circulation for the laid sheaves. Farmers located their stacks on high ground in the area where the threshing would take place, generally near the barn or shed where the stock was wintered and the bulk of the straw used for bedding and feed. Those people planning to use the mechanical threshing machines widely available on an itinerant basis by the 1860s built their stacks in adjacent pairs. This design allowed the machine owner to set the grain separator between two stacks from which the threshing crew could pitch bundles to either side of the machine (Photo 1).

Construction of grain stacks required at least two persons, though three men working together was the regional norm. As a minimum, one man pitched bundles to the stack from a wagon carrying the grain brought or "drawn in" from the field. The other person, working on the stack, arranged the sheaves in a careful and systematic pattern. Other participants usually worked in the transporting and pitching of the bundles (Thrasher, July, 1877; Page, July and August, 1844; Hubbard, August, 1844). Two men labored together in loading bundle wagons: one pitching the sheaves from field or shock while the second built a tiered load on the wagon bed. Three-man crews using two wagons and teams could typically stack the harvest of four to six acres in a full day's work (Yerkes and Church 1918:13-14; Jones 1980; Cravens 1981; Edger 1980). Stackers preferred to have bundles thrown to them from both sides of the stack with the pitchers laboring in an alternating rhythm. This system ensured even distribution of weight in the completed stack and prevented the structure from leaning as a consequence of loading from only one side. Builders could not always detect weight errors on lower tiers; often, imbalances became evident only as the problem compounded with the laying of successive tiers. Improperly constructed stacks, marked by asymmetric bulges or uneven settling, sometimes had to be torn down and rebuilt before they toppled in a storm or grew sodden from retained moisture. In the summer of 1844, for example, Illinois farmer Charles Hubbard "pulled down" a wheat stack "which had grown badly. The stack bulged a little on one side below the ring which deranged the position of the top sheaves" (August 16, 1844).

Labor divisions at stacking time reflect the unique responsibilities and status of the master stacker. Every man charged with this task had his own system and idea of proper construction; thus, variations in form existed in each locale. Building stacks that would shed water, remain standing through heavy winds, and provide necessary air circulation for the grain was a rural folk art developed through long practice and experience. Each neighborhood had a few individuals who were recognized by the community as expert or master stackers and who worked for a number of farmers during the harvest season. If two persons arranged the sheaves on the pile, one was always a master stacker and the "second" was generally an apprentice or farmer assisting the man in charge (Boyle 1966:17-18; *Indiana Farmer's* 1899:420). In most cases, farmers repaid the master stacker through providing reciprocal labor for other tasks. Wealthier farmers or large landowners who hired stackers on a daily rate always paid them a higher rate than that given for other harvest labor. Lewis Lesher, who farmed near New Carlisle, Ohio, in the 1840s, paid reapers and cradlers from 60 to 75 cents a day while the stacker received one dollar daily (Lesher 1848). In 1838 in Mercer County, Illinois, John Drury (1838) paid binders and reapers, respectively, 87 and 1/2 cents and one dollar per day, whereas a stacker earned $1.50. Binders attending their "stations" behind the reaper on Albert Dorringh's farm in Adams County, Illinois, received a daily rate of $1.25 in 1853. Two weeks after the grain was cut, a local stacker earned $2.50 a day to build four stacks near the "cow barn" (Dorringh 1853).

The basic components of stack construction are the foundation, lower courses or tiers, bulge or eave formed by the widest course along the horizontal plane, higher tiers sloping from bulge to peak, and cap. Beginning with the base of the stack, builders first decided how to keep the bottom sheaves elevated, and thus protected from both ground moisture and the appetites of rats, rabbits, and other animals. Stack construction providing some sort of air passage under the pile also aided the drying process as warm currents could more easily circulate through the bundles. A layer of rails placed in a single tier three or four feet apart, a double layer of boards laid in a lattice-work pattern, or a wood platform were the most common techniques used throughout the region. For example, platforms of rough lumber were used by Lee Smith, who built stacks with his father about 20 miles north of Cairo, Illinois (Smith 1981). He began the foundation by placing six planks on their edges along the length of the stack area. Smith then laid six- to eight-inch wide boards on their faces at foot intervals along the top edges of the foundation pieces. Other builders simply used a layer of old straw, hay, or other farm product to provide at least some protection from vermin. Some German-American farmers in Mercer County, Ohio, used straw left over from the previous year (Kotter 1979; *Prairie Farmer* 1849:5), while farmers in Iowa (Shutes 1968:5) or other areas in which slough hay was available could form a stack on a pile of local grass. Demonstrations of variation include one Benton County, Illinois, neighborhood where farmers built their stacks on a cross-laid grid of cornstalks (Cravens 1981). There is no evidence of Midwestern farm use of manufactured pole structures or cast pilings such as were sometimes used in nineteenth-century Great Britain.

Builders set the size and shape of the stack with placement of the first tier of sheaves. Average circular stacks had a radius of eight to twelve feet. The stacker placed the first tier's bundles either on their sides or standing on their butt ends. The latter technique was especially appropriate for a base when no foundation was used, for the butts could rot and the bundles settle without immediate damage to the grain heads. The cardinal rule of almost all Midwestern stack formations is to pack tightly the center with more bundles per cubic foot than any of the side areas. As stacks of all sizes and shapes settle during the drying period, a more dense center settles less and thus aids in promoting water runoff to the edges.

The two primary styles of Midwestern stacks were circular and rectangular in design. Most builders began the lowest tier of round formations in the middle by leaning a group of four to eight bundles against one another to form the stack "core." They "carried" the tier out to the edges of the planned structure by placing circular rows, usually called "ranges," around the core. As the builder approached the edge, he laid the bundles more horizontally with the sheaf heads always leaning towards the center. As a rule, stackers worked their way around the pile in continuous circular "rounds." Carrying the rows to the edge of the stack form constituted completion of a stack tier or "layer."

Isaac Tate, who built wheat and oat stacks near Macon, Missouri, during the 1880s and 1890s, described one method of circular construction using this technique (1935:16-18). With no base platform of foundation, he began in the center of the planned shape with the placement of four bundles standing upright on their butt ends. He then laid circular ranges of sheaves, also standing upright but with their heads inclined to the center. At the outside row, Tate took the bundles and bent them at the first joint along the straw below the grain heads. The builder placed the bundle stems upright with the heads facing into the stack. Because he bent the bundles, Tate used two layers to reach the height of the other ranges. The weight of this circle, leaning towards the center, helped to brace the stack.

He continued the process until the stack reached a height of around eight feet. Each succeeding layer in the lower section extended out a little further along the horizontal plane. Stackers often referred to this technique as "building out the stack." The result was the stack bulge that acted as an overhang to protect the base. As Tate raised the stack, the center rose more quickly because these sheaves were placed perpendicularly while the butts of the exterior ranges sloped downward towards the edge. He worked on his knees when laying the courses, using his weight to press in and down on each sheaf. No adjacent circular ranges began or ended at the same place in order to inhibit water penetration.

Once the main body of the stack reached the top of the bulge, Tate slightly changed his construction process to taper the pile up to the "cap." He formed a simple eave by projecting the butt ends of the last exterior row about a foot outside of the stack body. The builder then "brought in" succeeding tiers from the eave to the peak by decreasing by one the number of ranges in each new course. Tate continued with this process until a tier occupied a space no more than three to five feet in diameter. At this apex, he placed a single center sheaf with other bundles laid around it leaning towards the center. The stack builder wrapped a rope around the peak tier and tied the two ends to the base of the stack to prevent the "crown" from being blown over by a heavy wind. When the stacks were to stand until late fall or winter, Tate added extra ties in a criss-crossing pattern over the sides and tops.

In 1900, George Hendricks of Hancock, Iowa, offered readers of *Wallace's Farmer* his plan for stack construction. His method illustrates a second common method used in the Midwest, notably different from Isaac Tate's process in that the Iowa farmer began on the outside of each tier and worked towards the middle:

> Begin by setting sheaves upright, as in shocking, increasing the slant of the sheaves until the desired size of the stack is obtained. Then mount the stack, fork in hand; a light two or three-tined fork is preferable. If "right-handed" then stand with the right hand to the outside of the stack. Now with the fork place the sheaf for the outside row, then place the second sheaf—for next inside row—on first one, so the butt will cover the band of the first sheaf and step on the inside sheaf: continue with two outside rows at once, placing the same number of sheaves in each, walking on the inside row only. The reason for placing an equal number of sheaves on the two outside rows is that the inner row of the two being the smaller circle, the sheaves will be the harder packed, which allows the outside row to settle more than on the inside, thus giving the desired slant for the rain to run outward. Continue with third and subsequent rows towards the center, placing as many sheaves and packing as hard as possible, keeping the inside full, hard and higher than outside. A slight bulge in the stack will aid in securing the proper slant to the sheaves. [1900:783]

A final example, from the Shutes family of Carroll County, Iowa, in the 1890s, includes other variations in construction techniques, but also reveals continuities in the basic circular style and building design:

> A good stack was made by first setting a long sturdy stake firmly in the center where the stack would be built, then slew [slough] hay, if available, was stacked on the ground around the stake, higher in the center to drain any moisture to the outside. A shallow ditch was dug around the outside and away from the stack, to keep the water away. A starter shock of bundles was fastened to the stake, and then carefully placed bundles built around it in a circle. Care had to be taken not to give too much slant to these rows, or when the stack was getting high, the weight might cause a lower row to slip and ruin the stack. It would have to be rebuilt—after the stack settled [there was] no danger. The outside row had the butt ends of the bundles out, and the next layer was extended a few inches towards the outside, until the stack was up several feet, to shed rain away from the base. Then the bundles were gradually drawn in, to give taper, all the way to the top, to shed rain and snow. It was not unusual for snow before all the stacks in a run were threshed. At the

top when the last bundles were used to cap the stack, an extra cap of hay was put on top and a stake driven through it, to keep the cap from blowing off. [1968:2-3]

All of these examples have strong European antecedents, particularly in the British Isles where conical shaped stacks of similar construction were popular throughout the eighteenth and nineteenth centuries (Collins 1972:18-21; Fenton 1976:73-76; Hennell 1936:136-41; Jenkins 1976:47-50). One major difference between the stacks of the British Isles and Midwest was that the latter constructions were rarely thatched for protection, whereas it was customary for English and Scottish farmers to use rye or wheat straw to cover their conical caps. Midwestern farmers likely eschewed thatched coverings for two primary reasons. The mechanization of Midwestern threshing was widespread by the mid-nineteenth century (Rikoon 1988:20-27) and itinerant machine owners normally completed their seasonal runs within a few months of harvest. In England, stacks often remained standing for six or more months, and thus were subject to increased crop losses from inclement weather. It is probable, moreover, that few Midwestern farmers even knew how to thatch as that craft was not used, except on rare occasions, to roof houses, barns, or other outbuildings. The Midwestern counterpart to thatching was a farmer's layering of hay, straw, or grasses over the top of the stack. Ohio landowner George Brown, for example, preferred to use swamp or long rye grasses. One year he found neither was available and substituted last year's straw. He discovered that this covering worked well for a few weeks, but had to be replenished three times before threshing (1912:760). Temporary shields were usually held fast with tie lines draped over the piles. Some stackers in the late nineteenth-century used large sheets of canvas or burlap to cover the caps, a practice promoted by the agricultural press much as plastic wraps are used on today's hay bales. Other stackers used no coverings, but drove a long wooden stake down the center from the top, as in the Shutes example above, or attached "riders"—stones tied together with a length of cord or wire and draped saddle-fashion over the cap (Hager 1975:27-28; Logan 1975:130; Smith 1981).

Midwestern stacks do resemble British Isles constructions in their overall shapes and bundle placement patterns. It is not surprising, then, to note that farmers often cited first or second-generation English or Scottish settlers as the master stack builders in their communities. In south-central Ohio, where Welsh immigrants settled to work charcoal kilns and coal mines, they also became known for their grain-stacking abilities. Whereas it is uncommon to find references to women employed as stack-builders, this community had at least two women with reputations as expert stackers (Jones 1980). A correspondent to the *Wisconsin Farmer* wrote in 1866 that "every farmer who has not yet learned the art himself, should secure the services of some English, Welsh, or Scotch farmer to do that job for him, until he has thoroughly acquired the art himself" (Todd 1868:-398).

The stacking descriptions presented thus far emphasize circular designs. This form was the most common one throughout the nineteenth-century Midwest, but some grain producers constructed stacks shaped like oblong rectangles. These structures resembled hay ricks and were often called "grain ricks" by the farmers who built them. In general, while Midwesterners may use the term "stack" to refer to any systematic piling of grain sheaves, "rick" almost always denotes a rectangular design. Mid-nineteenth century rick constructions were normally associated with experiments in harvesting grain with headers produced by the Easterly and other companies (Johnson 1976:48-51; Quick and Buchele 1979:71-81). These machines cut the grain close to the head, thereby leaving the straw stems in the field and forcing stackers to build structures with the grain lying on its side. Longer ricks between 12 and 20 feet wide were built, most of them with rounded tops covered with hay or straw. The following description of a method used in Stephens County, Illinois, is typical of mid-century patterns:

> After preparing old rails, brush, etc., for the bottom of my stacks, I laid up for each stack a rail pen, 8 rails square, and 12 rails high, by having a boy in the pen or stack to keep it level and round up to the top nicely before putting on your cover of prairie hay, which should be done immediately after getting as much grain as you can; and unless the grain stands so uneven as to make it necessary to cut a good deal of straw with the heads, such a stack will hold from 12 to 15 acres of headings, which is about a common day's work; and rails enough for two such pens is all that is necessary during the harvest, for after the stacks have stood one day and two nights, if kept level while they were building, will have settled sufficiently so that the rails may be taken away from them and laid up for other stacks in the same manner. [Stephens County 1848:179]

Ricks of headed grain were part of the cultural landscape for only a short period, though, as Midwesterners did not adopt these machines in large numbers. Headers were never successfully designed for the region's uneven fields and climate, and farmers preferred to save their straw for bedding, feed, and domestic uses.

During the last two decades of the nineteenth century, rick constructions became increasingly employed by mid-sized farmers as final storage for bound sheaves. Rising grain acreages and average yields per acre between 1880 and 1900 supported the use of rick constructions because the design was more expandable than the circular stack for holding additional grain. The settlement of larger numbers of central and northern European immigrants, more inclined to oblong constructions than their British Isles counterparts, provided the technical expertise that made rick constructions a familiar grain storage procedure. As a general rule, though certainly with exceptions, north and central Europeans opted to build rectangular grain and hay storage structures in greater numbers than British-American farmers, the latter continuing cultural styles emphasizing circular designs.

Most builders laid their ricks on a north-south axis in order to provide the greatest sun-drying exposure to the bundles. The favored shape resembled a loaf of bread, with the outside profile slightly bulged from the lowest tier to near the middle of the total stack height (Photo 2). As in circular constructions, the bulge or "bridge" is the widest part of the rick, with builders decreasing the width of the tiers from that point to the peak. William Brandston (1980), of Miami County, Ohio, noted that "you made that stack wider by keeping the outside of the stack higher than on the inside. Then you placed each layer on a little farther out [than] that one underneath. . . . When you overlapped the layers, reaching them down towards the center, that tied those outer layers down and prevented them from slipping off."

A fundamental difference between circular and rectangular constructions occurred in the laying of the sheaves. In rick formations, farmers typically placed the bundles flat in rows along the length of the design. Sheaves were laid, as Brandston notes, in overlapping fashion so that the butt ends of one layer held in the grain heads of the layer just below. A builder could also "tie in the rick" by placing the sheaves of any one layer over the space between any two adjacent bundles in the preceding tier. Within each course itself, the butts and heads of adjacent ranges overlapped to increase the strength of the tier. The stackers generally worked around the circumference, beginning from the outside, attempting to compress the center as much as possible and completing one entire range before moving on to the next (Brandston 1980; and Pepsen 1980). The overall building pattern resembles laying roof shingles, with bracing provided in all directions.

After reaching the bulge level, builders began "bringing in" the stack through the use of progressively smaller tiers up to the peak. Farmers could retain the rick's shape simply by holding in each succeeding tier six to twelve inches from the outside of the course just below. The stacker's most difficult and dangerous task was to set the outside sheaves without tramping them down or affecting their later settlement. If one walked too close to the edges of the loosely laid outside ranges, the stack sides would lean or, possibly, topple over. Joseph Pepsen (1980) recalled that a young man near Portland, Indiana, once suffered a broken leg and bruised ribs from stepping on "a soft place near the edge of a stack," and many older Midwestern residents note children were constantly admonished, for occupational and safety reasons, to stay off the irresistible stacks.

Farmers formed the roof or cap of most grain ricks by decreasing the width of sheaf tiers until they reached the "peak layer," generally two or three bundles—laid butt to head—in width. Builders often referred to this last stage as "topping out" or "topping off" the rick. The peak of an oblong stack is similar in slope to a moderately-pitched gable roof. Tops with greater pitch shed water more effectively, but were also more prone to toppling from heavy winds or storms. Since any peak construction has a tendency to settle, especially after rains, the caps of roof stacks invariably appeared flat a few weeks (and rains) after construction.   To tie the rick together and ensure its longevity, some farmers saddle-draped their stacks with stones or poles tied together with rope or wire.

Descriptions of rick constructions indicate that more workers were generally used for oblong constructions than the number employed for building circular stacks. Although two men could comprise a rick crew, the median number of persons involved was four, with two teams of horses to draw the sheaves from the field (Edger 1980; *Farmer's Guide* 1899; Yerkes and Church 1918:13-15). Bundles were normally pitched up to the rick from both sides, with extra men joining the master stacker when the pile's height required middlemen to transfer bundles from the center part of the rick up to the head stacker. Although the large sizes of some ricks would seem to require two people to place bundles on each structure, expert builders could lay sheaves almost as quickly as they were received, thus freeing extra workers for loading, pitching, and transferring the crop.

The construction of stacks as a regular part of the grain harvest remained the regional norm until the latter decades of the nineteenth century. Agricultural patterns began to shift in the 1870s, primarily as a result of the itinerant thresherman's adoption of steam engines to power grain separators. The single most important innovation in farm power in the nineteenth century, the steam engine used in threshing was for many farmers the first on-farm use of the same energy designs that powered the urban industrial complex (Wik 1955). The use of steam engines stimulated changes in the progress and process of the threshing work and led to changed ideological perceptions of the thresherman and the threshing season (Rikoon 1988:79-88).

The increased horsepower provided by steam engines motivated a regional shift from stack to shock threshing because the additional power allowed threshermen to utilize larger, more complex separators that quickened the threshing pace and released farmers from the need to stack or mow their crops. On an ideal level, each person could reap his grain, allow it to go through a ten-day to three-week "sweat" in the shock, and then thresh by bringing the bundles directly from the field to the threshing machine. The grain would thus be in the granary or at the mill well before the need to tackle such fall tasks as harvesting corn or planting winter wheat. Adherents of shock threshing noted that it took about the same time to haul the sheaves to the machine as it did to bring them to the stack or barn. Further, pitching sheaves to a stack required more skill and labor than throwing the bundles onto the feeding table or self-feeding conveyer of a threshing machine. During the 1880s and 1890s, as larger threshing machines and steam engines multiplied on the rural landscape, it appeared likely that stacking would be an abandoned rural art by the turn of the century.

In addition to the speed of threshing from the shock, there were other good reasons for farmers to abandon the use of grain stacking. Elimination of stacking relieved the farmer of one extra harvest chore and meant that the grain would be handled one less time, thus avoiding yield loss due to the shattering of the grain head during transportation and handling. Stack or barn storage also increased the potential of crop damage due to what Walter Schmidt of Shelby, Iowa, called "rattage and birdage"; that is, the grain appetites of animals that squatted in and near farm outbuildings. Farmers used to storing their unthreshed grain in barns were also facing increasing demands on available barn space due to changes in other cropping patterns. For example, the amount of cultivated grass crops increased dramatically between 1880 and 1890, yet the use of mechanical balers was very limited before 1900. Unless one had one or more large barns, which was not common outside of certain German-American communities, mow space could be entirely filled with hay.

Although we do not have any comprehensive surveys of harvest techniques at the end of the nineteenth-century, there is ample evidence that farmers at this time were finding it increasingly difficult to locate men who could build effective stacks. Correspondents to state agricultural journals were complaining by 1903 that stacking experts were available only in the "good old times." An issue of

Wallace's Farmer in 1910 carried a large headline proclaiming that "Stacking is a Lost Art." This loss no doubt varied greatly between locales, and had a number of causes in addition to those previously cited as motivations for farmers to shift from stack to shock threshing. By 1910, there was a new generation of farmers who had grown up after neighborhood shifts to shock threshing systems and thus never learned how to construct a stack. It is relevant to note also that shock threshing was promoted heavily as a quicker and more efficient process by agricultural schools, Farmers Institutes, Farm Clubs, and the regional agricultural press. Although the widespread impact of these information conduits on general farm practices is certainly questionable, the art of stack building was neither encouraged nor taught in formal educational contexts. Finally, there was never any extensive settlement in the Midwest of a capable labor class that seasonly traveled to seek employment building stacks. European immigrants familiar with stacking procedures tended to settle in ethnic communities among people already familiar with the process.

Complaints about the loss of good stackers reveal, however, that Midwestern farmers periodically reconsidered their decisions to abandon the stack, particularly at those times when the apparent efficiency and advantages of the newer system proved to be less than had been anticipated. Manufacturing statistics claiming new highs in machinery purchases between 1890 and 1910 were little comfort to farmers when a thresherman's promise to arrive within a week or two of shocking stretched to a wait of a month or more. Most families in a neighborhood tended to follow similar agricultural cycles, with a result that the grain in that area ripened and cured at roughly equal intervals. Operators all threshing from the shock needed a thresherman at approximately the same time. Turn-of-the-century rural diaries and newspapers document repeated incidents in which harvest plans were undermined by an itinerant thresherman's tardy arrival. A delay in getting a machine to thresh grain standing in shocks engendered anxiety over the year's profits, hindered the progress of other fall tasks, and prevented the growth of pasture grasses planted to follow grain in the most common regional rotation. Umphrey Stump, of Darke County, Ohio, recalled (1903:771) the problems of his 1902 harvest:

> A party of neighbors and myself having in all about two hundred acres of grain decided to thresh from the field. As most of us raised tobacco and the sheds had to be gotten ready for the grain, we thought it would save work at so busy a time. There are four or five machines within as many miles of here and we were almost sure of getting one when we wanted it. We had the promise of one the first week of oats threshing and waited for it until the second week and still seeing no chance of getting it we decided to get another machine which was promised within one

week. We waited on it for nearly two weeks and still no machine. Then we had
to fall back on the first one and wait till it came. Of course they took on every job
on the road as they knew we had to wait. The last two weeks it rained nearly every
day and the grain was thoroughly soaked. Caps had blown off the wheat and the
oats, having been badly lodged before cutting, was in big squatty heaps upon the
ground. The machine arrived between showers and they were determined to thresh
before the grain was dry enough. It was either thresh or let them pull away so we
all threshed. The grain was damp and musty and not fit for market.

A farmer's decision to change from stack to shock threshing was
not a choice made simply on the basis of efficiency and speed. People
long used to stacking developed not only a tradition of harvest skills,
but shared cultural patterns of attitudes and values associated with the
agricultural cycle and with judgments of an ideal farm plan. Neighbors
evaluated the quality of a crop, and by extension the expertise of the
producer, not only by statistical means such as bushels per acre, but
also in the way the harvest and threshing were conducted. Displays of
carefully built stacks laid in a symmetrical pattern in the barnyard or
sheaves placed in neat rows in grain ricks could be measured by others
in terms of gross dimensions, for the largeness of the crop, and in
form and style, for the quality of the farm and farmer. Aesthetics of
farm appearance and tillage practices continue to play a part in
agricultural decision-making. For example, contemporary farmers on
sloping, highly erodible land who share the idea that clean fields and
straight, smooth crop rows are symbolic of a "good" farmer are most
likely to resist adoption of conservation tillage with high percentages
of crop residue, contour planting, or other innovative tillage practices
that decrease soil erosion.

Nineteenth-century farmers contemplating a switch from stack to
shock threshing could not alter their harvest cycles without considering
their neighbors. Although there were instances where only one or two
families in an area stacked their grain, most often everyone in a
neighborhood threshed with the same process due to the need to
coordinate reciprocal work arrangements. Shock threshing began soon
after harvest, or about the same time that most stacking normally took
place. If only a few men wanted to stack their grain and postpone
threshing, it could disrupt work cycles and require the thresherman to
make extra trips to that area. Around the turn of the century, Ohio
farmer George Petit (1901) stacked grain after his neighbors turned to
shock threshing, "and for years [we] were hindered with our stacking
by having to go help thrash." Most grain raisers who stacked their
crop wanted it to cure for at least four additional weeks before
threshing. Custom threshermen wanted to do all of their itinerant
work in one continuous seasonal run, however, and did not favor short

trips in the fall to "pick-up men who didn't think their grain was ready" (Edger 1980; Tracey 1981). In areas equally divided between shock and stack threshing, machinery owners often serviced the families that shocked at the beginning of the season and returned later for stack threshing.

Farmers who continued stack threshing well into the twentieth century normally did so because of ecological considerations or as the continuation of long-practiced cultural systems that emphasized the careful construction of grain stacks or the maintenance of large barns or sheds for crop storage. Ecological and environmental factors included the locations of the year's grain acreage and the likelihood of damage due to excessive moisture. Grain producers who farmed creek or river bottoms prone to summer flash floods preferred to stack their grain on safe higher ground near farm outbuildings. Threshing wet bundles often resulted in considerable grain left in the heads or blown over as "white caps" into the straw pile. Also, farmers in marginal grain-cropping areas with few reliable threshermen often stacked due to the need to hold their crops for extended periods of time.

Ethnoagricultural patterns in threshing style were particularly evident in Midwestern areas settled by central and north European immigrant groups. Neighborhoods of German-American farmers from central Missouri to northern Wisconsin, and from central Ohio to eastern Kansas continued to stack or mow their grain until they adopted combined harvester-threshers around 1940. In some cases, a desire to raise specific kinds of grain correlated well with local harvest systems. Farmers who continued to raise barley for regional breweries, for example, were better off stacking this crop as it required a lower moisture content than oats and wheat to cleanly pass through the separator's cylinders. Similarly, barn storage and threshing remained closely tied with the ownership and maintenance of outbuildings with ample storage areas. A former thresherman who operated in Darke County, Ohio, recalls two German-American farmers who continued to barn thresh long after their Anglo-American neighbors had changed to shock threshing:

> Those two men, well they had two of the biggest barns in the area, and I used to have to go out there two or three times over the winter to barn thresh their crop. They had a lot of grain, but they never wanted to thresh it all at once, so I had to go out to their place a few times. They'd just a-pile all their wheat in the lofts of those German barns and call me out whenever they needed me. . . They were about the only ones who'd ever want to thresh in the winter. [Edger 1980]

In areas such as northeast Iowa and southwest Minnesota, where Scandinavian immigrants settled among already-established Anglo-American communities, descriptions of harvest procedures at the end of the nineteenth century reveal a general persistence of the older pattern within immigrant neighborhoods. Lloyd Johnson, whose family farmed south of Rochester, Minnesota, learned the art of stacking from his uncle, a second-generation Norwegian-American. "The way he taught me was with the building of three stacks near the old barn on his home place," he noted. "I would just stand up there on the stacks as he laid out the bundles with his fork. Those stacks were not as easy to build as they looked, but they sure held up against the rain" (Johnson 1978; Main 1927-28:308; Hager 1975:25-8). As late as 1925, stack threshing remained the norm among Norwegians in both these areas and in southwest Wisconsin.

The process of change that marks the dynamism of traditional culture in contexts of developing industrialization is one of reorganization and adjustment to contemporary situations. The popularity of grain stacking in the middle decades of the nineteenth- century reflects its relevance to the cultural heritages of Midwestern farm families and the availability of competent stack builders. The form and style of the stacks resemble Old World antecedents, but also include modifications in design and placement due to the use of mechanical grain separators powered by horse sweep and treadmill devices. Changes in the technologies employed by threshermen motivated a sweeping change in harvest patterns to accommodate the availability and speed of innovative machinery. Farmers did not discontinue stacking until they first decided on another method, one that they believed would be a more efficient way of conducting the harvest, and coordinated their activities with the agricultural cycles of their neighbors. Stacking was thus more than a technique for storing unthreshed grain; it connoted a cycle of harvest, of labor and social relations, and of farm management. Decisions to continue older patterns due to environmental demands or cultural propensities did not denote the rejection of technological advances in other agricultural tasks. Rather, traditional cultural practices continued through an ability to modify the use of new technologies within culturally familiar patterns.

REFERENCES CITED

Boyle, Victor M., ed.
   1966 Reminiscences of a Hill-Billy.   *Indiana Magazine of History* 62:5-50.
Brandston, William
   1980 Interview by author, Piqua, Ohio, December 2, 1980. Tape and transcript in possession of author.
Brown, George
   1912 Untitled correspondence. *The Farmer's Guide* 24:760.
Collins, E. J. T.
   1972 *From Sickle to Combine: A Review of Harvest Techniques from 1800 to the Present Day.* Berkshire: Museum of English Rural Life.
Cravens, William
   1981 Interview by author, Springfield, Illinois, May 6, 1981. Tape and transcript in possession of author.
Dorringh, Albert
   1853 Diary, Indiana Historical Society, Indianapolis, Indiana.
Downer, Fred
   1863 Diary, Illinois Historical Society, Springfield, Illinois.
Drury, John
   1838 Diary, Illinois Historical Society, Springfield, Illinois.
Edger, Ira
   1980 Interviews by author, Greenville, Ohio, December 2-5, 1980.   Tapes and transcripts in possession of author.
Farmer's Guide
   1899 Unsigned correspondence, 11:420.
Fenton, Alexander
   1976 *Scottish Country Life.* Edinburgh: John Donal Publisher.
Hager, Gayle
   1975 Striking it Rich in the Northwest Iowa Hills. In *Conversations with the Recent Past.* Ed. Luis Torres, pp. 24-32. Decorah, IA: Luther College Press.
Hendricks, George
   1900 Signed correspondence to *Wallace's Farmer* 25:783.
Hennell, Thomas
   1936 *Changes in the Farm.* Cambridge: Cambridge University Press.
Hubbard, Charles
   1844 Diary, Illinois Historical Society, Springfield, Illinois.
Indiana Farmer's Guide
   1899 Anonymous article May 2, 1899.
Jenkins, J. Geraint
   1976 *Life and Traditions in Rural Wales.* London: J. M. Dent & Sons.
Johnson, Lloyd
   1978 Interview by author, Decorah, Iowa, August 5, 1978. Tape and transcript in possession of author.
Johnson, Paul
   1976 *Farm Inventions in the Making of America.* Des Moines: Wallace-Homestead Book Company.
Jones, Dan
   1980 Interview by author, Oak Hill, Ohio, June 5, 1980. Tape and transcript in possession of author.

Kotter, Jake
 1979 Interview by author, New Bremen, Ohio, July 23, 1979. Tape and transcript
 in possession of author.
Lesher, Lewis
 1848 Farm ledger, Ohio Historical Society, Columbus, Ohio.
Logan, Ben
 1975 *The Land Remembers.* New York: Viking Press.
Main, Angie Kumlien
 1927-28 Annals of a Wisconsin Thresherman. *Wisconsin Magazine of History*
 11:301-308.
Page, Thomas
 1844 Diary, Illinois Historical Society, Springfield, Illinois.
Pepson, Joseph
 1980 Interview by author, Troy, Ohio, July 17, 1980. Tape and transcript in
 possession of author.
Petit, George
 1901 Signed correspondence. *Ohio Farmer* 100:65.
Prairie Farmer
 1849 Unsigned article, 9:95.
Quick, Graeme R. and Wesley F. Buchele
 1979 *The Grain Harvesters.* St. Joseph, Mich.: American Society of Agricultural
 Engineers.
Rikoon, J. Sanford
 1986 From Flail to Combine: Folk Culture and Technological Change in the Rural
 Midwest. Ph.D. Dissertation, Indiana University.
 1988 *Grain Threshing in the Midwest: 1820-1940: A Study of Traditional Culture
 and Technological Change.* Bloomington: Indiana University Press.
Schmidt, Walter
 1980 Interview by author, Shelby, Iowa, August 8, 1980. Tape and transcript in
 possession of author.
Shutes, Leroy
 1968 Stack Threshing, Ioway–1890s. Manuscript, Indiana State Historical Society
 Library, Indianapolis, Indiana.
Smith, Lee
 1981 Interview by author, Unionville, Indiana, April 14, 1981. Tape and transcript
 in possession of author.
Stephens County
 1848 Anonymous letter in *Prairie Farmer* 8:179.
Stump, Umphrey
 1903 Signed correspondence. *The Farmer's Guide* 15:771.
Tate, Isaac
 1935 Recollections of a Pioneer Farmer. Manuscript, Joint Collection of University
 of Missouri Western Historical Manuscript Collection-Columbia and State
 Historical Society of Missouri.
Thrasher, Benjamin
 1877 Diary, Joint Collection of University of Missouri Western Historical
 Manuscript Collection-Columbia and State Historical Society of Missouri.
Todd, S. Edwards
 1868 *The American Wheat Culturist: A Practical Treatise on the Culture of Wheat.*
 New York: Taintor Brothers and Company.
Tracey, Kenneth
 1981 Interview by author, Seymour, Indiana, June 24, 1981. Tape and transcript
 in possession of author.

Wik, Reynold M
   1955   *Steam Power on the American Farm.* Philadelphia: University of Pennsylvania
      Press.
Yerkes, Arnold P. and L. M. Church
   1918   *The Cost of Harvesting Wheat by Different Methods.* United States Department
      of Agriculture Bulletin, Number 627. Washington, D.C.: United States
      Department of Agriculture.

Figure 1. Stack threshing in northeast Missouri, ca. 1925, with grain separator set between stacks. Credit: State Historical Society of Missouri.

Figure 2. Building a grain rick in central Ohio, ca. 1900.

Casă Frumoasă: An Introduction to The House Beautiful in Rural Romania

JAN HAROLD BRUNVAND

Despite the inevitable changes that folk traditions undergo, both in the natural course of person-to-person transmission and as a result of being reproduced for wider consumption, much may still be preserved in a culture full of old ways and crafts handed down from one generation to the next, always absorbing or developing new themes in each succeeding period. Thus, the traveler in The Socialist Republic of Romania who has the time and inclination to leave the planned tour and walk (or even just drive slowly) through the village streets, will find that sometimes weddings, funerals, and festivals there are occasions for traditional costuming, song, and dance; that women and girls still spin, weave, sew, and embroider some of their own clothing and household textiles; that men still carve and decorate wooden tools, gateposts, or cheese molds; that village potters still sit at their wheels creating pieces in the regional ceramic styles; and that other artisans may be making leather coats, belts, or vests, building furniture, manufacturing barrels, baskets, or musical instruments, and (in a few rare instances) painting icons on glass.

While no modern Romanian village is a beehive of traditional activity with virtually every need of daily life supplied by the local folk, at the same time, hardly a village in Romania is without its vestiges of such traditional production, most of them revealing various accommodations to modern times, whether in the use of new materials (such as chemical rather than vegetal dyes) or of new techniques (such as sewing machines in place of needle and thread). A prime example of the survival and resiliency of tradition in contemporary Romanian

191

life is the decorated peasant house, what I call "the house beautiful" in rural Romania—or **casă frumoasă**, as the Romanians would phrase it.

Though often lying fairly close to modern cities with their tall apartment blocks and smoky factories, or near sprawling collective farms, most houses in the villages and rural areas of Romania today are still, like those of many past generations, individual family homes, built by hand according to regional traditions of material, form, and decor. They constitute *folk housing* in the classic sense of the term. The often lavish decoration of the interiors and exteriors of their houses by people following traditional means and designs is an on-going practice in Romania, as indeed it is, to some degree, in neighboring Eastern European countries and elsewhere.[1]

As I have written elsewhere, "In some Romanian villages virtually every house seems to be slathered with embossed and brightly painted stucco designs, adorned with intricate wood or metal ornaments on gables and roofs, and dripping with sawed fretwork and wood applique" (Brunvand 1975b:66). It is true, however, that in other Romanian villages most of the houses are drab and commonplace with only the dimmest traces of any decorative efforts, or else they may be so over-decorated in kitschy modern colors and designs that contrast with the good taste and eloquent harmony characteristic of the finest specimens of old peasant houses preserved in open-air museums. Still, I have never been in a Romanian village that completely lacked at least a few examples of very *interestingly* (if not always *beautifully*) adorned houses. The sheer number of these decorated houses, and the mere fact of the vigorous survival of this tradition in the midst of modernization and rapid industrial growth in Romania, are reasons enough to appreciate and study them, especially when one considers how really abstracted from reality and how non-functional a carefully decorated house in a remote village is.

This point becomes more clear if we compare exterior house decoration with most other traditional folk arts in Romania. While the components of *interior* decor (textiles, icons, ceramics, furniture, etc.) are detachable from their settings and have distinct handicraft and utilization traditions in their own right, the decorated house facade is fixed in place and exists only as an eye-pleasing but apparently "useless" artifact. The richly decorated "clean room" inside a peasant house is both a family wealth display and a guest room or stage for special celebrations; its contents have functions beyond mere decoration. But a fancy exterior is just packaging, and the house seems no better or no more usable for the effort. Folk costumes are worn away from the home, and artifacts like wooden spoons, woven goods, or homemade musical instruments are sometimes used or are sold and traded at fairs and markets, but the decorated house is seen only by those who live in it or by people who happen to pass by.

What a decorated house contributes to the world is beauty, or at least an attempt at beauty, this being applied to a human residence, which in essence is a functional tool for survival. When the resulting building is truly pleasing, there is a temptation simply to rhapsodize about it, as one Romanian traveler, Tereza Stratilesco, did while gazing over the distant prospect of a peasant village some eighty years ago:

> Seen from the distance, a Roumanian village will always strike the traveler as a nest of peace, of comfort and homeliness, with those little white cottages peeping among the trees, in their own yards, more or less large, all away from each other, separated by large stretches of green and irregular roads meandering about in all directions. . . . A Roumanian village looks at its best in spring, when all Nature is green and fresh; after Easter, the cottages are still shining with cleanliness, with their white walls and red wood-work under the thatched roof, like Roumanian black-eyed country girls, with their glistening strings of bright-colored beads around their necks. [1906:206-207]

That passage sketches a very pretty picture, and one that it is still possible to view in our own time. But such enthusiasm and appreciation do not provide any understanding of what this complex and ancient tradition of decorating the exterior of houses with multifarious patterns, colors, and textures is all about. Besides, everything looks best on a sunny day in the spring—the country girls as well as the houses—and if Nature (with a capital "N") should unkindly give us a spell of dull wet weather after Easter, or if we should simply stroll a bit closer to the village houses and their often muddy or dusty yards, then the view may not seem so idyllic. William Wilkinson, for instance, British Consul in Bucharest in 1820, had only this to say about Wallachian dwellings:

> The villages throughout the country are principally composed of peasants' huts, all built in the same style and of the same size. The walls are of clay, and the roofs thatched with straw, neither of which are calculated to protect the lodgers from the inclemency of the bad seasons. [1971:157]

Wilkinson concluded that these inadequate shelters—the same kind that Stratilesco praised so highly—contributed materially to the "natural stupor and apathy" he believed to be typical of the oppressed, hard-working, and heavily-taxed, but patiently resigned peasantry of Wallachia and Moldavia. Similarly, Queen Marie of Romania (who was also English, it should be remembered), despite her enthusiasm for

Romanian folk culture—to the extent of sometimes donning peasant costume herself—summed up the villages she visited with the one word "miserable." She described one house as "absurdly ramshackle, with an over-bulky maize-covered roof" (1971:355,371).

It may seem odd that sources disagree so sharply about whether the Romanian village houses are attractive or not, and even whether they are decorated at all, beyond a coat of whitewash over the mud walls, but it is almost as if the earlier travelers and writers each saw completely different countries. Take William Jänecke, for example, a German military engineer stationed in Romania for about one year at the end of the First World War in order to direct highway construction; this put him in Wallachia considerably after Wilkinson, shortly after Stratilesco, and some time before Queen Marie. Jänecke was captivated by the village houses he saw, to the extent that his preoccupation while he lived in Romania was to sketch and photograph them avidly as he travelled by car in the vicinity of Bucharest and in the present-day states (*judeţ*) of Ilfov (renamed Giurgiu in 1981), Ialomiţa (partly re-designated as Călăraşi in 1981), Gorj, Mehedinţi, and Teleorman.[2] He published *Das Rumänische Bauern- und Bojarenhaus* (1918) containing 109 drawings and photos, including floorplans, elevations, many details of decoration, and one excellent cross-section representation printed in color of a typical decorated house. Jänecke's work shows painted outlining, carved wood trim, and embossed plaster decor, and he documented both the geometric designs used in house decoration and such other more representational motifs as trees, birds, stars, dates, initials, and even two portraits.

But had all of these beautiful houses completely vanished and the tradition died out by 1975 when one bicyclist, touring through some of the same countryside that Jänecke wrote about, reported his own thoroughly *opposite* impression? He claimed that all the villages looked like "shantytown," and that "the only bright spot can be found in the peasants' cemetery"; he wrote that for tourists seeking comforts and beauty "Rumania has little to offer" (Rakowski 1975:42-45). One wonders when reading this why anyone with a high regard for comforts would choose to go through Eastern Europe by bicycle in the first place, but one also observes that this traveler (as his mapped route showed) seemed to use only the main highways (such as the fast, but notoriously dull stretch of freeway between Piteşti and Bucharest), that the weather during his trip was rather bad, his bicycle broke down several times, and that he was really more interested in reaching the seacoast than in seeing the Romanian countryside anyway.

My approach has been objective and eclectic. I have tried to look closely at whatever the Romanian people who build houses and decorate the outsides have actually done, rather than at what the previous scholarly literature, or someone's current idea of "good taste" suggest that they *should* have done in order to preserve a supposedly pure peasant art tradition.

My first goal was simply to describe and illustrate the very rich tradition—both archaic and modern—of house building and exterior decoration in Romania. Second, I attempted to relate this continuing practice both to the broader subject of old Romanian peasant art and to the current needs, tastes, and desires of people who build and occupy these decorated houses. I have drawn on numerous published sources concerning folk architecture by Romanian scholars, and also examined pictures of old houses in Romanian archives. I studied the houses included in all of the open-air museums of Romania. But, above all, I traveled widely in Romania to find and photograph the decorated houses—old or new—in all regions. While I cannot claim that my data are "complete," or even that my geographical coverage has been perfectly systematic (highway and weather conditions sometimes interfered with careful plans), I believe that what I have collected is representative of the material that exists, both in documentation and in the field.

Early in my research I discovered the writings of the influential Romanian art historian and critic George Oprescu (1881-1969) whose enthusiastic appreciation of "the wonderful paradoxical blending of primitive taste and extreme refinement" (1926:35) in Romanian folk art was partly communicated in three works published in English. As I viewed decorated Romanian houses I kept coming back to the following description by Oprescu, somewhat idealized though it is, as representing very well the way many of the older village households still appeared:

> . . . do not certain parts of that house and of the church, which is everyman's house, being that of God—both of them built in the majority of cases by the villagers themselves—fall within the province of peasant art? The monumental gate, the royal entrance to the yard, at the far end of which nestles a tiny cottage—always clean but usually humble—the row of carved and decorated pillars which runs round the "Prispă"—a terrace and peristyle in front of the house—the rafters of the ceilings decorated with notches cut out with the knife and arrayed in accordance with ancient canons, the stucco flowers and animals, the figures which crest the roof, popularly known as "larks," the doors, the windows and their embrasures, the railed cellar openings, the panels of the carved doors and a host of other things, the railings and the stove, the wooden bench before the door and the bucket of the well—all this is the work of peasant hands. [1929:12]

The major paradox *I* felt, however, was the discrepancy seen in many Romanian villages nowadays between the balanced, harmonious, and entirely homemade nature of older traditional Romanian peasant house decoration and the absolute frenzy of new patterns and colors—often rendered in bright and garish colors and using metal, tiles or glass as often as wood, adobe or plaster. When I once asked a man living in a village in Moldavia that contained house after house done up in this new style how he could account for it, he replied very straightforwardly: "Well, first one man decorates his house, then his neighbor does, and soon everyone wants his own house to be just as beautiful as the rest."

It could be said, perhaps, that my whole interest in Romanian house decoration stems from a desire to get beyond that Moldavian's statement, and to reconcile it with George Oprescu's praise for an earlier tradition.

If you were to walk through a Romanian village you might receive an object lesson in the history and current status of traditional folk housing there. Whatever the region or the proximity of the village to modernized sections of the country, you would be likely to find a broad spectrum of house types, ranging from a few remains (perhaps now in ruins) of that area's oldest most traditional houses, up to modern dwellings that follow the latest fads and fashions in construction, material, or decoration. Most houses, in fact, combine traditional and innovative aspects, perhaps having adobe walls decorated with contemporary realistic murals, or metal roof trim (plus a television antenna) placed atop a hand-hewn log house. And everywhere people may often be seen (depending on the day of the week and the time of year) at work—building, maintaining, and modifying their houses—or else gathering and processing such raw materials for house construction as reeds, logs, bricks, or shingles. Folk housing is definitely a living tradition in Romania, and assimilation of new trends is the norm rather than the exception in the folk process.

The many influences—environmental, cultural, historical, political, ethnic, etc.—on Romanian folk housing have been so bewildering in their variety and complexity that it is impossible to characterize the current tradition as simply as Stratilesco did in 1906: "A peasant's cottage in the Carpathian region," she wrote, "is easily built, and is always made by the peasants themselves. . . . The material needed for the making of the house is at hand: mud and wood; in the districts richly wooded more of the latter; in the districts where wood is scanty, more of the former" (207-205).

Nor is it acceptable, as another writer on Romania did in the period between the World Wars, merely to compare the various house types of Romania to a supposed similar style in another country,[3] though there are certainly some useful descriptions of construction methods in the following passage:

> In the mountains, the houses are built of wood and shingled, and the peasants vie with one another in the wood-carving which adorns not merely the porch and railing but even the barn-yard gate. In the plain, the better houses are built of brick, with tiled roofs; the poorer classes live in what much resemble the adobe dwellings of the Spanish and Portuguese tropics and like them are gayly colored, often with elaborate decorative designs against the background of clear color. The typical mud hut is built as in Turkey; at the four corners strong piles are rammed down, to support the beams for the roof, and these piles are then connected by straight lines of sticks, held in place with branches and brush. Then a mixture of dirt, cut straw and manure is built up around this frame-work to form the walls; they dry under the sun outside and with the fire inside. The roof is thatched with bundles of reeds in the lowlands, straw and grass on the steppe. The more ambitious surround their house with a porch; vines and flowers, combined with the gay outer painting or kalsomining, make them very attractive in summer. [Clark 1932:265-269]

Probably the most misleading kind of general view taken of Romanian folk housing—and it is a surprisingly common one—is that which equates elements of twentieth-century peasant culture directly with the ancient Dacian traditions. One example, from a political history of 1932:

> The most amazing characteristic of the Roumanian people is that they have been able to maintain their language, culture, and religion throughout centuries in spite of war and servitude. Through all these thousand years and more they not only preserved but even intensified their faith in themselves. The peasant has preserved his ways and customs so remarkably that even today the villagers wear Dacian dress and build homes just as when the Emperor Trajan found them. [Roucek 1932:62]

The constituent elements of specific artifacts produced in any folk-cultural tradition are not explainable, as these writers believed, simply in terms of the availability of raw materials, competition among craftsmen, the relative ambition or wealth of different people, or even of their common cultural heritage, though each of these factors does *partly* explain the artifacts. *All* such influences plus many more (such as popular and academic cultural trends, the state of the economy, and contacts with foreign cultures) contribute alike, in almost incalculable ways, to determine the nature of such "folk" artifacts.

Ideally, each individual house needs a separate case study to sort out its distinctive features, account for its development, and compare it to "the tradition," which itself is to be understood only through other case studies of many dozens of houses. In practice, however, some generalizations about Romanian folk housing are possible.

First, the traditional materials used to build village houses in Romania are common and rather simple ones. Romanian folk housing is constructed of wattle and daub (that is, woven sticks and mud), wood (either logs or heavy planks), reeds, earth and adobe, stone, or brick. Roofs are made of straw thatch or reeds, wood shingles, tile, and sheet metal. These materials appeared chronologically in approximately the order listed, but they also varied in relation to the most plentiful raw materials in different districts and according to specific village, ethnic, and regional traditions. All of these building materials and several different construction techniques are found in active use today, often several co-existing in a single house.

Each building material has its own distribution, history, and methodology. Wattle and daub, now mostly used for rural outbuildings (corn cribs, pig sties, etc.) probably predates log construction, which requires some metal for cutting down trees and preparing the logs. Wattle and daub construction is also the typical house-building technique found in Neolithic sites such as Cucuteni and Hăbășești in Moldavia (MacKendrick 1975:11,14). The Romanian log building technique belongs to the great tradition of wooden construction extending from Scandinavia across to the forests near the Volga River and originally found also further south in western Europe (Petrescu 1972). Unlike some of the northern-European log work which has vertical members, however (such as the Norwegian "stave churches"), all Romanian log construction is done with horizontal logs that are notched at the corners and held together without the use of metal fasteners. Generally, these logs are first shaped to an oval or rectangular form and then quite tightly fitted along their lengths. Both log and heavy plank walls often have sticks or laths nailed close together and then are plastered over both inside and out.

Mostly in the Danube Delta some houses are made of reeds tied to a wooden frame with mud packed between and over them. The adobe or packed-earth house construction is found mainly in the regions poor in timber, particularly in Dobrogea. Stone houses appeared first in the late nineteenth and early twentieth centuries, largely in an area in the southern part of the country extending from Dobrogea westward to the Banat and in a few parts of Transylvania where good building stones are readily available (Petrescu 1973a). Brick is a relatively recent building material now in quite general use; it is most frequently plastered over, so that in common with most of the older building styles it offers a ready surface for the application of painted, stencilled, or embossed decoration.

A second series of broad generalizations may be offered about the design and floorplans of typical Romanian folk houses. While most specimens of Romanian peasant houses in the open-air museums are from the nineteenth or twentieth centuries, and only a few existing houses may be dated as early as the eighteenth century, it is clear that their basic form and structure were followed in antiquity. The houses excavated in the Dacian sanctuary of Sarmizegethusa in the Orastie mountains, for example, were log cabins set on stone footings with painted clay-daubed walls; and those shown on Trajan's Column being burned by the Roman invaders are one- or two-room cabins made of horizontal members (probably log) and with shingle roofs (MacKendrick 1975:64,79-80). It is certainly an oversimplification to select, as MacKendrick does, a single example of a current "house" (actually, his sample illustration is of a *mill* used for processing gold ore) from the Village Museum in Bucharest in order to "give an idea what ancient Dacian dwellings were like" (p.46), but many old wooden houses do seem to be relatively pure examples of an archaic type. This is true especially in the more remote sections of Transylvania such as Maramures, Hateg, and the Western Carpathians (Stahl 1961, Stahl and Petrescu 1966, Dunare 1973).

The simplest—and the oldest—of these Romanian peasant houses are rectangular (or nearly square) single-unit log structures ranging in size from four to eight meters on the shorter side and seven to fifteen meters on the longer, and with a very high thatched or shingled roof extending sometimes as much as three times above the wall height (Stahl 1958). The base logs (or **talpă**) rest upon huge boulders at each corner, or else on a row of stones which isolate the wooden wall from the moist earth.   Only a few peasant dwellings—usually temporary shelters—were circular, although other rural buildings are occasionally found in this form (Petrescu 1963). A larger semi-sunken house type that had its floor excavated one or two meters into the earth was found mostly in western Muntenia and in Oltenia; these are known as **bordei** (huts).

The floorplans of Romanian houses traditionally include a "clean room," (**cameră curată**), for guest or festive use, that is richly decorated with ceramics, woven hangings, rugs, icons, and impressive furniture; and a "hearth room" (**cameră a focului**) that is much more simply furnished for everyday family use.   Larger plans may add a small parlor to the front, or a separate room (generally at the rear or side) for the storage of food, clothing, and tools.   A narrow porch (prispă) may extend along the front and perhaps also across one or both ends of the house, and an extension of the porch—a sort of balcony or belvedere (foișor)—may thrust forward either from the center or at one end of the front porch. A common two-story floorplan (especially in Oltenia, Muntenia, and Dobrogea) has this projection placed directly above the ground-level entrance to a cool dry basement area (pivnița) where food, plum brandy (țuica), and wine are commonly stored.

The roofs, porches, and balconies of these houses, with their extending overhead protection, shelter the house walls somewhat from the elements and provide a pleasant place (especially in hot weather) for socializing and for food preparation. Also, their exposed beams, pillars, door and window frames, and railings are prime areas for decorative additions to the houses. Most Romanian traditional houses are aligned with the facade directly facing the street, or tilted at a slight angle from streetside. The larger two-story houses found in the hills of Oltenia and Muntenia have their first level closed with massive doors, and they are protected with heavy house walls and narrow defensive slits, in the manner of the nearby boyars' fortified houses which are called cula (Balș 1954, Stahl 1962).

In most regions of Romania the smoke from the centrally-placed hearth rises directly into the attic space and then escapes through chinks in the thatch or shingles. An adobe spark-catcher—like a second oven—is built into the house roof, directly above the flame, to prevent fires; the rafters of the house may then be used for hanging meats and other food to dry, smoke, and cure. The smoke probably also retards mold and repels vermin from the straw roofs, and its warmth melts snow that might otherwise collapse the roof. In Mehedinți (Oltenia), however, tall pyramidal chimneys (coș) are found (Popilian 1975), and other houses have eyebrow slits in the shingled roofs where smoke may escape or, at times (especially in Moldavia) houses have simple functional central chimneys.

The roof structure itself on Romanian traditional houses is usually composed either of two or four planes or watersheds; apă (literally, "water") is the word used to describe these forms. A roof with "two waters" will have the house entrance on the front wall (the long side of the rectangular plan) under the eave; this creates triangular sections, which are often decorated, at the gable ends. A hipped-roof variant creates a trapezoidal section there instead. A roof with "four waters" will extend downwards evenly all around the house and sit, it is said, like a fur cap (căciulă) upon the four walls. When the roof of a foișor has two watersheds, a triangular section faces forward, and with three watersheds this roof too is cap-like (the fourth side being joined to the house roof proper). A very few houses, mostly those that were built originally as taverns or shops, have gable-end or corner doorways.

Such, in brief outline, are the traditional materials, construction techniques, and designs of Romanian folk houses. All of these elements have steadily undergone modifications in response to social, political, economic, cultural, and technological influences. In general terms, the "new" peasant houses (i. e., those built since World War II) are larger (both in terms of number of stories and of rooms), make more use of modern materials, have irregular floor plans, and employ much more colorful and elaborate exterior decor. But several of the most traditional elements of Romanian folk houses—the **prispă** and **foişor**, the house's alignment to the street, the typical uses for various areas, and especially the dwelling being owner-built from local materials, have all persisted to some degree (Stahl 1964).

The major specific influences on post-War Romanian folk culture generally were the collectivization of agriculture and the increased contacts of rural and urban people. These factors resulted in such changes as the disuse and eventual disappearance of individual farm buildings, urban house plans being duplicated more often in the villages, brick (and sometimes cement) replacing wood or adobe for house walls, thatch or shingle roofs giving way to metal, tile, or asbestos; and moulded plaster or cement trim substituting for carved wood or embossed stucco (Petrescu 1975). In a striking instance of a traditional art, closely associated with the house, evolving as it is taken up in a new medium, certain gate carvings in the Bacău region of central Moldavia—once rendered in wood or stone—now appear in cast concrete, and with three "generations" of design features (Petrescu 1973b). First (up to about 1890) there were simple lofty wooden gates with minimal geometric decorations carved on them. Next (from about 1930 onwards) the wood or stone gates acquired richer geometric patterns, plus some symbolic images; and third (after the War) the gates began to receive decor combining geometric designs plus vegetal and animal motifs, but were now almost exclusively rendered in concrete with the designs embossed by means of pre-shaped wood or metal forms.

In the same way that modern forces have altered peasant houses, the influence of village houses on urban styles is also evident. Peasant-style house plans and decoration have been identified in such towns of northern Muntenia as Pucioasa, Pietroşiţa, and the old Wallachian capital, Tîrgovişte (Lăzărescu 1972). Even Bucharest has (or had until recently) many houses reflecting rural styles that became popular in the metropolis from the eighteenth century onwards (Petrescu 1971).

Since the mid-1970s, change has greatly accelerated in Romanian folk housing, and some of the earlier "innovations" now seem to constitute almost a new tradition. I can compare most easily my own field observations made in 1973-74 with those I made in February through August 1981 (see Brunvand 1976b).

On my earlier trip (as well as in 1970-71 when I looked only casually at decorated houses) larger house types were still exceptional in most villages, painted porch murals had become popular, and the colorfully-glazed factory-made ceramic tile was just beginning to appear as a frequent decorative medium. By the later trip, in many villages, huge (five or more room) two- or even three-story new brick houses with elaborate balconies, turrets, porches, and all sorts of wood and metal eave trim had all but replaced the traditional house forms. The ceramic exterior wall trim (on the relatively small percentage of new houses that were actually completed) had become the most common decoration in use in every region. There was also a veritable epidemic of fancy glass and metal window treatment on porches and house facades. Obviously, then, a Romanian house-building boom was on in the 1980s, but it was for the most part not simply a revitalization of traditional material culture but rather a new mode of (questionably) "folk" housing that was going up.

Fortunately, many older, simpler, and more traditionally-decorated folk houses still remained—and I saw some of these types under construction as well. Also, several open-air museums had been newly established or recently enlarged to ensure the survival of representative examples of earlier eras of Romanian folk architecture. In exceptional cases—such as the ongoing construction of a wooden church in the old traditional style in the Maramureş village of Ocna Şugatag—I saw instances of the deliberate revival of traditional folk architecture springing from the grass roots. But, in general, it was clear to me in 1981 that any folklorist hoping to document the house beautiful in rural Romania *now* would need to be quite broadminded and nonsentimental about the subject. The classic traditional styles had their great enduring value as part of the folk art heritage of Romania, but they probably had also already passed their prime and were being replaced by a new and quite different set of modern traditions. The recent news (1988) of the Romanian government's plan to raze thousands of peasant villages in the name of "progress" poses a terrible threat to the tradition of house decoration, and even of Romanian village life itself.

NOTES

This essay is adapted from an unpublished book-length work of the same title in which three further chapters and numerous illustrations present my findings on Romanian house decoration. When this book is published, it will be dedicated (as is this essay) to Warren E. Roberts.

I studied the folktale at Indiana University with Professor Roberts in the pre-folklife days, but my subsequent work in material culture has been strongly influenced by Roberts' writings and talks on the subject.

My research in Romania was supported by a Fulbright Research Grant and a Guggenheim Fellowship in 1970-71 and fellowships from the International Research and Exchanges Board (IREX) in 1973-74 and 1981.

1   This sentence is slightly revised from the opening statement in Brunvand 1980.

2   In referring to places in Romania I use the old names of all thirty-nine județ (i.e., "states") because this is how they are cited in the earlier literature. The larger regions mentioned in this essay are geographic, not political, units—Transylvania, Moldavia, Oltenia, and so forth. It should be noted that Romanian scholars have identified about eighty "ethnographic zones" distinguished by costumes, customs, dialect, folk art, and the like. These zones seldom coincide exactly with boundaries of județ, although some have the same names.

3   This author was mistaken in thinking that the building method in Turkey is identical to the one described here.

REFERENCES CITED

(Abbreviations: RRHA = *Revue Roumaine d'Histoire de 1' Art*, Seria Beaux-Arts. SCIA = *Studii și Cercetări de Istoria Artei*, Seria Arta Plastică. Both are published by the Institute of Art History, Bucharest.)

Balș, Stefan
    1954 Vechi locuinte boieresti din Gorj. *SCIA* 1(3-4):83-95.
Brunvand, Jan Harold
    1975a Traditional House Decoration in Romania. *The Romanian Bulletin* March:8.
    1975b Gingerbread in Romania. *Natural History* 84(6):66-71.
    1980 Traditional House Decoration in Romania: Survey and Bibliography. *East European Quarterly* 14:255-301.
Clark, Charles Upson
    1932 *United Roumania*. New York: Dodd Mead.
Dunare, Nicolae
    1973 Mijloace traditionale în agricultura Muntilor Apuseni în prima jumătate a Secolului XX. *Apulum* 11:573-634.
Jänecke, Wilhelm
    1918 *Das Rumänische Bauern-und Bojarenhaus*. Bucharest: König Carol Verlag.

Lăzărescu, Elena
1972 Aspecte ale arhitecturii urbane din nordul Munteniei. *SCIA* 19(2):295-305.
MacKendrick, Paul
1975 *The Dacian Stones Speak*. Chapel Hill: University of North Carolina Press.
Marie, Queen of Romania
1934 *The Story of My Life*. 2 vols. New York: Arno Press edition, 1971.
Oprescu, George
1926 Roumanian Peasant Art. *Art and Archeology* 21(1):5-41.
1929 Peasant Art in Roumania. Special autumn number of *The Studio*. London.
Petrescu, Paul
1963 Les Constructions circulaires des paysans Roumains. *Actes du VIe Congrès Internationale des Sciences Anthropologiques et Ethnographiques*, Paris, 1960.
1971 Condiţii sociale şi istorice reflectate în arhitectura urbană-Locuinţe ale ţăranilor şi tîrgoveţilor din Bucureşti secolelor XVII-XIX. *SCIA* 18(1):77-105.
1972 Holz und Stein in der bäuerlichen Baukunst in Rumänien. *RRHA* 9(2):161--219.
1973a Arhitectura ţărănească de piatră din România. *SCIA* 20(1):29-47.
1973b New Trends in the Wooden and Stone Popular Sculpture of Central Moldavia. *RRHA* 10(2):205-225.
1975 Transformări în arhitectura populară românească (1945-1974). *SCIA* 22:139-147.
1978 Unite et diversite dans l'architecture populaire roumaine. Formes regionales de la maison paysanne au XIXe siecle. *Objets et Mondes; Revue du Musee de l'Homme* 18(3-4): 127-140.
Popilan, Marcela Bratioveanu
1975 Locuinţa tradiţională din Podisul Mehedinţilor. *SCIA* 22: 149-165.
Rakowski, John
1975 Around-the-world Cycle Tour, Part V: Rumania and Bulgaria. *Bicycling!* March:42-45.
Roucek, Joseph S.
1932 *Contemporary Roumania and Her Problems: A Study in Modern Nationalism*. Stanford University Press.
Stahl, Paul Henri
1958 *Planurile caselor romîneşti ţărăneşti*. Sibiu: Muzeul Brukenthal. *Studii şi Communicări* 9.
1961 Case ţărăneşti din Maramureş. *SCIA* 8(2):339-361.
1962 Die befestigten Bauernhäuser in der Walachei. Ursprung und Entwicklung. *Deutsches Jahrbuch für Volkskunde*. 8(2):363-367.
1964 Case noi ţărăneşti. *SCIA* 11(1):15-33.
Stahl, Paul Henri and Paul Petrescu
1966 Construcţii ţărăneşti din Haţeg. *Anuarul Muzelului Etnografic al Transilvaniei, 1962-1964*. Cluj-Napoca.
Stratilesco, Tereza
1906 *From Carpathian to Pindus: Pictures of Roumanian Country Life*. London: T. F. Unwin.
Wilkinson, William
1971 *An Account of the Principalities of Wallachia and Moldavia*. New York: Arno Press edition. Originally published in 1820.

Figure 1. Map of the **județ** of Romania, from Petrescu 1978; note that the general regions and the surrounding countries are given in French spellings.

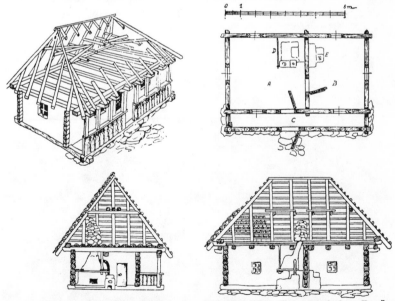

Figure 2. Elevations and plans of a house from Bulz, Jud. Bihor, Transylvania, from Dunăre 1973. The "hearth room," "clean room," and porch are marked as A, B, and C respectively. The construction of the stove and spark-catcher are shown in the section drawings.

Figure 3. Old log house, plastered over, and with carved pillars, in Racoviṭa, Jud. Vîlcea, Oltenia, photgraphed by Paul Petrescu ca. 1960.

Figure 4. Decorated house in Iaslovat, Jud. Suceava, Moldavia, photographed by Jan Brunvand in 1981.

Figure 5. Wooden house construction with dovetail corner notching in Sirbi, Jud. Maramures Transylvania, photographed by Jan Brunvand in 1974.

Figure 6. Men sawing timbers for use in house building, photographed by Paul Petrescu ca. 1960.

The Sisters Leave Their Mark:
Folk Architecture and Family History

HOWARD WIGHT MARSHALL

Introduction

In 1969, a historic farm came under the University of Missouri's care in the estate of the two elderly daughters of the nineteenth-century pioneer couple who developed the farmstead.[1] The 1,200 acre property known as the Cornett farm includes a collection of domestic furnishings and structures in the sort of pleasant rural landscape much admired by outsiders. This paper offers, in the spirit of Warren Roberts' way of closely studying cultural phenomena and traditional architecture in context through field research, a consideration of the story of the Cornetts and their Midwestern farm home. Near the county seat of Linneus in Linn County, Missouri, the farm lies in the fertile north-central part of the state in a region that is rarely studied.

In 1986, a multidisciplinary research effort was developed at the University to include field documentation, inventory, analysis, and preservation of the farmstead and its material culture. As the university's cultural research office, the Cultural Heritage Center mounted the project and joined discussions of partial restoration and preservation of the farm. The College of Agriculture funded research by our graduate student, Toni M. Prawl, and she conducted research in family history, furniture, and vernacular architecture. Laurel Wilson of the Department of Textile and Apparel Management inventoried and conserved historic textiles in the Cornett house. My work, in addition to running the project as a joint venture between my office and the College of Agriculture, attended to the architectural history of the 1884 house, the buildings of the steading, and the farm's cultural landscape.

In the house there is an array of furniture and furnishings left largely intact when the two daughters, Misses Bracy and Winnie Cornett, passed away. On the site are a one-room schoolhouse, the family graveyard (where slaves are interred as well as their owners), old agricultural implements, and a stand of hardwood timber (black walnut, hickory, and species of white oak) as well as the buildings. While this paper will discuss only features of the house, our team documented all the pieces of the material culture assemblage here. The main structures of the farmstead include the central-hall I house, and a side-opening, three-bay "English" barn built in the mortise-and-tenon construction tradition common to barn-building long after houses were being built of balloon frame.[2] Other outbuildings are less distinctive—a frame chickenhouse, wash house, smokehouse, and contemporary automobile garage. The Cornetts were practical conservationists and forbade plow tillage of the prairie and pastures they loved. The site and the saga of the Cornett family span some 150 years of Anglo-American settlement in Missouri.

The Place. In a study of regional folk architecture and local history, I described the patterns and traditions in an area often called "Little Dixie" out of which farmsteads like this one were formed.[3] In that study there is documentation of many buildings across a wide swath of the central-Missouri landscape; it provides a framework for the discussion of the vernacular design of the W.L. Cornett farmhouse. Little Dixie is a dynamic folk region of several counties in north-central Missouri defined by various criteria. The criteria include settlement history (heavy settlement by assertive and often well-off farmers and gentry from the piedmont, bluegrass, and gentle valleys of Virginia, the Carolinas, Kentucky, and Tennessee), voting patterns, pre-Civil War slave population and agricultural practices, patterns of rural vernacular building and other localized traditions with antecedents in the piedmont and Upland South. The story of the Joseph Moore and W.L. Cornett farm families fits within the historical outline of the classic Little Dixie scene as suggested in the 1981 book, and yet the farm is located beyond the arbitrary borders of the region.

In this paper, the Cornett farmhouse and the stylistic personality of the building's symbolic features are examined—architectural details that were possible to enunciate within the broad and flexible Anglo-American vernacular design tradition. I point to the venerable tradition behind the shape of the Cornett house, but my emphasis is equally on the specific people involved. They altered the received dwelling concept with additions—a new basement, rooms, and an intriguing new portico. We must ask how their additions suit motivations, community social conditions, economic circumstances, and individual design sensibilities.

Will and Mattie Cornett

William Lewis Cornett was the grandson of Kentucky emigrant William Cornett. W.L. established his farm in Locust Creek Township near Linneus, the principal town in Linn County until Brookfield was laid out by the Hannibal and St. Joseph and the Chicago, Burlington and Kansas City railroads in the late 1850s. The railroad towns grew quickly and surpassed the older agricultural market villages in population, commerce, and influence.

Young W.L. Cornett fought as a private with the legendary confederate general Sterling Price during the Civil War. After Appomattox, Cornett did what many other defeated Southerners did and went west; he became a freighter and drove ox teams from Nebraska across to Denver, Colorado. Later, he drove horse-drawn street cars in San Francisco. Still looking for his place, Cornett had moderate success in the Colorado gold and silver mines and helped organize the town of Telluride. He was among the first white men in the San Miguel Mountains and such landmarks as Cornett Gulch, Cornett Creek, and Cornett Falls are named for him. He christened his mines "The Golden Reef" and "The Silver Chief" in good frontier custom.

Cornett came back to Missouri and married Miss Martha Kansas Moore in 1881 in the old Moore homeplace in Linn County. He was 37, she 28. "Mattie" Moore was the daughter of prominent, affluent agriculturist and entrepreneur Joseph C. Moore. Moore came from North Carolina in 1840 to claim the 150 acres of untouched, rolling, northern Missouri prairie he had been awarded as a veteran of the War of 1812. He built a carding and grist mill and was active in community affairs. He organized Locust Creek Township school district Number One and donated the land for the one-room white frame school house that still stands at the Cornett Farm. Moore helped organize the Methodist circuit in Linneus in 1844. He became a respected judge and enjoyed a long and influential career in local politics and society. Moore's wife was Sophia Root, born in Tennessee, and some Root family furniture is part of the Cornett Farm collection today.

The Young Couple Settles Down. In 1883, after a sojourn in Kansas during which Mr. Cornett flirted with cattle speculation, Will and Mattie bought the old B.H. Mullins farm.   They lived at the Mullins place and developed their agricultural activities while their two-story "southern" house was being built on Turkey Creek a mile to the east. The house was constructed between March, 1883, and February, 1884 (the dates of the land purchase and the insurance policy covering the house).

Mattie and Will Cornett reared five children—Buena Vista, Bracy Vilas, Carlyle Cleveland, Winnie Davis, and Josie Lee. Such names conjure telling images for us of historical events and figures, and of the family's values; the last two children were named for Confederate States of America president Jefferson Davis's daughter and for Confederate commander Robert E. Lee.[4]

Carlyle ("Carl"), Miss Bracy, and Miss Winnie returned to the home place and figured in its consequent history and later development by the University of Missouri. "Jo Lee" was the only Cornett child to marry, was childless, and thus the Cornett family left no heirs in the community.

The Cornett children were well-educated. Three attended college. Bracy (who took a masters from Columbia University) and Winnie were noted schoolteachers before returning to the farm to help their brother Carl care for their aged mother, Mattie, who died in 1942 at 87. Will passed away at 85 in 1929.[5]

The Farm and the University. At the suggestion of their late brother Carl, a skilled farmer, in 1965 Miss Winnie and Miss Bracy gave control of the major part of their farm to the University for twenty-five years. The legal instrument required the University to create the agricultural research station where experiments are now conducted on cattle and pasturage.

The legal papers also ask the state university to "preserve and maintain the furniture, furnishings, and other contents of such residence as long as the University owns the farm." Miss Winnie hoped that the University of Missouri would develop the historic buildings and their contents as a museum to preserve, interpret, and honor the daily life of a farm family in rural Missouri. The house and the landscape are in very good shape. In the house, only the kitchen and back porch have been substantially remodeled. Most of the members of the Moore and Cornett families are buried in the Moore graveyard at the farm and in the Odd Fellows cemetery in Linneus.

The legacy of the Cornetts and Moores endures in the impressive materials they left us. Fortunately, we are able to study and appreciate the wealth of artifacts and material culture available in the house, the farm buildings, and the cultural landscape itself. We are in their debt.

The I House in North-Central Missouri. A traditional house known as an "I house" dominated the nineteenth-century central and north Missouri landscape on prosperous farms and in fine neighborhoods in town as well. The old British Isles-based house type was versatile and accomodated certain kinds of additions and stylish masks as it was rendered across the United States. The I house form could withstand the fresh ideas and variation an individual might bring to the building of the home.

The balanced central-hall I house is found wherever Southerners settled, especially those who shared cultural traditions of the largely protestant, Anglo-American life style familiar in the tidewater and piedmont areas of Maryland, Virginia, the Carolinas, and the lowland valleys of Tennessee and Kentucky.[6] The house type demonstrates a degree of economic success and intended social position, and these aspirations are played out in the selection of a solid Georgian appearance or the kind of decoration that lends a fashionable look of, say, classical revival architecture to the building.

The I house was until the early twentieth century a major dwelling form in European-America. Its layout is based on a dwelling one-room deep (though generally augmented by additions to the rear), two stories high, with the front door or doors on the long front aligned with the ridge of the gabled roof.[7] Indeed, the I house furnished with a central hall and symmetrical facade—like the W.L. Cornett house— came to be the ideal farmhouse for successful north-Missouri farmers in the nineteenth century, particularly those with a southern heritage.

Many I houses in Missouri, like those in the South, have a stately hallway as the home's focus. The hallways were built in imitation of and reference to larger, two-room-deep, more substantial Georgian houses of the prosperous earlier generation back in Kentucky, Tennessee, and Virginia. They seem scrunched up and tiny by comparison with their commodious antecedents, but they provided a graceful reception area and a conservative formality much favored by well-to-do farm families ("planters") with southern origins, lifestyles, and proclivities. The I house became more than shelter, it became a visible emblem of an attitude of Old Southern gentry transplanted to Missouri in the fifty years of settlement before the Civil War.

The I house as the farmer's standard desired dwelling was beginning to be eclipsed by the time the Cornetts completed their fine central-hall I house in the 1880s. In this period, several factors led to the popularity of new house types. These factors included the growing influence of designer's manuals, builder's patternbooks, and mail-order house plans from companies like Sears-Roebuck. Many of the new kinds of houses could be built more efficiently, less expensively.

One of the important factors that led to the demise of the "old Southern" I house was the desire for dwellings that indicated a person's sense of progress, patriotic vigor, and acceptance of the new order of rapidly-modernizing life in late Victorian America. While it was a heroic time of great inventions and technological marvels, the twenty-five years after the Civil War was a time of difficulty for "Southern sympathizers" in Missouri. There were maudlin popular ballads of lost comrades and despoiled honor, stories of yankee militia scalawags—all part of the romantic Gothicism of the post-Civil War era. Modern times brought a growing sense of national reality, industrial might, and technological change in domestic living; the "Gay Nineties," the "age of elegance" cultural landscape was beginning to look more "American" and less regionally distinct (Andrews 1969).

Today the old-fashioned I houses are often regarded as monumental relics of a past way of life. The "southern mansions" are the locus of legends and a community's reflections on its heritage. If one of the old Southern houses happens to date back to the antebellum period and if it happens to be constructed of red brick and dressed in Federal style finery (with an impressive Greek Revival portico, perhaps), the building may be the location of the local historical museum or be nominated to the *National Register of Historic Places*.

The Cornett House

In its vernacular pattern the Cornett farmhouse represents a continuation of the British-based upland and piedmont Southern I house. In its "style," the Cornett house represents a moment in architectural history when there was a transition from the old Southern models to more contemporary house types like the T house and to house types disseminated in patternbooks and catalogs, like Victorian Gothic cottages and twentieth-century bungalows.

Many people in the 1880s, like the Cornetts, devised an impressive home that was in essence a structure standing half-way between the old Southern dwelling and the contemporary patternbook Gothic Revival houses. In its plan it is a perfectly traditional central-hall I house, familiar and comfortable to conservative people like the Cornetts. Yet its original 1884 *style* suggests "Gothic cottage," complete with stick-like porch with turned posts and Gothic wall dormer over the front door.

But the house we see today appears more Greek Revival ("colonial" in the local tongue)—due to the handsome classically-inspired portico added on the front. The Cornetts' house in 1884 drew on their heritage and not on the more popular architectural trends that called for complete acceptance of the patternbook housing and Gothic style that were coming to be predominant throughout much of the Midwest.

The time of construction is important. On the rim of Little Dixie, the Cornetts' home is in perfect synchronization with the assertive ex-Southerners in the 1880s. It was in this period that the idea of a Little Dixie began to take hold in north-central Missouri. It reflected a partial rejection of repatriation for the Secessionists. The idea of Little Dixie is visible and symbolized in the houses these people built. The image of a "lost glory" was fortified by a desire to call on the noble, mythic motifs of Greece and Rome that had in earlier generations helped define for the nation the landed, slaveholding gentry of the antebellum South.

In architectural terms, variation could be expected in a house such as the Cornett house. Variation is almost always present when builders re-enact the customary forms of folk housing familiar in their families, communities, and regions. Once planting the traditional pattern, the Cornetts gave their house a "popular" 1880s' dash of fashion in the application of colors (contrasting buff colors), the small Eastlake-style porch, and in the steep wall gable centered over it.

Yet the house had sprinkles of classicism mixed in compatibly with the prevailing Gothic Revival look of the house—in the corner boards that are classic pilasters, in the cornice treatment, in the harmonious and symmetrical balance of the facade, and in interior details such as the ceiling medallion supporting the lamp in the fancy north parlor.

One of the errors we sometimes make is to think that these ideals and design motifs—the Gothic, the Greek—are concepts in conflict. For the people who shape and use these buildings, they are not.[8] When people build their own houses, they do not fuss over architectural terms or worry about agreement with the dictates of elite designers in distant cities.

Details. This 1884 house is special in several ways. There are distinctive elements which accumulate to form a unique building constructed within the community's tradition. As in many cases, the role of personality and personal history is probably larger in the articulation of individual buildings than we sometimes think. In looking at the changes in the house, one becomes interested in the sensibilities of Mr. Cornett's educated daughters, the last residents in the house who left it for us to visit and ponder.

Among the notable details are the basement's evolution, the kitchen T addition, the original color scheme, the hallway layout, the northwest dining room and bedroom addition, and the Greek Revival portico. The hallway, the dining room and bedroom addition, and the new portico will be discussed in some detail.

The basement evolved in three stages from a dirt-floor root cellar excavated under the back porch. The first addition was a limestone-walled cellar under the kitchen, and the second addition was a similar room under the dining room. The kitchen T was original to the house and not an addition. The kitchen is located in the customary way in an I house of this period.

The original Victorian colors are no longer evident. The house was painted stark white in about 1925, and the shutters green. Green asphalt shingles were put over the split shingle roof. A look at paint layers on the building suggest that the house was originally buff and earth tones (such was the scheme recommended by design manuals such as Downing's 1850 *Architecture of Country Houses*). The horizontal weatherboarding was probably a light buff color with contrastingly deeper shades applied to the cornerboards, the shutters, the cornice details, lintels, pilasters, eaves, and other trim.

The hallway. The house contains a perfect example of the formal hallway that became an essential ingredient in the proper I house in late nineteenth-century central Missouri. The hall as passage and reception area was common in medieval British vernacular houses. As Fraser Nieman notes, the kind of formal, enclosed hall seen in the Cornett house evolved in eighteenth-century Georgian Virginia from the medieval English cross-passage that in the seventeenth century was an open, informal space where gentry, neighbors, servants, and slaves mingled, a common hall with many social and agricultural functions (Nieman 1986:307ff).

The hall gradually became a special place for symbolic formality and ceremony: the stage for public and not private society. The hall has since then been considered as "foyer" and entry space where people are greeted and dealt with as they enter the family domain. The hallway thus serves as a threshold giving admittance to the home. The open hallway had become unpopular in eighteenth-century America in part due to the unstable, unsettled and rapidly changing nature of American society. People needed dividers; they needed separation, symbolically and physically, from others.[9] Architectural change echoes social change. People began to rely on their built environment and chosen artifacts, to create and define social position and personal intentions and to control the behavior of visitors and other people in the house (Upton 1986:321).

The Cornett house's central hall is typically a "closed" rather than an "open" space, with doors to other spaces. Just as in the fine Georgian home on a Virginia or Carolina farm, Missouri hallways were set with the finest furnishings the family could afford.

One of the interesting hallway details is the low landing at the top of the stairs. The difference in height between the landing (the upper hallway floor) and the doors to the room could be due to practical engineering needs of construction of a fancy stairway in a small space. But more likely—or in addition, perhaps—the lowered landing functions as a physical and psychological threshold where a home's public arena (its formal hall) gives entry to its private chambers of personal use.

Another interesting feature in the upstairs hall is the separate cross-walk hall on the front of the house where the balcony door is located. The hallway is sufficiently narrow that it was inconvenient to carry the landing fully around. Thus each of the upstairs front bedrooms has two doors in the inboard walls; the front (east) doors open onto the small separate walkway between the rooms, and the rear (west) doors open onto the landing at the head of the stairway.

The dining room and bedroom addition. These were added to the northwest corner of the house at the same time. The date of the addition has not been determined, but I believe it was between about 1900 and 1921. The bedroom was certainly added by necessity, but the dining room was probably added for social reasons and a desire for the special "dining room" (a new term) becoming fashionable in the Missouri countryside.

The addition carefully but incompletely supports the balanced appearance of the original front of the house. But the resultant construction slightly disrupted the exterior symmetry as one views the house from the north: the outside windows do not line up because the Cornetts placed a built-in china closet in that northwest inside corner. Having built the addition this way, the lower window had to be moved slightly inward toward the other window, thus off-setting the ordinarily perfect symmetry of a house like this one. The trick works so well that the casual visitor does not notice this subtle imbalance.

The dining room and the full-height bedroom above were added in such a way that they fill in the northwest side of the house. From the outside, the house takes on a squarish look and the additions blend with the original "T" shape of the house. Such additions were used earlier in the southeastern United States to contain new rooms, ordinarily bedrooms and kitchens (Upton 1986:325), and had become a standard element in the substantial I house and an accepted part of the tradition in nineteenth-century Missouri. The addition itself is not elaborate. There are no pocket doors in the passage between the more elegant front parlor. The "good" front parlor has very nice baseboard and a plaster medallion in the center of the ceiling where an electric light fixture now hangs. It was in the fancy front parlor where the Cornetts placed their fine piano about 1908. Bought in Brookfield for $100, the piano is typical of the big uprights (labored over by generations of correct young ladies) that are still an important, if little-used, possession displayed in American homes.

The new portico. This feature is critical to understanding the story of the Cornett house, the family, and the sisters Winnie and Bracy. The new front porch had always been assumed to have been an original part of the 1884 house. It looks like it has always been there. Indeed it furnishes the old southern I house with a familiar and appropriate finishing touch. It lends to the otherwise decently plain house the aura of mansion that people hold dear as an image of the cultural past. This classical portico is two full stories high, supported by a pair of white wooden Doric columns and topped with a plain classical pediment and roof.[10] If it was not original to the building, one might suppose the portico to have been the result of the Colonial Revival fashion in 1910 or 1915. Not at all.

Architectural research and family album photographs indicate that the portico was added by Bracy and Winnie Cornett between 1956 and 1962. In building the classical portico, the original Gothic wall dormer centered over the front door was simply brought forward and furnished with pediment, trim, and paired white columns.

Americans have that "Greek" image deeply embedded in our consciousness. Columns sprout on old as well as brand new buildings with every spring rain. Columns are important ingredients in the way institutions as well as families present themselves to the world. Motifs of classical Greek architecture have long been the favorite posture for American buildings whose designer wished to project power and authority in marketplace, government, and religion as well as in the mansions of the successful landowner; the style has been "copied on and off for some 2,500 years" and "never been superseded" (Fleming, et al 1976:212). "Greek" columns have a mythologizing force today just as in the past.

What does the Cornett sisters' portico suggest about the personality and motivation of the two women who had it built? Consider Bracy and Winnie Cornett. Both girls were named after famous Southerners who championed the glorious lost cause of the Confederacy—one after Robert E. Lee and the other after Jeff Davis's second daughter. They were talented, educated, traveled women who liked classical learning and taught school for many years. They remained unmarried and lived in the house in their elderly years.

In 1956, Winnie would have been 69 and Bracy 71 years old. It was at about this time that they had a classical portico put on the front of the old house. Allow a tenuous conjecture: Instead of thinking they were merely altering the family mansion, could it be that Bracy and Winnie understood they were creating the final chapter in their family history? They were growing old. They knew the University would soon take charge of the estate. Perhaps they did not want to leave the world with an impression of their father and family as railroad-town Victorians whose house was but a half-hearted embrace of the Gothic cottage style of the 1880s and 1890s.

Perhaps Winnie and Bracy wanted to leave the world with an impression of their family as educated, if perhaps old-fashioned, conservative gentry of whom Thomas Jefferson might have been proud. That front porch was the last palpable testament to a way of life that was very largely gone. Gone but not forgotten.

The portico may make the ghosts of Palladio and Inigo Jones smile (as it must make scholars blink). In the final chapter of a proud family, however, a sense of classical education and Missouri's Jeffersonian heritage was not unskillfully contrived by the children of an old Southern veteran.

Conclusion

Stylistic details and ornament present on the outside of the Cornett house are of sufficient importance that some architectural historians would classify it on these elements alone. Based on the prominent new porch, it might thus be called a "Greek Revival" house (looking at it today) or a "Gothic cottage" (looking at its original Victorian shape in historic photographs).[11]

In thinking about the case of this family and their experiences, I grow dissatisfied with standard generalizations about the rigor of vernacular design. While for the ethnologist, folklorist, and geographer formal characteristics and typology will remain paramount, a more congenial approach seems useful in our ability to incorporate style and psychological forces as we think about folk buildings.[12] Traditional concepts are elastic. Variation and the owner's sense of style are often neglected in the study of vernacular design. To come to fuller understandings of the process of folk building, we more and more wish to stress the roles that personality and personal history play.[13]

Where knowledge of the families and builders and users is available, personality and motivation along with economics often prove as instructive as theories of replication of patterns for understanding vernacular houses like the Cornett house. Buildings emerge as unique to their specific landscape. Far from being a dilemma, individuality and improvisation are present in folk architecture and these issues merit increased attention from researchers.

Mr. Cornett was aware of style and sought it—but he sought it conservatively. His children were sentimental and successful. They added to the domain, and the sisters Winnie and Bracy left their own mark on the old home place. At the historic Cornett farm in Missouri, we have an opportunity to realize the kind of creative action that is part and parcel of vernacular design. Information on pattern, and equally valuable information on variation and personalization, help us understand the process by which character is generated in folk culture.

NOTES

This paper is dedicated to Warren E. Roberts, in whose classes at Indiana University in the early 1970s I learned much about the nuances and pleasures of folklife studies. In forming this essay, I thank James M. Denny and Osmund Overby for bringing the matter of style more deeply into my considerations of vernacular architecture. This essay grows from papers presented to the Missouri Folklore Society (Columbia 1986) and to the Vernacular Architecture Forum (Salt Lake City 1987); a brief version appears in Carter and Herman (1989).

1   As part of the agreement bringing the farm to the University, the College of Agriculture developed a research facility to study beef cattle production and experiment with forage grasses. The College of Agriculture's attention to historic properties is timely because the centennial of the Hatch Act occurred in 1987, the sesquicentennial of the University in 1989, and because of growing interest in cultural heritage studies and historic preservation in Missouri. (William Henry Hatch was from Hannibal and in Congress developed legislation providing for agricultural experiment stations at land-grant universities in the United States.)

The project resulted in publications (Yancey 1986a, 1986b); an exhibition; a brochure ("The Cornett Farm Historic Preservation Project"); and a thesis (Prawl 1986). More can be done, such as historical archaeology at the original Joseph Moore farmstead and a study of the farm's original forestation along Turkey Creek and its alteration and preservation by the Cornetts.

2   To the south and east in the heart of Little Dixie, a county or so away, side-opening barns like this one used to be called "Yankee barns" in the dialect of the nineteenth century; see for barn types in central Missouri with discussion of their origins and associations in Chapter Four of Marshall (1981:72-88).

3   See Marshall (1981); I refined Little Dixie's flexible borders in a map of Missouri's vernacular regions developed with Walter A. Schroeder for *The WPA Guide to 1930s Missouri* (1986:frontispiece).

4   Davis and Lee were household words in the uneasy years during and after Reconstruction as southerners rebuilt livelihoods and communities; adjustment and rejuvenation was most painful in parts of Missouri where Unionists had been dominant and influential (as in much of northern Missouri).

5   For more on local history and the family, see Prawl (1986); Birdsall and Dean (1882); and Edwards Brothers of Missouri (1886).

6   For the vernacular architecture of early Missouri's southerners in this region, see James M. Denny (1983,1984,1985).

7   The dwelling which scholars know as the "I House" was first identified as a distinctive form by cultural geographer Fred Kniffen; the essential reference is his article "Folk Housing: Key to Diffusion" (1965), reprinted in Upton and Vlach (1986:3-26), quote p.8. Kniffen stressed the primacy of the floorplan in establishing a structure's "type" (following Estyn Evan's lead in Northern Ireland), and in this article coined the still-troublesome term "I House" (p.7). Also see Glassie (1968); McAlester (1986:78,96-97,309-17); and Marshall (1981:62-71).

8   John Summerson points this out in *The Classical Language of Architecture* (1963:7).

9   See Neiman (1986:310). The manor house's hall was "becoming less the shared center of everyday life on the plantation for the planter and his laborers and more the isolated domain of the planter and his family." The central hall developed into a "receptacle for outsiders" (p.311), the finest example of which is seen in the plan of Stratford Hall.

10   For the Doric order, see Summerson (1963); Doric often has a "soldierly bearing" (p.13).

11   The style of the new porch may pass under several revival titles (Greek Revival, Colonial Revival, Neoclassical); in McAlester (1986:342-43), the portico would be used to specify the entire house as Neoclassical. I prefer not to categorize vernacular houses according to decorative ingredients like the style of an added porch, but rather according to structural layout and function. In the original shaping of the house, layout and function prove more essential than exterior decoration or style for the purposes of folk and vernacular design.

12   In *Folk Architecture in Little Dixie* I add decoration as the fourth ingredient to be weighed, in an early expansion of Henry Glassie's (1968) formulation of "form, construction, and use" as the three criteria in analysis of folk buildings.

13   For an example of the need for including personality and intention in one's architectural investigations, see Marshall (1986); here a talented and individualistic German-American made a very old-fashioned housebarn out of personal motivation and not to suit local or family tradition.

REFERENCES CITED

Andrews, Wayne
> 1969 *Architecture, Ambition, and Americans.* New York: Free Press.

Birdsall and Dean
> 1882 *History of Linn County, Missouri.* Kansas City: n.p.

Carter, Thomas and Bernard L. Herman, eds.
> 1989 *Perspectives in Vernacular Architecture III.* Columbia: University of Missouri Press.

Denny, James M.
> 1983 Vernacular Building Process in Missouri: Nathaniel Leonard's Activities, 1825-1870. *Missouri Historical Review* 78(1): 25-50.
> 1984 A Transition of Style in Missouri's Antebellum Domestic Southern Architecture. *Pioneer America Society Transactions* 7: 1-12.
> 1985 Early Southern Domestic Architecture in Missouri, 1810-1840: The 'Georgianization' of the Trans-Mississippi West. *Pioneer America Society Transactions* 8: 11-22.

Edwards Brothers of Missouri
> 1886 *An Illustrated Historical Atlas of Linn County, Missouri.* Reprinted in 1976. Marceline: Walsworth Publishing Company.

Fleming, John; Hugh Honour; and Nikolaus Pevsner
> 1976 *A Dictionary of Architecture.* Woodstock,N.Y: Overlook Press.

Glassie, Henry
> 1968 *Pattern in the Material Folk Culture of the Eastern United States.* Philadelphia: University of Pennsylvania Press.

Kniffen, Fred
> 1965 Folk Housing: Key to Diffusion. *Annals of the Association of American Geographers* 55(December):549-77.

McAlester, Virginia and Lee
> 1986 *A Field Guide to American Houses.* New York: Alfred A. Knopf.

Marshall, Howard Wight
> 1981 *Folk Architecture in Little Dixie: A Regional Culture in Missouri.* Columbia: University of Missouri Press.
> 1986 The Pelster Housebarn: Endurance of Germanic Architecture on the Midwestern Frontier. *Material Culture* 18(2): 65-104.

Nieman, Fraser D.
> 1986 Domestic Architecture at the Clifts Plantation: The Social Context of Early Virginia Building. In *Common Places.* Dell Upton and John M. Vlach eds. Athens: University of Georgia Press. Pp.292-314.

Prawl, Toni M.
> 1986 The W.L. Cornett Farmhouse, Linn County, Missouri: Cultural Expression and Family History through Architecture and Furniture, 1884-1986. M.A. Thesis, University of Missouri.

Summerson, John
> 1963 *The Classical Language of Architecture.* Cambridge: M.I.T. Press.

Upton, Dell and John Michael Vlach, eds.
> 1986 *Common Places: Readings in American Vernacular Architecture.* Athens: University of Georgia Press.

Writer's Program of the Works Projects Administration in the state of Missouri, Comp.
> 1986 *The WPA Guide to 1930s Missouri.* Lawrence: University Press of Kansas.

Yancey, Kate
  1986a Cornett Farm Project Preserves Heritage of Rural Life in 19th Century
      Northern Missouri. *Tradition* No. 3 (Fall): 4-5.
  1986b Exploring the Legacy of Mattie and Will. *Rural Missouri* 39(10): 8-10.

Figure 1. The Cornett farmstead looking south; the house faces east. (Photo by H. Marshall 1986)

Figure 2. Regions of Missouri by Walter A. Schroeder and H. Marshall. (*WPA Guide to 1930s Missouri,* 1986)

Figure 3. The Cornetts pose with their children at a reunion in about 1927. Front: William Lewis Cornett (1844-1929), Josie Lee Cornett-Wood (1894-1970); rear, L-R: Bracy Vilas Cornett (1885-1967), Winnie Davis Cornett (1887-1981), Martha Kansas Moore Cornett (1855-1942), and Carlyle Cleveland Cornett (1889-1964). (Cornett family album, University of Missouri)

Figure 4. Among items in the Cornett collection that came down through Mrs. Cornett's side of the family is an exceptional handmade press (cupboard) in the Empire or Neoclassic style, made by a member of the Root family in Virginia ca. 1830-1840 and brought to Missouri by the Roots from Tennessee in 1844; the front is maple, the back walnut; the press disassembles into three parts for transportation. (Photo of author and researcher Toni Prawl by Kate Yancey, *Rural Missouri* 1986)

Figure 5. I house with Gothic wall dormers (left) next to a somewhat more fashionable T-shaped house (an I house turned sideways with the gable to the street) built at about the same time (ca. 1880) in the up-and-coming railroad town of Brookfield some ten miles east of the Cornett Farm. (Photo by H. Marshall 1986)

Figure 6. The Cornetts on the front porch of their house in 1900–the "two story shingle roof frame Dwelling" detailed in the $19.00 1884 insurance policy covering the house up to $1,000, and the "commodious rural home" to a local newspaper of the day; the photograph shows the Victorian paint scheme and Eastlake porch that were later replaced with pure white and the classical portico. (Cornett family album, University of Missouri)

Figure 7. The author photographs the Cornett house. (Photo by Kate Yancey, *Rural Missouri* 1986)

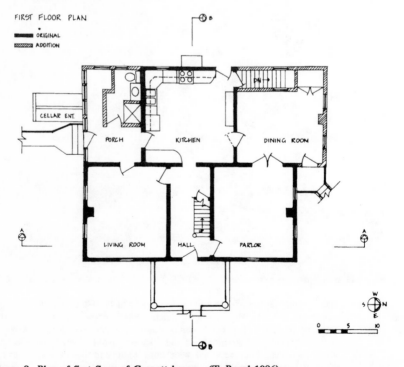

Figure 8. Plan of first floor of Cornett house. (T. Prawl 1986)

Figure 9. The itinerant carpenter, whose name was forgotten, built this handsome neoclassic walnut staircase and newel post as well as pieces of furniture while living with the Cornetts and finishing their house in 1883-1884. (Photo by Howard Wilson 1986)

Figure 10. A storefront in Linneus, the county seat, exhibits the application of power and trustworthiness–columns–to anchor the corners of the hardware store. (Photo by H. Marshall 1987)

Summer Kitchens of
Harrison County, Indiana

CHRISTOPHER K. BOBBITT

Until the mid-twentieth century in southern Indiana, most rural households, and many in town, did their summertime cooking and many other chores in a small building separate from the main house. For nearly five months out of the year, this summer kitchen served as the center of all of the family's activities except sleeping and entertaining company; the main house could thereby be kept clean and cool. The building was put to a variety of different uses in the winter. The yearly move to and from the summer kitchen was a major but welcome event, a ritual marking the changing seasons.

While much has been written on the subject of traditional folk architecture of houses, and somewhat less on barns, very little to date has been written about the structure and function of the smaller outbuildings so necessary to the preindustrial household.[1] Fred Kniffen commented on this lack 20 years ago (Kniffen 1969:1-4). This study is a survey of one such type of building, and its physical structure, uses, and social significance in one small geographic area. I renew the call for such studies in other parts of the country.

Harrison County, some 25 miles west of Louisville, Kentucky, is still quite rural, if no longer preindustrial. Small-scale farming of corn, popcorn, vegetables, tobacco, cattle, hogs, and poultry is widespread. Home canning remains a way of life for many families. Summer kitchens were very common until the 1940s and many of them are still standing. "Everybody had one" (Leffler), or at least "Most people would have had them" (Lang 239).[2] Harrison County was chosen as the site for this research partly because I have done additional fieldwork on folk housing in the county, and partly because my own grandparents had a summer kitchen there.

The construction and use of these buildings mark a specific era in the history of folk architecture in southern Indiana. Sometimes a summer kitchen was the original settler's first home, put to new use. "And I remember being up in the Flatwoods area and my mother would go around to various of my cousins, and nearly every one of them had a summer kitchen, and I'd say half of them . . . were the first house they had built, or were the first house that they had, just pulled into the back yard" (Griffin 225). Some were originally another building, such as a springhouse or smokehouse, converted for this purpose (S. Turpin 294; Mauck). Of the structures I studied, however, most had been built specifically as summer kitchens, some as late as the 1930s (Atkins; Leffler; Lang 336).

The summer kitchens I saw in Harrison County were remarkably consistent in size and proportion, being 12 to 14 by 20 to 22 feet (cf. Milspaw 1983:80).

One such structure which no longer stands, dating from the 1840s, had been of log construction (Griffin 210); all the rest, including one whose main house was log (Lang 194), were frame. Some of these were vertical board and batten (Bickel 333; Griffin 289) but most used horizontal weatherboarding.

Many floors were wooden, perhaps covered with linoleum (Bickel B110); the back room might have only a dirt floor (Duggins). One 1930s summer kitchen had a poured concrete floor (Leffler)—a long term investment at a time when external economic changes were soon to alter the summer kitchen's original purpose.

The present-day roofs I saw were "tin" (galvanized iron), but at least one summer kitchen in the county still has a wooden shingle roof (Bickel B181; G. Bickel B189). Most of the main houses had tin roofs as well.

All of the summer kitchens I saw or heard about had gable roofs, and the main door (sometimes with an attached porch) was in a gable end. The other door was either in the other gable end or on one of the long sides near the end (Atkins 36; Bickel 118, 333, 356; Lang 86; Griffin 108; Leffler). This is in marked contrast to the predominant style of folk house in Harrison County, the double pen, whose main doors are in the long wall facing the road (see Bobbitt 1985). I suggest that this departure from the classic housing pattern has a very practical reason. In the summer kitchen, ventilation was of paramount importance. In the main house, the primary center of winter activities, ventilation (i.e. a draft) is *not* a particularly desirable attribute. The summer kitchen door, which usually faced south or southeast, might have to remain closed to keep out the chickens and pigs (Lang 66), but two windows in each of the long walls, in line with the west to east prevailing wind, would provide excellent cross ventilation as well as light in morning and afternoon.

Several of these summer kitchens have or had a central or slightly offset chimney, intended for use with either a single stove or one in each of two rooms. Others had one end chimney opposite the main door (cf. Milspaw 1983:80). All chimneys that I saw were built of brick.

Most had two rooms, one slightly larger than the other, and a loft. The partition between the rooms might be temporary or permanent; if permanent, there would probably be a door between the two rooms. The windowless loft would be used for storage (Leffler; Duggins), a children's play area (Wiseman), or sleeping quarters for itinerant workers (Lang). A few had no loft (Atkins 40) or only a sheet of muslin stretched across as a ceiling (Bickel 360; Bickel 1981:31).

The summer kitchen was usually very near the back of the main house, occasionally attached as a lean-to (S. Turpin 295). Almost invariably it was oriented so that the windows faced east and west. There might be a stone walkway between it and the main house, and a grape arbor over this breezeway appears to have been very traditional—as well as delightful when fruiting in July and August (Griffin 240; E.Turpin 300, B105; S.Turpin B100; Bickel 128).

Folk houses normally face the road (or where the road used to be). In Indiana, roads tend to follow north-south and east-west range and section lines because the state was surveyed before much homesteading had taken place. What happened when a house must face due north in order to face the road? The summer kitchen was still oriented for best light and ventilation.

A source of water was always close to both the summer and main house kitchens. This might be a spring (Atkins 84; Mauck), a well with a hand-operated pump—one inside was deluxe (Leffler; Bickel 280; Griffin 150; Bickel 1981:30-31)—or a cistern (E. Turpin B60; Griffin 155; Lang 200). My grandparents had an elaborate system of drain pipe, barrels, and an old washing machine to collect rain water from the roof.

Other small farm outbuildings usually located near the summer kitchen might include a bakeoven (Griffin B84), a separate dryhouse (Griffin B180), a smokehouse (Griffin B191; Flock 42), wellhouse or springhouse, and woodshed (Atkins 96; Griffin B93; Bickel 28, B12). A woodbox inside the summer kitchen would be replenished by the children every evening. ". . . this was wood split in small pieces, wrist sized, which made a good fire 'cause you didn't have a big place to put wood into [in a wood-burning range]" (Bickel B38). "It was a little further distance to carry it into the main house in winter. The wood box in the main house sat in the kitchen fairly close to the stove. We had another woodbox out on the side porch which was filled with the big wood for the heating stove" (Bickel B50).

"The woodpile would be between the kitchen and the outhouse so that every time you went to the outhouse you'd come back with a load of wood. Or if somebody saw you headed for the outhouse you could just go as far as the woodpile instead" (E. Turpin B195).

Most obviously, the summer kitchen was used for summertime cooking. In this way, heat was kept from the main house, making it a cooler place to sleep (Duggins; Griffin 27; Flock 26). Odors and clutter were also kept away from the parlor, where company might be entertained (Griffin 37; Flock 29). The hazard of fire in the main house was also eliminated for nearly half the year (Flock 126). Opening the house's windows in the summer while there was a fire in the fireplace or stove might well create a backdraft, causing the house to fill with smoke. Summer kitchens were designed with such cross ventilation as to prevent this from happening (Griffin 42).

In addition to cooking, people generally ate in the summer kitchen (Duggins; Griffin 210; S. Turpin 93, 310; E. Turpin 95). Adults might sit in chairs around a drop-leaf table while the children would sit on backless benches or eat outside (Griffin 214). Occasionally, when company came, a meal might be prepared in the summer kitchen but served in the more formal main house parlor (Flock 385; S. Turpin 310; E. Turpin 316).

The wood stove provided not only heat for cooking, but also hot water for laundry and bathing. "Mother used part of it [the summer kitchen] when she washed clothes, and heated the water to wash the clothes on the stove" (Atkins 44). A few families had a separate wash house (Griffin 270; cf. Long 1972:244-257; Leach and Glassie 1968:56-61), and some would boil clothes in a large kettle underneath the grape arbor near the summer kitchen (S. Turpin 356; E. Turpin 366; Flock B20-45; Griffin 194). Unless the stove had a built-in hot water reservoir, water for bathing would be heated in a large oblong copper kettle placed across two burners (S. Turpin B53; Griffin 186).

On cool nights, children might sleep in the summer kitchen rather than in the main house. This was akin to camping out (Leffler). Apprentices and long-term hired hands might also sleep there, as might a cook or housekeeper in a more affluent home in town (Flock

210; Griffin B59). One summer kitchen in Ramsey, Indiana, served as headquarters for several ten-year-olds who published a local children's newspaper from 1940 to 1942 (Wiseman).

During the summer, food would be stored in the loft, if there was one. Milk, butter, and other perishables would be stored in the springhouse or root cellar which was underneath or very nearby (Wiseman). It was the children's job to get fresh food from the refrigeration of the springhouse or root cellar (Wiseman; Lang 175). Unless there was a separate dryhouse (cf. Long 1972:197-205), the summer kitchen would be used for drying fruits and vegetables such as apples, pears, peaches, beans, hot peppers, and pumpkin (Griffin B180; Wiseman; Bickel 363).

With the exceptions of sleeping and entertaining company, family summer life in the old days centered around the summer kitchen, just as in winter around the main house kitchen.

At summer's end came the canning season. Ball jars from Muncie had been readily available since the 1890s (Birmingham 1980:70), and the summer kitchen was ready to receive the onslaught of tomatoes, beans, corn, and other vegetables. "They done all the preparation for the canning out there, like they snapped their beans, and like if they were making jams or jellies, you know, all the fruit preparation and such" (S. Turpin 318). Most people did their canning within the summer kitchen on the wood cookstove, but some would set up a tripod and large kettle outside. Straw would be put between the jars to keep them from bumping together, for in "open kettle" or "cold pack" canning, the jars need to be boiled vigorously for several hours. As many as 65 jars at a time could be processed in a 30-gallon kettle (Flock 310; S. Turpin B173; E. Turpin B385). Canning can be an all-day affair and then some. "Mother did some canning, most of it out there, and then some of it at home, because there she could be with us of a nighttime, see, with the children" (Atkins 60).

Despite its name, the summer kitchen was used all year round. In winter, the building would be used to store things brought in out of the weather (Atkins 93; Lang 86, 319; Flock 378). It would also be used to store food which would not freeze, such as flour, sugar, dried food (Duggins; Griffin 145; Bickel 383; S. Turpin 17), and smoked meat (Leffler). The summer kitchen was usually vermin-proof (Leffler).

A homemade drum stove might be brought out to take the place of the cookstove which had been moved back into the main house kitchen (Bickel 42). One reclusive grandmother lived for many years in the back room of a summer kitchen; the wall calendar has not been touched since she turned it to April, 1966 (Leffler; P. Flock).

The drum stove would provide heat when needed to dry laundry in inclement winter weather (Bickel 58), and men might gather inside to play euchre or checkers or just to talk (Bickel B81, B100). But because it was usually *not* heated in winter, the summer kitchen was the ideal place for the messy job of cutting up meat after slaughtering (Bickel 70, 95; Bickel 1981:24-25). Most farms which raised animals had a smokehouse, for in the days before electric deep freezes, smoking meat was be best way to preserve it. For occasional use, however, part of the summer kitchen might be pressed into service: the closet under the stairway to the loft (Leffler), or the dirt-floored back room, shut off with a heavy rug as a curtain (Duggins; Lang 86; cf. Milspaw 1983:71,80). Meat would be hung on greenwood hooks over an iron kettle containing slowly burning hickory knots and stumps —wood not suitable for use in the stove (Leffler; Lang 98). After the meat was cured, the summer kitchen served as a walk-in refrigerator until spring (Duggins; Leffler).

Central to each of my informant's memories of summer kitchens was the twice-yearly ritual of moving tables, chairs, dishes, and most likely the cookstove itself. The exact dates would vary from year to year, but the summer kitchen was generally used "soon as it got nice and warm" (Lang 112), ". . . probably May, . . . but we can have some pretty cold spells" (Flock 258). "Usually there was a thing amongst kids, your mother would let you go barefoot the first of May. . . ." (Bickel 82). Children helped with the move.

"In the spring, I was just a real small kid [about 1907], why, Mom would take newspapers and we'd paper that building; it was an old building. We would paper that anew every spring, and she'd move our cookstove and she'd move our table and chairs and I don't know what else. Now we didn't have that much to, I doubt if there were any cabinets; I guess she had something else to put the dishes in" (Lang 33).

"Paper was scarce, and they put clean paper on. I've heard Aunt Kate Funk say . . . they always entertained themselves . . . by reading what the newspaper said, papered on the wall. Yes, I think that it wasn't so much people being stingy, they just *used* what they had" (Griffin B296).

Additional spring cleaning at this time might include removing the tacked-down rag rugs and sweeping out the straw insulation underneath (Lang 44). "And we'd go out to the straw stack where they'd thrashed, and we'd done throwed our old straw bed away, and go and get our fresh straw, and clean it all and change it, and put it in our straw bed, and boy we'd have a nice clean bed" (Lang 48).

The stove, too, would be cleaned. A winter's accumulation of soot and grime would be scrubbed off in the yard, so that the summer kitchen began the new season afresh (E. Turpin 270; Bickel 1981:31).

I did not find any Harrison County summer kitchens which used fireplaces. One 1820s main house fireplace was used for year-round cooking (Flock 160). The close proximity to Louisville may have enabled the use of stoves earlier than in the rest of the state. In the mid-19th century, Shaker step-stoves were popular (Griffin 373; they are used at the old state capitol in Corydon, Harrison County seat). These heating stoves were long and narrow, with three levels for cooking at different distances from the fire.

Later came wood ranges, designed specifically for cooking. A two burner stove (Leffler) would be replaced by the standard four or six burner one (Leffler; Duggins). A side reservoir for warm water was a special convenience (Atkins 55; Leffler; Mauck; E. Turpin 280). In the 1920s came coal oil (kerosene) stoves. Those who could afford to bought such a stove for use just in the summer kitchen (Leffler; Wiseman; Duggins; Bickel 42; S. Turpin 286), as they were far cleaner, more convenient, and above all cooler to operate.

The move back to the main house usually occurred in September, or whenever the weather began to get cool, "when the men would start shredding," that is, cutting cornstalks into fodder (Leffler). If the wood cookstove were to be brought back, it would first be given another cleaning. Many of my informants recalled the excitement of the moves, spring and fall—a family affirmation that a new season was at hand.

The summer kitchen can be seen to have been a symbol of community in this rural, pre-industrial part of southern Indiana, not only as expressed in the statement, "everybody had one," but also in the family (and hired help) all working together in the common labor of production, preparation, preservation, and consumption of food. The work done and the pleasures enjoyed in the summer kitchen—its place in the rhythm of the seasons—were integral to their way of life.

In Harrison County, summer kitchens as such fell into disuse in the 1930s and 1940s (Leffler; Griffin B167; Bickel 179, 190; Flock 64; Atkins 15). "It took a few years for people to make the change. Some people, I remember hearing people say, oh the food just wasn't *good* cooked on an electric stove, you know. I never could figure out how the food knew the difference. But it took a few years before people made the change" (Flock 90).

And indeed the coming of electricity was probably the most important factor in the phase out of the summer kitchen as an institution. In the southern two-thirds of the county, people could tap onto the high tension power line between Louisville and Evansville by the mid-1930s. One man sold $400 worth of standing timber to obtain a spur from S & K Electric Company (Bickel 220). In northern Harrison County, "electricity came through here in '39, and after that those things [old time ways] sort of went into demise. There aren't as many of them anymore" (Flock 72).

For some households, the remodeling of the house, perhaps after a son's marriage, resulted in the abandonment of the summer kitchen (Leffler; P. Flock; Bickel 190; cf. Milspaw 1983:71). The availability of clean, cool, coal-oil [kerosene] stoves, and later electric ranges, meant that cooking might be done inside the main house year round with a minimum of heat. "It's when they done away with wood stoves. When they had coal-oil stoves, you know, they could afford to have more inside" (E. Turpin 322).

"Give electricity the credit, I suppose. An electric range to cook on, a fan to move the air, a refrigerator to provide ice, a freezer to keep foods in, a pump to provide running water, and one had the comforts, yes, luxuries of life right in the winter kitchen" (Bickel 1981:31).

Why else are there no more summer kitchens? "Modernization. Modernization. Everybody likes to have everything in one place" (Leffler). "I don't know. They couldn't have air conditioning and all that sort of stuff, could they? Ceiling fans. Think they could have a ceiling fan? I don't know. It's just a different way of life. My dad worked for 50 cents a day, worked a thrashing machine" (Lang 258). "Well, we have all this new stuff, microwave, you know, electric. We cook with electricity or cook with gas, and you don't need that big an area. You don't have to process food anymore; you go buy frozen food and canned goods. People don't process food and they don't have need for that area, and they don't have any reason to keep the heat out of the house anymore. And of course [electric] stoves don't make that much heat. And everyone wants things more efficient now. They don't want to do things the hard way like they used to" (Griffin B170). "It's fast, a fast world. People just don't want to take the time to sit down and eat" (Atkins).

Although Harrison Countians are now less tied to the land than they once were, their rural, conservative values are still manifest. While summer kitchens, once the norm, were rendered obsolete by the introduction of electricity, the buildings which once housed these kitchens have not been demolished but rather transformed, with new uses, into workshops, storage sheds, and smokehouses. Some may even become guest houses (Milspaw 1983:80).

Does the summer kitchen have applications today? I believe that it does. With increased use of wood as a heating fuel in recent years, people should consider the entire complex of burning wood as a cooking fuel as well. Even those who continue to use electric stoves might well benefit from the example of the summer kitchen. After all, does anyone in Indiana really enjoy cooking indoors in July?

NOTES

[1] This annotated bibliography is indicative of the sparsity of published research on summer kitchens.

Bickel, George Robert. 1981. *Way Back When.* Corydon, Indiana: George R. Bickel. Anthology of articles originally published in *The Corydon Democrat.* One article is his reminiscences of his family's summer kitchen in the early 1900s.

Dawson, Roger R. 1969. Greenway Court and White Post: Virginia Home of Thomas, Lord Fairfax. *Pioneer America* 1(1):33-39. Description of elite homestead in 18th c. Va. Mentions "adjacent kitchen house nearby" (p. 37).

Franklin, Linda Campbell. 1976. *America in the Kitchen: From Hearth to Cookstove, an American Domestic History of Gadgets and Utensils Made or Used in America from 1700 to 1930.* Florence, Alabama: House of Collectibles. Illustrated encyclopedia of equipment used in both main and summer kitchens. Period line drawings.

Glass, Joseph W. 1986. *The Pennsylvania Culture Region: A View from the Barn.* Ann Arbor: UMI Research Press. Mentions in passing that summer kitchens would be oriented toward the main house and that their absence today is not proof that they never existed (Pp. 169-170).

Johnson, C. 1974. Missouri-French Houses: Some Relict Features of Early Settlement. *Pioneer America* 6(2):1-11. Proposes survivals of French colonial architecture in eastern Missouri. Kitchens were lean-to sheds or preferably separate structures (p. 9).

Jordan, Terry G. 1978. *Texas Log Buildings: A Folk Architecture.* Austin: University of Texas Press. Mentions in passing the existence of separate kitchens (Pp. 161, 173).

------- 1985. *American Log Buildings: An Old World Heritage.* Chapel Hill: University of North Carolina Press. Mentions Swedish precedent for free-standing kitchens (p. 75) which were formerly quite common in midland U.S. (p. 38).

Kauffman, Henry J. 1975. *The American Farmhouse.* New York: Hawthorn Books. Photographs, floor plans, descriptions of farmhouses and outbuildings including summerhouses (Pp. 119, 191-202, plate 9).

Long, Amos, Jr. 1965. Pennsylvania Summer-Houses and Summer-Kitchens. *Pennsylvania Folklife* 15(1): 11-19. Antecedent to following work.

_____. 1972. *The Pennsylvania German Family Farm: A Regional Architectural and Folk Cultural Study of an American Agricultural Community.* Breinigsville, Pa.: The Pennsylvania German Society. Definitive work on architecture and farm folklore of Pennsylvania Germans, all outbuildings including summer kitchens (Pp. 122-133).

Loomis, Ormond H. 1980. Tradition and the Individual Farmer: A Study of Folk Agricultural Practices in Southern Central Indiana. Ph.D. dissertation, Folklore Institute, Indiana University.   Mentions heritage of smaller domestic farm outbuildings but declares them beyond the scope of his study.

Milspaw, Yvonne J. 1983. Reshaping Tradition: Changes to Pennsylvania German Folk Houses. *Material Culture* 15(2): 67-84. Includes changes in physical structure, uses, and significance of smaller outbuildings, including summer kitchens (pp. 71, 80).

Ridlen, Susanne S. 1972. Bank Barns in Cass County, Indiana. *Pioneer America* 4(2):25-44. Incidental photograph of one summer kitchen with "traditional projecting roof" (p. 36).

Wacker, Peter O. 1971. Cultural and Commercial Regional Associations of Traditional Smoke-Houses in New Jersey. *Pioneer America* 3(2):25-34. Mentions (p. 25) that not every farmstead had a smokehouse because meat smoking could be done in the detached kitchen.

Wilhelm, Hubert G. H. 1971. German Settlement and Folk Building Practices in the Hill Country of Texas. *Pioneer America* 3(2):15-24. German settlers of Texas adapted their previous folk architecture to a hot climate, adding shed kitchens (p. 18).

2   Number in text reference is counter number in tape recorded interviews.

REFERENCES CITED

Bickel, George Robert
    1981 *Way Back When.* Corydon,IN: George R. Bickel.

Birmingham, Frederic A.
    1980 *Ball Corporation: The First Century.* Indianapolis: Curtis Publishing Company.

Bobbitt, Christopher K.
    1985   Central-Chimney Double-Pen Houses of Harrison County, Indiana. Typescript.

Leach, MacEdward, and Henry Glassie
    1968 *A Guide for Collectors of Oral Traditions and Folk Cultural Material in Pennsylvania.* Harrisburg: Pennsylvania Historical and Museum Commission.

Long, Amos Jr.
    1972 *The Pennsylvania German Family Farm: A Regional and Folk Cultural Study of an American Agricultural Community.* Breinigsville: The Pennsylvania German Society.

Milspaw, Yvonne S.
    1983   Reshaping Tradition: Changes to Pennsylvania German Farm Houses. *Material Culture* 15(2): 67-84.

INFORMANTS

Atkins   Dorothy K. Atkins, Depauw, IN 47115.
Bickel   George Bickel, Mulberry St., Corydon, IN 47112.
G. Bickel   Gertrude Bickel, Mulberry St., Corydon, IN 47112.
Duggins   Lloyd Duggins, Mauckport, IN 47142.
Flock   June Flock, Rt. 1, Ramsey, IN 47166.
P. Flock   Phil Flock, Rt. 3, Depauw, IN 47115.
Griffin   Fred Griffin, Walnut St., Corydon, IN 47112.
Lang   Gay Lang, Rt. 3, Depauw, IN 47115.

Leffler	Jim Leffler, Rt. 1, Ramsey, IN 47166.
Mauck	Mrs. Eugene Mauck, Dixie Rd., Corydon, IN 47112.
E. Turpin	Earl Turpin, Rt. 3, Depauw, IN 47115.
S. Turpin	Susan Bobbitt Turpin, Rt. 3, Depauw, IN 47115.
Wiseman	Geneva Wiseman, Woodland Ave., Corydon, IN 47112.

Figure 1. Jim Leffler's childhood homestead. The summer kitchen, built in the 1930s, has a poured concrete floor.

Figure 2. Leffler's summer kitchen as seen from the back yard. His grandmother lived in the rear room for many years.

Figure 3. Gay Lang's log double pen house, dating from the 1850s, and nearby summer kitchen built over the root cellar.

Figure 4. The offset gable-end door of the summer kitchen near Ramsey is unusual.

Nomadic Architecture: The River Houseboat in the Ohio Valley

JENS LUND

During the late 1940s, Kentucky artist and author Harlan Hubbard and his wife, Anna, floated down the Ohio and Mississippi Rivers from Cincinnati to New Orleans in a homemade houseboat. Their journey, which took nearly three years, was chronicled in Hubbard's book, *Shantyboat: A River Way of Life*, published in 1953. The book captured the public imagination and inspired children's writer Lois Lenski to research and write *Houseboat Girl* (1957) for her American Regional Series. At the time these two books appeared in bookstores and libraries across the country, the way of life which they celebrated had nearly come to extinction. From the early decades of the nineteenth century to the middle of the twentieth, thousands of Americans lived a nomadic life on homemade houseboats, sometimes floating from one landing to the next one downstream on a regular basis, sometimes merely mooring for years at the same landing, but avoiding both house and ground rent. The nomadic and semi-nomadic houseboat-dwelling population that lived on Midwestern rivers produced a characteristic architectural form, the "houseboat," "cabin boat," "camp boat," or "shantyboat."

There are very few floating houseboats of the original type on Midwestern rivers today, although a few beached examples still exist on riverbanks in various places. There are, however, probably still a few afloat here and there in the South, at least there were up to five years ago (Crawford 1984; Freeman 1977). Many itinerant houseboat folk were commercial fishermen and fish-marketers, at least seasonally, so it is not surprising that a few similar structures are still used as floating fish-markets (Comeaux 1978:86-87).

During the late 1970s, in the course of researching Lower Ohio Valley commercial fishing traditions, I was able to locate a few examples of river houseboats now dragged up on shore, and even a few still-afloat fish-markets, one of which had once been a real houseboat (Lund 1983:720-43). In the course of interviewing fishermen, marketers, and their descendants, I heard about houseboats again and again and was shown many a snapshot of a parents' or grandparents' houseboat or floating market (or combination of the two). In no case, did I ever hear a river person refer to one as a "shantyboat," although all were familiar with the term, which they considered derogatory (Bogardus 1959). The term, "houseboat," may be somewhat confusing, as it most often refers to elaborate craft used for recreation or as summer houses. Here the term, "houseboat," refers specifically to a type of locally built barge, with a cabin superstructure, commonly used by itinerant people on the rivers of the Midwest and South, and sometimes modified for use as a floating business, usually a fish-market or fish-house (Comeaux 1978:85-87).

The typical Midwestern and Southern river houseboat was strongly suggestive of the dimensions of today's single-wide mobile home. Aspects of it also strongly suggest the shotgun house, a structure often found in river communities and associated with Afro-American settlement (Vlach 1976). The most typical houseboat seems to have been one room wide and two or three rooms long, with the superstructure the same width as the hull, but several feet shorter at each end. It was single-story, with a flat or slightly arched roof. Early examples, seen in nineteenth century photographs, sometimes had a very low-pitched gable roof. Each end had a door and a small open deck, covered by the roof, which extended the full length of the hull. The decks were typically used as work-platforms and as places to land fish from the open johnboat or skiff that a fisherman also had. The roof typically extended the full length of the boat, thus supplying a porch roof at each end. Below the superstructure was a square scow-type barge with identical bow and stern. The superstructure was built of light framing timbers, such as two-by-fours, using balloon frame construction and sided with flush boards or occasionally clapboarding; the material used was often entirely or largely salvaged driftwood. Each room had one window on either side, so a two-room houseboat had four windows. The typical two-room houseboat had one room serving as a bedroom (often with an impractical large iron bed) and the other (with a central woodstove) serving as a combination kitchen, parlor, and work area.

The houseboat's form suggests the flatboat, which served as the chief form of transportation on the Ohio and Mississippi Rivers in much of the nineteenth century. The pioneer flatboat also consisted of a box-like superstructure mounted on a scow-end barge, with or without open deck space. Like the houseboat, the flatboat could only be navigated downstream, at least in common practice.

Historians of the Ohio Valley often divide the early settlement years into "eras," named after a preponderant form of river transportation in the period. "The flatboat era," 1800-1810, was succeeded by "the keelboat era," 1810 to 1830, which was, in turn succeeded by "the steamboat era," 1830 into the twentieth century (Ambler 1932; Baldwin 1941). The problem with this system is that these "eras" overlapped. In sheer numbers, flatboats continued to increase after the keelboat and steamboat made settlement and commerce more efficient. The flatboat was still the cheapest form of downstream (frontierward) transport, when speed was not important. One historian has suggested that during the prime of the "steamboat era," there were more flatboats on the rivers than ever, because they were still the cheapest and most practical way of floating goods and people downstream when time was not a factor, and when it was easy for a person to catch a steamer upstream after delivering goods and abandoning an inexpensive and easily replaced craft (Carmony 1964:306). In 1826 and 1833, travel writer Timothy Flint noted that the rivers were full of singular boats reflecting only the idiosyncracies of their builders (Flint 1826:14; 1833:160). The entire nineteenth century saw Midwestern rivers awash with various manifestations of the flatboat, and it is out of this enormous fleet of locally built boats that the houseboat and its itinerant population evolved.

Ease of building and economy of materials led to the use of large flatboats (also called "arks" or "barges") as the chief form of transportation on the Ohio and Mississippi Rivers by 1800. Their classic form is attributed to a Mr. Hodgen, who built them on the Juniata River, an Ohio River tributary in Pennsylvania, beginning in 1793. Some observers noted "Kentucky boat" and "New Orleans boat" subtypes. The former was crude and only partly enclosed. The latter was well-built and completely enclosed and could conceivably make it all the way from Pennsylvania to New Orleans (Carson 1920-21:27-30; Ashe 1808:75). But all flatboats had one serious disadvantage: they could only be navigated downstream. The invention of the keelboat about 1810 obviated this difficulty, but for many purposes a barge floating downstream was still practical and economical (Baldwin 1941:56-59).

It is worth taking a brief look at how flatboats were built, for purposes of comparison to later river craft. John Calvin Gilkeson, a professional flatboat-builder who built flatboats on Little Raccoon Creek (a Wabash tributary) in Parke County, Indiana, near Terre Haute during the mid-nineteenth century, left a detailed description of the process of building a Gilkeson flatboat. First, one laid the gunwales (their length ranged from twenty to over 100 feet (or 6.5 to 33 meters). Then the frame was added, consisting of cross-timbers (parallel to the ends) and streamers (parallel to the sides). He then pegged on the cross-planks from gunwale to gunwale to make the bottom, and then turned over the hull, so that the superstructure could be built. The result was a flat-bottomed double scow-end boat, with a perpendicularly-planked hull, on which stood a large cabin that served as its superstructure (Carmony 1964).

Scow-end boats became the predominant home-built boat type throughout the Midwest and South from frontier times to today (Comeaux 1978:84; Dablemont 1978; Marshall and Stanley 1978). Now they are called "johnboats" rather universally, but traditional names include "joeboat" and "dogboat." Small boats built by professional boatbuilders were usually skiffs (Comeaux 1978:76-82). All houseboats used by fishing families needed two or three auxiliary boats, usually johnboats or skiffs, and one was often mounted with an engine and could be used to push the houseboat short distances upstream or across the river. According to Lenski's description of Henry Story's houseboat, he also had a heavy wooden barge with an inboard engine covered with a small shed, which he used as a towboat and which he called his "cabin boat." His johnboat, powered with an outboard, was used for fishing (Lenski 1957:8).

The houseboat can be considered a variant of the flatboat, essentially a one-room-wide superstructure on a scow or barge. During the period when many nomadic people lived on houseboats, a typical example often had a long sweep, especially if it was being navigated. Early houseboats generally had slightly curved or shallow gabled roofs. Most of the later ones usually had completely flat roofs sealed with hot-mopped asphalt, which needed frequent repair.

Descriptions of early examples of houseboats are difficult to find. One that did turn up was a deed in the Recorder's Office of the Dearborn County Court in Lawrenceburg, Indiana, dated 1885: "House or shanty boat with hull twenty-eight feet [8.5m] long and ten feet [3m] wide, the said boat being painted blue" (Dearborn 1885:467). On the other hand, early picture books and articles on local scenery in river towns often included houseboat photos, with such romanticized captions as "A Home on the Rolling Deep" (Hodge 1902:51; Johnson 1905:81-91; 1906:148-59; Marshall 1900:102; Tait 1907:473-78; Theiss 1910:699-701; Vincennes 1916:42).

Interviews with river people in the Lower Ohio Valley during the late 1970s produced a number of descriptions of houseboats and floating markets that were consistent with the generalized type. Harold Weaver of Antioch Harbor, Tennessee, who grew up on a Lower Ohio River houseboat, and who fished commercially for most of his life near Cave-in-Rock, Illinois, grew up on a forty-seven-foot (15.3m) by eighteen-foot craft. His father was a Pentecostal preacher and fisherman, who used large fish-fries as a way of attracting people to "bush harbor" (brush arbor) camp meetings along the Ohio River (1978). Roy Lee Walls of Urbandale, who operated the Cairo Point Fish Market in Cairo for decades, once owned a three-room houseboat sixty feet (18.3m) long by fourteen feet (4.7m) wide. This is the largest example of which I have heard (1978). Curtis Lang, commercial fisherman and musseller of Metropolis, floated from Metropolis to Memphis during the 1950s on a twenty-four foot (7.3m) by nine-foot craft (1978).

Sandra Cunningham Hartlieb of Indianapolis described her fishing parents' houseboat at Owensboro, Kentucky, which they used from 1935 through 1945. It was thirty-six feet (11.1m) long and twelve feet (3.7m) wide, and had three rooms, with two-foot (61cm.) porches fore and aft. At one end was an adults' bedroom with a double bed, a chest of drawers, and a dresser. A room amidships held a child's bed, a wood stove, two chairs, and a corner closet. At the other end was a kitchen, containing a wood stove (with oven), a table and three chairs, a cupboard, a work table, and an icebox. It had a slightly curved roof, doors in both ends, and six windows, and was plank-sided and painted white (Hartlieb 1980; Lund 1983:724). (See Figures 4 and 5)

During the 1950s most of the surviving houseboats in the Ohio Valley were hauled up on land. There most were either abandoned or disassembled, but a few continued to be used as dwellings, usually by former river folk. Diligent searching over a two-year period led to only two examples. One was a forty-four-foot (13.4m) by fourteen-foot (4.7m) three-room houseboat still owned by Joe "Bunk" Owens of Metropolis and stranded in his back yard near the riverfront. It was six feet (182cm) from deck to ceiling, and had two three-foot (91.5cm) porches, one of which was only twelve feet (3.66m) wide, because part of it was enclosed to make a six-foot (183cm) square storage closet. The Owens houseboat has a flat roof, a door in each end, and was sided with clapboards, painted white. (See Figures 7 and 8)

The other example found was a twelve-foot (3.7m) by eighteen-foot (5.5m) one-room houseboat, with a six-foot-three-inch (191cm) ceiling, which serves as a gatehouse and caretaker's cabin for Ralph Carver, watchman for the Forrest Shelton Carver Marina on the Clark River in Woodland, Kentucky, just east of Paducah. In 1978, Carver still lived in it year-round. He had built it in 1963, and hauled it ashore in 1977 (Carver 1978). All its lumber, except ceiling and floor, was driftwood, and its barge, on which it still stood, consisted merely of a platform enclosing watertight steel drums. It also had a flat roof, doors in both ends, and was sided with corrugated sheet-metal roofing.

Some houseboat-like structures have been built in recent years as floating markets or as enclosed fish docks, where fish were landed and dressed, but not sold. An interesting case is the Lueke Fish Market on the Wabash River in Maunie, Illinois, near New Harmony, Indiana. It consists of two structures, built by Fred and Dennis Lueke in the mid-1970s, each about sixty feet (18m) long and fifteen feet (4.5m) wide. They are tied parallel to the shore and float on steel drums. One is full of deep freezers, and is used primarily for storing frozen fish. The other contains two hand-winch-operated live-baskets, raised and lowered through rectangular holes in the deck. It also has a large workbench used for dressing fish and fitted with power tools for scaling, skinning, and scoring. A door opens directly out onto the river, for loading fish. A door at the upstream end leads to the other market and one at the downstream end leads to a small, open boat dock. A door on the bank side is connected to land by a long gangplank. The freezer market is accessible only through the other market, as it has only one door, in its downstream end, connected to the other market with a short gangplank. Lueke's floating markets are balloon-framed with two-by-fours, and covered with prefabricated plastic sheet siding.

An older floating market is the Cave-in-Rock Fish Market, just outside the entrance to Cave-in-Rock State Park and close to a ferry landing, convenient to heavy tourist traffic. It consists of seven docks, all supported by watertight steel drums. Its open docks also serve as a marina and as a marine filling station. The enclosed portion is the market proper. It is about fifty-five feet (15m) long by twenty feet (6m) wide. In it are a large retailing area with freezers, dressing tables, an old iron bathtub used for rinsing fish, scales, and counters. In the far end is an insulated windowless room loaded with several hundred pounds of crushed ice. It serves as a walk-in icebox. The market is connected by cable to an old farm-tractor ashore. When the water level rises, the marketer starts up the tractor and pulls the market further ashore, and when the level lowers, he lets it back down again. The Cave-in-Rock Market was built in 1955 by fish-marketer Bob Garland, and it has changed hands at least five times (Patton 1978).

Smaller enclosed floating fish-docks are found here and there in the Lower Ohio Valley. A small unique example built by Jack Emory floats in the Little Wabash at Carmi, Illinois. At the mouth of Bonpas Creek, where it joins the Wabash at Grayville, Illinois, there are seven small markets, all about eight-by-ten feet (2.4x3m). Five are enclosed, and four have small porched decks. All but one have winch-powered live-boxes. One built in 1976 by the Young Brothers Fish Market is wired for electricity and aluminum-sided. Fisherman Orval Loven of Grayville built three of them, the last in 1978. First he built the platform of wooden planks, with rectangular holes in both ends to accommodate live-boxes. Then he built the cabin frame of two-by-fours. With his welding outfit, he fashioned two steel winches to raise and lower the live-boxes. After that, the structure was roofed with plywood and asphalt, and sided with prefabricated plastic siding, and hauled to the river (about a mile [1.6km]), by trailer. On the bank, he turned it on its side and mounted the platform with six drums. He then righted it and slipped into the Wabash, pulling it by rope into the mouth of Bonpas Creek. He mounted it with a work table and a drained dressing table, and finally installed two live-boxes of wire and wood-slats (Loven 1977). (See Figures 9 and 10)

As late as the early 1980s, a traditional houseboat served as a fish market and seasonal home for Howard Durham at Old Shawneetown, below the Illinois State Route 13 bridge to Kentucky, and dwarfed by the enormous levee that cuts off Old Shawneetown from the Ohio River. The barge, long-since rotted away, had been replaced by a dock held up by watertight fifty-five-gallon drums. Originally it had belonged to the Jimmy Yakely family, who still live in Old Shawnee-town, and it had been tied up at Wabash Island, a delta at the confluence of the Wabash and Ohio, where Illinois, Indiana, and Kentucky join (Durham 1977). The Durham market had two rooms, one with freezers, tables, and scales, and the other a living room with easy chairs, a dining room table, a television set, and a folding bed. (See Figure 6)

The Yakely/Durham houseboat-fish market represents the transition of the houseboat form from dwelling to place of business. Many river fishing families operated floating markets permanently moored where a river town adjoined a levee. Such markets were often similar in form and structure to houseboats, but not used as dwellings. Cave-in-Rock, Golconda, and Old Shawneetown, Illinois, and Paducah and Smithland, Kentucky, were places which had several such floating markets for long, continuous periods. Floating markets often had live-boxes which could be raised and lowered through a hole in the deck by means of a winch. The Cox family market and houseboat at Golconda, also had a catwalk extending about a foot or two over the water and running the entire length of the boat (Cox 1978; Lund 1983:728). (See Figures 2 and 3)

Understanding the river houseboat necessitates familiarity with the nomadic houseboat subculture. This transient population began some time in the early nineteenth century and persisted as late as the mid-1950s, when regulations pertaining to waste disposal, craft safety, and tie-up began to be enforced (Comeaux 1978:87). The larger barge trains used after the building of the high lift dam system also produced wakes that were so strong as to make houseboat life uncomfortable, unsafe, and impractical, and by then the competition of industrial and construction wage-labor was too great for formerly self-sufficient houseboat folk to ignore. Houseboaters were most numerous during the Great Depression, and during the late 1930s sociologist Ernest Theodore Hiller conducted a major field study of houseboaters tied up in Illinois waters (Hiller 1939).

Houseboat folk were engaged in many different livelihoods, and most of them regularly changed activities, depending on what resources and opportunities were available. Many were fishing families, but there were probably more sedentary fishing families living on the river's banks than there were nomadic fishermen (Comeaux 1978:86). Despite this, many of the surviving commercial fishermen in the Lower Ohio Valley in the 1970s grew up in houseboat families. The negative stereotype of the "river rat" (an epithet often applied to houseboat folk by land-dwellers) was equivalent to "poor white trash," but most houseboat folk were industrious and self-reliant, though poor (Lenski 1957:2, 110-12, 126-27; Johnson 1906:262). Several former house-boaters did say, however, that certain urban concentrations of moored houseboats, such as the one on Pigeon Creek in Evansville, Indiana, had reputations for crime and violence.

During the nineteenth and early twentieth centuries, many books and articles were written about the great rivers of the Midwest, parti-cularly the Ohio. The authors were often fascinated by the lives of nomadic river folk and paid a great deal of attention to these people

(Jakle 1977). Reuben Gold Thwaites, writing in the 1890s noted that land-dwellers considered them larcenous, but he called them "a race of picturesque philosophers" and "followers of the apostle's calling." He noted their colorful speech, their occupation as fishermen, and their folktales which, "told with an honest-like open-faced sobriety, would do credit to a Munchausen." He also noted their complaints of pollution's harmful effects upon their livelihoods (1897: 107,259). In 1906, Clifton Johnson described them thus:

> Of all the dwellers in the valley of the great river,
> those who live in the houseboats have, by far, the most
> picturesque environment. You find them everywhere,
> from St. Paul to New Orleans, and not only on the main
> river, but on all the larger tributaries. There are many
> thousands of these water-gypsies, in all. [1906:251]

He described the diversity of their architecture, the circumstances of poverty or disaster that periodically swelled their ranks, and their varied occupations, including driftwood-gathering, peddling, stove-wood-sawing, preaching, shake-splitting, and, of course, fishing, and he found Cairo, Illinois, to be a concentration of them (1906:251-65). Most writers were relatively kind in their description of the houseboat folk, but a few emphasized the negative "river rat" stereotype (Marshall 1900; Tait 1907). The United States Commission on Fish and Fisheries also took notice of these people and their craft, counting 153 house-boats engaged in commercial fishing in Illinois, Indiana, and Kentucky in 1894, 220 in 1899, but only 84 in 1922. Most were tied up in Kentucky (Smith 1898:518,524; Townsend 1902:673,679,685; Sette 1925:222,227,237).

In 1913, Raymond S. Spears actually wrote an instruction book on how to become a houseboater! It was directed primarily at sportsmen and alienated city people who desired to establish an independent, nomadic life. Spears gave complete and detailed plans for building and equipping a houseboat. He seems to have derived his plans from observing traditional houseboats and building them himself. Spears' houseboat was twenty-eight feet, eight inches [8.74m] long, nine feet [2.74m] wide, and thirty inches [76cm] deep in the hold. Its cabin was eighteen feet ten inches [5.74m] long, eight feet six inches [2.59m] wide, and six feet, five inches [1.96m] between floor and carlins (rafters), allowing two decks, five feet, four inches [163cm] forward, and four feet, four inches [132cm] aft. For the hull, he recommended heavy hemlock and oak planking (1913:57-65).

Spears' directions are detailed and complex and can be summarized as follows: The hull is constructed first, and built upside down. First the gunwales are laid, and then the bumpers are laid and spiked on, after which the sides and then the ends are planked. Then the bottom is planked perpendicular to the sides, after which inside and outside stringers are attached. The hull is then turned over, which takes four or five men. Timberheads for mooring are bolted on, fore and aft. Then the planking of the fore and aft decks are nailed on. At that point the builder decides whether or not to have a hold, and if he decides to have one, he nails the floor of the cabin at the same height as the decks, supported by rafters. If not, the floor is nailed directly on to the inside stringers (1913:61-70). (See Figure 1)

The builder then builds the cabin frame, first the corner uprights and then the struts. Then the carlins (roof rafters) are nailed in place, and the door-frames are put in the two ends of the cabin, and the cabin is boarded up, leaving spaces for the doors and windows, where they are desired. He recommends using store-bought casings and frames for the windows. The doors and windows are hung, and the roof is first planked, then covered with canvas and roofing paper. Finally, details are completed, such as a hole for the stovepipe, an interior partition (making it a two-room cabin), interior mouldings, door-jambs, a trap-door down into the hold, and so on. The boat, which has been built on the riverbank, is then slid down into the river on skids, and finally fitted and furnished (1913:70-75).

The author also describes how to make a lighter and narrower model, and notes that a single person could do quite well by merely decking and cabining over a skiff or scow (1913:75-80). He also suggests that a cabin could be built on a log raft (81-83).

Spears suggests that the aspiring nomad pursue hunting, trapping, driftwood-gathering, photography, or fishing (1913:48-136,239-41). He had floated all the way from the Ohio to New Orleans supporting himself by peddling fish, and he wrote articles on the subject for publications such as *Hunter-Trader-Trapper* and the *Saturday Evening Post* (1922, 1931). Another outdoor writer, Walter S. Chansler, writing in 1922, described the practice of setting out by houseboat from a Midwestern riverbank and floating all the way to New Orleans by peddling fish. Chansler was fascinated by the sheer variety of homemade boats found in one small area of the Lower Wabash, and provided photographs and descriptions of several houseboats there (1922:10-11,15).

The most prolific author on the subject was local-color fiction and travel writer Ben Lucien Burman (1929, 1933, 1938a, 1938b, 1949, 1951, 1953, 1973). He gathered material for his books while traveling as a tramp along the Ohio and Mississippi Rivers, toting a mandolin, on which he played folk melodies to allay people's fears that he was a Revenue Agent (1973:68). During the early 1930s, many houseboaters practiced moonshining, a pursuit which Burman heartily defended (Ibid:133). Burman's interest in folk culture led him to describe such activities as basketmaking, boatbuilding, fishing, hunting, trapping, root-and herb-gathering, and willow-furniture-making. He also described varieties of religious worship among houseboat folk, and emphasized the people's close familial and clan ties.

The most detailed and reliable account of houseboat life is Ernest Theodore Hiller's study, based on fieldwork on the Ohio River and the Illinois River-Mississippi River confluence. Hiller estimated that in 1935, there were 50,000 houseboat folk in the entire Greater Mississippi-Ohio Basin (1939:14). He found them industrious but poor, and described their "river self-help occupations," the same as those listed above, with the addition of "musselling"—fishing for freshwater mussels for their pearls and mother-of-pearl—quilting, woodcarving, and chair-bottoming. Most of Hiller's informants were Southerners, and he noted the similarity of their lives to lives on the Southern frontier (Ibid:33-65,129-32).

> The free squatting and floating privileges and the
> pursuits of the self-help opportunities supplied by
> the stream are survivals of the frontier traditions,
> rather than unique adjustments induced by the depression.
> [1939:133]

> The people of the river environs are seen to have a like
> background of skills and occupational attitudes which,
> since pioneer days, have enabled and predisposed them to
> use the opportunities supplied by the river. [1939:46-47]

There is also some evidence that nomadic fishermen specialized in the fabrication of gear for use by other river people. James "Harry" Linville (1980), of New Harmony, Indiana, remembered a houseboat family who floated down the Wabash seasonally preparing rived wooden hoops for hoop-nets, which they sold to other fishing families.

Hiller found that many houseboat folk had once been tenant farmers forced off the land by hard times (1939:211-12). Their larcenous reputation he attributed to the traditional habit of foraging for available resources, such as game or timber, stray chickens or standing green corn (Ibid:47,126). Although Hiller was not explicit about it, his research, others' articles, and my own interviews suggest that almost all houseboat folk in the Midwest were white. Despite this, many of their fish-buying customers were black (Hubbard 1977:72;

Walls 1978). There were, however, black houseboaters in the South (Freeman 1977).

Typically, a houseboat would be built in the Midwest or Upper South and, over a period of a few years, it would be floated downstream, perhaps all the way to New Orleans. Occasionally boats could be moved upstream by hitching a ride with a steamboat. Some houseboaters also tied ropes to trees and hand-pulled their houseboat upstream for relatively short distances—a technique called "pardelling" or "cordelling" (Tillson 1919:69; Walls 1978). Once powered skiffs and johnboats were available to houseboaters, they could be used to push a houseboat upstream, but this would be impractical and uneconomical for more than a few miles at a time.

One excellent source of information on houseboat life, still unpublished, is the collection of photographs made by former houseboater Maggie Lee Sayre on the Ohio and Tennessee Rivers from 1939 through 1965. Ms. Sayre, who was born on the river near Paducah, Kentucky, and now lives in Parsons, Tennessee, photographed hundreds of scenes of houseboat life. Many of her photographs were recently toured by the Tennessee Folklore Society in the exhibition, "A Pictorial Narrative of River Life," which is now permanently located at the Tennesse River Folklife Center in Eva, Tennessee. The folklorist who discovered her work, Tom Rankin, is presently compiling a book-length anthology of Ms. Sayre's work, slated for publication in 1990 (Rankin and Bobby Fulcher: Personal communications).

The twilight years of houseboating, the 1950s, were described by Harlan Hubbard in his travel account, *Shantyboat: A River Way of Life*, and by Lois Lenski in her ethnographic children's book, *Houseboat Girl*. The Hubbards, floating in their own houseboat from Cincinnati to New Orleans, supplied themselves with river fish, and also learned to build johnboats, a skill they considered necessary for any river-dweller (1977:47-49). They also noted that houseboat folk often planted squatter gardens on bottomland near where they were tied up (Ibid:56-57). Lenski spent time with the Henry and Lou Story family of Metropolis, Illinois, visiting them at various places along the river, while they floated from Metropolis to Memphis, Tennessee. She renamed them the Fosters, and made their daughter Irene into the heroine-protagonist Patsy Foster. Her descriptions are consistent with those above, emphasizing in particular the importance of close family ties (Ibid:2, 110-12, 126-27). The negative stereotype was depicted in a confrontation between "Patsy" and some land-dwellers who harassed her by calling her a "river rat" (Ibid:81). Lenski also noted that both women and girls fished alongside men.

By the end of the 1950s, houseboat folk had practically disappeared from most rivers, except for a few cutoffs and sloughs, in most of the Deep South. Louisiana seemed to have had more later, and they were described as numerous there in the 1950s (Knipmeyer 1956:130-32). "Cabin boats" was the prevailing name in Louisiana. Geographer Malcolm Comeaux found a few survivors in the Midwest and Louisiana in the early 1970s (1972: 21-22,25-26,53; 1978:85-87; 1985:170-72). *Mother Earth News* reported on one in a Louisiana bayou in 1982, and the Louisville *Courier-Journal* described one on the Kentucky River near Frankfort as late as 1984 (Carpenter 1982; Crawford 1984).

Most houseboats were gone after the 1950s, but some of the houseboat folk who settled on land continued to work the river as seasonal fishermen, trappers, mussellers, and salvagers. Most of the fishing families on the river in the 1970s were of houseboater background, and some seem to have maintained the tradition of the riverman as raconteur. Hardin Dome Wentworth of Henderson, Kentucky, told two lengthy *Märchen* to a visiting University of Evansville student in 1976 (Lacy 1977; Lund 1983: 815-17). Harold Weaver, an Ohio River fisherman from the Cave-in-Rock, Illinois, area, who later retired to Antioch Harbor, Tennessee, on Kentucky Lake, recited dozens of *Schwanken* and tall tales, sang several ballads, and told scores of jokes (Lund 1983:808-13). Roy Lee Walls of Urbandale, Illinois, also sang ballads and told numerous tales, including an amusing family saga about two houseboater relatives stealing a cook stove with a pot of beans on it from a farmer's cabin (Lund 1983:772-73, Walls 1978).

The age of the river houseboat is now almost forty years past. The floating market is practically gone, too, for pollution and siltation have destroyed most of the river fish resource. Catfish, the mainstay of today's river fishery, is now mostly farm-raised in the Deep South. Howard Durham even sold frozen farm-raised "fiddlers" (baby channel catfish) from his Old Shawneetown market in 1979.

The river houseboat was never an attractive or elegant piece of folk architecture. Most examples were probably considered eyesores by land-dwellers. But the houseboat was indispensable to a little-known way of life that persisted on North American rivers for almost 150 years. No one knows how many nomadic river folk lived on the Midwestern and Southern rivers from the 1820s through the 1950s, but the total was probably in the hundreds of thousands. Some of them and their descendants continued to fish for a few decades afterwards, as a very few still do today. Scale and building materials have changed, but Orval Loven's fish-dock on Bonpas Creek, built in

1978, still follows the form of the river flatboats of the early nineteenth century. The river houseboat was cheap, practical, easy to build, and perfectly suited for a nomadic way of life.

REFERENCES CITED

Ambler, Charles Henry
  1932 *A History of Transportation in the Ohio Valley.* Glendale, CA.: Arthur H. Clark.
Ashe, Thomas
  1808 *Travels in America Performed in 1806 For the Purpose of Exploring the Rivers Alleghany, Monongahela, Ohio, and Mississippi.* London: R. Phillips.
Baldwin, Leland P.
  1941 *The Keelboat Age on Western Waters.* Pittsburgh: University of Pittsburgh Press.
Bogardus, Carl R.
  1959 *Shantyboat.* Austin, IN.: Muscatatuck Press.
Burman, Ben Lucien
  1929 *Mississippi.* New York: Farrar and Rinehart.
  1933 *Steamboat 'Round the Bend.* New York: Grosset and Dunlap.
  1938a *Big River to Cross: Mississippi Life Today.* New York: John Day Co.
  1938b *Blow For a Landing.* New York: John Day Co.
  1949 *Everywhere I Roam.* Garden City, NY.: Doubleday and Co.
  1951 *Children of Noah: Glimpses of an Unknown America.* New York: Julian Meissner, Inc.
  1953 *The Four Lives of Mundy Tolliver.* New York: Julian Meissner, Inc.
  1973 *Look Down That Winding River: An Informal Profile of the Mississippi.* New York: Taplinger Publishing Co.
Carmony, Donald F. ed.
  1964 Flatboat Building on Little Raccoon Creek, Parke County, Indiana. From a manuscript by John Calvin Gilkeson. Contributed and illustrated by Sam K. Swope. *Indiana Magazine of History* 60: 305-322.
Carpenter, Gwen
  1982 A Barge on the Bayou. *Mother Earth News* 76, July-August. Pp. 30-32.
Carson, W. Wallace
  1920-1921 Transportation and Traffic of the Ohio and Mississippi Before the Steamboat. *Mississippi Valley Historical Review* 7: 26-38.
Carver, Ralph
  1978 Notes to interview by Jens Lund, Woodland, Paducah, KY. August 2.
Chansler, Walter S.
  1921 Water-craft of the Lower Wabash. *Fur News and Outdoor World* 34, September. Pp. 10-11, 15.
Childs, Marquis
  1932 River Town. *Harper's* 165, November: 710-718.
Comeaux, Malcolm L.
  1972 Atchafalaya Swamp Life: Settlement and Folk Occupations. *Geoscience and Man 2.* Baton Rouge: Louisiana State University, School of Geoscience, 1972.
  1978 Origin and Evolution of Mississippi River Fishing Craft. *Pioneer America* 10: 72-97.

1985 Folk Boats of Louisiana. In *Louisiana Folklife: A Guide to the State*. Ed. Nicholas R. Spitzer. Baton Rouge: Louisiana Folklife Program, Office of Cultural Development, Department of Culture, Recreation, and Tourism. Pp. 161-178.

Cox, Bob
1978 Notes to interview by Jens Lund, Golconda, IL. July 3.

Crawford, Byron
1984 Floating home: Conways buoyed by life on the river. Louisville (KY.) *Courier-Journal*, May 5, P. 2.

Dablemont, Larry
1978 *The Authentic American Johnboat: How to Build It, How to Use It*. New York: David McKay Co.

Dearborn County [IN.] Recorder's Office
1885 Deed of George Eikler, November 21. Lawrenceburg, Indiana. Book 42. P. 467.

Durham, Howard
1977 Notes to interview by Jens Lund, Old Shawneetown, IL., April 22.

Flint, Timothy F.
1826 *Recollections of the Last Ten Years Passed in Occasional Residencies and Journeyings in the Valley of the Mississippi from Pittsburgh and the Missouri to the Gulf of Mexico and from Florida*. Boston: Cummings, Hilliard, and Co.
1833 *The History and Geography of the Mississippi Valley to Which is Appended a Condensed Physical Geography of the Atlantic United States and the Whole American Continent*. Cincinnati: E.H. Flint and Carter, Hendee, and Co.

Freeman, Roland
1977 Folkroots: Images of Mississippi Black Folklife (1974- 1976). In *Long Journey Home: Folklife in the South*. Ed. Allen Tullos. Southern Exposure 5. Chapel Hill, NC Southern Exposure, 1977: 29-35.

Hartlieb, Sandra Cunningham
1980 Houseboat Living: A Folklife Study. Unpublished paper. Indiana University--Purdue University, Indianapolis.

Hiller, Ernest Theodore
1939 Houseboat and River Bottoms People: A Study of 683 Households in Sample Locations Adjacent to the Ohio and Mississippi Rivers. *Illinois Studies in the Social Sciences* 24: 3-146.

Hodge, J.P.
1902 *Vincennes in Picture and Story: A History of the Old Town, Appearance of the New*. Vincennes: Privately Printed.

Hubbard, Harlan
1977 *Shantyboat: A River Way of Life*. Revised Edition. Lexington: University Press of Kentucky. (Orig. pub. 1953).

Jakle, John
1977 *Images of the Ohio Valley: A Historical Geography of Travel, 1740 to 1860*. New York: Oxford University Press.

Johnson, Clifton
1905 Houseboat Life on the Mississippi. *Outing Magazine* 46, April. Pp. 81-91.
1906 *Highways and Byways of the Mississippi Valley*. New York: Macmillan.

Knipmeyer, William B.
1956 Settlement Succession in Eastern French Louisiana. Unpublished doctoral dissertation, Louisiana State University.

Lacy, Mac
1977 An Afternoon With Hardin Dome Wentworth: A Study of a Southern Indiana Riverman. Unpublished paper. University of Evansville.

Lang, Curtis
    1978 Taped interview by Jens Lund, Metropolis, IL. August 3.
Lenski, Lois
    1957 *Houseboat Girl*. Philadelphia: J.B. Lippincott Co.
Linville, James "Harry"
    1980 New Harmony Remembers. New Harmony (IN.) *Times*. August 28. P. 4.
Loven, Orval
    1977 Taped interview by Jens Lund, Grayville, IL. October 23.
Lund, Jens
    1983 Fishing as a Folk Occupation in the Lower Ohio Valley. 2 vols. Unpublished
        doctoral dissertation. Indiana University.
Marshall, Dexter
    1900 The River People. *Scribner's Magazine* 28, July. Pp. 101-111.
Marshall, Howard Wight and David H. Stanley
    1978 Homemade Boats in South Georgia. *Mississippi Folklore Register* 12: 75-94.
Patton, Harold
    1978 Taped interview by Jens Lund, Boyd's Addition-Cedar Point, Cave-in-Rock,
        IL. July 4.
Sette, Oscar
    1925 Fishing Industries of the United States, 1923 [actually 1922]. U.S. Commis-
        sioner of Fisheries. *Report for 1924: Appendix 4*. Pp. 141-359.
Smith, Hugh M.
    1898 Statistics of the Fisheries of the Interior Waters of the United States [1894].
        U.S. Commission of Fish and Fisheries. *Report of the Commissioner for 1896*,
        Part 22: Appendix 11. Pp. 489-574.
Spears, Raymond S.
    1913 *The Cabin Boat Primer*. Columbus, OH.: A.R. Harding Co.
    1922 Commercial Fishing. *Hunter-Trader-Trapper* 44, July. Pp. 64-65.
    1931 Vagabond Specialists of the Open Country. *Saturday Evening Post* 204,
        November 14. Pp. 28,86,89-90.
Tait, John Leisk
    1907 Shanty-boat Folks. *The World To-Day* 12, May: 473-478.
Theiss, Mary and Lewis
    1910 Homes Without Ground Rent. *Good Housekeeping Magazine* 50, June:
        699-701.
Thwaites, Reuben Gold
    1897 *Afloat on the Ohio*. Chicago: Way and Williams.
Tillson, Christiana Holmes
    1919 *A Woman's Story of Pioneer Illinois*. Ed. Milo Milton Quaife. Chicago: The
        Lakeside Press and R.R. Donnelly.
Townsend, C.H.
    1902 Statistics of the Fisheries of the Mississippi River and Its Tributaries [1899].
        U.S. Commission of Fish and Fisheries. *Report of the Commissioner for 1901*,
        Part 27: 659-740.
Vincennes Fortnightly Club
    1916 *Vincennes, 1702--1816--1916: Views of Vincennes*. Vincennes, IN.: The Western
        Sun.
Vlach, John Michael
    1976 The Shotgun House: An African Cultural Legacy (Part 1). *Pioneer America*
        8:36-56. (Part 2) 8:57-70.
Walls, Roy Lee
    1978 Taped interview by Jens Lund, Urbandale, Cairo, IL. July 14.

Weaver, Harold
    1978 Taped interview by Jens Lund, Antioch Harbor, Kentucky Lake, Springville, TN. July 13.

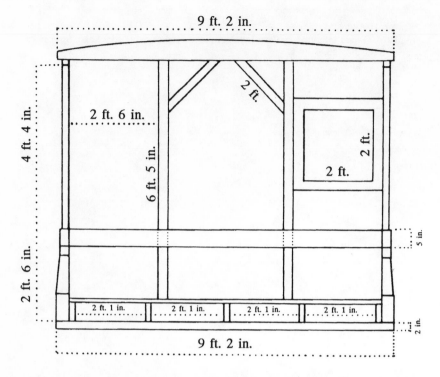

Diagram of End of Houseboat

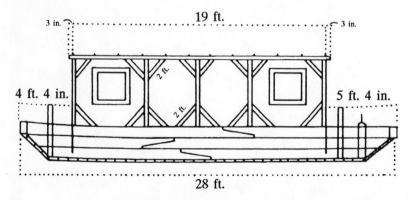

Diagram of Side of Houseboat

Figure 1. Redrawn from *The Cabin Boat Primer* (Spears 1913).

Figure 2. Cox family houseboat, ca. 1880, Wabash River, near New Harmony, Indiana. (Photo courtesy Bob Cox).

Figure 3. Bill Cox family houseboat and fish-market (Bob Cox foreground). Ohio River, near Golconda, Illinois, ca. 1950. (Photo courtesy Bob Cox).

Figure 4. Cunningham family houseboat on bank of the Ohio River, near Owensboro, Kentucky, ca. 1950. (Photo courtesy Sandra Cunningham Hartlieb).

CUNNINGHAM HOUSEBOAT INTERIOR

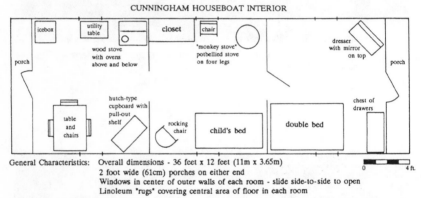

General Characteristics: Overall dimensions - 36 feet x 12 feet (11m x 3.65m)
2 foot wide (61cm) porches on either end
Windows in center of outer walls of each room - slide side-to-side to open
Linoleum "rugs" covering central area of floor in each room

Figure 5. Cunningham family houseboat, ca. 1950, Owensboro, Kentucky. From drawing by Sandra Cunningham Hartlieb, Indianapolis, Indiana.

Figure 6. Former Yakely family houseboat, now Howard Durham's Fish Market, Ohio River, Old Shawneetown, Illinois, 1977. (Photo by Jens Lund).

Figure 7. Joe "Bunk" Owens family houseboat, 1978, Metropolis, Illinois. (Photo by Jens Lund).

Joe "Bunk" Owens Family Houseboat
Metropolis, Illinois 1978

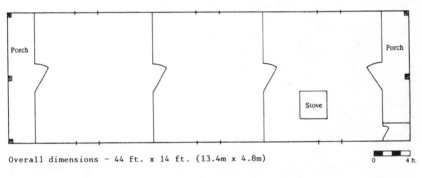

Overall dimensions – 44 ft. x 14 ft. (13.4m x 4.8m)

Floor Plan

Figure 8. Joe "Bunk" Owens family houseboat, 1978, Metropolis, Illinois.

Figure 9. Fish dock built by Orval Loven, 1978, Bonpas Creek-Wabash River confluence, Grayville, Illinois. (Photo by Jens Lund).

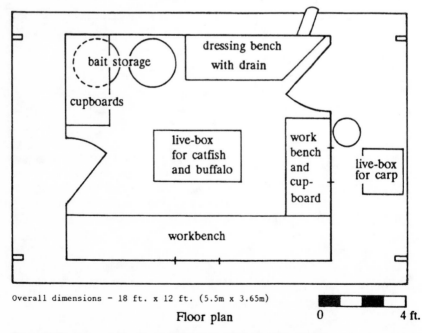

Overall dimensions - 18 ft. x 12 ft. (5.5m x 3.65m)

Floor plan   0   4 ft.

Figure 10. Floorplan of Orval Loven's fish dock, 1979, Grayville, Illinois.

Puyallup Valley Hop Kilns:
Preliminary Findings

PHYLLIS A. HARRISON

Since the 1860s, Washington State has been one of the nation's leading producers of hops, a flavoring agent used in the brewing of beer. The large curing sheds or kilns used to dry the hops are landmarks in hop producing areas, and the early wooden structures provide particularly distinctive markers on the landscape. The following observations on hop kilns and hop production in the Puyallup Valley of western Washington constitute a preliminary investigation into the kilns, the work and social activities associated with them, and the emotional and cultural significance of the kilns for current Puyallup Valley residents.

Hop production began in western Washington when pioneer Jacob Meeker brought the crop to the Puyallup Valley in 1865. Hop production spread quickly to other portions of western Washington, particularly to the Boistfort Valley in Lewis County, to Snohomish and Snoqualmie in King County, and to the Skagit Valley in Skagit County. In the 1880s, with the onset of irrigation in central Washington, hop production began in the Yakima Valley where it increased steadily in subsequent decades. By 1940, central Washington had taken over as the state's main producer. Common to hop production throughout the state was the curing shed, basically a wooden box with a ground floor furnace, an elevated drying floor, a cupola for ventilation, and an attached baling area. The early kilns were wooden, either log or frame. Contemporary kilns in central Washington follow the same basic model, though made of metal and using conveyor belts for

263

moving the hop cones from truck to drying room to baler (Lindeman and Williams 1985:29).

Hop production in the Puyallup Valley began in 1865 when Jacob Meeker obtained a few roots from a brewer in Olympia. Although the elder Meeker died before he could see the full success of his experiment, his son Ezra Meeker continued hop production, earning a reputation as the state's leading producer of and expert on hop cultivation; at one time, he devoted some five hundred acres to the vines. From the late 1860s to 1891, hops comprised the primary commercial crop of the valley. In the mid-1880s, cultivators were achieving 3000 pounds per acre and Puyallup Valley hops were being shipped all over the world. During this period, the crop is estimated to have brought some twenty million dollars into the valley. In 1891, a combination of plant lice and mold devastated the hop fields in western Washington. The remedy, brought to Washington from London by another Meeker son, Fred, required such quantities of whale oil soap and quassia wood chips as to prove nearly as fatal to the crop as the original pests (Lingreen and Tiller 1981:13). By 1895, crop production was still faltering in the Puyallup fields. A generation later, Prohibition added to the difficulties of hop growers by decreasing the demand for what had become a much more difficult and costly crop. Although hop farming continued on a much reduced scale as late as the 1960s, it never regained its earlier place of prominence in the economy of the valley. Area farmers responded by diversifying their crops, adding berries in the early 1900s, rhubarb and bulbs (tulip and daffodil) in the 1920s, and Christmas tree farms in the 1960s.

Jacob Meeker cured his first harvest of hops in the loft over his living room, and most of the earliest hop crops were cured in the producer's home. By the late 1860s, due in part to the research and experimentation of the Meekers, specialized curing sheds or kilns came into use, and by the 1870s the typical hop kiln was a familiar sight in the valley. The general model for a Puyallup Valley kiln is "approximately twenty-four feet square with interior walls of lath and plaster, normally suspended on stone foundation blocks several inches off the ground with drying rooms seventeen feet above the kiln floor and built with floors of slats laid one and a half inches apart" (Graham 1978:7). Ezra Meeker's 1883 publication, *Hop Culture in the United States*, contains fairly specific guidelines for the overall dimensions of the kilns, and most Puyallup Valley kilns fall easily within his guidelines. Still, by the time Meeker's work appeared, many kilns had been in operation for over a generation in the valley, and those built after 1883 suggest that construction details were determined as much by a grower and his neighbors as by Meeker's treatise as no two seem to follow precisely the same plan. A forty acre farm generally possessed two kilns separated by a single baling room, all housed under one roof. (See Fig. 1)

In 1884, while the Meeker family had the most notable hop farms in the valley, some twenty-seven other farmers had smaller hop operations, and their kilns literally dotted the valley (Adventures 1987:31). As late as the 1940s many of the kilns remained, the large structures proving fairly adaptable to crops such as bulbs. "I could see ten from where we stand now," said Louise Koehler-Anderson in a recent interview. In 1978, six of the kilns remained; in 1988 the number is down to four.

One of the four is the Woolrey-Koehler kiln, remarkable for being one of the oldest kilns in the valley and for the use of both log and frame construction. The kiln itself was built in two stages. Jacob Woolrey acquired his farm in the 1860s and by 1869 had constructed one log kiln for curing hops. The charred cedar logs, some as large as thirty inches in diameter, are square notched and appear to lack any stone foundation. The kiln measures twenty-five feet six inches by twenty-six feet and the interior of the stove chamber is plastered. According to Pierce County records, Woolrey added a second kiln of frame construction in 1890 (although current occupants believe that their father, Karl Koehler, built the 1890 addition). Measuring approximately twenty-four feet square, the second kiln is sided with horizontal fir and the interior is lath and plaster. A large baling room was added at the time the second kiln was built. It measures forty-six feet ten inches by thirty-four feet, and is of frame construction with vertical board and batten siding. A single roof ties the three together.

Karl Koehler, an immigrant from Saxony, Germany, purchased the Woolrey farm in 1902, and whether or not he built a portion of the hop kiln he did continue hop cultivation on the farm through the 1930s. A firm believer in diversification, Karl Koehler had an apple orchard and a dairy along with his hops, and in the 1930s he replaced his hops with tulip and daffodil bulbs, using the baling room of the old kiln for the sorting and storage of bulbs.

Harvesting the hops required much labor and so involved family and neighbors. Hops were probably the first crop to bring migrant workers to the Puyallup Valley, and in the earliest days of cultivation some of the migrant workers were Chinese. Prejudice, anti-Chinese legislation and violence in the 1880s drove the Chinese workers from the hop fields, and current residents remember the majority of migrant workers being Native Americans from British Columbia. Frank

Swalander, eighty-nine, remembers harvesting hops when he was about ten years old:

> I picked hops. All the kids did. If you were a kid or an Indian, you picked hops. I remember the Indians would come from British Columbia, down the Sound and up the Puyallup River in the dugouts. Dugout canoes as long as from here to the road. They'd camp by the Puyallup River and hop farmers would hitch a team to bring them out to their farms. They'd set up camp on the hop farms. They'd catch salmon in the river and smoke it while they were here.

Louise Koehler-Anderson, daughter of Karl Koehler, remembers hop harvests during the 1920s:

> We had a special crew that came down from British Columbia. They were Indian families, and they were the same families that came every year. We had sheep and they would take the wool back with them and bring us sweaters and socks and caps and everything. . . . It was like a United Nations. . . . And there were white people who helped here too. Quite a number of white people. In fact, when the hops were done over at my Aunt Annie's, . . . then they would get together and if there was still work to do over here, they would come over and help finish up. . . . It was like any other thing here in the valley, like the berries or any other crop. There would be school kids and there would be older people from the town, people who wanted to get out and make themselves a little extra money to eat and pay their taxes.

Pickers filled baskets which were dumped into larger boxes in the fields for transport to the kilns. Frank Swalander remembers his uncle Carl who, crippled and unable to work in the hop fields, built containers for pickers to take to the fields. Using a froe, he split sections of fir and nailed them to two rectangular frames, creating an open-topped box slightly larger on top than on the bottom. He also nailed a board seat across one corner of the box, so the picker could push the basket under the hop vines and sit while he picked. The finished box was about thirty inches tall, thirty inches wide, and twenty-five inches deep. (See Figs. 4 and 5)

Frank Swalander also remembers the dangers of hop production. "Hardly a year went by without a barn burning. They'd just explode from the dry hops. They were log barns, mostly, logs lined with plaster, and they had to be air tight. The furnace would get red hot, and that would start the fire. You could see the light for ten miles. A year's hops and all your equipment gone."

A happier recollection is of the dances following the harvest. "The crews would move around, and every time you'd get done in a field, you'd have a big dance in a hop kiln. Sliding those burlap bales over the floor [bales of hops were wrapped in burlap] would polish them to a shine. You'd have a big dance, usually three or four in a season. . . . Square dances." The music he remembers is "violins, mouth harps, guitars, and maybe an accordion," and the food, "oh, sandwiches and cakes, and probably beer and wine, but we kids weren't allowed near that!" Late nineteenth and early twentieth-century photographs of hop pickers in the fields, festooned with cone-filled hop vines as they posed for the camera, add to the picture of festivity that accompanied at least the conclusion of the harvest.

Despite the fact that hops have not served a vital role in area agriculture for over fifty years, and despite the fact that the number of kilns in the valley has decreased steadily as hop production declined, these unusual structures still play a vital role in resident's definitions of themselves and their region. Joe and Delores Meshke bought a hop farm with a kiln dated 1907, which they have incorporated into their Christmas tree farm. They were horrified when "newcomers" down the road bought another old hop farm and demolished the kiln to make room for more trees. Frank Swalander summarizes the dilemma, "I wish they'd save those darn things, but, I guess you can't save everything." Occasionally a stray hop vine reappears. One such vine is carefully noted in the locally-produced volume on Orting history. Louise Koehler-Anderson described another:

> Every once in a while you find a spot where there is still an active root, and you just kind of nurture that and just love seeing it grow. We had one down at the golf course for quite a while and it was quite a topic of conversation. Wally Statz really loved showing it off and Bill Copeland would get his hand on it and then there'd be a little article in the paper and it would revive the good old days. . . . The days when hops were king.

REFERENCES CITED

Adventures, Ms. Guided
  1987 *Orting Valley: Yesterday and Today.* Orting, WA: Heritage Quest.
Graham, Oscar
  1978 Hop Kilns of the Puyallup Valley. *National Register of Historic Places Nomination.* City of Tacoma, WA:Community Development Department.
---------and Caroline Gallacci
  1983 The Woolrey/Koehler Hop Kiln. *National Register of Historic Places Nomination.* City of Tacoma, WA:Pierce County Planning Department.
Koehler-Anderson, Louise
  1988 Interview conducted at her home near Orting, Washington. 22 August.
Lindeman, Glen and Keith Williams
  1985 *Agricultural Study Unit.* Unpublished ms. revised by the Washington State Office of Archaeology and Historic Preservation, Olympia, Washington.
Lingreen, Minnie and Priscilla Tiller
  1981 *Hop Cultivation in Lewis County, Washington, 1888-1940: A Study in Land Use Determinants.* Chehalis, WA:n.p.

Meeker, E. [Ezra]
    1883 *Hop Culture in the United States: Being a Practical Treatise on Hop Growing in Washington Territory, from the Cutting to the Bale.* Puyallup:E.Meeker and Co.
Swalander, Frank
    1988 Interview conducted at his home near Orting, Washington. 9 December.

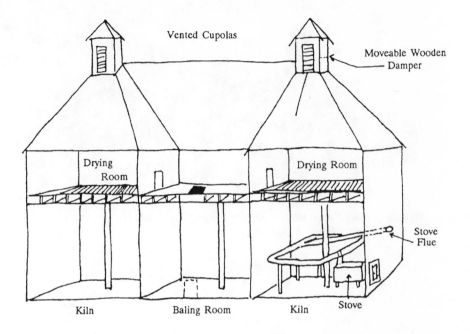

Figure 1. Basic design of a Puyallup Valley hop kiln. Hops were loaded into the drying room via a system of exterior ramps which ran to doors leading into the drying rooms. Heat, maintained at 150 degrees for fifteen to twenty hours, rose from the stovepipes through the slatted drying room floors. The slatted floors, covered with burlap, held freshly harvested hops, piled two feet deep. Rising heat carried moisture from the curing hops out through vents in the cupolas. Once cured, the hops were moved to the baling room and dropped through the floor into a compressing device which formed burlap-wrapped bales for shipment. (Graham/Gallacci 1983:7)

Figure 2. Undated photograph of Woolrey/Koehler kiln, 1890-1940. Photo courtesy of Louise Koehler-Anderson.

Figure 3. The Woolrey/Koehler kiln as it stands in 1988.

Figure 4. Undated photo of workers on Koehler hop farm. Note hop boxes on deck, team and wagon on ramp leading to kiln. Photo courtesy of Louise Koehler-Anderson.

Figure 5. Undated photo of workers on Koehler hop farm. Note picker's baskets and boxes. Photo courtesy of Louise Koehler-Anderson.

Here Today, Gone Tomorrow: Determining the Disappearance Rate of Agricultural Structures in Pike County, Ohio

ALLEN G. NOBLE
DEBORAH PHILLIPS KING

In 1981, several oversized corn cribs elevated on pillars stood on the floodplain of the Scioto river just south of Waverly, Ohio (Figure 1). Four years later, in 1985, a team of geographers from The University of Akron visited the floodplain in Pike County, Ohio, to look for additional elevated, elongated corn cribs, and other historic structures associated with the corn economy of the late 1800s and early 1900s and to document these structures (Noble 1988). One of the corn cribs photographed on the first trip, in 1981, was no longer standing. The grassy ramps which stood at each end of the corn crib, and the stone support pillars were in the process of being bulldozed down. One more structure in the Scioto River floodplain was in the process of disappearing.

This sequence of observations and the loss of a large agricultural structure raised the question of the disappearance rate of farm buildings in Pike County. Agricultural structures, which in an earlier time manifested distinct functions, rapidly are disappearing from the landscape. It is not surprising that relic structures disappear. Once a building becomes obsolete or its original function disappears or changes, it is likely to be abandoned or removed. In agricultural areas, obsolete structures may be destroyed in order to provide additional space for planting crops. Some abandoned structures become the victims of time and simple neglect. An obsolete structure does not warrant much effort and expense in maintenance. A strong incentive to remove relic structures lies in the fact that taxes are often based upon buildings and their removal may reduce taxes. Finally, fire insurance rates may be lowered by removal of obsolete buildings, especially those built of wood and close to other buildings. Since structures stand as testimonials to a different age, it seems valid to ask, "How quickly are structures disappearing from the landscape?"

The purpose of this study is to determine the disappearance rate of agricultural structures in Pike County, Ohio. Pike County is located in south-central Ohio, 60 miles south of Columbus, the nearest major city (Figure 2, inset). Historically, the economy of Pike County has been based upon the land. The western part of the county is a hilly, timber-producing area, while in the east, the hills flatten and the soils improve for farming. The floodplain of the Scioto River, which traverses the eastern part of the county, is its most fertile and intensively farmed section. This study concentrates on the floodplain and the agricultural structures built to take advantage of the floodplain soils.

For the sake of easing field observations for this study, and to facilitate map and aerial photograph interpretation, the floodplain is considered as the area between the old Ohio and Erie Canal on the west side of the Scioto River, and the Norfolk and Western railroad on the east (Figure 2). The floodplain is approximately one and a half miles wide as it traverses the county. Structures within the incorporated areas of Piketon and Waverly have not been included in this study.

Methodology

The first step in this investigation involved counting the number of structures in the floodplain study area on U.S.G.S. 15 minute maps dating from 1906 and 1915. Secondly, a comparison was made to see if any of the same structures were symbolized on 7.5 minute maps from 1961. The comparison was made solely on the basis of location since the map symbolism for structures changed between the early maps and the 1961 maps. Figure 3 depicts part of the study area and illustrates the procedures and difficulties of identifying the structures. On the 1906 map, two buildings are mapped along a field road south of the river. These two structures do not appear on the 1961 map.

On the early maps, the legend indicates that the small, square, black symbols on the maps are "buildings". Map users cannot be certain exactly which kinds of structures fall into this general category. On the 1961 maps, two types of structural symbols appear: an open black square or rectangle can represent a barn, outbuilding or warehouse; while a solid black square or rectangle represents a dwelling place or place of employment. It is possible that cases exist where an early structure was demolished and replaced by a structure built on the same site. If this occurred, the early building was counted as still standing. Since this study deals with the disappearance of structures, this inconsistency in symbolism did not cause a major problem. However, simple counts of building symbols from maps with different dates could yield misleading information.

The third observation was based upon 1977 aerial photographs viewed at the County Engineer's office in Waverly. The large-scale aerial photographs made it very easy to count the structures within the study area and often even to differentiate their uses.

The fieldwork was completed prior to examining the aerial photographs. Since structures dating from 1915 were the basis for determining the rate of disappearance, field checks were essential to ensure that newer buildings would not be counted on the aerial photographs.

One caveat should be mentioned regarding the accuracy of U.S.G.S. maps. Researchers traditionally put considerable faith in the reliability of 7.5 and 15 minute maps, as basic research tools. During this study, we realized that the maps are not perfect. In field traverses, some structures, as well as roads, were located which did not appear on any of the maps. While these minor inconsistencies did not materially affect this study, those working in the field should keep these deficiencies in mind.

Results

What do observations made from the maps, aerial photographs and fieldwork tell us about the disappearance of structures in the Pike County floodplain? Figure 4 shows the results of five observations based on different sources over a 72 year time period from 1915 to 1987. Initially, there were 89 structures in the floodplain study area. By 1961, 50 structures remained. In 1977, 37 of the original structures were indicated on aerial photographs, and in 1986 and 1987, fieldwork confirmed that 31 of the original structures were still standing in various states of repair. Based on these figures, the mean disappearance rate over the entire time period is: 1 structure every 15 months. By breaking the time period down by observation periods, the rates vary:

1915-1961	39 structures disappeared OR 1 every 22 months
1961-1977	14 structures disappeared OR 1 every 13 months
1977-1987	5 structures disappeared OR 1 every 24 months

These numbers indicate that the disappearance rates vary, and over the last 10 years the rate has been slower. The slower rate can be explained by four factors: 1) the process of urban sprawl and suburbanization in Pike County has slowed; 2) the structures that were poorly constructed or maintained have already met their demise and the sturdier structures remain; 3) a limited number of structures have been given a different function and because of this their maintenance has improved; and 4) the cost to remove the structures exceeds the benefits and the economy of Pike County in recent years has not been very healthy.

If we look at the results geographically, more structures remain in the central and southern sections of the floodplain than in the north (Figure 5). Most of the structures near Waverly, the county seat, have disappeared. In contrast, Piketon, being the less prosperous of the two towns, is still surrounded by several original structures. Looking at the disappearance of the structures by township (except Newton), considerable variation is revealed. Virtually all of the structures in Jackson township have disappeared (Figure 6). Seven structures remain in both Pee Pee and Seal townships, but more of the original structures have disappeared in Pee Pee township. Scioto township comprises a large part of the floodplain, and just over half of the original structures are still standing. Finally, all of the structures have disappeared in Camp Creek township, but the floodplain in that township is very narrow. Because of insufficient air photo coverage Newton township could not be included.

Analysis

Why have the structures disappeared in the floodplain, despite an overall population increase of 25 percent from 1900 to 1980? Clearly, the rate of disappearance of structures is not related directly to population levels. As figure 7 shows, population declined from 1900 to 1930, experienced a growth spurt in 1940, and has generally increased since 1950. However, the agricultural statistics for Pike County reflect more accurately what has happened in the farming area of the floodplain (Table 1). The early 1900s represented a prosperous period. At the turn of the century, there were four times as many farms as there are today, the number of acres being farmed was at its peak, and corn yields were high. In the 1950s, a drastic change occurred both in the number of farms and the average size of farms. Even as farm consolidation began, employment alternatives in Pike County and nearby areas became available. The federal government picked economically depressed Pike County to be the site of a Uranium Enrichment Plant. As a reaction to this investment, Waverly built housing to accommodate 4000 new residents; 1800 jobs actually materialized. Bristol Village, one 400 unit subdivision built on the floodplain, went up for sale due to foreclosure in 1961. Today, Bristol Village is successfully operated as a retirement village by a nonprofit church organization.

Few scholars have given much attention to the question of the disappearance of vernacular structures other than to bemoan the loss of a part of our collective cultural heritage. Probably because of this lacuna, many students of material culture make the mistake of assuming that the current relic landscape is a faithful representation of earlier periods. At least one scholar recently has shown that such is not the case (Herman 1987). Fortunately, in Pike County the farm structures are overwhelmingly built of wood so that the rates of disappearance are not influenced by differences in building materials.

Overall, several factors contribute to explain why structures have disappeared in the floodplain:

1. Consolidation of farms has taken place, thus requiring fewer farm structures;

2. Corn is no longer stored in the large, elevated corn cribs which were a characteristic feature of the landscape in the early years of the century;

3. Storage requirements for farm machinery have changed;

4. People have various perceptions concerning what structures have "historical" value, and farmers cannot afford to be sentimental, therefore maintenance becomes an issue;

5. On the better managed or more prosperous farms, the cost of fire insurance works to eliminate the obsolete wooden farm structures;

6. Land use in the floodplain has changed, especially since 1950;

7. Abandoned and poorly maintained structures are simply falling down.

Summary

Why is this information on disappearance rates and patterns important? If we base a projection on the slowest rate of disappearance, and the rate remains constant, where one structure disappears every 2 years, it will take 62 years for the remaining structures in the floodplain, dating back to 1915, to completely disappear. This seems like a long time, but in 62 years the structures will be at least 130 years old. How many structures are standing today that date back to 130 years?

Several structures remain in the floodplain of the Scioto River—elongated corn cribs, scale houses and many distinctive houses which symbolize more prosperous times. These structures are valuable keys to understanding the settlement, economy and the resources of Pike County. Hopefully, a few structures representative of different technologies and a more lucrative time will be preserved. As scholars with map, aerial photograph and fieldwork skills, we can perhaps motivate and assist efforts to preserve some of this material cultural heritage for future generations, before it is too late.

REFERENCES CITED

Herman, Bernard L.
    1987 *Architecture and Rural Life in Central Delaware, 1700-1900.* Knoxville: University of Tennessee Press.
Noble, Allen G.
    1988 Crib Death: The Demise of Elevated Corn Cribs in Pike County, Ohio. *The East Lakes Geographer* 23 (in press).

Table 1: Agriculture in Pike County, Ohio
(Sources: U.S. Census)

Year	Number of Farms	Acres of Farmland	Average Acres/Farm	Corn Yields (bushels)
1900	2385	243,270	102	1,053,680
1910	2189	242,226	111	1,092,432
1920	1940	229,343	118	731,603
1930	1592	204,806	129	873,513
1940	1720	209,214	123	915,948
1950	1656	169,268	102	719,419
1960	919	133,004	145	710,094
1970	770	126,298	164	444,061
1980	607	110,466	182	592,800

Figure 1. The elevated corn crib of the Scioto Valley.

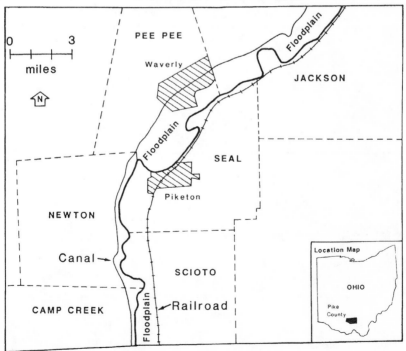

Figure 2. Eastern Pike County.

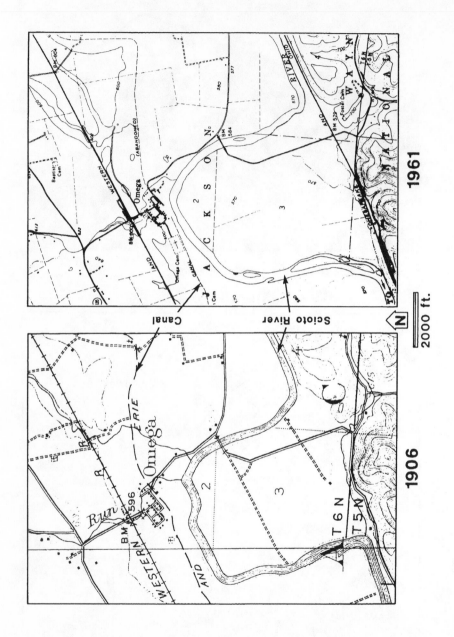

Figure 3. Topographic maps showing rural structures, 1906 and 1961.

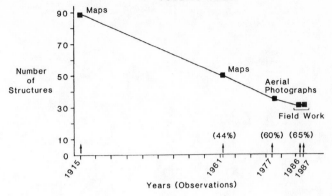

Figure 4. Disappearance of rural structures.

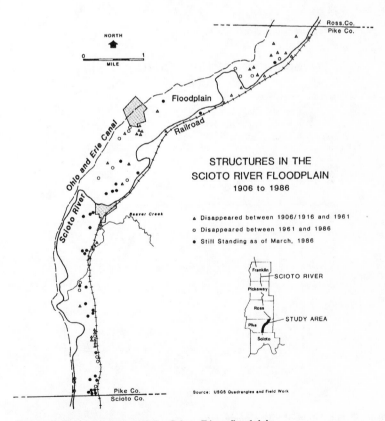

Figure 5. Rural structures of the Scioto River floodplain.

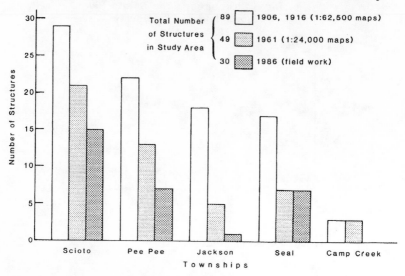

Figure 6. Disappearance of structures in Pike County.

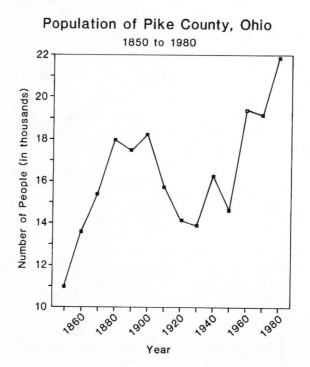

Figure 7. Population of Pike County, Ohio.

Folklife Starts Here: The Background of Material Culture Scholarship in Pennsylvania

SIMON J. BRONNER

During the bicentennial celebration in Philadelphia of the American Constitution, a time for celebrating and cogitating democratic principles, Pennsylvania billboards told travellers that "America Starts Here." America's political history is indeed wrapped up in the momentous deliberations which occurred in Pennsylvania. Let notice be additionally served of the social and cultural legacy important to the work of Warren Roberts which also lies there: America's first plural society and a folklife studies movement geared to its study. Roberts reflected on this influence in his "Autobiographical Note" for *Viewpoints on Folklife*; in the piece he acknowledged how he kept coming back to Pennsylvania to inform his budding folklife research. He relied on the nation's first folklife journal, *Pennsylvania Folklife*, and in what he describes as a kind of initiation into the folklife fraternity, in 1967 he trekked to a conference in Harrisburg, Pennsylvania, where he "met many of the scholars studying traditional material culture," including his life-long folklife comrades Henry Glassie and Don Yoder. In this essay, I want to examine reasons for the historical priority within Pennsylvania of material culture (particularly folk art and architecture) and folklife scholarship, and consider the future as this priority has become a national movement, thanks greatly to the missionary efforts of Warren Roberts.

Pennsylvania among the states holds the distinction in folklife studies of boasting probably the most extensive record of articles and

books on folk art and craft. The record reaches well back into the
nineteenth century and continues to build today. This legacy has
helped to convey the image of Pennsylvania as a place where hand--
wrought tradition is momentous. It is an image filled with bank barns,
fraktur, painted furniture, paper cutting, decorated stoves, baskets,
quilts, and pottery. It is an image combining the hardy practicality
associated with Pennsylvania's settlers and the beauty they carved into
their lives. This image undergirds much of today's folk art scholarship
in general—emphasis on handwork, rural life, and domestic goods—and
reflects several patterns that call particularly on the Pennsylvania
experience.

The first noticeable pattern has to be the ethnic context of art
and crafts. As opposed to the relative homogeneity of the early
southern and New England settlement, Pennsylvania encouraged, even
legislated, multicultural and multi-religious settlement from groups
outside the English mold. Coming into Pennsylvania, they formed
distinctive ethnic and religious communities, often isolated from one
another, that helped preserve Old World customs and language. In
Pennsylvania, the character of group life in America became defined.
As historian Michael Zuckerman emphasized, "The very diversity of the
area demands the requisite attention to variation. Tribalism may have
emerged among the Quakers of New Garden, but a far different fam-
ilialism appeared close by among the Friends of the Welsh Tract. Sects
may have solidified in revolutionary Philadelphia, but privatism
prevailed in the revolutionary countryside a few miles up the Schuyl-
kill" (1982:23-24). Unlike New England where studies of communities
leap to national generalization, in Pennsylvania, study by geographic
and cultural necessity is essentially local, primarily ethnic and religious.
Yet it is in this local arena that studies in Pennsylvania more often
grasp the meaning rather than the events of the American experience.

The contrast of Pennsylvania to the nation is less a matter of
landscape than ethnicity, amply demonstrated by the coverage of
German heritage among Pennsylvania's many groups. Even in this nod
to the dominance of German material culture and folklife in Pennsylvania's history, there is a plural, fragmented story. The Dunkards and
Brethren had their towns, while those known as the Amish diffused
sects from Old Order Mennonite to the Byler Amish. Even as the
sectarian emphasis has eased, residents still distinguish between Old
German, or the "Dutch" of colonial Pennsylvania, and New German
brought over in the wave of late-nineteenth-century immigration.
Pennsylvania's identities, its sense of ethnicity, are bound up in its
history and settlement.

The second pattern is an emphasis on decorative and pre-industrial arts. The combination of practicality and beauty is an oft-cited theme in the work on Pennsylvania's material culture. Some of this emphasis is a matter of ethnic cultural values, but often it is also a consideration of agrarian community life. In Pennsylvania there is a kind of national model for the conflict of industrialism and agrarianism. This hearth of American industrialization and great cities built around it, also is home to one of America's largest rural populations, a population that clings fiercely to small-town life. The abundance of communities in Pennsylvania inspired a variety and profusion of pre-industrial arts and crafts for localized use lasting to this day.

The attention to small-town life leads to a third pattern of emphasis on arts of regional and local concern within Pennsylvania. To be sure, the role of family and occupation, especially on the farm, in the shaping of folk art comes through in many works of Pennsylvania folklife research, but even when these themes are developed there is usually a strong connection to the many small communities emerging on the broad Pennsylvania landscape.

The fourth pattern is one of approach: studies of Pennsylvania's crafts commonly emphasize the role of crafts in everyday life. This emphasis is at the heart of what emerged as the "folklife" perspective, the consideration of crafts, architecture, custom, and lore in a total culture, rather than the life history of the item under scrutiny. Some academic influences particularly color this perspective in Pennsylvania: one can detect special consideration in many entries to historical, religious, and geographical topics.

The Ethnic Connection

Pennsylvania began its settlement late, when compared to the other colonies on the Eastern Seaboard. The Commonwealth also differed from its neighbors in the kind of settlers who came. Consistently, Pennsylvania attracted disenfranchised religious and ethnic groups from Europe. First came the English Quakers during the late seventeenth century, who were joined by Dutch and Welsh brethren. Almost immediately the principle of a plural society emerged with this mixing of European peoples in a "holy experiment." Attracted by promises of ethnic and religious tolerance and a landscape reminiscent of their homeland, persecuted religious sects from German-speaking countries came next to give a contrasting image to the English roots of most of the Eastern Seaboard. Mennonites, Amish, and Dunkers from Switzerland and the German Rhineland spread inland into Pennsylvania establishing close-knit farming communities. Further rooting their culture onto the landscape were their sectarian ties, which came out in various religious arts and sectarian costumes. Showing the cultural strength of these Pennsylvania communities, the German language, art, and life of the Old Country persisted well into the twentieth century.[1] Near to the Pennsylvania-German settlements were lowland Scots who had lived in northern Ireland, including many Presbyterians who had come during the eighteenth century to southeastern Pennsylvania for religious and economic opportunities. The result of this early settlement was an association of Pennsylvania's landscape with strong ethnic areas—particularly German and Scots-Irish communities. The distinctiveness of the arts and customs of these peoples, when compared to the predominant English background of the other colonies, helped create an image of folk-cultural islands within the new American nation.

When waves of southern and eastern European immigrants came to Pennsylvania during the late nineteenth century, they found encouragement from German and Scots-Irish precedents for maintenance of ethnic customs. Nonetheless, the life preserved by the Germans was not matched by later immigrants who tended to maintain aspects of their culture such as food, domestic arts, dance, and music in a more ethnically mixed environment. By then spreading out across the state from Philadelphia to Scranton and Pittsburgh, the new waves of Italian, Ukrainian, Serbian, Croatian, Polish, and Hungarian immigrants—to name a few of the nationalities—settled more into an urban experience than their German predecessors. Today, we see a new kind of immigration from Asia—particularly from Vietnam, Cambodia, and Laos—following almost a century after the influx of Asians mostly from China. The literature on the urban Chinese harped on the carry-over of exotic religious customs, medicine, arts, societies, and games of the immigrants mostly in Philadelphia, while from the new Asian immigrants studies have taken note of textile arts, lore, foodways, and beliefs of the Southeast Asians settled across Pennsylvania (Culin 1890; Peterson 1988:6-22; Miska 1980:20-23).

Against this background, the study of folklife in Pennsylvania typically stressed ethnic connections. The first local chapter of the American Folklore Society in Philadelphia, formed in 1889 to study the forms of folklore in America, diverged from the national society by organizing its work around ethnic "fields." It identified these fields as Anglo-American, Africo-American, and other "Local Foreign," such as "The Chinese Quarter," "The Italian Quarter," "The German Quarter," and "Gipsies" (Philadelphia Branch 1893:71-72).

Other indications of this ethnic bias can be seen in nineteenth-century studies and societies. The Pennsylvania-German Society was formed in 1891 and featured many folklife topics in its publications, and other periodicals such as *Pennsylvania-German*, *Penn Germania* and *German American Annals* began at the turn of the century. Thirty years earlier, *Atlantic Monthly* featured Phebe Earle Gibbons's essays on Pennsylvania folklife. His organization revolved around ethnic connections: under "Pennsylvania Dutch (Properly German)," he covered Quiltings, Festivals, and Manners and Customs, and he discussed similar topics for Swiss Exiles, Dunkers, Moravians, Schwenkfelders, Irish Farmers, and English. Sydney George Fisher, writing his classic *The Making of Pennsylvania* in 1896, characterized the state and its folkways by its "mixture of languages, nationalities, and religions," and the way "these divisions led a more or less distinct life of their own in colonial times." Pennsylvania was no melting pot, according to the literature, and the studies of immigrant crafts verified this fact by showing the "extremely varied and interesting," as Fisher called it, character of Pennsylvania.

The Celebration of Decorative and Pre-Industrial Arts

The lateness of Pennsylvania's settlement allowed until-then, rarely-heard-from immigrant farming settlements of the Germans and Scots-Irish to spread out over central Pennsylvania. The lateness also encouraged the rapid introduction of industrialism that began sweeping Europe in the eighteenth century into the port of Philadelphia. Fisher believed that Pennsylvania's reputation for tolerance also contributed to the acceptance of innovation in the region. The same immigrants that brought masterful craft skills to the United States found themselves highly sought after by the growing numbers of manufacturers in Philadelphia and its outskirts. By the 1790s, more than one-third of all exports of the United States came from Philadelphia. In 1795, Oliver Evans introduced his automated gristmill in the Philadelphia area; to the amazement of the public, the mill received raw material and delivered a finished product on a large scale with little human intervention. Similar transformations were occurring in the printing, cloth, leather, and iron industries. The American factory system took shape in these technological advancements; artisans and small farm operations, a mainstay of the Philadelphia economy for more than a century, felt squeezed out by more mills and iron furnaces. By 1800, at least 167 furnaces and forges had been established in Philadelphia; by the early nineteenth century, Philadelphia led the nation in manufacturing and population.

Pennsylvania's populations, especially its German settlers, were known for their practicality bred by agricultural life. Out of this tradition, Pennsylvanians offered the nation the Conestoga Wagon and the Pennsylvania Rifle, known for their durability, efficiency, and economy. The German bank barns so much a fixture on the Pennsylvania landscape were architectural machines similarly built for use and efficiency. Larger than English barns, the bank barns used the hillsides for extra support and created extended space on the second level with an overhanging forebay. The forebay additionally served to protect livestock and equipment underneath (Glass 1986). Yet it was hard to miss the attention to decorating these barns. Builders formed ventilation holes in the second level in geometric and natural shapes; elaborate weathervanes graced the tops of the barns; hex signs colorfully marked the front of the barn. The decoration often worked in consistent motifs of tulips, birds, swirls, and hearts which added symbolic meanings of good fortune to the equipment of agriculture and farm living, but they also seemed to certify the masterwork of practicality by covering it in pleasing designs that drew attention to the value of the utilitarian object. To be sure, decoration often indicated a maker's cultural insignia and background, but it also marked the object as one made to last and to be cared for. This approach to the built environment carried over into the household, where rugs, quilts, towels, coverlets, documents, stoves, and furniture often carried decorative touches. Even after the landscape appeared more industrial, the domestic interior perpetuated traditional arts, and the hearth and bed became the dominant symbol of traditional ethnic life in Pennsylvania.

Pennsylvania folk-art scholarship emerged to recognize the force of industrial change in the region, and to celebrate the domestic domains of stability. One can look to some of the nation's first folklife collections to see these influences on the attention to pre-industrial and decorative arts. John Fanning Watson created a stir in the early nineteenth century, for example, by publishing his *Annals of Philadelphia and Pennsylvania in the Olden Time* (1830), in which he romantically recorded accounts of proud artisans. During his lifetime, he claimed, great changes had occurred in the lives of the artisans. "In less than twenty years," wrote Watson, "our exports have grown from twenty to eighty millions . . . Our inventions and improvements in the arts, which began but yesterday, make us, even now, 'a wonder unto many'"(Ibid:2). Thus he sought to document the handskills of the aged before their proud traditions associated with the bonds of community and spirit passed; he recorded the reminiscences of wheelwrights, blacksmiths, and furniture makers. Many of these pre-industrial arts did not disappear, as Watson feared, but the belief that their extinction was imminent, coupled with the assumption that Pennsylvania's conservative rural German settlers preserved the old ways, guided the hunt for folk arts for many years to come. Indeed, the use of the term "folk art" and the decorative crafts it described during the late nineteenth century were particularly associated with Pennsylvania researchers before the term became generally popular in American studies during the 1930s (Robacker 1959:20-29; de Jonge 1972:10-13; Bronner 1984a:xi-xxvii).

A pivotal figure in the late nineteenth-century boom of interest in pre-industrial and decorative arts is Henry Mercer of Doylestown, Pennsylvania. Repeating some of Watson's rhetoric, Mercer claimed that "mechanical improvements in human handicraft at the beginning of the nineteenth century have suddenly transformed the American farmer from a pioneer relying for equipment upon his own skill and industry to a husbandman abundantly supplied with labor-saving devices." For Mercer, the value of preserving the old crafts was that "they give us a fresh grasp upon the vitality of the American beginning." Himself an industrialist, Mercer appreciated the integrity of handwork and its closeness to nature. In 1897, he compiled an influential exhibit entitled *Tools of the Nation Maker*, and followed with essays on fraktur and decorated stove plates. He then began building his dream of a folklife museum to house the collection and re-create the setting of pre-industrial life, now known as the Mercer Museum. His collection was not alone, as indicated by the publication of F.J.F. Schantz's *The Domestic Life and Characteristics of the Pennsylvania-German Pioneer* (1900) and, later, the famed collecting of the Landis Brothers which led to the establishment of the State Farm Museum near Lancaster, Pennsylvania (Landis 1939:71; 1945:43,46,49).

The Community Emphasis

In Pennsylvania, the idea of community is a material, not abstract, concept. When Pennsylvanians talk about community, they're talking about their towns and ethnic settlements (Zelinsky 1977:127-47; Hopple 1971-72:18-40). Just travel the old pike in Central Pennsylvania from Harrisburg to Carlisle, a distance under twenty miles, and you can go through a dozen towns. There's no thought here of incorporating into a larger unit, as cities in the Midwest have done. And residents maintain fierce loyalties to their small towns, manifested in Old Home Days, local historical societies, and town festivals. Another indication is that residents still identify where they live by the small town name rather than the large urban center around which it may revolve. Considering the historical roots of this town identity, geographer Wilbur Zelinsky noted that the process of town founding advanced more vigorously in eighteenth-century southeastern and central Pennsylvania than over any other extended tract in British North America.

The Pennsylvania town has several distinctive characteristics. One peculiarity, when compared to other American regions, is the tightness of the settlements. Residences are built close together and close to the street, and as Zelinsky observed, this tendency "appears in those attenuated one- or two-street villages that straggle far into the countryside." Unlike town plans elsewhere, Pennsylvania towns often mix dwellings, shops, and offices in a single area and relegate churches, cemeteries, and schools to peripheral locations. Other common features in the Pennsylvania town are the diamond or square, often where a public market once stood, and a network of attractive alleys running through the town. Similar to many settlements in Germany, the compactness of the towns is contrasted with sprawling outlying areas of farmland or woods that are kept fairly pristine. The effect is to attain an "urbane intimacy and lively visual variety" in town while maintaining a pastoral landscape on its outskirts. This pattern reflects the varied settlement characteristic of the plural sectarian society that originally came into Pennsylvania, and fosters the bonds of tradition working in tightly knit communities. Part of the reason that folk arts are associated with these communities is the location of crafts and services in each town. The compact town commonly featured blacksmiths, wheelwrights, tinsmiths, and other craftsworkers along the main street in addition to the farmers who brought crafts to sell at market. The profusion of towns throughout the landscape encouraged the establishment of many craft services and apprentice traditions through Pennsylvania. Documentation of crafts in Pennsylvania was often a way to recall town life and the quality of goods found within one's town. It also spoke to the speculation that along with industrial change, urbanization threatened Pennsylvania's customary folk life revolving around the almost-communal towns. Folk arts particularly showed local variation, and projected an "intimacy and lively visual variety" reminiscent of the towns.

Hence, local study of folklife and history have been strong in Pennsylvania. Watson's *Annals*, reprinted in many editions to the end of the nineteenth century, was an influence on the efforts to record folk traditions as part of town histories in Pennsylvania. The guide for study published in 1893 by the Philadelphia chapter of the American

Folklore Society made the emphasis of community explicit. It urged the study of "usages of a community which are peculiar to itself, and which, taken together, constitute its individuality when compared with other communities." Henry Mercer's fame in folklife studies was indeed based on the study of his beloved Doylestown and surrounding towns in Bucks County for the Bucks County Historical Society. In this light, with the community holding the key to tradition and creative expression, we might better understand his particularly Pennsylvanian boast in 1897 that when considering folk crafts, "we need not look so far ahead to imagine the time when if we do anything like our duty, the student of these things, whoever he may be, will not go to Washington, Boston, New York, Chicago or anywhere else in the country to study American history from this fresh point of view, but will be compelled to come to Doylestown" (1897:289).

The communities of Pennsylvania relate well to one another partly because of ethnic connections and the paths of transportation that tied the state into a region. Unlike the pattern in other states, migration from the eastern port of entry, namely Philadelphia, tended to stay within state lines. A reason, then, for the attention to arts particularly framed by Pennsylvania is that the state demarcates cultural as well as political lines. The Pennsylvania-German influence dips down below the Mason-Dixon line into north-central Maryland and northwestern Virginia, and north-central Pennsylvania bears a New England stamp, but generally the state uniquely represents a cultural region tucked between the older regions of New England and the South (Glassie 1968; Zelinsky 1973; Gastil 1975).

As with other aspects of Pennsylvania's life, the tradition of fragmentation works on the state's regional identity. Many views of folk arts typically take in the state's subregions representing its ethnic and occupational variety. The roughest division, often offered by residents, falls into eastern Pennsylvania revolving around Philadelphia, central Pennsylvania working around Harrisburg, and western Pennsylvania orbiting near Pittsburgh. But the arts commonly spring from more closely defined regions. North-central Pennsylvania up from Scranton has a Yankee feel to it, and the slags near Hazleton announce what many call the Coal Region. A great deal of attention has also been given to identifying the "Pennsylvania Culture Region" formed by German settlement, art, and architecture in south-central and eastern Pennsylvania (Glassie 1968; Zelinsky 1977; Glass 1986).

The Folklife Perspective

The close integration of language, art, and custom in the ethnic and sectarian enclaves of Pennsylvania suggested to many nineteenth-century chroniclers an approach that examined the arts within the life of Pennsylvania's distinctive communities and regions. The arts were seen as part of the daily round of life and an expression of the cultural inheritance maintained in the New World experience. Contributing to the appropriateness of this approach to Pennsylvania was the influence of German anthropological methods which were widely read in intellectual circles in Pennsylvania academies. Referring to *Volkskunde*, or "folklife," and *Volkskunst*, or "folk art," nineteenth--century German scholars understood arts as part of the cultural life and spirit of community-based societies (Bronner 1984b: 57-73; Möller 1964:218-41; Yoder 1963:43-56). Scholars in Pennsylvania picked up on this idea, especially because they could observe similar patterns among the state's Amish, Quaker, Irish, Italian, Chinese, and Welsh communities, to name a few.

The folklife approach in Pennsylvania differed from the British-inspired approach prevalent in the American Folklore Society, formed in 1888. In this latter approach, oral traditions were often considered separately from material traditions, and compared cross-culturally, rather than in the context of a single community or culture, to compile an evolution of the tradition's development. The distinctiveness of the Pennsylvanian, and especially Pennsylvania-German, scholars' approach helps explain the relative independence of Pennsylvania folklife studies from the main movements of American folklore study until the late twentieth century.

Pennsylvania study stressed the crafts and arts as part of folk tradition, and related it to social and oral parts of a community or regional culture. A sign of this emphasis to American folklorists came in 1888 with the first volume of the American Folklore Society's journal, the *Journal of American Folklore*. In it, Walter James Hoffman published "Folklore of the Pennsylvania Germans," in which he described flax raising, barn design, marriage custom, foodways, and quilting parties all related to the cultural history of Pennsylvanians around his native Reading.

Interest after World War II in fading community life and folk arts in America promoted renewed consideration of Pennsylvania's folklife studies by American scholars. Mercer's museum was already in place in Doylestown, and the Landis brothers developed their collections near Lancaster. The Pennsylvania Folklife Society was formed in 1951 with support from Pennsylvania-German researchers at Franklin and Marshall College.[2] Don Yoder, a long-term editor of the society's journal, *Pennsylvania Folklife*, and a teacher at Franklin and Marshall College and the University of Pennsylvania, described the move toward folklife studies as a "20th Century re-discovery of the total range of the folk-culture (folklife)" (Yoder 1963). Folklife studies, in particular, built on folklore, anthropology, and cultural history; and in Pennsylvania, with its close relation of landscape to the built environment, folklife studies prominently added a geographical aspect. Folklife research, he announced, "is oriented toward holistic studies of culture regionally delimited and toward 'life,' the life of the society under study and of the individual within that society" (Yoder 1976). Crafts and arts were particularly expressive of folk life because they expressed not only the skills important to survival, but also the spirit and values basic to the culture. The folklife studies movement has spread around the country, although much of its initiative remains strongest in Pennsylvania.

Emerging Patterns

Although the patterns I have discussed still set the stage for much of folklife research in Pennsylvania, changing trends are apparent from recent studies. The new trends reflect a concern for post-industrial Pennsylvania following on the legacy of pre-industrial life. Urban and industrial crafts, modern children's crafts, suburban yard arrangements, and memory arts of the aged are coming under increasing scrutiny. Revival and tourist arts, especially in regard to the image they convey of traditional Pennsylvania life, are the subject of several significant studies. More attention is also being given to individuals maintaining their craft in modern society, their life stories, their performances before the public and their communities. More than documenting arts for posterity, many students are questioning the vital roles that traditional craftsmanship can and should play in our society, today and in the future. Scholarship is becoming more active, chronicling the past and present with an eye toward interpretation, and indeed conservation, in the future. Coincidentally, the inspiration of American folklife studies in Pennsylvania's plural society and vernacular spirit informs Warren Roberts's own wish for the future that the appreciation of America's craftsmen provides "an intellectual basis for democracy, a basis not anchored on the belief that all progress comes from a handful of elite geniuses but from great numbers of intelligent, hardworking people, both men and women, who work with their hands and their minds and constantly improve the things they make or grow and thus contribute to creating a better life for everyone" (1988:311).

NOTES

[1] This pattern drew Warren Roberts's attention when he studied German-Catholic communities in Dubois County, southern Indiana. See his "German-American Log Buildings of Dubois County, Indiana," in *Viewpoints on Folklife*, pp. 289-310; and "Field Work in Dubois County, Indiana: A Project of the Folklore Institute, Indiana University" (1976).

[2] In addition to offering courses on folklife, Franklin and Marshall College had a Pennsylvania Dutch Folklore Center and during the 1950s sponsored "Seminars on the Folk-Culture of the Pennsylvania Dutch Country" intended for "serious students of American folk-life" who wanted to study "folk culture on an academic plane"; see *Pennsylvania Dutchman* 4 (May 1952), p. 2. The Center published *The Pennsylvania Dutchman* devoted to the Pennsylvania-German folklife. The Center's faculty included Alfred L. Shoemaker (Folklore, Arts, Crafts), Don Yoder (History, Religion, Genealogy), and J. William Frey (Dialect, Literature, Music). Although the Pennsylvania scholars emphasized German sources and subjects for their study of folklife, they also recognized folklife efforts in the British Isles which were appropriate for the study of Pennsylvania's substantial Scotch-Irish population.   Indeed, the switch in title from the limiting *Pennsylvania Dutchman* to the broader scope of *Pennsylvania Folklife* was inspired by the appearance of *Ulster Folklife* in 1955. As Don Yoder explained, "The scientific study of folklife (traditional culture) in the United States is an academic migrant from the universities of the Continent of Europe and the British Isles in the 20th Century. Our work in Pennsylvania very much reflects this European emphasis." This statement appeared as an editorial note attached to Donald M. Hines, "The Development of Folklife Research in the United Kingdom," (1972:8).

REFERENCES CITED

Bronner, Simon J.
    1984a *American Folk Art: A Guide to Sources*. New York: Garland Publishing.
    1984b The Early Movements of Anthropology and Their Folkloristic Relationships. *Folklore* 95: 57-73.
Culin, Stewart
    1890 Folk Custom and Medicine of Chinese Americans. Reprinted in: Simon J. Bronner, ed., *Folklife Studies from the Gilded Age: Object, Rite, and Custom in Victorian America*. Ann Arbor, Michigan: UMI Research Press, pp. 87-103.
de Jonge, Eric
    1972 The Thing about Folk Art. *National Antiques Review* 4 (February): 10-13.
Fisher, Sydney George
    1896 *The Making of Pennsylvania*. Philadelphia: J. B. Lippincott.
Gastil, Raymond D.
    1975 *Cultural Regions of the United States*. Seattle: University of Washington Press.
Gibbons, Phebe Earle
    1882 *"Pennsylvania Dutch," and Other Essays*. Philadelphia: J. B. Lippincott.

Glass, Joseph W.
  1986 *The Pennsylvania Culture Region: A View from the Barn.* Ann Arbor, Michigan: UMI Research Press.
Glassie, Henry
  1968 *Pattern in the Material Folk Culture of the Eastern United States.* Philadelphia: University of Pennsylvania Press.
Hines, Donald M.
  1972 The Development of Folklife Research in the United Kingdom. *Pennsylvania Folklife* 21(Spring): 8-20.
Hoffman, W.J.
  1888 Folklore of the Pennsylvania Germans. Reprinted in: Simon J. Bronner, ed., *Folklife Studies from the Gilded Age: Object, Rite, and Custom in Victorian America.* Ann Arbor, Michigan: UMI Research Press, pp. 75-85.
Hopple, C. Lee
  1971-72 Spatial Development of the Southeastern Pennsylvania Plain Dutch Community to 1970: Part I. *Pennsylvania Folklife* 21 (Winter): 18-40.
Landis, H.K.
  1939 Local Folk Museums. *Chronicle of the Early American Industries Association* 2 (April): 71.
  1945 Landis Valley Museum. *Chronicle of the Early American Industries Association* 3 (Sept):43,46,49.
Mercer, Henry C.
  1897 Tools of the Nation Maker. Reprinted in: Simon J. Bronner, ed., *Folklife Studies from the Gilded Age: Object, Rite, and Custom in Victorian America.* Ann Arbor, Michigan: UMI Research Press, pp. 279-91.
Miska, Maxine
  1980 Folk Arts of Southeast Asia: Persistence and Change. In: Jack Santino, ed., *Festival of American Folklife 1980.* Washington, D.C.: Smithsonian Institution, pp. 20-23.
Möller, Helmut
  1964 Aus den Anfangen der Volkskunde als Wissenschaft. *Zeitschrift für Volkskunde* 60:218-41.
Pennsylvania Dutch Folklore Center
  1952 Seminars on the Folk-Culture of the Pennsylvania Dutch Country. *Pennsylvania Dutchman* 4 (May):2.
Peterson, Sally
  1988 Translating Experience and the Reading of a Story Cloth. *Journal of American Folklore* 101: 6-22.
Philadelphia Branch of the American Folklore Society
  1893 Hints for the Local Study of Folk-Lore in Philadelphia and Vicinity. Reprinted in: Simon J. Bronner, ed., *Folklife Studies from the Gilded Age: Object, Rite, and Custom in Victorian America.* Ann Arbor, Michigan: UMI Research Press, pp. 71-72.
Robacker, Earl F.
  1959 The Rise of Interest in Folk Art. *Pennsylvania Folklife* 10 (Spring): 20-29.
Roberts, Warren E.
  1976 Field Work in Dubois County, Indiana: A Project of the Folklore Institute, Indiana University. *Echoes of History* 6:12-14.
  1988 *Viewpoints on Folklife: Looking at the Overlooked.* Ann Arbor, Michigan: UMI Research Press.

Schantz, F.J.F.
  1900 *The Domestic Life and Characteristics of the Pennsylvania-German Pioneer.* Lancaster, Pennsylvania: Pennsylvania German Society.
Watson, John Fanning
  1857 *Annals of Philadelphia and Pennsylvania in the Olden Time.* (Orig. 1830) Revised edition. Philadelphia: Elijah Thomas.
Yoder, Don
  1963 The Folklife Studies Movement. *Pennsylvania Folklife* 13 (July): 43-56.
  1976 Folklife Studies in American Scholarship. In: Don Yoder, ed., *American Folklife.* Austin: University of Texas Press, pp. 3-18.
Zelinsky, Wilbur
  1973 *The Cultural Geography of the United States.* Englewood Cliffs, New Jersey: Prentice-Hall.
  1977 The Pennsylvania Town: An Overdue Geographical Account. *Geographical Review* 67: 127-47.
Zuckerman, Michael
  1982 Introduction: Puritans, Cavaliers, and the Motley Middle. In: Michael Zuckerman, ed., *Friends and Neighbors: Group Life in America's First Plural Society.* Philadelphia: Temple University Press, pp. 3-25.

Charles Fletcher Lummis: The Man Who Lived the Life

W. K. M c N E I L

Most writers dealing with the history of American folklore scholarship have taken one of three stances. Either they have argued that there is no American folklore story of value before the twentieth century, or they have concerned themselves solely with the major figures such as Newell, Boas, and Child, or they have devoted themselves to the study of the major folklore organizations and movements.[1] While all three approaches have much to commend them, they all also somewhat miss the point, for they leave out much of the story of American folklore scholarship. There were personalities whose connection with the various folklore societies was tenuous, who were active prior to the twentieth century, and who made significant, albeit perhaps not major, contributions to the field. For example, there is the case of a Harvard dropout who became renowned as an expert on the Southwest. Charles Fletcher Lummis (1859-1928) became known later in life as a man perhaps too serious and too preoccupied with intellectual concerns, but in his college years he was primarily interested in athletics and having fun, an attitude that led to his premature exit from Harvard. This failure must have been shocking to all those who knew the young Lynn, Massachusetts, native who had mastered Latin, Greek, and Hebrew before he was a teenager and who later memorized an entire German dictionary in four days to pass his college entrance examination. This unexpected setback did not greatly concern Lummis, whose enthusiasm for the university life had always been mild. Calmly and somewhat philosophically he reflected late in life on his schooldays:

I had no violent personal ambition for college. I went because Father had gone, because he had trained me with years of personal concentration. And because it was the cultural convention of New England—to which I acceded as I did in most things. Up until Harvard. . . . I studied reasonably for my classes but for a restrained encircled son of a Methodist minister there were so many other things than lessons to study. My escapades certainly brought me no credits—but I am not sure they were not the most important part of my college courses and of the most lasting benefit. From my cloistered life I had come to the Tree of the Forbidden Fruit. I climbed that tree to the top. . . . What I needed, you see, was not so much to learn books as to Find Myself.[2]

Soon after his expulsion from Harvard, Lummis gained fame as great, if not as lasting, as that of any of his former classmates, but not for any intellectual activity. Instead his initial entry into the public eye came as a result of a flamboyant adventure of the type that Lummis's life seemed to be filled with. After leaving school he moved to Chillicothe, Ohio, to manage his father-in-law's farm and, liking the area, remained for three years. Possibly he would have stayed longer had he not come down with a severe illness that spurred him to perform the deed that catapulted him to sudden fame. In his autobiographical reminiscences, "As I Remember," Lummis describes how he arrived at the decision:

It never occurred to me that I could slow down to the Chillicothe gait. But one night without warning the Old Familiar of the region made me an unexpected call—old Fever-'n'-Ager. I burned and tossed and leaked at every pore. In the morning I was pounds lighter and weak as a drowned rat. The bed was as though I had turned a hose on it.

I am not abrupt nor impetuous, but that one night's lesson that even I was mortal, was enough for me. I was fond of Chillicothe and its courtly people, but before night I decided that I was going to move, that I was going to move a long way, that if I could arrange it, I would make it to California. And I was going to walk there.[3]

In these days of rapid transportation it is not easy to visualize either the difficulties of crossing the country on foot in 1884 or the great appeal such a feat would have for the newspaper readers of that day. During his five month trek which began in Cincinnati and ended in Los Angeles, Lummis braved desolate plains where food was scarce, Indian attacks, freezing winds on the mountaintops, blistering heat on the desert floors, sleeping on the ground in rain and blizzards. One day near the top of the Continental Divide he fell through the ice of a shallow pool and had to walk eight miles to shelter with his clothing frozen to his body. Despite all of these problems Lummis never failed to write every day about his journey, for prior to departure he had contracted to produce a weekly letter dealing with his adventures for the *Los Angeles Times* and the *Chillicothe Leader*. These articles soon began to be reprinted by other papers and before he had progressed very far on the cross-country trek Lummis was already widely known and his trip a *cause celebre*. When he passed through Seymour, Indiana, he "just tore up the burg. Six hundred or more people witnessed his entrance into the town, and since his departure he has been the leading topic of conversation" wrote a local reporter. One editor puzzled over Lummis's sudden fame noting that "the articles have a strange, indescribable interest and people have got to talking about Lum all over the country. He is the most noted man in the West just now and carries in his shoes a pretty fair-sized circus" (Fisk and Lummis 1975:16-17).

This cross-country trek was also important in Lummis's career, aside from the publicity it provided him, for it was on this trip that he first saw the Southwest, the region he eventually came to be most closely associated with. Despite certain prejudices he previously held, Lummis almost immediately thought of the area as his own special province:

> . . . once I had reached Spanish America and the hearts of its people, I realized that this was where I belonged.
> Though my conscience was Puritan, my whole imagination and sympathy and feeling were Latin. That is, essentially Spanish. Apparently they always had been, for now that I had gotten away from the repressive influence of my birthplace I began to see that the generous and bubbling boyish impulses which had been considerably frosted in New England were, after all, my birthright.[4]

In January, 1885, the walk ended in Los Angeles and Lummis never again lived outside the Southwest. He got a job as first city editor of the *Los Angeles Times* and began the first of his writings advocating his newly adopted home region. Initially this activity was carried on only in newspaper articles, but in 1891 the first of many subsequent books about the Southwest appeared. This work, *A New Mexico David and Other Stories of the Southwest*, was successful enough to encourage Lummis a year later, in 1892, to pull together the letters from his 1884-1885 cross-country trek, which appeared as *A Tramp Across the Continent*. Thereafter folklore and non-folklore books were about equally divided in his literary output.

Although Lummis found his niche in the Southwest he was still an adventurous person ready to set off on any journey that promised to be exciting. In 1886 he spent several months with General George Crook's troops in Arizona after the outbreak of Indian wars in that state, performing so well that Crook offered him the position of chief of scouts (Fisk and Lummis 1975:37-38). Moving to New Mexico in

1888, Lummis was determined to take photographs of the flagellation ceremonies of the secretive Herman de la Luz cult. His friends, believing the Penitentes would kill anyone who tried to get such pictures, warned him against going through with this plan, but the danger inherent in the task was one of the prime reasons it appealed to Lummis. Earlier he explained his love of taking risks, noting that nothing was:

> . . . more dreamily delicious than to tease a rattler with some object just long enough to keep those grim fangs from one's own flesh. I have stood thus, thoughtless of discomfort, carried away by the indescribable charm of that grisly presence. Perhaps the consciousness of playing with death and as his master contributes something of that spell. . . . No one who has ever played with a rattlesnake can disbelieve the superstition that it fascinates its prey. I have felt it . . . a sweet dreaminess which has tempted me to drop that stick and reach out my arms to that beautiful death. [Lummis 1892b:22-23]

Anyone with such a love for accomplishing dangerous feats was bound to succeed or die, and so it was that Lummis eventually obtained the desired pictures of the Penitente ceremonies and later used them in several of his books.

Lummis's love of exploration soon brought him into contact with a like-minded scholar, Adolph Bandelier, and the two traveled together on many trips throughout the Southwest and on the Villard Expedition to Peru in 1892. In 1911, when he was fifty-two, Lummis headed a field trip to Guatemala sponsored by the School of American Research. Later, in 1926, despite the onset of blindness, he joined a "dig" in New Mexico sponsored by the Southwest Museum. On these numerous rambles, Don Carlos (a nickname given by Lummis's friends) rarely missed an opportunity to gather lore from those he met. While in New Mexico recovering from the paralyzing effects of a stroke, he collected songs from local sheepherders. In his unpublished autobiography, "As I Remember," he describes his methodology in some detail:

> For months I hung by night around the sheep camps of Don Amado, squatting with the quiet Mexican herders in the little semi-circular brush shelter by a crackling fire of juniper. March and spring nights are chill up there at 7,000 or 8,000 feet on the north shoulder of Mt. San Mateo.
>
> There were no musical instruments, save now and then a mouth organ and more frequently the "bejuela"—a stick maybe a foot long, strung like a little bow with a piece of linen thread and played at the mouth precisely like a jew's harp. There were few good voices but all had what is much more important than a good voice, the will to sing and express their emotion. And beyond that, an invariable sense of time and rhythm which only our best musicians can match. And they were such human, friendly folk! Glad to sing a song over and over until I had it note-perfect

and then to repeat the words while I wrote them down. They were greatly pleased when I could sing their songs back at them.

So we sang and talked and smoked cigarettes under the infinite stars of a New Mexican sky or the even more numerous flakes of a mountain snowstorm.

Folksongs of Spanish origin had a special appeal for Lummis who found in them "a peculiar fascination, a naivete, and yet a vividness and life, a richness of melody with a certain resilience and willfulness which give it a preeminent appeal. It has more music in it, more Rhythm, more Grace (sic). It is more simpatica. It not only joys my hearing and tickles my pulses but cuddles my heart more happily than the songs of any of the score of other nationalities to which I have given friendly ear."[5] He soon came to the belief that the songs of the pastores were the musical record of a vanishing way of life in the Southwest, an idea that spurred him on to record these numbers before they were lost. So for a reason common in the history of folklore collecting, Lummis gathered in the forty years from 1888 to 1928 nearly 600 songs. A sampling of fourteen pieces appeared in his *Spanish Songs of Old California* (1923).

In his various explorations, Lummis was constantly running across interesting personalities, and an encounter with one such "character" in New Mexico led to a minor controversy. In the 1890s he met Martin Valle, a Pueblo statesman who was seven times governor of the cliff republic of Acoma, who told him about Katzimo, the Enchanted Mesa, an extremely steep and rocky cliff where according to tradition the Pueblos once lived. Valle said that the Indians would have remained on Katzimo except for an unfortunate occurrence:

One summer in the time of the harvest all came down from the rock to gather their corn and beans, men, women and children, with buckskin bags to bring the harvest home. All but three women who stayed behind because one was sick. And while they were all away at their fields, down in the Long Valley, there came such storms as no one ever saw; and the rains did not stop; and floods ran down the cliffs of the Valley of Acoma and the waters ran against the foot of Katzimo and ate away the sands and rocks that grew there and burrowed under the great rock that was their ladder. And it fell out into the plain shaking the earth. When the storm ended the people crawled out from under the ledges where they had taken refuge and came home. But their ladder rock was gone and from the top of the sand hill to the cleft was higher than a tall pine. So they could never get up there any more. Neither could the three women on top come down. And there they died after a long time—except one who threw herself off the cliff. And then the people came to this Acoma that is today and built it, a town like the one they lost.

When Lummis published the story it caught the attention of a Princeton professor, William Libbey, who felt it his duty to debunk this Indian "fairy story," and after scaling the Enchanted Mesa during a storm and finding no evidence that any human had ever set foot on the mountain concluded that Lummis's tale was nonsense. But the argument was ended in 1897 when Frederick Webb Hodge of the Bureau of American Ethnology led a small party to the mesa top and found numerous artifacts caught in the rocks in such a way that they had not been washed off the cliff despite centuries of violent storms. This was indisputable evidence that the mesa had been inhabited. Savoring his victory, Lummis chided Libbey, calling him a "tenderfoot" (Fisk and Lummis 1975:59-60). This handling of the Princeton professor was typical, for Lummis was never one to be gracious, and correctly noted that he did not have the ability to say things softly (ibid:103). This trait was particularly true when anyone ventured to comment about things within Lummis's areas of knowledge. He regarded the Southwest as his own, and he was quick to criticize others who dared to deal with the subject. George Wharton James, a clergyman turned western authority, described the effect of Lummis's acid pen:

> . . . Mr. Lummis took upon himself the task of being the censor of everything dealing with the Southwest. When it came to matters dealing with this subject, his virile pen became an instrument of torture to all those who were dealing in an incompetent and incapable manner with subjects connected with this region. It became the standard question, not only in California and the Southwest but even in the libraries and magazines in the East, "Who will Lummis pillory next?" Many a man who deemed himself almost above criticism found himself stripped naked, as it were, shot through with arrows and even scalped because he had presumed carelessly to handle subjects that were within the domain of Mr. Lummis' interests. [James 1923:10]

Not even friends were exempt from Lummis's caustic commentary, as Mary Austin found out. When she was starting out as a writer, Miss Austin had been aided both by Don Carlos and his wife, but this did not prevent him from criticizing her in the most acerbic manner. Concluding a review of her writing he remarked: "She has the most oracular impudence of anyone that ever wrote about the Southwest. . . . A brilliant lady but without conscience and without sense of humor; above all, she has the misfortune of Doubling for the Almighty. She never would study anything for it all comes to her by divine revelation but she, naturally, with her oracular way and her incalculable nerve, imposes on a lot of people to believe her a wonder of wisdom."

While he was quick to find fault, Lummis was just as rapid with praise when he felt a work merited commendation, for he believed that "the privilege to criticize severely or even savagely carried with it the obligation to praise as heartily when it was called for (quoted in Fisk and Lummis 1975:106). In discussing John Muir's *Our National Parks* he wrote enthusiastically:

> A man who writes only because he has something to say on subjects it is worthwhile to say something about and who says it in a medium as unanilined as the Word, is nowadays one of the rarest bipeds without feathers. It would be a little of an impertinence to "review" John Muir's "Our National Parks." It doesn't need it. There are only a few people alive competent (by equal parts of knowledge of the theme and an equivalent literary gift) to appraise it. But all that have the Breath of Life in them are competent to read it and grow by it; nor will any of them find it hard reading . . . And it is one of the books everyone should read who cares for beauty either in nature or in letters. [Lummis 1902:313]

Another feature of Lummis's personality was that he loved to found societies. Among the numerous groups he started was the first of many Landmarks Clubs in the United States. In the early 1890s he had become concerned about the condition of the unoccupied Franciscan missions of southern California, which he regarded as cultural treasures ultimately of more value to the State than all her gold mines. His plan to preserve these monuments found opposition from several quarters, much of it arising from the American Protective Association and its anti-Catholic propaganda. To this kind of thinking he angrily replied: "Those mighty piles belong not to the Catholic church but to you and to me, and to our children and the world. They are monuments and beacons of Heroism and Faith and Zeal and Art. Let us save them—not for the Church but for Humanity" (Fisk and Lummis 1975:88). In 1894, Lummis was able to realize his dream with the founding of the Landmarks Club that took as its goal the preservation of the Missions and other historic monuments of California. Eight years later, in 1902, Lummis organized and christened the Sequoya League which was devoted to the welfare of the American Indian. This organization was designed "To make better Indians by treating them better" and included noted scholars such as Frederick Webb Hodge, John Wesley Powell, Washington Matthews, and Alice Cunningham Fletcher. Lummis's determination that Los Angeles should have a museum led to the formation of the Southwest Society in 1903, and his eagerness to improve the city library and its personnel inspired the establishment in 1906 of the Bibliosmiles, a group he referred to as "the best joke of my ulterior decade." This organization started when Lummis went east to attend the 1906 convention of the American Library Association. He noticed a number of bored members of the audience and gathered a dozen of them at his table, where he pointed out that the ALA was far too

serious.   Therefore he proposed as a remedy an association of
"Librarians Who Are Nevertheless Human," an idea that was readily
accepted, and thus the Bibliosmiles were formed "to keep the dust off
our own top shelves." The group convened at the annual meetings of
the American Library Association and had special signs of membership
including a seal, badge, grip, high sign, password, anthem, and, in lieu
of dues, a "dew," apricot brandy being selected. The Bibliosmiles and
the Los Angeles chapter met yearly until 1920 and was always
something of an embarrassment to the American Library Association.
Yet even that august organization noted that the Bibliosmiles and
their founder made some important contributions (Fisk and Lummis
1975:129).

As the library association he founded demonstrates, Lummis was
a character, a fact he recognized and relished. Proudly he boasted
about his love of the unconventional:

> . . . for 40 years my easy and invariable corduroys and sombrero have reflected
> independence without rebellion and the conclusion that the clothes and English were
> made for me and not I for either. I know Academic English and several other Dead
> Languages—and respect them all too deeply to be their parrot and reverently enough
> to insist that all my liberties with their crystallization shall be true to type and not
> pyrites instead of gold.

Certainly no one ever accused Lummis of being a "parrot," for he was
truly a unique personality. In dress, as in most other matters, he did
exactly as he pleased. At one of his frequent parties, or "noises" as he
called them, he usually dressed up in his "charro" suit, a skin-tight
riding costume of soft suede worn by the caballeros of Mexico, and at
the most formal meetings he would appear in his sombrero and
corduroy suit. Such individualism invited criticism, and throughout
Lummis's career numerous writers published sneering remarks about
his "unusual" dress. Referring to a talk before a ladies club in
February of 1904, a reporter for the *Los Angeles Graphic* became irate:
"Never before was a body of refined ladies so insulted with his cowboy
hat and dirty corduroy suit . . . with the unspeakable odor of
perspiration. . . . Perhaps Lummis is so filled with Indian lore that he
is acquiring their antipathy for water" (Fisk and Lummis 1975:93-94).
A journalist for the *New York Evening Post* dismissed Lummis as "an
apparition simply seeking publicity and trading on an outworn
tradition." A *Washington Post* writer was kinder in noting that the
Californian "is famed not only as a scholar, traveler and writer but as
a wearer of clothes so picturesque as to astonish folks . . . last night
his raiment was toned down a bit, yet it could be distinctly heard as

far as Baltimore. . . . Mr. Lummis' peculiar dress is his own affair and does not mitigate against his reception in the most cultured homes in the nation. . . he has a fine command of language . . . profound information . . . regarded by competent critics as without peer" (ibid:95).

Eventually Lummis produced a number of folklore books of which the most important now is the slender volume *Spanish Songs of Old California* (1923), a work that has never gone out of print and is still selling more than sixty years after its first publication. This small sample of his vast folksong collection is the only one of Lummis's publications that is not extensively reworked, and also one of the few that does not contain a sermon lecturing readers to "See America First." In one of his first books, *Some Strange Corners of Our Country*, he set the tone for the message he would preach throughout his life:

> Other civilized nations take pride in knowing their points of natural and historic interest but when we have pointed to our marvelous growth in population and wealth, we are very largely done and hasten abroad in quest of sights not a tenth part so wonderful as a thousand wonders we have at home and never dream of. . . . There is a part of America—even of the United States—of which Americans know as little as they do of inner Africa. [1892a:1-2]

Thereafter in all his publications the thesis never changed and in some cases overshadowed the other purposes of the book, a point that reviewers did not miss. When *The Land of Poco Tiempo* appeared in 1893, various critics overlooked its folklore content to comment on the author's "enchanting descriptions" of New Mexico. Some focussed on Lummis's "curious" linguistic ability, noting that his "language . . . is not our own" and adding that "familiarity has not endeared it to our minds." They found such adjectives as "the roily pulse of the river" and "devoluted donkey" particularly puzzling (Fisk and Lummis 1975:120).

Lummis's folklore interests and publications dealt with what he considered the strange and the oppressed. New Mexico, the "enchanted" land he "discovered" as a young man, which he believed to be a little known and understood part of the United States figured in *A New Mexico David* (1891), *The Land of Poco Tiempo* (1893), *The King of the Broncos* (1897), *The Enchanted Burro* (a book that caused the author some consternation when the jacket appeared with the caption: The Enchanted Burro Charles F. Lummis) (1897), and *A Bronco Pegasus* (1929). His second great passion, the American Indian, was considered folklorically in *The Man Who Married the Moon and Other Pueblo Indian Folk-Stories* (1894), a book reprinted sixteen years later

in 1910 as *Pueblo Indian Folk-Stories*, and *The Enchanted Burro*. All
of these volumes consist of attempts to convert oral traditions into
literary art. Lummis was aware that not all would approve of such
"improving" but he offered in defense the argument that "Our notions
are far more influenced, in the aggregate, by the local color of fiction
than by the cold lines of monographs" (1972:prefatory note).

Although much of Lummis's work consists of touched up materials
this is not to deny that there is some wheat among the chaff. In *The
Land of Poco Tiempo* he published the first collection of New Mexican
folksongs, one that was not surpassed for more than sixty years. As
usual, Lummis had some strong opinions regarding both the songs and
singers he encountered. Most people were without any "real" understanding of music. In contrast to Californians, New Mexican folksing-
ers came off a dismal second. There were few people with "beautiful"
voices and Lummis definitely didn't care for the style of the husky-
voiced paisano vocalizers. "He slurs his notes oddly, and is prone to
reduplicate them. He sings always *con espresione*, but to him
expression has but two devices. The more he is inspired, the higher
he clambers after his pitch in falsetto and the more conscientiously
nasal he becomes" (1952:166-67). Yet, despite all the marks against
them, Lummis confessed that "there is something far from contempt-
ible in the humblest singing of these humble songs of the soil."
Moreover, the worst singer always had one saving grace, for "the
Mexican is invariably a master of time. His technique may fail at
other points, but the tempo is faultless" (ibid:170).

Lummis found love the favorite motive of New Mexican folksongs,
which was no surprise to him as it also lay at the bottom of most
songs. He also surmised that the total lack of pieces about sheep-
herding, the life led by most men in New Mexico, could be predicted,
for there, as elsewhere, singers like to dwell on subjects more exotic
than the harsh realities of everyday life. That there were no indigenous songs dealing with the saddle, the guitar, the dance, and the
cigarette was not inexplicable to Lummis since all of these items were
commonplace in the territory. Lummis admitted that one song lauding
the soothing cigarro did exist in the repertories of some natives but
admitted that he had written it himself in 1889 "to please my paisano
friends in return for their patience in teaching me real songs of the
soil" (1952:190).

Despite presenting a considerable body of songs and discussing
singers in generalities, Lummis spends remarkably little ink discussing
specific informants. Those who provided the texts are described only
in passing references. From a "tuneful Mexican" who shared a lonely

stage drive of eighty miles in western Arizona he acquired the song "Angel De Amor" (Angel of Love) (1952:168), while a "tattered sixteen-year-old shepherd of San Mateo" contributed "Suzanita" (171). One of the best ballads in his collection came from "two bird-voiced little girls" in the remote village of Cerros Cuates (186). These few glimpses of New Mexican singers entice the reader who wishes more information, but the desire is unfulfilled.

The failure to go beyond generalities in discussing his informants and subjects characterizes the rest of the book. In an essay titled "The City in the Sky" he speaks of the "quaint people" of Acoma although no actual cliff dweller appears in detail; the subject of discussion is merely a typical composite. Only in a consideration of "The Penitent Brothers" is the reader introduced to a real person rather than a hypothetical one. Lummis vividly describes the torture several of the Penitentes inflict upon themselves. He is particularly fascinated by one man, Antonito Montano, a short, stocky man who seemed to take a special delight in self-castigation. During the course of one day this brother absorbed more than two thousand blows of a whip and lay for some time on a bed of thorns. Although young, he was an awesome looking and unforgettable figure. His face had been caved in by a mule and his skull smashed by a soldier in a drunken quarrel but, amazingly, "he is still keen to enjoy such tortures as the most brutal prizefighter never dreamed of" (1952:78).

In a subsequent book, *The Enchanted Burro*, Lummis presented fourteen stories, most about South America but a few about New Mexico. Proudly he skewered library scholars by noting that it was impossible to really know a people or a country without living with the average family, and then added the point that most of the material here came from "episodes I was some part of" for he had gone among these "strange" people and become one of them (1972:preface). Despite this boast, the title story was a legend kept alive by the Pueblos and rewritten by Lummis. The specific source of this narrative is not revealed, but in some portions of the book he gives considerable detail about the context in which he collected stories. He deftly describes the situation when he first heard his friend Don Jose, a hunter from Rio Arriba, tell the legend of "The Witch Deer." He also recalls several encounters with a conjurer he refers to as "The Great Magician" but, generally, his remarks about informants are minimal. This is hardly surprising, for to Lummis the tale, not the teller, was important.

The hero who triumphs against great odds is one of the two major themes that run throughout Lummis's works. In the title story of *A*

New Mexico David he recalls the life of Lucario Montoya, who as a youth in 1840 avenged the death of his family by slaying the gigantic Ute Indian who had killed them. This book also recounts the career of Manuel Chaves, a veteran of more than one hundred Indian battles. *The King of the Broncos* deals with several heroic types that Lummis admired and contains very little folklore. These people include a man who survived the bite of the deadly Pichu-cuate by chopping off his hand, and a friend who triumphed over illness and tragedy to become an example for others. Only a legend about "Poh-Hlaik, The Cave Boy", set five hundred years in the past, and an account of a youth known as Baby Bones could make any claim to be folklore.

Magic is the second theme that occurs throughout Lummis's volumes. In *A New Mexican David* he relates a Pueblo legend of "The Enchanted Mesa," a story set in fifteenth-century New Mexico. Repeatedly he returns to the topic of enchantment and witchcraft. The same volume contains an account of Lummis's meeting with "Three Live Witches." *The Enchanted Burro* includes a Pueblo fairy tale rewritten as "Pablo's Deer Hunt," the story of "The Great Magician," and the tale of "The Witch Deer." *The Land of Poco Tiempo* contains no chapters devoted entirely to witchcraft and the like, but Lummis does spend several pages discussing the "irrational" belief of New Mexicans in witches.[6]   This preoccupation with enchantment is merely an expression of Lummis's love of the odd and unusual. Nothing could be more strange and unique to him than the blind acceptance of belief in fairies and other supernatural creatures.

Today the bulk of Lummis's work seems dated, but it is noteworthy for reaching readers that otherwise might never have looked at a folklore book. This public was really the only audience he wanted, for he was not so much the scholar as the illuminator of misunderstood things and people; he saw all of his writings "as a fingerboard along the path to comprehension" (Fisk and Lummis 1975:121). His success as an interpreter of the Southwest is due to the fact that he had "lived the life," for none of the people discussed in his publications were known only at second hand. Lummis realized the value of fieldwork and insisted on becoming "one of the family" of any group in which he became interested.   If he had any fault in this regard it was that he got too involved with his informants, for he was not content merely to study the Indian, the New Mexican sheepherder, or the "charro"—he also had to live their lives. While these experiences certainly gave his books the stamp of authenticity, they also worked against the author, for Lummis the adventurer became far more interesting than any of

his writings, to such an extent that now his own career and personality
overshadows all of his publications.

NOTES

[1] At a meeting of the American Folklore Society in Austin, Texas, in November, 1972,
Richard M. Dorson responded to a question from the audience on why he had not
written a history of nineteenth-century American folklore scholarship by saying that
"There weren't any American folklorists at that time." Some representative articles and
books that illustrate my contention in the sentences above include Bell (1973), Wilgus
(1959), Vance (1893), and Dwyer-Shick (1979). Of course, many other works could be
cited, but these are sufficient to prove the point.

[2] See "As I Remember," the handwritten autobiography of Lummis which is on file
at the University of Arizona, Tucson, and at the Southwest Museum, Los Angeles. Also
quoted in Fisk and Lummis (1975:7).

[3] See "As I Remember," and Fisk and Lummis (1975:16).

[4] See "As I Remember," and Fisk and Lummis (1975:20-21).

[5] See "As I Remember," and Fisk and Lummis (1975:45-46).

[6] See the first chapter in Lummis (1952).

REFERENCES CITED

Bell, Michael J.
    1973 William Wells Newell and the Foundation of American Folklore Scholarship.
        Journal of the Folklore Institute 10(1-2):7-21.
Dwyer-Shick, Susan
    1979 The American Folklore Society and Folklore Research in America 1888-
        1940. Ph.D. Dissertation, University of Pennsylvania.
Fisk, Turbese Lummis and Keith Lummis
    1975 *Charles F. Lummis: The Man and His West.* Norman: University of Oklahoma
        Press.
James, George Wharton
    1923 Founding of the Overland Monthly and History of the Out West Magazine.
        Overland Monthly (May): 7-11.
Lummis, Charles F.
    1892a *Some Strange Corners of Our Country.* New York: The Century Co.
    1892b *A Tramp Across the Continent.* New York: The Century Co.
    1902 Untitled. *Out West* 16(3): 313.
    1952 *The Land of Poco Tiempo.* Reprint of 1893. Albuquerque: University of New
        Mexico Press.
    1972 *The Enchanted Burro: Stories of New Mexico and South America.* Reprint of
        1897. Freeport, N.Y: Books for Libraries Press.
Vance, Lee J.
    1893 Folk-Lore Study in America. *Popular Science Monthly* 43: 586-98.

Wilgus, D.K.

   1959   *Anglo-American Folksong Scholarship Since 1898.*   New Brunswick, N.J: Rutgers University Press.

Some Overlooked Aspects of Propp's *Morphology of the Folktale:* A Characterization and a Critique

ROBERT A. GEORGES

Following its translation into English thirty years after its initial publication in Russian, Vladimir Propp's *Morphology of the Folktale* (1958, 2nd ed. 1968) created a noticeable stir in scholarly circles. It stimulated Claude Lévi-Strauss to pursue a multi-decade inquiry into the nature of myth structure (see, e.g., Lévi-Strauss 1964, 1966, 1967), provided Alan Dundes with a model for his doctoral dissertation on North American Indian folktales (Dundes 1964b), and motivated individuals such as Claude Bremond to determine its applicability to analyses of non-Russian *Märchen* (Bremond 1977) and researchers such as Daniel Barnes to explore its relevance for studies of selected literary works (Barnes 1970). In an astonishingly short period of time, folklorists accorded Propp's *Morphology* the status of a classic; and it quickly became one of a small number of works on a folklore form to attract the attention of non-folklorists as well. What was it that made the English translation of Propp's book an "instant hit," and why did it become one of the all-time best-sellers on the American Folklore Society's publication list?

Although one could no doubt advance several hypotheses to account for the immediate success of the English translation of Propp's book, two stand out as being particularly defensible and important. First, the translation of *Morphology of the Folktale* appeared during what W. Nelson Francis has called the "revolution in grammar" (Francis 1954). In the 1950s and '60s, increasing numbers of scholars joined the ranks of critics of historical and prescriptive approaches to language, arguing instead for a synchronic and descriptive perspective grounded in the systematic analysis of language structure. The growing interest in, and popularity of, structuralism did, indeed, revolutionize language study, resulting in the creation of linguistics as a discipline readily distinguishable from philology, both conceptually and method-ologically. Furthermore, as it evolved, linguistics provided a stimulus and model for those in other fields, suggesting by example that intangible phenomena other than language could also be conceptual-ized and analyzed structurally. Thus, the English translation of Propp's work found a ready audience, for it appeared when structu-ralism was emerging as a promising analytical mode, not only in investigations of language, but also in the study of other behavioral and cultural phenomena (see, e.g., Piaget 1970 and the essays in Ehrmann 1966 and Laine 1970).

A second—and related—reason for the instant popularity of the *Morphology*, one can posit, is Propp's explicit and incisive critical stance. He begins the book by taking students of *Märchen* to task for their failure to advance inquiry. He scoffs at the prevailing views that collecting must take priority and that generalizations must await the establishment of a more extensive data-base. "It is impossible . . . to say that 'the material already collected is still insufficient,'" he states, adding, "What matters is not the amount of material, but the methods of investigation" (p. 4).[1] Propp accuses researchers of proceeding "according to instinct" (p. 6) and asserts that the preoccupation with trying to classify fairy tales "according to theme leads to total chaos" (p. 7). He admits that Antti Aarne's *Verzeichnis der Märchentypen* (1910) "is important as a *practical reference*" (p. 11, Propp's emphasis), but adds that it is also "dangerous" because it "suggests notions which are essentially incorrect" (p. 11). He asserts that "the problem of classification of the tale finds itself in a somewhat sorry state" and that classification studies "are still in their 'pre-Linnaen' stage" (p. 11). As these characterizations and quotations reveal, Propp does not mince words. By the time his *Morphology* appeared in English translation, enough folklorists had come to share his misgivings about the state of folktale research to bring the book and its author the immediate attention and acclaim both received.

Although Lévi-Strauss' work has replaced Propp's as the principal model and inspiration for an avid, but steadily waning, group of structuralist-oriented researchers, *Morphology of the Folktale* retains its classic status and maintains a place on most folklorists' required reading lists. Propp's discernment and characterization of the patterning phenomenon in fairy tales and his demonstration that structure is more stable and predictable than content and style continue to ring true and to be borne out by structural studies of narratives and other folklore forms (see, e.g., Dundes 1961, 1962, 1964a, 1964b, 1975, 1976, and Georges and Dundes 1963). Yet despite its obvious historical importance, Propp's book is filled with seldom–noticed and rarely-noted statements that warrant scrutiny and discussion.[2] My purposes in this essay are (1) to characterize selected aspects of Propp's *Morphology* that folklorists either have overlooked or have been reluctant to discuss, and (2) to consider some of their implications.

As is well known, Propp discerns and describes a recurrent structural pattern in *Märchen* consisting of a maximum of thirty-one functions, or acts of the dramatis personae. Some of these functions, he indicates, are obligatory, in that they are always present, while others are optional, meaning that they may or may not occur. Because many functions configure into sets, the presence of the first in a set of optional functions makes the other members of the set obligatory. Interdiction, for example, is an optional function in Propp's scheme; but when there is an interdiction—whether it is explicitly stated or implied—it is invariably violated, since, according to Propp, function II ("AN INTERDICTION IS ADDRESSED TO THE HERO," p. 26) and function III ("THE INTERDICTION IS VIOLATED," p. 27) "form a *paired* element" (p. 27, Propp's emphasis). Similarly, if optional function XII, "THE HERO IS TESTED, INTERROGATED, ATTACKED, ETC., WHICH PREPARES THE WAY FOR HIS RECEIVING EITHER A MAGICAL AGENT OR HELPER" (p. 39), is present, then the two functions with which it configures into a set will necessarily follow—that is, function XIII, "THE HERO REACTS TO THE ACTIONS OF THE FUTURE DONOR" (p. 42), and function XIV, "THE HERO ACQUIRES THE USE OF A MAGI-CAL AGENT" (p. 45).

Propp's distinguishing between obligatory and optional functions and his illustrating how optional functions become obligatory when they configure into sets and when the first member of a set is present are intended to enable one to understand better the readily-apparent conventionality and predictability in fairy tale plots. But the seeming elegance, simplicity, and significance of the patterning Propp describes are considerably lessened when he notes that of the maximum total number of thirty-one functions, only a single pair is really always obligatory—*either* function VIII, "THE VILLAIN CAUSES HARM OR INJURY TO A MEMBER OF A FAMILY, " *or* function VIIIa.,

"ONE MEMBER OF A FAMILY EITHER LACKS SOMETHING OR DESIRES TO HAVE SOMETHING," *and* function XIX, "THE INITIAL MISFORTUNE OR LACK IS LIQUIDATED." If, in fact, a story needs to have inherent in it only a single pair of functions in order for it to be identifiable as a *Märchen*, then Propp's scheme cannot be regarded as one that defines the fairy tale and distinguishes it from all other phenomena, which is what he indicates he has accomplished. As Dundes has illustrated, for example, narratives other than *Märchen*, and even such non-narrative phenomena as superstitions, can be shown to be built on a lack/liquidated pattern, demonstrating that that pair of functions is not unique to fairy tales, as Propp implies (see, e.g., Dundes 1963, 1964b).

The waters are muddied further when Propp finally presents his structural definition of the *Märchen*: "Morphologically," he writes, "a tale (*skázka*) may be termed any development proceeding from villainy (A) or a lack (a), through intermediary functions to marriage (W*), or to other functions employed as a dénouement" (p. 92). Noticeably missing from this definition is any mention of the need for liquidation, a function that Propp earlier states is always paired with villainy or lack. One might infer that Propp does not mention the second member of the obligatory pair because he assumes it is implied by mention of the first member of the set. But it is difficult to be certain of this, particularly since Propp later states, "A (villainy) or *a* (lack) *are the only . . . obligatory elements*" (p. 102, my emphasis). Moreover, if all functions other than lack or villainy—or the pair villainy or lack and liquidation of the initial misfortune or lack—are optional, then what are the "intermediary functions" and "other functions" that Propp mentions in his definition? He specifies neither number nor kind, leading a reader to infer that for a tale to be identified as a *Märchen*, it need have only a lack or a villainy and some other functions; and such a definition is obviously neither very specific nor very satisfying.

Late in the *Morphology*, Propp offers a second definition of the fairy tale, which further clouds the matter about the obligatoriness of functions in *Märchen*: "The stability of construction of fairy tales," he writes, "permits a hypothetical *definition* of them which may be stated in the following way: a fairy tale is a story built upon the proper alternation of the above-cited functions [i.e., his list of all thirty-one functions] in various forms, with some of them absent from each story and with others repeated" (p. 99, Propp's emphasis). No mention is made here of the necessity for the presence of a villainy or a lack, either by itself or in combination with what Propp elsewhere describes as its "paired element," liquidation. Furthermore, this second definition of the fairy tale is even more vague and imprecise than the first, as such word groups as "*proper* alternation," "in *various* forms," "with *some* of them absent," and "with *others* repeated" clearly reveal. While the first definition indicates that at least one of two functions--villainy or lack--is always obligatory, the second one reveals that no *specific* functions need be present in *Märchen* at all!

Propp is also inconsistent in his discussion of function sequencing. Early in the *Morphology* he states, "The sequence of functions is always identical," noting that "by no means do all tales give evidence of all functions," but insisting that the "absence of certain functions does not change the order of the rest" (p. 22). Propp reveals his surprise at having discovered, early on in his research, this fixity in the sequencing of functions ("This is, of course, a completely unexpected result," p. 22); and he repeatedly reiterates its inviolability and importance:

> What conclusions does this scheme present? In the first place, it affirms our general thesis regarding the total uniformity in the construction of fairy tales.
> This most important general conclusion at first does not coincide with our conception of the richness and variety of tales.
> As has already been indicated, this conclusion appeared quite unexpectedly. It was an unexpected one for the author of this work as well. This phenomenon is so unusual and strange that one somehow feels a desire to dwell upon it, prior to going on to more particular, formal conclusions. Naturally, it is not our business to interpret this phenomenon; our job is only to state the fact itself. Yet one still feels inclined to pose this question: if all fairy tales are so similar in form, does this not mean that they all originate from a single source? The morphologist does not have the right to answer this question. At this point he hands over his conclusions to a historian or should himself become a historian. [pp. 105-06]

Despite this repeated emphasis on structural "uniformity," it soon becomes apparent that the sequence of functions is not so fixed and inviolable as Propp asserts, for he illustrates that sets of functions can be--and frequently are--transposed. "In comparing a large number of tales," he writes at one point, "it becomes apparent . . . that the elements peculiar to the *middle* of the tale are sometimes *transferred to the beginning* . . ." (p. 36, Propp's emphasis). Elsewhere, he states, "The assertion concerning absolute stability would seem to be unconfirmed by the fact that the sequence of functions is not always the same as that shown in the total scheme. A careful examination of the schemes will show certain deviations" (p. 107). Propp admits to the occasional presence of such "transpositions" or "transformations," as he alternately calls them; but he also tends to dismiss them, as the following quotation reveals:

All of these deviations do not alter the deduction concerning the typological unity and morphological kinship of fairy tales. These are only fluctuations and not a new compositional system or new axes. There are certain cases, as well, of direct violations. In isolated tales the violations are rather significant . . . , but a closer examination will reveal these to be humorous tales. A transposition of this kind, accompanying the transformation of a poem into a farce, must be recognized as the result of dissolution. [p. 108]

The sequencing of functions that Propp initially insists is fixed and inviolable in fairy tales, then, turns out to be ideal rather than real, even insofar as the selected *Märchen* he presents and analyzes structurally in the *Morphology* are concerned.

One could, of course, excuse these inconsistencies and contradictions by attributing them to Propp's careless rhetoric or to the translator's imprecision. One could, as well, dismiss them as being relatively insignificant, arguing that the real contribution of *Morphology of the Folktale* is that Propp succeeds in describing a pattern of actions that not only recurs in *Märchen*, but that also defines the form and differentiates fairy tales from all other phenomena. Yet while he is explicitly self-congratulatory about his success in defining the *Märchen* as a distinctive category of phenomena and in doing so "scientifically" rather than intuitively as he judges others to have tried unsuccessfully to do, Propp makes assertions which indicate that the structure he characterizes throughout the bulk of his book as being unique to *Märchen* is actually not really found only in fairy tales at all, but that it is also discernible in other kinds of narratives as well. At one point, for example, he states that "non-fairy tales may also be constructed according to the scheme cited," adding, "Quite a large number of legends, individual tales about animals, and isolated novellas display the same structure" (p. 99). At another point he states, "If tales of this class [i.e., *Märchen*] are defined from a historical point of view, they then merit the antique, now discarded, name of mythical tales" (p. 100). Moreover, Propp's structural connection between myth and fairy tale is made even more explicit when he notes:

From the historical point of view, this signifies that the fairy tale in its morphological bases represents a myth. We fully realize that, from the point of view of contemporary scholarship, we are expressing a totally heretical idea. This idea has been considerably discredited by adherents of the mythological school. On the other hand, this idea has such strong supporters as Wundt, and now we are coming to it by way of morphological analysis. [p. 90]

Myth comes up again later in the *Morphology;* and Propp's words are worth quoting in full:

It might also be pointed out that a similar construction is displayed by a number of very archaic myths, some of which present this structure in an amazingly pure form. Evidently this is the realm back to which the tale may be traced. On the other hand, the very same structure is exhibited, for example, by certain novels of chivalry. This is very likely a realm which itself may be traced back to the tale. [p. 100]

By noting that the structure inherent in fairy tales is also discernible in such other kinds of narratives as legends, novellas, "novels of chivalry," and myths, Propp seems to discredit the very thesis he sets out to develop and prove: that *Märchen* constitute a distinctive kind or category of narrative and that their distinctiveness is demonstrable on the basis of the uniqueness of their structure.

There are numerous other examples of inconsistency and self-contradiction in Propp's *Morphology* (some of which are discussed in such works as Taylor 1964:121-27 and Nathhorst 1969:16-29). Let me mention just two more related matters. First, despite his criticisms of other folktale scholars and his self-proclaimed effort to make the study of *Märchen* more "scientific"—and hence, from his point of view, more objective and respectable—Propp is actually more indebted to, and dependent on, works and views he criticizes or dismisses than he is willing to admit. He is critical of Aarne's type-index, for instance, because of its thematic bases. "Clear-cut division into types does not actually exist," he states, adding that "very often it is a fiction. If types do exist," he continues, "they exist not on the level indicated by Aarne, but on the level of the structural features of similar tales . . ." (p. 11). Yet when he describes his method and material, Propp states, "The existence of fairy tales as a special class is assumed as an essential working hypothesis. *By 'fairy tales' are meant at present those tales classified by Aarne under numbers 300 to 749*" (p. 19, my emphasis). Thus, despite his insistence that "the division [of *Märchen*] according to theme leads to total chaos" and that "the division of fairy tales according to themes is, in general, impossible" (p. 7), Propp uses Aarne's theme-based index to define his data corpus and to determine what kinds of tales to analyze structurally. In addition, his rejection of theme-based tale types does not deter him from noting, at several points, that the fairy tale which comes closest to embodying the overall structure he discerns and describes is, in fact, the first story that Aarne includes in the subdivision of his index of which Propp makes use—that is, Type 300, *The Dragon Slayer*. Writes Propp:

Were we able to unfold the picture of transformations, it would be possible to satisfy ourselves that all the tales given can be morphologically deduced from the tales about the kidnapping of a princess by a dragon—from that form which we are inclined to consider as basic. [p. 114]

A theme-based tale type, then, becomes the proto-narrative structurally for all fairy tales, despite Propp's dislike both of tale types based on themes and of Aarne's index of such tale types.

While Propp criticizes theme-based types and Aarne's index of them, he does not reject the tale-type *concept*, as attested by his repeated utilization of the word *type* throughout the *Morphology*. But he is neither clear nor consistent in his use of the term. At times, Propp seems to equate type with genre, as is the case, for instance, when he states, "All fairy tales are of one type in regard to their structure" (p. 25). Implicit in this assertion are the notions that the only defensible conclusions one can draw about *Märchen*, based on the nature of their structure, is that they are all *Märchen* and that further subdivision by type is impossible, at least on structural grounds. At another point, however, Propp takes a different stance when he states:

> Tales with *identical functions* can be considered as belonging to one type. On this foundation, an *index of types* can then be created, *based* not upon theme features, which are somewhat vague and diffuse, but *upon exact structural features*. If we further compare structural *types* among themselves, we are led to the following completely unexpected phenomenon: functions cannot be distributed around mutually exclusive axes. [p. 22, my emphasis]

Later in the *Morphology*, Propp adds to the confusion concerning his conception of type when he discusses tales containing two pairs of functions: (1) XVI, "THE HERO AND THE VILLAIN JOIN IN DIRECT COMBAT," and XVIII, "THE VILLAIN IS DEFEATED," and (2) XXV, "A DIFFICULT TASK IS PROPOSED TO THE HERO," and XXVI, "THE TASK IS RESOLVED." Since *Märchen* can contain either, both, or neither of these sets of paired functions, Propp notes, their absence or their presence singly or together reveal the existence of "four types of tales" (p. 103). "Does this not contradict our assertion concerning the complete uniformity of all fairy tales?" asks Propp (p. 103). He states that it does not, noting that each of these pairs of functions is found in only one move of multi-move tales and that when both are present, the fight and its paired function always occur in the first, and the task and its paired function appear only in the second, move. Hence, what seem like four types structurally are really only two types, according to Propp. "It is quite possible," he speculates, "that two types existed historically, that each has its own history, and that in some remote epoch the two traditions met and merged into one formation" (p. 103). He adds, "But in speaking about Russian fairy tales we are compelled to say that today this is one tale, to which all tales of our class are traced" (pp. 103-4).

It is obviously confusing, if not actually ambiguous or even contradictory, to characterize *Märchen* as all being "of one type in regard to their structure" while at the same time asserting that only "tales with identical functions" can belong to "one type" and that an index of multiple fairy tale types can be created, since fairy tales can differ in type because different sets of tales are distinguishable from each other on the basis of the combinations of the specific functions they exhibit.

Given the nature and number of ambiguities, inconsistencies, and contradictions in Propp's book, one is understandably motivated to ask whether *Morphology of the Folktale* is as important or significant a work as many judge it to be. Does it deserve to be accorded the status of a "classic," and should the book be included on folklorists' required reading lists?

The answers to such questions will necessarily vary, depending on the interests and biases of the respondents and the evaluative criteria they judge to be most important. From those who place greater value on effort than on achievement, the *Morphology* will undoubtedly receive high marks. Propp attempts to make the study of fairy tales multidimensional and more analytic by demonstrating the possibility and value of distinguishing conceptually among structure, content, and style and by illustrating that it would seem to be structure that accounts for the fairy tale's "striking uniformity" and "repetition," while content and style are responsible for its "amazing multiformity, picturesqueness, and color . . ." (p. 21). For those who value achievement over effort, on the other hand, the *Morphology* will, understandably, not fare well. Propp does not carry out the objectives that he sets for himself and that he repeatedly states he has achieved. He neither provides an "exact description" (p. 15) of the *Märchen* that he feels a structural analysis makes possible, nor does he demonstrate that "fairy tales possess a *quite particular* structure which is immediately felt and which determines their category" (p. 6, my emphasis). He purports to depart conceptually and analytically in his pursuits from the paths taken by his predecessors and contemporaries, who, he claims "have proceeded according to instinct" and whose "words do not correspond to what they have actually sensed" (p. 6). But he is dependent on the fruits of the labors of those he criticizes (particularly Aarne's) to advance his own position; and he shares many of the same assumptions and concepts—e.g., that myth preceded *Märchen* in time, with fairy tales being modeled after, or derived from, myths; that *Märchen* have deteriorated with the passage of time and their movement through space; that fairy tales contain "very little pertaining to [modern-day] everyday life" (p. 106).[3]

Morphology of the Folktale has inspired many, and will no doubt stimulate others in years to come, principally because of Propp's aspirations and his critical stance. It seems unlikely, however, that the work will be able to retain its status as a classic and maintain its position on required reading lists once folklorists study and analyze it more systematically and critically, and once they come to realize that the book's ambiguities, inconsistencies, and contradictions—selected ones of which I have characterized and discussed in this brief essay—are too numerous and significant to excuse or dismiss.

NOTES

[1]   This and all subsequent page references provided parenthetically throughout the essay are to the second (1968) edition of the English translation of Propp's work.

[2]   While an overwhelming majority of folklorists who mention or discuss Propp's *Morphology* are positive and often even reverential in their remarks, some have also been critical. See, for instance, Lévi-Strauss 1960, Fischer 1963:288-89, Taylor 1964:121-27, and Nathhorst 1969:16-29.

[3]   For further discussion and exemplification of the pervasiveness of early folktale scholars' concepts and assumptions in the work of their successors, see Georges 1986.

REFERENCES CITED

Barnes, Daniel R.
    1970 Folktale Morphology and the Structure of Beowulf. *Speculum* 45:416-34.
Bremond, Claude
    1977 The Morphology of the French Fairy Tale: The Ethical Model. In *Patterns in Oral Literature*. Ed. Heda Jason and Dimitri Segal, pp. 49-76. The Hague: Mouton.
Dundes, Alan
    1962 The Binary Structure of 'Unsuccessful Repetition' in Lithuanian Folk Tales. *Western Folklore* 21:165-74.
    1963 Structural Typology in North American Indian Folktales. *Southwestern Journal of Anthropology* 19:121-30.
    1964a On Game Morphology: A Study of the Structure of Non-Verbal Folklore. *New York Folklore Quarterly* 20:276-88.
    1964b The Morphology of North American Indian Folktales. *Folklore Fellows Communications* 195. Helsinki.
    1975 On the Structure of the Proverb. In Alan Dundes *Analytic Essays in Folklore*. pp. 103-18. The Hague: Mouton.
    1976 Structuralism and Folklore. In *Folk Narrative Research: Some Papers Presented at the VI Congress of the International Society for Folk Narrative Research*. Ed. Juha Pentikäinen and Tuula Juurikka, pp. 75-93. *Studia Fennica: Review of Finnish Linguistics and Ethnology* 20. Helsinki.

Ehrmann, Jacques, ed.
   1966   Structuralism. *Yale French Studies* 36-37:1-272.
Fischer, J. L.
   1963   The Sociopsychological Analysis of Folktales. *Current Anthropology* 4:235-95.
Francis, W. Nelson
   1954   Revolution in Grammar. *Quarterly Journal of Speech* 40:299-312.
Georges, Robert A.
   1986   The Pervasiveness in Contemporary Folklore Studies of Assumptions, Concepts, and Constructs Usually Associated with the Historic-Geographic Method. *Journal of Folklore Research* 23:87-103.
------------, and Alan Dundes
   1963   Toward a Structural Definition of the Riddle. *Journal of American Folklore* 76:111-18.
Laine, Michael, ed.
   1970   *Introduction to Structuralism*. New York: Basic Books, Inc.
Lévi-Strauss, Claude
   1960   L'analyse morphologique des contes russes. *International Journal of Slavic Linguistics and Poetics* 3:122-49.
   1964   *Mythologiques I: Le cru et le Cuit*. Paris: Plon.
   1966   *Mythologiques II: Du Miel aux cendres*. Paris: Plon.
   1967   The Story of Asdiwal. In *The Study of Myth and Totemism*. Ed. Edmund Leach, pp.1-47. ASA Monographs 5. London: Tavistock.
Piaget, Jean
   1970   *Structuralism*. Translated and edited by Chaninah Maschler. New York: Basic Books, Inc.
Propp, Vladimir
   1968   *Morphology of the Folktale*. Second Edition. Translated by Laurence Scott, revised and edited by Louis A. Wagner. Publications of the American Folklore Society, Bibliographic and Special Series 9. Austin: University of Texas Press.
Taylor, Archer
   1964   The Biographical Pattern in Traditional Narrative. *Journal of the Folklore Institute* 1:114-29.
Waugh, Butler
   1966   Structural Analysis in Literature and Folklore. *Western Folklore* 25:153-64.

Antti Aarne's Tales with Magic Objects

CHRISTINE GOLDBERG

Stith Thompson's book *The Folktale* has for forty years been the principal English-language source of American folklorists' and literary historians' knowledge of oral tales. Thompson accepted the ideas of Kaarle Krohn, who developed the historic-geographic method for the study of folktales. Krohn put other people to work (including both Thompson and Antti Aarne) testing *his* predecessors' sweeping statements concerning the place of origin of many or all folktales. Impressive amounts of data were gathered to determine whether a certain tale could be shown to have originated in any particular region, and what its paths of dissemination had been. For some tales, where all the evidence points in the same direction, these conclusions are convincing even today. For others, the authors may try to reach back into a hoary antiquity beyond the available evidence, and I for one become skeptical. It was the intellectual fashion at that time to search for and to accept *origins* as being the ultimate (perhaps I should say primary) explanation of phenomena. The historic-geographic conclusions as to the original form and place of origin always are a heuristic device that simplifies a lot of complicated data, "so," as Thompson says, "one can secure a comprehensive view of the whole tradition" of a tale (1946:440). Intellectual fashion now prefers ahistorical, dynamic, process-oriented explanations. Fortunately, the tale studies' presentation of their considerable data is also useful for this kind of analysis. One has to sift carefully through the material and pick out the relevant details.

In *The Folktale*, Thompson generally provides a plot summary of each tale type, and answers when possible the questions of when? and where? He presents only a couple of studies in more detail (24-32,432-433). He tells very little about any of Aarne's studies. In part this is justified by their naiveté: they do present overly simplistic notions about the relationship of variants to an Ur-form, and are careless in reporting the composition of each individual variant. Nevertheless, Aarne's studies, as they describe and analyze many variants, are full of information relevant to the folklorist's perpetual interest, stability and variation in tradition. Aarne was a hard worker, who set himself a project, worked on it, finished it, and went on to the next project. He created the original index of tale types (*Verzeichnis der Märchentypen* 1910). His *Übersicht der Märchenliteratur* (1914) proves that he was a careful bibliographer (Krohn 1926). I think he completed thorough studies of more tales than anyone else ever has. Working as he did on the formation of the concept of the tale type, Aarne was a pioneer in a field where Thompson became an adherent. Many of Aarne's discoveries have been overlooked in the intervening years. Space limitation here restricts me to only a few of his studies. I chose "tales with magic objects" because these complex tales have enough variables to show both how such tales can change, and how they can remain fixed.

In *The Folktale* (440-443), Thompson discusses some then-recent objections to the historic-geographic method. The gist of his reply is that "things are better now," more or less allowing that earlier the objections would or might have been valid. Walter Anderson's *Kaiser und Abt* is singled out as an example of a tale study that properly takes into account many old literary variants of the tale. Though he does not find so many as Anderson did, Aarne gives old examples that are given full weight. Two sources that appear repeatedly in the studies discussed below are the Mongolian *Siddi-Kür* with its suggestion of Indian origin (Cosquin 1913:1-11) and Basile's *Pentamerone*. The *Pentamerone* (1634-1636; Penzer 1932) establishes a *terminus ante quem* for the genre of the European magic tale, but, often surprisingly, not necessarily for the tale types as they exist in recent oral tradition.[1] Thompson credits C. W. von Sydow and his students with the idea of studying groups of related tales. Aarne did this too: he displayed pairs or sets of tale types that follow a similar outline and share a significant idea or episode. Within each pair, one tale may be distinctly European and the other tale (which may be found in Europe, too) be Asiatic. The European form will have an apparent center of dissemination in that region, and will have stylistic traits later described by Max Lüthi as characteristic of European folktales. Thompson's praise of the living did an injustice to the dead. While specific additions or emendations are always appropriate, Aarne's tale studies need no general apology.

AT 563, *The Table, the Ass, and the Stick*
AT 564, *The Magic Providing Purse and Out, Boy, of the Sack*
(Aarne 1911)

Although it comes from sixth-century China, the oldest version of AT 564 is typical of modern versions which are found in Europe, Asia, and Africa. A poor man gives offerings to a religious man, and receives from him a jar that will produce anything he wants—but he must not tell the king. He grows rich and invites the king to be his guest. The king takes the jar. The hero goes back to the religious man who gives him a vase that produces attacking sticks and stones, which he is to give to the king. The contents kill the king's men, and the king returns the jar. The hero becomes rich and does good deeds (Chavannes 1962).[2] The frame here is moralistic, and there are two contrasting episodes within it.

The Table, the Ass, and the Stick (AT 563) is a more popular tale, found throughout the same Old World region. The strong contrasts in AT 564—the rich and poor men (who in oral tradition are often brothers), the similar containers with opposite contents—are weakened. The motifs in their place are more like those characteristic of wonder tales: the adventures take place away from home (at an inn); the magic gifts are trebled rather than doubled; the self-laying cloth and the gold-dropping donkey are more precise than the all-providing jar. Although in Asia AT 563 has neighbors instead of an innkeeper, the inn and the trebled objects are the crucial distinctions between the two tales. They bring *The Table, the Ass, and the Stick* completely out of the realm of supernatural legend and into that of humorous fantasy. The two tales are oikotypes, cousins which have been subjected to changes in different generic directions.

Because they are so similar and are known throughout a common region, AT 563 and AT 564 share introductory episodes. A poor man asks his rich brother for meat and is given some, and told to "go to the devil"—which he does, and the devil gives the jar in payment for the meat. Or the poor man's crops are spoiled by the weather and he goes directly to Frost or to the Wind to complain. These introductions are regional, and occur in both tales. They are markedly humorous, in that the poor man takes one or another figure of speech literally and profits from this foolishness. Aarne was frustrated that the episode of going to the devil does not seem to occur as a separate tale (80-82). It is, however, an ancient motif. In Aristophanes' comedy *The Birds* (lines 27-29) two con men "go to the crows," where the phrase means "get lost," and find those birds quite helpful. Like the man in the folktale, they take a figure of speech literally and profit therefrom. The humor in the episode as it appears in AT 563-4 is of a piece with the slapstick humor in the rich brother's (or innkeeper's) beating.

In the Mongolian *Siddi-Kür*, a poor man takes a magic-providing sack from forest spirits in a cave. His rich brother copies him, and the spirits, thinking it was he who stole the sack, tie knots in his nose. The rich man has to use a hammer to remove the knots (Jülg 1973:139-47, no.14). The misunderstanding is that found in *Ali Baba* (AT 676); the knotted nose reminds us of the hump back in *The Gifts of the Little People* (AT 503). There are elements of AT 564 here, but the differences are also significant. In the *Pentamerone*, a tale with two brothers and two gifts (chest and flail) would seem to be AT 564, but the action takes place at an inn, the location usually associated with AT 563 (day 5, tale 2). Aarne remarked that when the rich brother begs the pardon of the poor brother, that is Basile's touch. There is also a typical version of AT 563 in the *Pentamerone* (day 1, tale 1).

Along with these tales, Aarne investigated a tale from northern Europe, *The Magic Mill* (AT 565). All three tales share a common structure: the hero obtains a magic object, the villain steals it (or uses it improperly), and the object or its double punishes the villain. These tales discuss poverty and abundance, and the magic-producing objects tie the episodes together into a coherent entity. Some of the changes from the sixth-century Chinese version make the tale more economical: the two brothers instead of a man and a king; riches as its own reward instead of as a means to do good. Others make it more fanciful: the comical source of the gifts; the tablecloth and donkey in place of the pot. In the introductory episodes with the bacon or the spoiled crops, the poor man's poverty, in the specific form of a lack of food, is made apparent. All these variations testify to a desire to make the story more interesting. Aarne thought that the form with the three objects was perhaps the original (77). If this be the case (which I doubt), then, in the change from three to two magic objects, greater symmetry and simplicity were achieved. Alterations are experiments at making a good tale better, but the meaning of "better" is certainly regional.

AT 560 *The Magic Ring*
AT 561 *Aladdin* (Aarne 1908:1-82)

A man buys a cat and a dog who would have been killed. He saves a snake or its son from fire, or from a dangerous opponent, or pays their debts. In return for this help, the snake gives him a magic ring (or stone or lamp). (In Finland and Russia, the role of the snake may go to a frog, a dead man, or a devil.) With the ring he obtains a castle and marries a king's daughter. In Europe, she steals the magic ring and castle and disappears; in Asia a villain steals the wife, the ring, and the castle. The cat and dog, with the help of a mouse and the hindrance of a fish, retrieve the ring for the hero. The cat causes a mouse to steal the ring from the thief as he sleeps. On their return, the cat rides on the back of the dog as he swims. The cat opens his mouth and the ring, falling out, is swallowed by a fish. The cat again recovers the ring and delivers it to its owner. The hero uses the ring to recover his wife and castle. If there is a separate villain, he is punished; if the wife is the villain, she may either be forgiven or be put to death.

The nature of the connection of the helpful animals with the magic ring tale is central to an understanding of this tale type. The variant in the *Siddi-Kür* has both parts (Aarne 1908:72-74). Aarne decided on an Asiatic origin for this Helpful Animals plus Magic Ring tale (AT 560), which is seldom complete in western Europe. *Aladdin* (AT 561), with the famous lamp in place of the ring, has no helpful animals (61-71). A late addition to the Arabian Nights, that tale has only a handful of oral variants (Ranke 1977); of those, many (in Aarne's study, ten of 17) are mixed with AT 560. In the *Pentamerone* there are two relevant tales, one of AT 560 with the magic ring and a helpful mouse (but no dog or cat) (day 4 tale 1), and the other with the dog, cat, and mouse, but no magic ring (day 3 tale 5). The helpful dog and cat are found in three-quarters (108 out of 144) of Aarne's variants. An important question not yet answered is, to what extent are these two independent tales (as they are in the *Pentamerone*) that have formed a stable combination in the East? Does the *Magic Ring* tale have two forms, a short one without the animals and a long one with them? Is there a separate Helpful Animals tale or episode?

The Magic Ring part alone discusses sexuality: adultery, infidelity, or rape. The helpful animals divert the interest, focusing the suspense on the mechanics of the recovery of the ring. In the combined tale, the Magic Ring episodes provide the motivation for the loss and recovery of the ring. But even so, other tales or episodes could have been employed to serve this purpose. The Magic Ring and the

Helpful Animals share a hero who is kind to animals, and who is helped in return. Basile's tales suggest that they may also share the helpful mouse. There is also repeated regurgitation of the ring (by the thief, who hides it in his mouth, the cat, who carries it in his, and the fish). These are the points of contact that give the episodes such affinity. Complex tales can derive stability from episodes that reiterate ideas.

AT 567, *The Magic Bird Heart* (Aarne 1908:143-200)

A man buys a magic hen that lays golden eggs, and grows rich by selling them. When he is away, a clerk learns that whoever eats the bird's head will become a lord and whoever eats her heart (or entrails) will find a piece of gold under his pillow every day. The clerk induces the owner's wife to order the bird killed, but instead of the clerk the owner's two sons eat the head and heart. Knowing that eating the sons will restore the magic properties to himself, the clerk tries to kill them but fails. (Sometimes an animal is killed in their place.) The son who ate the head becomes a lord. The other, with the golden coins, meets a girl and marries her. (Now for the second part). Helped by an old woman, the girl causes him to vomit the heart. He obtains magic grass (or fruit) that turns her into an ass (or makes horns grow on her head). She returns the heart and he restores her to human form. The clerk and the mother may be punished.

Aarne pursued a number of details in search of their original forms. At the outset, he thought, the buying of the bird was suggested by the sale of the eggs. Often the clerk learns about the bird's magic properties from a note hidden under its wing; Aarne thought that this was a later addition not originally in the tale. In about a fifth of the variants, dogs are killed in place of the sons. These precise details, not really necessary to the plot, are quite common. Their presence makes Aarne's goal of determining the details of the original form of the tale seem almost feasible. Extraneous, deceitful women can appear in both parts: the clerk acts in collusion with the treacherous wife of the bird's owner, and a scheming old woman often assists the wife of the second son. Eating the bird's head or heart enhances the lives of the sons; eating the magic grass disrupts the plan of the second son's wife. Other details are regional: in the Slavic countries and in Finland, the second son spits out the gold pieces, analogous to his having swallowed the heart and later vomiting it. (The substitution of the bird's entrails for its heart also reflects the vomiting.) The plot to kill the sons (a motif that repeats the killing of the bird) is absent in Mediterranean Europe.

There are two parts to this tale, the clerk's intrigue and the adventures of the gold-sleeper. The first part has next to no hero, only a villain and his victims. Aarne (182) and Krohn (1931:45-47) discussed whether the second part might be a later addition to the tale. The variant in the *Siddi-Kür* has both parts. The second part has been influenced by the similar tale of *The Three Magic Objects and the Wonderful Fruits* (AT 566), which makes its "original form" difficult to discover. Original or not, the second part sticks to the first because it repeats both the treachery against the owner of the magic bird (heart), and the magic effects that eating something can have on one's person.

AT 566, *The Three Magic Objects and the Wonderful Fruits*
(Aarne 1908:83-142)

Three men each receive a magic object: a travelling cape, a gold-producing purse, and a horn that can send forth an army. A princess or dragon steals the objects. One of the men obtains an apple that causes horns to grow and another that removes them. He tricks the princess into eating the apple, and she has to return the three magic objects so that he will remove her horns.

In western Europe, three enchanted girls give the magic objects, and the villain is able to steal them because the hero showed them off. In Finland and in Russia, the devil gives the objects and the hero loses them in a card game. In southern Europe and in Egypt, dates, figs, or grapes replace the apples. Many of the motifs are oriental, but the tale as a whole is definitely European, with its best form in western Europe (see also Uther 1987). In *The Folktale* (1946:74) Thompson complains that the tale is poorly motivated, and that the enchanted girls and the extra two comrades are left dangling.

Occurrences in this tale correspond directly to those in *The Magic Bird Heart*. The girl who steals the magic objects is the strongest point of similarity. Most of the other details differ, even as if the gory *Bird Heart* tale had been consciously rewritten into a typical European magic tale. The introductory domestic melodrama with the clerk is replaced by soldiers and lovely girls, trebled. The mistaken eating of the bird becomes three gifts. The blood and guts are replaced by three discrete objects. Vomiting the heart becomes a clean theft. In both tales the shape of the girl's punishment comes out of earlier motifs. In *The Magic Bird Heart*, her donkey form corresponds to the animal form of the hen; her horns (in *The Three Magic Objects*) correspond to the magic horn that contains the army. The donkey ears on the one girl match the horns on the other. *The Three Magic*

Objects is a string of cliches from the genre of the European magic tale. Max Lüthi (1984) has pointed out the artistic device of tripling and the qualities of typical magic objects that appear in European wonder tales; Vladimir Propp's *Morphology* documents many typical villainies and "donors." The tale of *The Three Magic Objects* hardly ever occurs in less than its full form (18 of 143 variants). It is sometimes mixed with *The Magic Bird Heart* (33 variants), and the horns and apples are found in the second part of both tales. This proves that the narrators of the tales recognized their similarity.

AT 313, *The Girl as Helper in the Hero's Flight*
AT 314, *The Youth Transformed into a Horse*   (Aarne 1930)

Most tale studies demonstrate the existence of a tale type, and prove that the tale exists (in its repeated variants) independently of other tales. This does not mean that it never mixes with other tales, either in isolated examples or in traditional combinations, nor that it never borrows details from other sources. But it does mean that it is easy to understand the tale as a discrete entity. Many tale types are easily described as a group of subtypes that all relate to a common (perhaps hypothetical) archetype. Most of Aarne's studies confirmed this idea of the tale type as a simplifying display of many variants. This concept was developed by Krohn and his successors as a tool for studying folktales. Studies in the historic-geographic tradition amply demonstrate its usefulness. But even in tale study, a single tool is not appropriate for all jobs, and in *The Magic Flight* Aarne encountered tales that, if they can be said to belong to tale types at all, demand a different idea of the tale type. In the course of this paper I have been moving away from an origin-oriented tale type, into one bound together by internal forces. This latter position brings a change in perspective that gives a clearer view of *The Magic Flight* in European tradition.

Aarne, Krohn, and Thompson all agreed that in Europe there are primarily two tales, with a lot of extra material annexed from other tales. The two tales have also borrowed from each other, back at least as far as the eleventh century. I think it significant that Aarne's study of *The Magic Flight* was published posthumously. Perhaps he was not really finished with it. He cannot have failed to see that this study is less satisfactory than his earlier ones. Actually the *study* is not so bad (although it lacks careful coding of variants): it is the *material* that shows no respect for order.

The outline of the Magic Flight in *The Types of the Folktale* follows Aarne's monograph:

Transformation Flight: The hero, in the ogre's power, is helped by the ogre's daughter. As they flee together, she transforms them into a garden and tree, church and priest, water and duck, etc. They escape.

Obstacle Flight: The hero, in the ogre's service, is helped by a horse. As they flee, they throw small objects that change into obstacles (mountain, forest, sea). They escape.

On the side of stability, it must be allowed that these sketches fit most of Aarne's material. He found 289 variants of the Transformation Flight, plus more from Finland and Estonia (p. 103). Of the Obstacle Flight, he found 69 variants, 13 (with more from Finland and Estonia) with animals other than a horse as helper, and 49 more with a girl as helper, and 46 more with the hero alone (50-52).[3]

Aarne pointed out that the girl as helper is appropriate with the transformation sequence, where both the characters and the magic objects into which they are transformed, come in pairs (45). The simultaneous transformations of the fugitives also demonstrate the girl's closeness to the hero. The horse that is so swift is appropriate to the obstacles that obstruct the villain's pursuit. Aarne decided that the Obstacle Flight was the original form, and that the Transformation Flight was a variant of that. He thought furthermore that all helpers were late additions, that originally the tale had only the hero, the villain, and the obstacles. This shifting of units from episode to tale is disconcerting. The situation with regard to whole tales is very complicated.

AT 314, *The Youth Transformed into a Horse.* Other episodes and tales that are important to AT 314 include the Service to the Devil (How is it motivated?); the Enchanted Horse (who helps the hero); Goldenhair (the hero breaks a prohibition and his hair turns to gold, which later causes a princess to fall in love with him); and Winning the Princess through Tests. Aarne's investigations into these other episodes yielded only negative results, making this part of the tale study rather unsatisfying. He was interested only in whether any of these motifs were original to the Magic Flight tale, and the answer is always No. They all belong to tales of helpful horses, AT 502 *The Wild Man* (Grimms' "The Iron Man") and AT 530-533. Aarne analyzed only those variants with the Magic Flight episode, which is insufficient for a good description of the Helpful Horse tales. His repeated assessment that all these episodes—the Helpful Horse, Goldenhair, Winning the Princess—and also the other episode (Service to the Devil) that is associated with other tales besides the Helpful Horse tales, are "later additions," is annoying, but it makes sense in terms of his attempt to find the original form of *The Magic Flight.*

Put correctly, the Obstacle Flight episode has associated itself with the Helpful Horse tales, where it demonstrates the horse's abilities, his cleverness, his power, and his speed.

AT 313, *The Girl as Helper in the Hero's Flight.* Aarne found several times as many variants of this tale as he did of AT 314. Boy Meets Girl is evidently more popular than Boy Meets Horse. Of 289 variants, most (229) have, in addition to the Transformation Flight, an episode of Son-in-Law Tasks, in which the ogre sets impossible tasks for the hero and the ogre's daughter helps him accomplish them. This rendering of help occurs in both the Tasks and the Flight episodes; it gives the girl's character consistency and is undoubtedly important to the continuing association of these episodes. A variant with these tasks from eleventh-century India, part of Somadeva's *Ocean of Story* (book 7 chapter 39), is exactly like modern tales—except that it has both versions of the Magic Flight, the Obstacle Flight as well as the Transformation Flight (book 7 chapter 39, Penzer 1924, III:222-239). Several of the most common Son-in-Law Tasks use images from the Magic Flight: chopping down a forest recalls the forest that grows magically, and taming a wild horse brings in the horse from AT 314. Plowing, sowing, and reaping all come out of cutting down the forest. Sorting grain and choosing the bride from among her sisters echo each other and play upon the fleeing couple whom the villain does not recognize when they are transformed. The less common tasks of building a church or a garden, or drinking the sea, repeat images from the Transformation Flight. The variations found in the specifics of the tasks imply that oral-formulaic principles are at work: the tale requires tasks, so a narrator chooses a few from a repertoire. But yet it is striking that the very tasks in Somadeva's tale are so common in oral European tales.

Another episode that frequently appears with the Son-in-Law Tasks and the Magic Flight is the Swanmaidens. This is a floating introduction that attaches itself to several tales. It provides a supernatural pedigree for the girl in AT 313. Her swan form foreshadows the transformation of the hero and heroine into a duck and water, during the Transformation Flight. Sometimes the couple flee in the form of birds, a detail which Aarne (48-49) thought came out of the Swanmaiden motif.

Several alternative introductions account for why the hero is in the ogre's service. He or his father often has made a bargain with the ogre. One, from eastern Europe, more complicated than most, says that "after war of birds and quadrupeds (Type 222) a wounded eagle is cared for by a man. Eagle gives man box not to be opened until he arrives at home. Man disobeys and castle appears. Man must get help of ogre to close box and must promise ogre his unborn son (Type 537)" (Thompson 1964 Type 313 I d, cf. 313B). This introduction foreshadows the Magic Flight. The castle that comes from a box is like the mountain that grows from a stone, or the church that is really a fugitive. The ogre who closes the box parallels the sweetheart who helps the hero accomplish impossible tasks. Other introductions are simpler: the ogre grabs a man's beard as he drinks (magic water as in the Magic Flight), and will not let go until the man promises his son (this is mainly Slavic); or the service may settle a gambling debt. Even more so than the tasks, the reason for the ogre's power over the hero is very much a pick-and-choose proposition, with a strong regional influence.

During the Transformation Flight itself, throughout Europe, there is often a formulaic conversation. The villain asks the person into whom the hero or heroine has been transformed, whether he has seen anyone running past, and the reply is always misleading. This is repeated for each transformation (75-79, 85). The villain often finds himself talking to a deaf bystander, which slows down the pursuit even more, and can add some "comic relief." Formulaic speech like this paces the story and adds to the suspense and excitement. It contributes to the stability of a tale by making it more memorable.

Preceding the Transformation Flight, there is an optional episode in which the heroine arranges a doll, drops of blood, or some such magic object, so that it will reply to the villain and lead him to believe that the fugitives are still at home (109-110). Aarne, in all his familiarity with tales, was not aware of this episode in any other tale (116). It comes out of the formulaic conversation in the Flight episode. It increases the suspense by making the Flight more complicated, and anticipates the formulaic conversation as a verbal delaying tactic. Folktale artistry works in two media: one is the sequence of images which, as tales with the Magic Flight repeatedly show, selects out images that anticipate or recall others in the tale. The other is purely verbal: to use verbal delaying tactics in the most exciting part of this tale shows consummate artistry. It proves the power that speech has, both over the characters in the tale and over the spellbound audience.

Of course the couple finally escapes, and generally the villain is killed or contained behind an insurmountable obstacle (65-74). When the final obstacle is a body of water, he may burst trying to drink it or be drowned in it. He may fall off the mountain or be burned in the fire, when these are the last obstacles. There is indeed variety but his fate often comes out of the final motif in the Magic Flight. Characteristically, Aarne declared that the destruction of the villain was a later addition—meaning that no conclusion about any original form is possible.

The tale can end here, or can move into "The Forgotten Fiancée" (mots. D2003, D2006.1). This episode has not been dignified with its own tale type number, but occurs as a conclusion to several tales including Swanmaiden tales and AT 425, *Cupid and Psyche*. Thompson tentatively gave the designation AT 313C to Magic Flight tales that have this extension. Aarne did not examine it in detail because it is so clearly "of an independent nature." In only a few Magic Flight tales does the villain actually cause the forgetting, in revenge against the fleeing couple (117). Why is this extension so common in the Transformation Flight tale? It reinforces the resourcefulness of the girl and may provide yet another opportunity for her to perform magic. It demonstrates how truly she loves the hero. A few of the particular details of this conclusion reiterate images that appeared earlier in the tale. When the hero overhears a conversation between the girl and animals or objects, it recalls the formulaic question and answer between the villain and the transformed fugitives. Talking birds, and a reflecting well, recall the magic transformation into a duck and a pool of water.

Basile's *Pentamerone* contains four tales that Aarne thought relevant (11-14). One has the episode of the Forgotten Fiancée following a flight (but not a magic one), and nothing else from the Magic Flight tales (day 3 tale 9; it has a parallel in Bello's *Mambriano*). In the second tale are the Son-in-Law Tasks and the Forgotten Fiancée (remembered because of a dove; day 2 tale 7). In the third, a wild man wins a wife by solving the riddle of the louse hide (AT 621), and carries her off into the forest. She escapes by means of an Obstacle Flight (day 1 tale 5). The fourth is a variant of AT 310, *Rapunzel*, in which the witch pursues the lovers who throw apples that change into wild animals (day 2 tale 1). In 1698 the Countess d'Aulnoy gave a well-developed version of the Transformation Flight in a tale with no other traces of AT 313-314 (Aarne 1930:14-15). I must take exception to Thompson's statement (1946:90) that the tales of Bello and Basile testify to the existence of the oral tales AT 313-314. Only one of these examples has even two episodes from these tales, and it has no Magic Flight. We know only that the separate *episodes* were known in Europe at that time. As is sometimes the case with Basile's tales, they fit the genre of the modern magic tale to perfection, but the actual combination of episodes are at variance with the bulk of the oral versions. This suggests that some of the tale types in the forms that we know them have solidified only during the last few hundred years. In Basile's time the episodes may have joined and rejoined more freely into different configurations.

Aarne turned up a number of occasional examples of the Magic Flight in other tales. *Rapunzel*[4] and *The Louse Skin* (after Basile) each have a couple of oral variants (120). *The Bird, the Horse, and the Princess* and *The Sons on a Quest for a Wonderful Remedy for their Father* (AT 550-551) have a Magic Flight in four variants that incorporate the Helpful Horse (119, 121). *Hansel and Gretel* (AT 327A) provides a rationale for the Service to the Ogre, and has a place for pursuit as the children escape. *The Dwarf and the Giant (Tom Thumb)*, AT 327B, also has a place where the ogre pursues the hero; eight examples from Slavic countries show that this combination has become traditional (18,105,115,118-9). The *flight* part of the Magic Flight is predominant in all these combinations.

The *magical* aspect is prominent in the combination with AT 325, *The Magician and his Pupil*. A boy is apprenticed to a magician, who intends to prevent his returning to his family (the rationale for the Service to the Ogre). The boy asks his father to help him escape, and the magician's daughter may help him also. In a final contest, the magician and the boy transform themselves into a series of animals that fight or flee from each other. Aarne found about twenty examples of AT 325 with a Magic Flight episode (84-85,119). AT 325 shares with AT 313-314 the ogre and his daughter, and magic transformations that allow the hero to escape.

Aarne concluded that the Magic Flight episode predated both AT 313 and AT 314. Thompson (1946:88-90) carefully separated these two (perhaps rather recent) European tales from world wide analogues that can not be said to have the same source. In the case of AT 314, the Magic Flight episode has been annexed to tales about a hero with a helpful horse. In AT 313, it has been attached to an episode of difficult tasks assigned by an ogre, and had developed a small dependent episode of speaking objects. This combination has accepted a variety of introductions and, sporadically, the conclusion of the Forgotten Fiancé. Thompson questions whether the version in the eleventh-century *Ocean of Story* (book 7 chapter 39, Penzer 1924 III:222-239) is actually a form of the European tale, or just coincidentally like it. It contains several of the more popular Son-in-Law Tasks and is incredibly similar to modern AT 313's. If he is suggesting an independent origin for this example, he opens up all sorts of possibilities of polygenesis for more of the modern material, destroying the concept of a tale type as variants that are "genetically" related. Happily we do not need to go that far. I only want to question the idea that tale types must be basically fixed patterns that are handed down in stable forms. For some tales, variants may be held together by internal tensions rather than in a rote sequence.

The occasional combinations, not only of the Magic Flight tales but of all folktales, however trivial to the histories of the tales involved, illustrate points of contact that lead to stable combinations of tales or episodes. Affinities can work through nouns like the repeated bird forms in the Swanmaidens, the Transformation Flight and the Forgotten Fiancée. They can work through verbs, like the swallowing and regurgitation in AT 560 and in AT 567 discussed above. Particular characters can link tales, like the helpful horse, the ogre's daughter, the man who is kind to animals (in AT 560), or the scheming old woman (in AT 567). General compatibility of character roles in the tales to be joined is often crucial: the couple fleeing the ogre can be his daughter and son-in-law, Rapunzel and her lover, Hansel and Gretel, or the (magician's) pupil and his father. Affinities like these, only stronger, are at the bottom of the more important combinations of the Magic Flight with the Son-in-Law Tasks and the Helpful Horse tales.[6]

Working out of oral rather than archival tradition, a contemporary of Aarne's, Cecil Sharp, introduced the concepts of *continuity*, *variation*, and *selection*, to account for evolution in folk tradition (1907:16-31, chapter 3, "Evolution"). As Aarne's concepts were patterned after those of Linneas, Sharp's followed Darwin's. Both approaches are valuable: without Linneas' system of species there would have been no basis for the Darwinian theory of evolution. Gyula Ortutay (1959) found Sharp's concepts particularly useful for analyzing Hungarian folklore, where tales are still obviously evolving and the tale types are not always congruent with those in western Europe.

Some folk tales have been refined almost completely, so that any alterations are more likely to mar the tale than to improve it. These tales make the most satisfactory subjects for tale studies. Other tales are still in a period of experimentation, where variations may more likely improve them (cf.Lüthi 1967; 1984:183 note 202). It is exciting that the Magic Flight tales were caught while still in this stage of development. Interestingly, the tales that they most mingle with (Goldenhair and the Helpful Horse tales, the Swanmaidens, and the Forgotten Fiancée conclusion) are also in various states of flux. These tales make for unwieldy studies, but because of that they reveal more of the forces that attract episodes to each other, than do tales that have already become solidified.

Aarne's tale studies demonstrate that each tale is unique. Saying that tales follow "laws" or "principles" of composition or dissemination is only a figure of speech, an expression of amazement that, yes, there *are* some regularities in this bewildering mass of data. There are also plenty of surprises. Professor Warren Roberts' study of *The Tale of the Kind and the Unkind Girls* is part of a scholarly tradition that respects the vicissitudes and fluctuations of folktales, a tradition that is exceptionally adept at relating and analyzing a great number of variants with clarity and economy. Their careful analyses have made permanent contributions to folklore studies, helping to provide "a comprehensive view of the whole tradition."

NOTES

1   Schenda (1977) gives a list of tale type numbers for the *Pentamerone*.

2   Thompson (1946:72) calls this example AT 563, but with only two objects and no inn it is much more similar to modern AT 564.

3   Aarne himself did not itemize like this, out of respect for the fact that the collection of folktales can never be considered complete. Here and elsewhere in this paper I have counted the variants to impress the fact that the tale type descriptions definitely are a convenient shorthand to represent many variants. Tales collected since the studies make the numbers even greater.

4   AT 310 with the Obstacle Flight is a tale type traditional in Mediterranean Europe (Lüthi 1970:117-119; 1984:116).

5   Gerould (1908:116-118,168-171) used this phrase to explain combinations of tales.

6   See Ortutay (1959) and other references in Voigt (1977), on the concept of Affinity. In some cases the term clearly refers to a mixing of tale types, or a tale type and an extraneous motif ("contamination"). In my discussion here, it refers to a combination of motifs or episodes that may or may not be firmly fixed into tale types.

REFERENCES CITED

Aarne, Antti
      1908 Vergleichende Märchenforschungen. *Mémoires de la Société Finno-Ougrienne* 25.
      1910 *Verzeichnis der Märchentypen.* FFC 3 (See also Thompson 1964).
      1911 Die Zaubergaben. *Journal de la Société Finno-Ougrienne* 27:1-96.
      1914 *Übersicht der Märchenliteratur.* FFC 14.
      1930 *Die magische Flucht: eine Märchenstudie.* FFC 92.

Basile
1634-36 *Pentamerone*. (See Penzer 1932).
Chavannes, Edouard
1962 *Cinq cent contes et apologues extraits du Tripitaka chinois*. Paris: Adrien-Maisonneuve.(Originally published 1910-1935) I:vii; III:256 (no.468).
Cosquin, Emmanuel
1913 *Les Mongols et leur pretendu rôle dans la transmission des contes Indiens ver l'occident Europeen*. Niort: G. Clouzot. (extrait de la Revue des traditions populaires, 1912).
Gerould, Gordon H.
1908 *The Grateful Dead*. London: Publications of the Folk-Lore Society, No.60.
Jülg, Bernhard ed.
1973 *Siddhi-Kür, Mongolische Märchen-Sammlung*. Hildeshein and New York: Georg Olms. (Originally Innsbruck, 1868).
Krohn, Kaarle
1926 *Antti Aarne*. FFC 64.
1931 *Übersicht über einige Resultate der Märchenforschung*. FFC 96.
Lüthi, Max
1967 Urform und Zeilform in Sage und Märchen. *Fabula* 9:41-54.
1970 *Once Upon a Time*. Translated by Lee Chadeayne and Paul Gottwald. New York: F.Ungar. (Originally *Es war Einmal*, 3. Aufl. 1968).
1984 *The Fairytale as Art Form and Portrait of Man*. Translated by Jon Erickson. Bloomington: Indiana University Press. (Originally *Das Volksmärchen als Dichtung: Aesthetik und Anthropologie*, 1975).
Ortutay, Gyula
1959 Principles of Oral Transmission in Folk Culture (Variations, Affinity). *Acta Ethnographia* 8:175-221.
Penzer, N.M. ed.
1924 *The Ocean of Story, Somadeva's Katha Sarit Sagara*. London: C.J.Sawyer. 10 vols.
1932 *The Pentamerone of Giambattista Basile*. London and New York: John Lane and E.P.Dutton. 2 vols.
Propp, Vladimir
1968 *The Morphology of the Folktale*. Austin: University of Texas Press. (Originally *Morfologiia skazki*, 1928).
Ranke, Kurt
1977 Aladdin. *Enzyklopädie des Märchens* 1:240-47.
Schenda, Rudolf
1977 Basile, Giambattista. *Enzyklopädie des Märchens* 1:1296-1308.
Sharp, Cecil
1907 *English Folk-Song, Some Conclusions*. London: Simpkin.
Thompson, Stith
1946 *The Folktale*. New York: Dryden Press.
Thompson, Stith and Antti Aarne
1964 *The Types of the Folktale*. FFC 184.
Uther, Hans-Jörg
1987 Fortunatus. *Enzyklopädie des Märchens* 5:7-14.
Voigt, Vilmos
1977 Affinität. *Enzyklopädie des Märchens* 1:154-55.

The Ethnography of a Folktale

LINDA DÉGH

AT 570 (The Rabbit Herd) is essentially a folktale of four episodes belonging to the large family of biographical hero-stories in which the lowly (poor, young, and simpleton) protagonist acquires a magic object in exchange for kindness to a supernatural donor, and thus succeeds in rendering impossible services to royalty and winning the hand of the princess. Within this range, the versions exhibit great episodic variety, and borrow liberally from similar content structures, causing the expansion of the narrative and the dilution of the main point it makes. Nevertheless, the most consistent four episodes that seem to be bound together by an inner logic and that make up a distinctive tale type with a very specific meaning, appear throughout its geographic distribution area:

(A) Sick king, princess seeks cure from healing fruit (fig, apple, orange, almond, peach, or other). Three sons of a poor woman try their luck by taking a basketful of magnificent fruits to the king;

(B) One by one the brothers encounter a poor old woman, a fairy, or a gray old man asking for food, assistance, or simply curious about the content of the basket. Older brothers deny help and rebut old woman by mocking answers: "potatoes," "frogs," "pig bristles," "shit," or "cuckoo's eggs;" whereby the fruits transform and the brothers are thrown out from the royal court. The fruits of the youngest (weakest, silliest) brother succeed in healing the princess; he also obtains a magic pipe (wand, bell) from the old woman for his kindness to her, or only because of his lowly condition.

(C) The king (or princess), reluctant to accept the young simpleton as marriage partner, attempts to set an additional impossible task to

338

him. He is to keep a herd of 900 (300, 100, 40, 25, 18, 12, or 10) rabbits (rarely roosters, sheep, goats, swans, partridges) on the pasture for three days; or he has to retrieve from the forest one, three, or twelve wild hares turned loose from a sack; or he has to tend, groom, and train one or three white pet rabbits. When the hero succeeds in bringing the animals back, the royal family tries to trick him into failure. One by one, envoys in disguise try to buy a rabbit (or the magic pipe) so that the youngster should not be able to perform the task. Sometimes a servant girl, a valet, or a royal official starts the negotiation, but usually it is the princess (occasionally three princesses), the queen and the king who tries to make a deal for a rabbit. They ask for a rabbit as a courtesy act, or promise money, even gold and silver, jewelery, a locket or a ring, as a token, but the rabbit-herd offers the rabbit only in exchange for forcing the royal family to perform an embarrassing act of self-humiliation. Besides milder, or more drastic and cruel forms of ridicule (kissing the rabbit-herd; accepting punches or whipping from him; allowing him to cut a piece of the nose or skin from the palm or strips of flesh from the back of the victim; jumping on one leg for half an hour while nose-picking; dancing to the tune of hero's flute; throwing somersaults; having a pot fastened to his ass; allowing to be branded on the rump; kneeling down and kissing the bare bottom of hero and eating his feces; kissing the donkey, the donkey's ass, or licking a dead donkey's ass; holding the dead donkey's carcass between his teeth and dragging it around; pulling a dead coyote by its tail with his teeth; kissing the horse's ass under its tail), the most prevalent bargain proposal is sexual. The rabbit-herd lies with both the princess, the queen, and sometimes the king, or forces him to commit bestiality with the mare he is riding. Despite the high prize, and precaution (placing the animal into a sack, a wooden or metal chest, an iron case, or killing and cutting it up into pieces), the rabbit returns at the sound of the pipe.

(D) Dismayed by the power of the magic pipe, the king tries to beat the hero by testing his wit. He has to fill one or three sacks, a basket, a copper chest, or a bowl with lies, or with truths, spoken or sung. Often he is to "lie truth" (Wahrheiten lügen; trois sacs de verites). The king stages the event by erecting a platform for public performance of the destruction of the hero, but soon discovers that the "lies" will turn out to be "truths." The rabbit herd tells two stories: the humiliation of the princess and the queen, but before he can complete the third the king interrupts him to avoid his public embarrassment; "the sack is full," and the rabbit-herd wins the hand of the princess.[1]

2

The earliest version of AT 570, published in 1791,[2] is already heavily interwoven with episodes belonging to other types. In this, the rabbit-herd incident blends with AT 554 (The Grateful Animals). The sick king promises his daughter to the brave one who heals him with figs. Aided by grateful animals (fish, a black and a white dove, ants) the youngest of the three brothers succeeds but must perform four additional tasks to win the prize. He has to retrieve a ring from the bottom of the sea, get a wreath from heaven and a flame from hell, separate the mixture of nine kinds of cereals into nine measures, and finally, herd nine hundred rabbits. Ultimately, he has to fill a bag with truths. Another early version, *Der Vogel Greif* (Grimm 165), published in 1837,[3] exhibits even more contamination and change of orientation, resulting also in the elimination of episode D. Although episodes A, B and C remain intact, two other tests—to build a ship that travels through water and land (AT 513 B); and to steal the feather of the Griffin Bird (AT 550), blended with elements of AT 461—brings the text close to Grimm 29, *Der Teufel mit den drei goldenen Haaren.*[4]

From the second half of the 19th century the Rabbit Herd tale appears in a variety of textual contexts while a clear pattern of affinial relationships emerge that limits its episodic combinations into two directions. In the one case, rabbit herding appears as one of the several domestic tasks given to the protagonist in hero tales, such as AT 300, 306, 314, 328, 425, 461, 502, 531, 550, 552, 554, 561, and 592. Despite the wide distribution of these combinations, the tone and the style of episodes C and D does not fit very well. In the other case, the Rabbit Herd tale is interlinked with trickster and cleverness test tale types—such as AT 559, 566, 571, 621, 650, 851, 852, 853, 854, and 860—and seems to be in perfect harmony with them. Here C and D does not play such a subordinate role as in hero tales. The whole story, as Kurt Ranke (1955-62:264-65) aptly remarked, is "Schwankhaft" and can either blend into or be linked up with any of the Schwänke on an equal basis.

In addition to these two kinds of content structures in which AT 570 appears, either in a subordinate or coordinate relationship with other stories, versions of the pure and uncontaminated Rabbit Herd tale type composed of episodes A-B-C-D, or B-C-D are also widely disseminated. Episode D on the other hand, tends toward greater independence to develop into a self-contained lie-contest story (AT 1920). The almost even distribution and coexistence of these formulations of type 570 indicate its existence in oral tradition prior to literary fixation.   There are, however, some questions that warrant caution in considering its age, spread, popularity, and meaning: Why was this tale not recorded prior to the end of the 18th century? Why is there still a scarcity in documentation from the large geographical area where it has been reported? How dependable are the texts available to researchers to analyze and determine its place in narrative tradition?

AT 570 is among the classic folktales in which an explicit sex act is featured as a turning point. Its topic and message is in open contradiction with the romantic concepts of 19th century folktale scholars of the purity and innocent ignorance of the folk. Therefore, the modest number of publications does not reveal much of its popularity and place among other, more covert sexual tales like Rapunzel, Snow White, or Sleeping Beauty.   In the majority of published texts, episode C is radically rewritten and euphemized[5] and only some limited editions indicate the true nature of the tale. One of the early versions appears in a modest book of "intimate tales" by Afanas'ev (1977:88-92) who felt that these "real treasures" (which had to be left out from his Russian tale collection) must be preserved for posterity because of their uniquely authentic, unadulterated expression of the feelings of the simple folk. Afanas'ev's story makes episode C into an elaborate labor contract story (AT 650, 1000) between serf and landlord. The peasant must herd the rabbits to pay for his debt, but the master does not want him to succeed and free himself from bondage. The mistress is slept with twice in exchange for a rabbit, and the third time the master has to mount his mare. He gives in, realizing his defeat and releases his serf. Another untainted version from 1884 comes from Brittany,[6] with reference to Afanas'ev, although this one returns to the more Märchen-like social milieu. The text is complete with all four episodes and resembles several of the French variants (Delarue and Tenéze 1964:254-58). The shepherd boy collects the evidences of the rabbit-bargain into three handkerchiefs: a piece of skin from the palm of a gentleman; another piece from the back of the king; and thirdly, the virginity of the princess to be presented as "truths." In a complete Bosnian version, collected in 1907, the boy has sex with the daughter and the wife of a pope, and he forces the pope to submit to sodomy.[7]

Two versions recorded by Vance Randolph (1952:17-19) from the same raconteur in 1927 suggest that the editing of the risque passages may not always be the work of the collector; the teller may formulate things differently for different audiences. The outspoken version published posthumously in 1976 is "for men only," while the earlier one—alluding only to the sexual abuse of the princess, the queen, and the king—was meant for "mixed audiences" (1976:47-50, No.29). In general, however, the fact remains that the bulk of the more or less accurately recorded variants of AT 570 remained in manuscript archives, and that only more recent field recordings provided dependable texts and related information concerning the nature of the tale.

3

Although the tale has been reported from almost every European country and from numerous ethnic regions, most of the versions come from the German-speaking areas,[8] the Nordic[9] and Baltic countries,[10] and France.[11] The bulk of the approximately 400 noted versions are from Germany, Finland,[12] Norway,[13] and France, while texts from Ireland, Spain, Italy, Portugal, Belgium, Holland, Russia, Poland, Czechoslovakia, Hungary, and Yugoslavia prove that the type has it established place within their national repertoires.[14] The Balkan Peninsula seems to be a checkpoint for the distribution of the tale: both Bulgarian and Greek versions are intermingled with elements and episodes borrowed from adjacent Middle Eastern-Islamic cultures.[15] Likewise, texts from Ireland, Scotland, England, and Iceland deemphasize the main orientation of the tale, as does the Gypsy version.[16]

There are further limitations in the dissemination of the type beyond Europe: it seems that it traveled with emigrants to the New World without being adapted by people on other continents. Sporadic versions appear from the Spanish Balearic Islands[17] and Portuguese Cape Verde Islands,[18] while a larger fund is known from Latin-American countries, particularly Mexico,[19] Brazil, and the West Indies.[20] The provenance of the four almost identical Anglo-American variants[21] would be hard to connect with a particular group, while the formulation of French-Canadian versions[22] indicate a direct link with France. A distribution map of the variants would suggest a possible French or Franco-German origin of the tale, not merely because of its relative frequency but also because of the currency of affinial types and motifs. These ingredients may have been pre-existent and crucial to the development of type 570 by the separation and integration of the constituent four episodes. In the practice of traditional storytellers knowledgeable of the pertinent stock of stories, consolidation of types occurs through frequent retellings, as well as spontaneous variation by the addition of stock episodes.

4

No oicotypes or local variants can be established, mostly because sufficient numbers of variants are not available from all regions of the distribution area. But even where there is enough material, no specific patterns emerge. Instead, the four-episode Rabbit Herd sequence usually coexists with the hero-tale and trickster-tale conglomerates throughout the distribution area, and remarkable parallel formulations can be found at places without direct contact. Even such a trivial element as the green or fresh fig as healing fruit does not seem to be tied to a particular source. It appears in French, Swiss, German, Portuguese, Polish, and Bosnian variants, and an Italian variant develops a unique feature: The princess' hunger for figs can be satisfied only by magic replenishment of the basket she speedily empties (Calvino 1959:145-47, No.47).

5

Because of the scarcity of contextual information, little can be said about the function AT 570 played in the social environments in which it was told through the ages. Most of the variants come from the 19th century or the first three decades of the 20th century when collectors seldom recorded even the name of a teller. Annotations accompanying the texts refer often to their scandalous nature. In 1853 Kulda, for example, mentions that "Er habe das Märchen nicht so veröffentlichen können, wie er es gehört habe—die auf der Weide gestellte Bedingungen seien so schimpflich und hässlich, das mein Ohr sich scheute, sie zu hören."[23] Depending on my own experience as a fieldworker in Hungarian peasant communities, the Rabbit Herd story, like other sparsely recorded magic tales with scatological implications, was reserved for the company of men. As János Nagy, a 76 year old fisherman from Sára, told me after I had recorded his version (he had two of diverse combinations), "This is one for the military. In the barracks after curfew, what else could you do in winter from eight to midnight until you really wanted to sleep? We were young kids, and needed more of this stuff than sleep. The pasture scene was interesting, he got his way and the princess had also her desires fulfilled."[24] Peter Pandur also had a witty version of the tale which had to remain unpublished,[25] and he referred to the construction workers' quarters where the workingmen found recreation in storytelling at night (Dégh 1969:67-69).

Lacking more information on the sociocultural background of AT 570, the text itself has much to reveal. The world it features, the ideas it presents, and the motivations of actors in their action are those of the traditional European peasant. In this story, the kind and the dull, lowly hero (der Dumme Hans, Ti Jean) begins his career story like in other magic tales. He obtains the magic object because of his miserable condition, not because of some skill—he is only modest and kind to older people, as peasant upbringing requires. This in itself makes him qualified to succeed as blind executor of the actions suggested to him by the protective adult donor. But as the story reaches the point of performing the task according to instruction, the hero is transformed into a shrewd trickster, with his own initiatives and projections. He appears as a ruthless businessman, a determined bargainer who takes everything and risks nothing, and who carefully gathers evidence for a final showdown; he also emerges as a speech artist, a storyteller. His purpose is not so much the royal wedding[26] as it is trading places with the mighty. As Thompson (1946:155) notes, "the hero's use of blackmail is the characteristic trait" of this tale.

The pasture scene has several specifics. The story would stand as is without the bargain over money or sex; it would have been enough to hand over the rabbit to the visitor and then whistle it back without much ado to restore the number of the herd. Or, it would also seem that to accept bribery from the visitors and collect cash would have been sufficient disclosure in the concluding episode (as in MI H1024.1.1). But this would not have been enough. The humiliation and embarrassment is complete only when it includes the sexual or genital area, where social tabu makes people most vulnerable and helpless. Herding small animals (geese, turkey, sheep) is the responsibility of young people in traditional peasant society, and the pasture is the place where fantasizing, courting, and exploration of sexuality begins. The staging of episode C is set in peasant reality: the princess brings lunch to the rabbit herd, an occasion to test their sexuality. But the test in this case becomes a calculated project on both sides. Royalty takes risks at any cost to avoid the victory of the lowly boy and submits itself to the danger of utter humiliation. The boy, on the other hand, fulfills a cleverly plotted attack on authority and dominance. In most versions the king (lord, master, landlord, pope) is desperate in the losing battle of giving in: "dem Popen, wie einem Popen tat es leid, die Tochter einen gemeinen Bauern auszugeben."[27] It is the brutal struggle between the rich and the poor, not the seduction of the princess. In fact, the women, or the sexuality of daughter and mother are blind tools in this power struggle. When the final showdown comes—the task he himself set for his rival, to lie truth—the king allows everyone to know of it. It is only in the revelation of his engagement in shameful and disgusting acts that he stops the rabbit herd.

Episode D seems an integral part of and logical conclusion to the tale, although it might have preceded its existence. It has also long been known as a self-contained test tale, independently or intertwined with dependent episodes of lying contest tales.[28] Unquestionably, this is a story of wish fulfillment for poor peasants, who are the bearers of Märchen tradition, in which the wit of the lowly hero conquers. To reveal what really took place through the act of telling a story ("a lie" in general folk-parlance) is not uncommon in folktales; unjustly accused or banished heroes or heroines often do it as, for example, in AT 407, 450, 706 and 707. In this story, however, to fill a container with lies is ambiguous and confusing in the variants. It is set by the king as an additional hard test in which a halfwit peasant boy must fail. In some versions he has to lie truth, in others he has to fill the sacks with truths, and in still others with lies. There is also a considerable discussion in some versions in which the royal family members protest, express their dismay with, or admit to the facts presented. The close affinity to lying-contest tales is obvious here. In a Sorbian version (Nedo 1956:276-80, No.61), for example, the narration is accepted and handled as trifle and believable until it becomes inadmissible: "that's a lie." In one Mexican-American version (Zunser 1935:161-64), two sacks are filled with lies and one with truths. But no matter how much episode D oscillates under the influence of lying-contest tales, anger bargains between master and servant, and the convention of village storytelling practices, the fluidity of the public show in AT 570 connects facts of peasant life with Märchen fantasy.

6

The above interpretation of AT 570 is drawn from the socio-cultural milieu, taking departure from native ethnography as much as it is discernible from the variants, and the commentaries of storytellers and attendant villagers. Alan Dundes' (1980) psychoanalytical reading of the Rabbit Herd tale draws on the subconscious (symbolic) level of making sense. Dundes' long-term concern with the symbolic-metaphoric meanings of folklore led him to this particular tale. He is critical of folklorists who look only at the literal (conscious), and not at the analytically constructed symbolic content of the tale, derived according to the rules of Freudian interpretation. He argues for the research of universal psychological symbols in folktales through an approach that combines the comparative method with structural analysis. Accordingly, he proposes to use the Proppian sequence of motifemes (functions), discerning allomotifs from field-collected variants that he sees fitting the motifemic slots which, he suggests, lead to the discovery of inter- and cross-cultural allomotific equivalences. Dundes hopes that his proposed approach will lead to more knowledge of oicotypification, national and local characteristics, and individual idiosyncrasies.

After constructing a plot outline of AT 570, Dundes selects a few tale traits for interpretation of their symbolic equivalents. The first example concerns a marginal trait, common to hero tales: the death threat to the hero in case of failure. The three equivalents are beheading, castration, and being thrown into a snake pit, chosen from three variants. The second example equates magic object, rabbit, and intercourse as symbolic equivalents of fertility to suggest the phallic nature of the tale. The third example is a test, marginal to the type and infrequent in the variants: the hero has to cut grass as far as the princess can urinate. This analysis, of course, raises the question of whether or not universal psychological symbols underlying artistic formulations such as folktales should be taken for granted when attempting the interpretation of the specific formulations and variations of individual tales.

NOTES

[1] My description follows the AT outline.

[2] See Ammenmärchen I, p.93, no.5.

[3] Obtained through Wilhelm Wackernagel from the Swiss Friedrich Schmid of Aargau. It was first published in the third edition (1837) of *Kinder-und Hausmärchen*.

[4] This relationship was noted in the third volume of *Kinder-und Hausmärchen*, published in 1856, p.256.

[5] The nature of rewriting to which the Rabbit Herd was subjected is well illustrated in the 17 variants published in Šmits, VIII, (1962-70:263-83).

[6] See Kryptadia II, pp.45-53, no.13.

7   See Antropophyteia IV, pp.393-98, no.621; another less complete version in II, pp.340-44, no.421, is so close that the collector notes that the two peasant informants learned it from each other or a third person (IV, p.393).

8   Bolte and Polivka 1918:268-69; Ranke, op. cit. It must be noted here that in collections, type-lists and catalogs, many texts are erroneously identified as 570. In numerous cases the identification follows the Grimm text or takes test episodes marginal to but sometimes coincident with the rabbit-herding test as equivalent. For example, out of six variants in the Berze Nagy catalog only two fit 570.

9   AT list 21 versions from Sweden, 29 from Denmark, and 13 from Norway.

10   Šmits (1962-70); Ambainis (1977); Böhm-Specht (1924); Jurkschat (1898); Viidalepp (1980).

11   Delarue-Tenéze (1964) has 36 variants.

12   AT refers to 70 Finnish variants.

13   B. Hodne lists 16 more Norwegian texts.

14   See national catalogs by Ó Súilleabháin and Christiansen (1963); Espinoza (1946-47); de Meyer (1968); Cirese and Serafini (1975); Andreev (1929); Barag et al (1979); Tille (1927-34); Berze Nagy (1957) and references in BP.

15   A Greek version begins with 325 and is otherwise imbedded in AT 561. Grateful horse and dog help to acquire the lamp with the servant spirit to fulfill additional tasks (Kretschmer 1919:34). In a Bulgarian story, the hero succeeds with the help of Negroes from a wonder bowl (Sbornik min.1901, vol.6, p.176).

16   In an Icelandic version, episode C is missing, only D (the sack to be filled with words) prevails as the disclosure what the princess, queen and the king did to get the magic objects: self-sewing needle, self-cutting scissors, and self-cutting axe (Arnason 1864:2, 482). The Scottish Gypsy version is totally without conflict. The smallest son picks the cake that is small but blessed, not big and cursed. He gets the flute from the donor, succeeds with rabbits, royal family rewards him with generous meals, he takes princess to town and they get married. Mother, donor join the royal family (Aichele 1926:289-95, no.69).

17   The text is a conglomerate of 304, 570, and 851. Among the tasks, one is to herd 13 roosters and fill the sack with lies—the king learns that the maid, daughter, wife slept with the herd (Amades 1950:194).

18   Child born with magic whistle that summons rats. Negress, princess, queen are blackmailed into having sex with the boy for not telling the king. King mounts the mare -seven sacks are filled with lies (Parsons 1923:83, Vol. I).

19   Robe (1973:105) has 12 variants.

20   See Hansen (1957).

21   Randolph's "polite" and "bawdy" texts and Chase's version are almost identical, and they are distinct from the European versions in two points: not a herd is hired for service but a competition is called to find the best husband for the princess, who would be able to keep a rabbit in a place for short time. In the first two a trained pet responds to a bell; in the third, a drill in the middle of the ring is installed to make a wild hare stay for 30 minutes (Chase 1943:89-95). These are tricks of training animals rather than magic tricks. Also, the "fill bowl, fill" episode as a cante fable is unique to the Anglo-American variants (Baughman 1966:14).

[22]   Lemieux (Vol.2, 1974:245-54; Vol.4, 1975:227-42; Vol.7, 1976:54-67) contains three variants. The first is complete containing all four episodes, the second begins with AT 850, continues with a complete 570 and concludes with 559 which debases a prince who competes for the hand of the princess. The third begins with episode A, but then more tests—cutting down a large tree, killing a giant—are added, and finally sheep and not rabbits are to be herded. Common to all three Canadian variants is the elaborate formulation of C and D episodes, lengthy bargain of maids, sisters, preceding the royal family. The contract year here is not the usual three-day year as in magic tales but rather a real year, with intervals of weeks and months between the visits. Bargaining dialogue, intercourse with the women and drastic degradation of the king (dragging dead animal's carcass between his teeth) are detailed, as is episode D as a public retelling of the bargain.

[23]   Jech (1961:494) notes that from Kulda's recently discovered field notes it became evident that in this tale the price for the rabbit is commonly to sleep with the herdsman.

[24]   A complex narrative of J. Nagy (see Ortutay, Dégh and Kovács Vol.2, 1960:549-70, no.96) combines three affinial types; the frame story is AT 935 within which 854 and 570 are fully included. Another variant of Nagy combines 400 and 570 (MS).

[25]   In this combination of 756B, 854, and 570, P. Pandur's hero is a prince with a butler who is his advisor. The three princesses who undress in payment for the rabbit and run away naked when the butler knocks on the door provide for the token (a bundle of clothes) to be shown at the sack-filling contest: "I went a-hunting, I shot the rabbit, it ran away but I kept its skin" (MS).

[26]   In some versions the king manages to pay the boy off (Haiding 1969:no.98); he gets 500 rubles (Šmits 1967:no.9); the princess turns against her father and elopes with the rabbit herd to wed in town (Aichele op.cit.); or he marries the chambermaid he loved (Massignon 1965:67-71, no.8), an orphan instead of the princess (Šmits 1967:no.8), or there is no daughter at all as a payment for the service (Afanas'ev 1977).

[27]   See Antropophyteia 4:393.

[28]   Parsons (op.cit.) does not contain episode C, but only D, handling the telling lies as much a skill as in 852.

REFERENCES CITED

Afanas'ev, Aleksandr N.
    1977 *Erotische Märchen aus Russland.* hg. u. übersetzt von Adrian Baar. Fischer
        Taschenbuch.
Aichele, Walther
    1926 *Zigeunermärchen.* (Die Märchen Der Weltliteratur, No.25) Düsseldorf-Köln.

Amades, Joan
   1950 *Folklore de Catalunya.* Barcelona: Editorial Selecta.
Ambainis, O.
   1977 *Lettische Volksmärchen.* Berlin.
Ammenmärchen
   1791 *Ammenmärchen.* 1-2 Weimar.
Andreev, N.P.
   1929 *Ukazatel' skazochnikh siuzhetov po sisteme Aarne.* Leningrad.
Antropophyteia
   1905 *Antropophyteia.* Vol. II.
   1907 *Antropophyteia.* Vol. IV.
Arnason, Jon
   1864 *Icelandic Legends.* London: Richard Bentley.
Barag, L.G.; Berozovskii, I.P.; Kabashnikov,K.P.; Novikov,N.V.
   1979 *Sravnitelnii ukazatel' siuzhetov.* Leningrad.
Baughman, E.W.
   1966 *Type and Motif Index of the Folktales of England and North America.* The Hague: Mouton.
Berze Nagy, J.
   1957 *Magyar népmesetipusok.* Pécs.
Bolte, Johannes and Georg Polivka
   1918 *Anmerkungen zu den Kinder- und Hausmärchen der Brüder Grimm.* Vol.III. Leipzig: Dieterich.
Böhm, Maximilian and F. Specht
   1924 *Lettische-Litauische Volksmärchen.*(Die Märchen Der Weltliteratur, No.15) Jena: Eugen Diederichs.
Calvino, Italo
   1959 *Fiabe italiano.* Torino: Einaudi.
Chase, Richard
   1943 *The Jack Tales.* Boston: Houghton Mifflin.
Cirese, A. and L. Serafini
   1975 *Tradizioni orali non cantate.* Rome.
Dégh, Linda
   1969 *Folktales and Society.* Bloomington: Indiana University Press.
Delarue, P. and M.L. Tenéze
   1964 *La conte populaire francais.* Vol.2. Paris.
Dundes, Alan
   1980 The Symbolic Equivalence of Allomotifs in the Rabbit-Herd (AT 570). *Arv* 36:91-98.
Espinoza, Aurelio
   1946-47 *Cuentos Populares españoles. Recogidos de la tradicion oral de España.* (3 Vols.) Madrid.
Haiding, Karl
   1969 *Märchen and Schwänke aus Oberösterreich.* Berlin: de Gruyter.
Hansen, Terrence L.
   1957 *The Types of the Folktale in Cuba, Puerto Rico, the Dominican Republic and Spanish South America.* Berkeley: University of California Press.
Hodne, Bjarne
   1979 *Eventyret og tradisjonsbaererne.* Oslo: Universitetsforl.
Jech, Jocomir
   1961 *Tschechische Volksmärchen.* Berlin: Rutten and Loening.

Jurkschat, C.
   1898 *Litauische Märchen und Erzählungen.* Heidelberg: C. Winter.
Kretschmer, J.
   1919 *Neugriechische Märchen.* Jena: Eugen Diederichs.
Kryptadia
   1884 *Recueil de documents pour servir a l'étude des traditions populaires.* Vol. II. Heilbronn.
Lemieux, Germain
   1974-76 *Les vieux m'ont conté.* Montreal: Editions Bellarmin.
Massignon, Genevieve
   1965 *Contes traditionnels des reilleurs de lin dun Trégor (Basse Bretagne).* Paris: Picard.
de Meyer, M.
   1968 *Le conte populaire flamand.* FFC 203. Helsinki: Suomalainen tiedeakatemia.
Nedo, P.
   1956 *Sorbische Volksmärchen.* Bautzen: Schr. d.Inst.f.sorb. Volksforschung der DAW.
Ortutay, Gy.;Linda Dégh; and A. Kovács
   1960 *Magyar népmesék.* 3 Vols. Budapest.
Ó Súilleabháin, S. and R. Th. Christiansen
   1963 *The Types of the Irish Folktale.* FFC 188. Helsinki: Suomalainen tiedeakatemia.
Parsons, Elsie Clews
   1923 *Folk-Lore from the Cape Verde Islands.* Part II. (Memoirs of the American Folklore Society, No.15) Cambridge, Mass: American Folklore Society.
Randolph, Vance
   1952 *Who Blowed Up the Church House and Other Ozark Folk Tales.* (Notes by Herbert Halpert) New York: Columbia University Press.
   1976 *Pissing in the Snow and Other Ozark Folktales.* Urbana: University of Illinois Press.
Ranke, Kurt
   1955-62 *Schleswig-holsteinische Volksmärchen.* 1-3. Kiel: F.Hirt.
Robe, Stanley L.
   1973 *Index of Mexican Folktales.* (Univ. of California Publications: Folklore Studies, No.26) Berkeley: University of California Press.
Sbornik--
   1901 *Sbornik za narodni umotvorenija nauka i kniznina izdava Ministverstvoto na narodnoto posvescenie.*Vol. 6. Sofia.
Šmits, Pēteris, ed.
   1962-70 *Latviešu tautas teikas un pasakas.* 15 Vols. (2nd Edition) Waverly,Iowa: Latvju Grāmata.
Thompson, Stith
   1946 *The Folktale.* New York: Holt, Rinehart and Winston.
Tille, Vaclav
   1927-34 *Soupis ceskych pohádek.* 1-2. Prague.
Viidalepp, Richard
   1980 *Estnische Volksmärchen.* Berlin.
Zunser, Helen
   1935 A New Mexican Village. *Journal of American Folklore* 48(April-June): 125-78.

Historicity and the Oral Epic:
The Case of Sun-Jata Keita

JOHN WILLIAM JOHNSON

Western-trained scholars have attempted to reconstruct a history of the great empire period of West Africa arguing that Sun-Jata Keita, the culture hero of one of those great empires, that of Old Mali, was an historical person.[1] Recent oral historians have refined their arguments concerning historicity in oral traditions, responded to criticism from anthropologists, and continue to keep their faith in oral tradition as evidence of past history. Unfortunately, they appear not to have read the work of folklorists or sociologists, who have recently contributed a great deal to theory in oral tradition and knowledge of its role in contemporary society.

The question of what Sun-Jata represents today remains easier to answer than who he may have been in the past. As the primary culture hero of the Mande peoples, Sun-Jata's memory is a part of the symbolic culture of those societies. The social role of this narrative appears to take precedence over concern for historicity and thus is an oral argument of contemporary social function and political power. This paper asks a major question of concern to scholars in several disciplines today: "How much of the actual past do traditions really reflect; and what can contemporary performance theory in folkloristics, and recent attempts by the sociologist Edward Shils and a number of other students of tradition as a concept, contribute to the understanding of historicity in oral literature?"[2]

I should state from the beginning that the search for history in oral lore is not and never has been one of my principal concerns as a folklorist. I can hardly be considered an expert in this respect, and to put my limited experience with this topic up against experts such as Jan Vansina, Joseph Miller, Yves Person, and others is somewhat intimidating to me. In truth, the ability of any scholar to actually glean historicity out of an oral text has always appeared to me to be just a little bit beyond the boundaries of possibility. The nature of oral tradition as I have come to understand it simply does not allow for such analyses. In addition, a recent attempt to look more critically into the nature of tradition would, I think, argue against the possibility of finding the kind of chronological history described by Yves Person in African oral tradition.[3]

The more I read, however, the more convinced I became that to bring studies in folkloristics and sociology to the attention of oral historians might be of some assistance to their scholarship. I must say from the start that I admire very much indeed the efforts by historians to reconstruct Africa's past, especially because such efforts go a long way toward lessening the still prevalent racism and prejudices held in the West about the indigenous populations of Africa. In the end, however, the need to reconstruct Africa's past in the way Westerners want to do it appears to me to be of primary importance to scholarship in the West. I am not certain of what use it will be to the people of Africa, who have and will continue to reconstruct their history in their own way and for their own uses.

What I propose to do in this essay is to state my views on the topic of the search for historicity in oral tradition, based upon some recently published studies concerning the concept of tradition and on theories expressed at a conference at Indiana University, as well as in a seminar I conduct at that institution concerning tradition as an ethnic and analytic construct.[4] In the light of newer ways of looking at tradition and what influence it has on human behavior, perhaps I may be able to stimulate oral historians towards solving the problems of separating symbolic and social function from chronological history, if the latter pursuit ever proves possible.

In a recent public address at a prominent university in the Midwest, an individual made the following statement (words to the effect): "This institution houses some of the finest collections of music from primitive, traditional, and modern societies in the Western hemisphere." Such a statement tells us more about the speaker's own worldview than it does about the nature of holdings in the archives in question. There is no such thing in the twentieth century as a primitive society.[5] Additionally, all societies are both traditional and modern at the same time. Edward Shils' recent book entitled *Tradition* (1981) has had an influence beyond his discipline of sociology.

His separation of the concepts of tradition from *traditum* (the latter of which he defines as a product of tradition) helps clarify one of the current folkloristic views that tradition is a process and not merely the products of that process. As a basis for beginning our understanding of this recent research and analysis, let me offer my own working definition of tradition, "working" because I am still in the process of retooling my understanding of this enigmatic concept.

Tradition is a form of learned behavior. It is not information deduced from reason or logic. It is not information that one learns by oneself. And it is not a part of instinctive behavior. As Shil's puts it:

All that human beings do is done within the limits imposed by their neurophysiological properties and ecological situations, but there is much room for variation within these limits. [1981:41]

In other words, social behavior, including tradition, is very humanistic and bound by human limitations and possibilities.

So, tradition is a form of behavior, but I should state that I am not a behavioralist in the theory I adhere to. Learned behavior of this nature represents a set of socially defined constructs, not a set of predictable mannerisms resulting from given social settings. Again paraphrasing Shils, societies learn most of what they practice. Where Shils' theory seems lacking, from the point of view of folkloristics, is his neglect of the marriage between tradition and its bearers, the folk of folklore. His book concentrates mostly on the lore of folklore. Let me elaborate a bit on this idea.

I noted that tradition is learned behavior, but it does not represent all of the behavior a person learns. It is learned behavior which contributes to group identity. It draws boundaries around groups and defines them, and reflects their beliefs and worldview. If one has learned most of what one knows from members of one's group, it only stands to reason that what one has learned will reflect the concerns and worldview of that group. Many folklorists in America now recognize that any group that practices traditions together qualifies as a "folk" group, and ethnicity is only one kind of group identity. There are multiple expressions of group identity in any individual's life, but further elaboration on that topic is beyond the scope of this essay. Suffice it to say that what constitutes "tradition" in any of the groups to which an individual belongs is defined and debated by members of that group. In other words, the specific forms of behavior that group members employ as traditional constructs are argued as such by those members; learned behavior does not become traditional just because it is learned.

We recognize that tradition is not always verbal; it is sometimes learned by observation. Indeed, an older definition of tradition expressed by many folklorists at one time—some, perhaps, still hold this view—is that tradition is a body of knowledge passed down from generation to generation by word of mouth or by imitation. This definition has recently come under fire from another set of scholars, perhaps most articulately represented by Richard Handler and Jocelyn Linnekin.[6] In an article in the *Journal of American Folklore*, Handler and Linnekin make the point that tradition must be understood as a set of wholly symbolic constructs, and that there is nothing "natural" about it. They make another important point with which I agree: As an interpretive construct, tradition is composed of elements of both continuity and change. This idea is not new to folklorists, nor perhaps to oral historians. But it does have important deeper implications with regard to the search for historicity.

Tradition comes to us in both a formalistic and a symbolic state, each of which undergoes change over time. Tradition may come *from* the past, but it is *of* the present. It is a contemporary set of constructs which influence the behavior of its practitioners and is used to *argue* the past, not *explain* it. The illusion that it is a flawless memory of the past is just that, an illusion. Whatever actual memory of the past it may represent, it is certainly a contextually-bound interpretation of the past for use in the present. Again, Handler and Linnekin argue that "an ongoing reconstruction of tradition is a facet of all social life, which is not natural but symbolically constituted" (1984:276).

At this point, it might be useful to give an example of what these two authors are attempting to analyze. In the twentieth century, American Indians of mixed ethnic identity practice traditions which their ancestors never heard of. In 1986, I served on the Folk Arts Board of the Indiana Arts Council, which reads grant proposals submitted by various groups in Indiana that request funding for projects of both a research-oriented and a performance-oriented nature. One such proposal last year came from an American Indian group found in both Michigan and Indiana. This group applied for a grant to expand a yearly powwow which they stage in Michigan. The previous year's advertising brochure was submitted as evidence of the potential success of the proposed powwow. In this brochure it was evident that Indians of several ethnic groups were a part of the former year's powwow, and that they had come from many parts of the country to participate. Indeed, certain skilled performers are actually sought after because they are good at some form of dance or craft. Thus it became evident that such powwows are a modern phenomenon which bears no historical connection to the past, only a symbolic one. There was no need for them in the past, as there is in the present. They function to maintain ethnicity in the midst of a majority which is not Indian. Nothing rallies the expression of ethnicity like external threat.

Another implication of Handler and Linnekin's views that I might mention in passing is that chronological history itself is a reconstruction of the past and not a description of it. (I should stress that this view is implied in their work and not explicitly stated.) Again, this idea is not new to folklorists interested in oral history or folklife. I have heard it argued for years, but it does have serious implications for historians who have spent a disproportionate amount of time attempting to reconstruct the history of a minority of the populations they study, namely the political elite and ruling classes of humankind. Perhaps I oversimplify the process of writing history, but scholars in folklife studies, on the other hand, have attempted to reconstruct the social history of the masses.

Folklife scholars have also argued that the function of history as a discipline cannot be disconnected from other social and cultural pursuits of the society in which it exists. It is important for us as Westerners to have a view of the past in order to help place ourselves in the worldview of our present. What is important for us as human beings practicing our various specialties as members of our own society is to reconstruct our past in order to give meaning to our present, and we reconstruct that past in the context of the present. The reconstruction of Africa's past is a part of the larger framework of the Western view of history. It is possible to argue that an understanding of any society's past is always accomplished in a manner meaningful to that society. It is also possible to demonstrate that chronological history, which is a Western methodology, is not meaningful universally.

Before turning to the epic of Sun-Jata as a case study in which to argue these views of tradition and history, let me present one more set of ideas in an effort to understand how the set of constructs which we call tradition actually work. I am indebted to a colleague at Indiana University, Roger Janelli, for these ideas. In many ways, Janelli anticipated the conclusions that led Handler and Linnekin to write their later article. In a seminal piece in *Folklore Forum* in 1976, Janelli attempted to reconcile the older definition of tradition as a body of handed-down knowledge with some of the newer arguments from the performance-centered focus of the school of folkloristics which has come to be called *contextualism*.

If tradition is not an inherited body of knowledge in the real world, Janelli asks, "how is it . . . that we can recognize textual or plot stability over centuries if each folkloric performance is unique to the immediate context in which it occurs?" (1976:61). Janelli attempts to reconcile the question with two levels of causality, which operate to produce the final *tradita*, or products of tradition. He calls these levels the macro-level and the micro-level of tradition. Let me describe these levels using my own understanding of, and additions to, Janelli's view.

If tradition is a memory of the past which is passed on to the present, what is the nature of this memory? Jan Vansina has argued that tradition involves a mnemonic code which is largely a collective memory of a group in a chain of testimony from the past, and from which historicity can be isolated in oral tradition because "collective views of the world are slow to change" (1980:273). Joseph Miller's own theories place a heavy emphasis on this collective aspect of memory (1980:11). But in the real world, groups do not have memories; only individuals can have memories. While the argument from psychologists for a theory of a mnemonic code in human memory is defensible, a mnemonic code in a collective memory is not. What actually exists is a group of memories attempting to act collectively, but in reality renegotiating memory while being under the illusion that a collective body of lore exists. It is this illusion of collective memory that Janelli calls the macro-level of tradition.

As the collective body of learned behavior practiced by a group, the macro-level of tradition is thus a fiction. Groups can only practice tradition in its actual performance. So it is at the performance level, or micro-level, where tradition is really negotiated and acted out using the individual memories of its practitioners. Macro-level tradition is often argued as a reality by members of a group, which may call such a notion "tradition," or they may use other terms for it, like "our heritage." Such a notion is thought to be a reality because the practice of traditions also occurs in groups. Each time a tradition is practiced at the micro-level the memory of how it was done before plays a role, and the memory of how it is redone gets stored in the memories of its participants, and thus becomes a part of the macro-level fiction, which will potentially influence the next micro-level performance of the tradition.

One may note in passing that Richard Schechner (1985) has argued that it is not so much in performance that tradition is renegotiated, but in the rehearsal of performance.[7] But this view of performance is too narrow for many scholars who view the concept of performance in a sphere larger than the formal theatrical performance.

To return to the main point, ways of behaving in the past must be remembered by individuals, and even Vansina argues that such social interactions involving memory as courtroom testimony from separate witnesses of the same event can lead to considerable disagreement. I have observed members of my extended family interact in this very manner. Terrific arguments ensue concerning the chronology of events in their early lives during the Great Depression. Topics are forgotten, changed, sometimes agreed upon, but often argued about. It is my view that they are reinterpreted according to the needs of the present context in which the family finds itself.

To cite an example, a family member will take my grandmother to a department store where she will purchase 12 pairs of hose at a time. Her explanation is that at 86 years of age and unable to drive a car, she can't get to the store often enough. Other members of the family argue that her behavior is the result of the Depression. She buys in great numbers, they argue, because she remembers when she could not afford any at all.

To sum up, macro-level tradition is a fictive notion held by individual members of a group who think it to be the inherited body of lore which has been passed down from generation to generation by word of mouth or by imitation. Micro-level tradition is the symbolic social interaction of tradition at the performance level, in which memories of past performances of tradition are reconstructed and re-negotiated among the active bearers of tradition and their audiences. Schechner employs the term "restoration of behavior" for this act. For him, tradition may be seen as a process of restoring a remembered form of behavior to a contemporary shape, form, and meaning through the act of recreating it in a performance (or rehearsal). Working within a remembered "set of rules" or literary conventions, the individual (or group) recreates a tradition, but at the same time influences the various ways it will be remembered in the future.

With this view of tradition from folklorists and sociologists in mind, let me now turn to some of the views put forward by the oral historian Joseph Miller. Miller has argued that "the historian must approach the oral tradition as 'evidence,' whatever scholars in other disciplines choose to do with the same narratives," and he defines evidence as "something that bears witness to a vanished time because it has *survived unchanged* from then until the historian examines it" (1980:1). But according to the newer views of folkloristics, nothing survives unchanged in human behavior. If everything is reinterpreted in each succeeding performance, let alone in each succeeding generation, to conform to new contexts and social needs, then the very premise upon which this theory is built is faulty.

In another work, Miller has defined a structural device he calls a *cliché*. The concept of cliché has been known in folkloristics as a *motif* since the heyday of its first prominent school of thought, the historic-geographic, or Finnish School (or Method), which began in the last century. While he does not argue that all clichés are the same, Miller does argue that some clichés are encapsulations of actual historical events from the past. He further states in the introduction to his edited volume *The African Past Speaks*:

> It is therefore the cliché that each generation hands down to members of the next, who may remember it and use it even after it has become archaic and has lost its original meaning for those who continue to pass it on. The cliché at the center of the episode, not the detail of the narrative, is what may bear information from and about the past. [1980:10]

Such a notion concerning the nature of folklore was held in folkloristics in the nineteenth and early twentieth centuries: essentially, folklore was seen as composed of mindless survivals from the past with no contemporary function. The folk, it was thought, were incapable of creative behavior; they simply carried on oral tradition by repeating motifs and tale types from one generation to another without knowing what they meant or where they had come from in the distant past. Such a theory minimizes if not eliminates any creative ability in the raconteurs of oral tradition. If we are to adopt this theory, we come close to insulting the African bard's abilities. Transcription and translation of texts I have collected in Mali indicate the opposite case. Bards are very creative, and the manipulation of motifs and larger narrative segments, as well as linguistic word play and ideophones, within the constraints of what these bards conceive of as a macro-level set of literary conventions indicate extremely creative ability. The violation of the macro-level conventions is in fact one of the ways bards act creatively, some bards being better at composition than others.

Miller argues that variation is due to the fact that bards place a positive value on individual elaboration of historical clichés. He states that the analysis of variation is a strength the historian may use to understand historicity in oral tradition. But he does not really explain the methodology of how this is to be done. Folklorists view variation as a contemporary phenomenon, based not upon the interpretation of the past by epic bards, but the interpretation of the present. Contemporary regional relationships between clans, for example, are often described in the epic of Sun-Jata, but the variations one encounters are easily related to present-day clan relations. Different regions have different relations, which are reflected in epic performance. In my recent book, *The Epic of Son-Jara* (1986), I have called this phenomenon "Law by Parable." Let me cite an example.

The Dabò clan, which Gordon Innes (1974) describes as a *masalen*, or royal clan, in the Gambia, is a casted blacksmith clan in Kita, a city west of Bamakò, the capital of Mali. In one episode, Sun-Jata is insulted by a Dabò blacksmith, and in wrestling with him, Sun-Jata pulls the head of the Dabò clansman completely off his neck. The bard explains that *"a d'a bò,"* "he pulled it off." This episode is an etiological legend explaining the origin of the name Dabò. With what tool of the oral historian are we to look for historicity in this story? Mande people are very fond of linking etiological legends to folk etymologies of proper names in their society. The variation in these legends is due to local politics and social relations, and it is not easy to prove that they are reflections of historicity.

In conclusion, I should like to return to my original thesis, the contention that what Sun-Jata represents today remains easier to answer than who he may have been in the past. Sun-Jata is a culture hero. The epic which celebrates his memory constitutes a social and political charter of Mande culture, both reflective of their cosmology and participatory in its renegotiation of the past in the present. The evidence argues that events from the real life narrative of Sun-Jata as a person are not necessarily incorporated into the stereotyped plot of the contemporary epic which celebrates his life.

In the same region, there are other epics which carry similar structural traits, including the use of many of the same motifs (clichés) with other culture heroes. A cross-cultural view of other epics in West Africa outside the Mande regions gives similar results. Scholarship on European and Middle Eastern culture heroes dating back to von Hahn's famous treatise in 1836 lends further weight to arguments supporting the use of oral tradition in contemporary social functions.[8] Too much similarity recurs in too many epics concerning the culture hero to lend weight to the search for historicity in oral epic. Consequently, that these themes and motifs (Miller's clichés) are chosen for their literary value in structurally symbolizing worldview, as well as in simply telling a good story, rather than for their value in recording chronological history, is still as reasonable a conclusion now as it was some years ago when oral historians renewed their attempts to answer their critics in anthropology.

The problem the folklorist must face lies in the idea behind the phrase I used above: "events from the real life narrative of Sun-Jata as a person are not necessarily incorporated into the stereotyped plot of the contemporary epic." While arguments from performance-centered contextualist folkloristics today appear to me to be stronger that those of the research methods of the oral historian, time has a way in academics of bringing down theories in one generation of scholars that seemed so sound in another. While I remain an agnostic with regard to the search for historicity in oral tradition, I am not a heretic.

NOTES

[1]   An oral version of this essay was presented to the 29th annual meeting of the African Studies Association in Madison, Wisconsin, from 30 October to 2 November, 1986. The culture hero under discussion is Narè Magan Konatè, founder of the empire of Old Mali (the Manden) in the thirteenth century and better known by his contemporary praise-name Sun-Jata (Soundiata, Sundjata) Keita. For a complete background to this culture hero and the epic recited to his memory in modern West Africa, especially Mali, see Johnson, et al. (1986).

[2]   Shils' general approach to the concept of *tradition* is thoroughly discussed in his book *Tradition* (1981).

[3]   For a discussion of his approach to this subject, see Person (1973).

[4]   The conference concerned culture, tradition, and ethnicity and was held at Indiana University in March of 1984. It was part of a binational research collaboration initiated by the American Council of Learned Societies and the Hungarian Academy of Sciences. The proceedings of this conference appeared in the *Journal of Folklore Research* 21:2/3 (1984). I should also like to thank all my students and colleagues in the Folklore Institute and in other departments at Indiana University who have participated in my seminar on "The Concept of Tradition in Folkloristics."

[5]   For a discussion and summary of the history of the concept of primitiveness in social evolution in Western academics, see Kuper (1988).

[6]   For their somewhat radical but stimulating views, see Handler and Linnekin (1984).

[7]   See especially chapters two and three of Schechner (1985).

[8]   Von Hahn (1836) was followed by several famous books on the subject of the stereotyped culture hero, namely Nutt (1881), Raglan (1936), Rank (1909), Campbell (1949), and De Vries (1963).

REFERENCES CITED

Campbell, Joseph
    1973 [1949] *The Hero with a Thousand Faces*. Princeton: Princeton University Press.
De Vries, Jan
    1963 *Heroic Song and Heroic Legend*. London: Oxford University Press.
Hahn, Johann Georg Von
    1836 *Sagwissenschaftliche Studien*. Jena, Germany: F. Mauke.
Handler, Richard and Jocelyn Linnekin
    1984 Tradition, Genuine or Spurious. *Journal of American Folklore* 97: 273-90.
Innes, Gordon
    1974 *Sunjata: Three Mandinka Versions*. London: School of Oriental and African Studies, University of London.
Janelli, Roger L.
    1976 Toward a Reconciliation of Micro- and Macro-Level Analyses of Folklore. *Folklore Forum* 9(2):59-66.
Johnson, John William, et al.
    1986 *The Epic of Son-Jara: A West African Tradition*. Bloomington: Indiana University Press.
Kuper, Adam
    1988 *The Invention of Primitive Society: Transformations of an Illusion*. London: Routledge.
Miller, Joseph
    1980 Listening for the African Past. In his *The African Past Speaks: Essays on Oral Tradition and History*. Pp. 1-59. Hamden, Conn: Archon Books.
Nutt, Alfred
    1881 The Aryan Expulsion-and-Return Formula in the Folk and Heroic Tales of the Celts. *The Folklore Record* 4: 1-44.
Person, Yves
    1973 Oral Tradition and Chronology. In *French Perspectives in African Studies* Ed. by Pierre Alexandre. Pp. 204-20. London: Oxford University Press for the International African Institute.
[Proceedings of] Culture, Tradition, Identity Conference
    1984 *Journal of Folklore Research* 21(2/3). March 26-28.
Raglan, Lord Fitz Roy Richard
    1949 [1936] *The Hero: A Study in Tradition, Myth, and Drama*. London: Watts.
Rank, Otto
    1959 [1909] *The Myth of the Birth of the Hero*. New York: Vintage.
Schechner, Richard
    1985 *From Theater to Anthropology*. Philadelphia: University of Pennsylvania Press.
Shils, Edward
    1981 *Tradition*. Chicago: University of Chicago Press.
Vansina, Jan
    1980 Memory and Oral Tradition. In *The African Past Speaks: Essays on Oral Tradition and History*. Ed. by Joseph Miller. Pp. 262-79. Hamden, Conn: Archon Books.

Family Settlement Stories
and Personal Values

SANDRA DOLBY STAHL

*It is difficult for us today to accept
the fact that a family could consider a
house with but a single room and a loft
adequate to their needs.* Warren E. Roberts [1984]

In *Log Buildings of Southern Indiana*, Warren Roberts asserts that
in the pre-industrial era the majority of people in the expanding
Midwest lived in what he calls "The Basic Anglo-American House," a
single-room dwelling of log construction with an overhead loft
(Roberts 1984:179). He spends some time addressing the question of
why people find that such a difficult fact to accept today. He contends
that because of our contemporary taste and technical advances we
project our own preference for larger, multi-roomed homes onto the
early pioneers. We address their needs through a worldview tied to
the present rather than the past.

This same failure to account for a contemporary perspective
influencing the interpretation of folklore materials is even more
apparent in studies of personal or family narratives from an earlier
era. To illustrate this difference in perspective, let me present a brief
overview of some work I have initiated with regard to family stories
relating to settlement on the frontier. Studies of migration during
America's frontier settlement period show that for every family that
moved from a place of long settlement there was "an initial period in
which an isolated nuclear family pioneered in a new territory" (Adams
and Kasakoff 1984:35). What this suggests is that the experiences of
families in settling a new territory were likely to be remembered as

362

adventures, as tests of character, stories that illustrate the resource-fulness, strength, and courage that allowed these early settlers to survive and succeed despite their isolation from a supportive kinship system. Scholars who determine to collect and study such stories must ask first what motive keeps such stories alive within the families, and perhaps as well what triggers their demise.

In my initial research into this topic in Huntington County, Indiana, I have found that family settlement stories are not so common as I had supposed. Mody Boatright (1958) led the way in identifying this genre of folk narrative in the American context and spurring others on to collect and analyze such stories. Many of the themes Boatright identified in Texas are indeed common in Indiana as well, but they are to be found in printed sources from the 1930's and 1940's, not in the current repertoires of families, especially not among the younger family members who must assume "ownership" of the stories if they are to be passed on to the next generation.

In part this is due to the typical context in which such stories are told. Often the primary storyteller for family narratives is an older woman, and the stories are usually told at family gatherings. In such situations, younger family members are passive bearers; they are receivers; they tacitly acknowledge the older woman's "ownership" and authority. So long as the stories function solely as "family history," chances are good that the active repertoire will remain attached to the older authority figure with few occasions in which other family members assume an active storyteller role.

There are, however, exceptions to this pattern. One exception is the use of family stories as cautionary tales. Many of the "Caddy Buffers" described by Kathryn Morgan (1980) function as fables or parables to illustrate how a significant ancestor (Grandmother Caddy) behaved in a particular situation that is perceived by the teller to be analogous to a current problematic situation. Another exception, and one I would like to focus on in this essay, is the use of family stories in the more subtle practice of characterizing the family for a current generation.

Both of these uses of family narrative are quite different from the "purely" historical use often envisioned for such narratives. In other words, while family stories do sometimes serve to inform "the family" about how and when ancestors came to live where they did—i.e., straightforward historical information—they may also serve needs beyond that of history for its own sake. They may represent a kind of "emic presentism," a "native" interest in history for the sake of throwing light on current individual concerns, such as how to teach a sense of "family character."

Anthropological historian George Stocking (1968) is critical of contemporary historiographers who trace a discipline's history with an eye toward current concerns and especially the theoretical perspectives that happen to be in vogue. He feels such "presentism" cannot accurately account for the actual historical development of ideas but rather offer only rhetorical support for the researcher's current perspective. His criticism may be sound with regard to historians, but the effects of presentism may indeed be welcome if the "historians" are family storytellers. Such emic presentism recognizes the truth reflected in inaccurate narrative. As Kay Cothran (1972) suggests, it treats the lie as truth. Emic presentism turns historical narrative to blatantly non-historical ends.

As narratives, family settlement stories serve literary as well as historical goals. In fact, as folk narratives, such stories follow fairly predictable structural patterns even though the content of family stories is typically not indexed. Like personal narratives, local character anecdotes, and some personal legends, family stories may through their variability of content serve the storyteller's personal literary goal of "narrative value endorsement" (see Stahl 1988). That is, such stories endorse specific values by illustrating fundamental themes or character traits. And often the historical accuracy of the narrative is sacrificed for the sake of the more compelling requirement of a literary or psychological goal, a personal value asserted boldly in the face of a collectively held counter-value.

Consider for example the following story recorded from my mother, Loretta Dolby of Huntington, Indiana. Present when the story was recorded was my sister, Carol, and myself. The time period of the reported incident is approximately 1850.

> Mom: My great-grandfather. Yeah, my Grandmother Henricks's father and mother. They moved from Virginia to Illinois. And they came in a Conestoga wagon. My grandmother walked most of the way behind.
>
> Carol: Ach! Women's Lib take note!
>
> Mom: It would be her job to keep the cow or two in line that was following this old Conestoga wagon. But her father was stricken by lightning while he was sitting on this wagon—and died.
>
> Carol: Probably from making his wife walk behind!

Mom: And Grandma Knupp–Great-grandmother Knupp–had to take–go to where
they were going in Illinois. And they buried him there. Then she raised all of
her family then by herself. Never remarried. I don't know how she did it.

This story is effective as a dramatic statement about the hardiness
of the great-grandmother who had to bury her husband in a sparsely
populated wilderness and raise a family by herself in an Old Northwest
pioneer setting. The notion of being struck by lightning is both
dramatic and symbolic. There is, in fact, a relevant motif in the
Thompson index: A285.1 Lightning as Weapon of the Gods. Carol's
joking comment that the father was struck by lightning as punishment
for his mistreatment of his wife (actually it was his daughter who
walked behind) is in reference to this longstanding belief that God or
the gods punish mankind by sending lightning to strike them dead.

The story is effective and interesting, but it is also historically
inaccurate. Great-great grandfather Knupp was indeed struck by
lightning while riding on a wagon, and he did die. However, it was
not while he was driving the Conestoga wagon which brought them to
the Midwest. Instead he was killed some three years after they had
settled in central Indiana (not Illinois; the widowed wife moved there
later). While still in Indiana, Jacob Knupp (the father) loaded furniture onto a regular flatbed wagon drawn by two horses and was driving
it to his newly-wed daughter's new home when he was struck by lightning. The father and one horse were killed. The chest upon which
he was sitting was scarred by the lighning bolt. The chest remains in
the family as a momento.

I have this more accurate account (plus supportive records) from
distant relatives (my mother's cousins) who live nearer to the family
homestead in Illinois and are indeed the family which has the burned
chest in its possession. My mother has heard this "accurate version"
of the story, but in most instances, when inspired or called upon to
tell the story, she tells her own version represented by the text above.
Why does she stick with this "folklorized" version? I think it is
because her version more dramatically and thus more effectively serves
to characterize our family ancestor as a strong and courageous woman
who survived the trials of pioneering on her own, without the help of
a man. There are other stories that characterize the male ancestors
in the family, but this one serves to convey a strong female role
model.

My sister and I are the audience for the story. My mother is eager
to pass along a sense of family character, a message that women in our
family are strong, they endure. She is less interested in historical
accuracy. The "history" she wants us to learn is what personal values

are significant for her, and by extention, for our family, what kind of character our family has chosen to identify as its own. This is emic presentism. History is skewed to serve contemporary developmental concerns and ideas. And, it is history skewed by a particular individual, a "native" historian, the primary bearer of my family's history.

My question in this instance is, what kind of transformation has occurred? Is it a simple matter of folkloric process, the kind that has given us the great spread of naturally occurring variants? Is it, perhaps, an example of social transformation inspired by the pervasive sweep of feminism specifically in this case, or more generally, simply American individualism? Or, is it my mother's bold assertion of her own values, gained through a long and unique lifetime, and reflective of her own personal philosophy? Ultimately, of course, it is both—it is both social and personal, both collective and idiosyncratic. Social transformation cannot occur without personal transformation, and folklore cannot exist unless an individual interprets and presents it. Stories, songs, and houses change over time, but that change reflects not simply a change in collective culture but the assertion of individual values as well.

REFERENCES CITED

Adams, John W. and Alice Bee Kasakoff
    1984   Migration and the Family in Colonial New England: The View from Genealogies. *Journal of Family History* Spring: 24-42.
Boatright, Mody
    1958 *The Family Saga and Other Phases of American Folklore*. Urbana: University of Illinois Press.
Cothran, Kay
    1972 The Truth as a Lie—The Lie as Truth: A View of Oral History. *Journal of the Folklore Society of Greater Washington* 3: 3-6.
Morgan, Kathryn L.
    1980 *Children of Strangers: The Stories of a Black Family*. Philadelphia: Temple University Press.
Roberts, Warren E.
    1984 *Log Buildings of Southern Indiana*. Bloomington, Indiana: Trickster Press.
Stahl, Sandra Dolby
    1988   *Literary Folkloristics and the Personal Narrative*. Bloomington: Indiana University Press.
Stocking, George W., Jr.
    1968 *Race, Culture, and Evolution: Essays in the History of Anthropology*. New York: Free Press.

Jamie Tamson's Legacy

MARY ELLEN BROWN

"Willy Weir's Legacy"

Here is a true and faithfu' list,
An' not an article is miss'd,
O' the utensils, gudes, an' gear,
That did belang to Willie Weir.

He left twa horse, baith strong an' stout,
  An' Jessy his auld mare,
Three halters, each five ells about,
  And six gude hooks to shear.

An' sour-milk barrels twa or three,
  An' twa gude new milk-stoups,
An' dishes for their drinkin' tea,
  An' chairs to ha'd their doups.

Some ducks and geese to gang about,
  To gather worms and snails,
A pair o' fanners, auld but stout,
  An' three gude threshin' flails.

A pleugh he left, the grund to till,
  An' sythe the grass that maws,
A kist wad ha'd four bows o' meal,
  A gun to shoot the craws.

An auld black-fac'd, auld-fashion'd watch,
  A coal-rake an' a paidle,
An angle-net the trouts to catch,
  A flesh-fork an' a laidle.

Twa curlin' stanes he also had,
  That ran out o'er the ice,
A leather-whip, to thresh his yad,
  A box for ha'ding spice.

He also had a reddin' kame,
  To redd his wither'd lock,
A belt that buckled round his wame,
  Four gude sacks, an' a pock.

He also had a muckle coat,
  To had him dry when foul,
A bag for powder an' for shot,
  An auld Kilmarnock coul.

A cow he left, worth guineas five,
  An' trunchers mae than twa,
Twa gude new carts as ane cou'd drive,
  Likewise a rattan fa'.

He also had a rusty sword,
  Lay ay on the bed-head,
A gude wair cage, to ha'd a bird,
  A girdle for the bread.

He left twa kettles an' a pat,
  A pair o' clips, a cran,
Twa bonny kittens, an' a cat,
  And an auld master-can.

He also had a gude oak-stick,
  A brazen-headed cane,
Three needles that were unco quick,
  A bodkin made o' bane.

He also left to them an axe,
  Twa baskets, an' a wheel,
A pair o' tawse, to gie them paiks,
  For he cou'd use them weel.

A candlestick he also had,
  A lantern, an' a lamp,
A pair o' sunks, a ridin' pad,
  An' a strong badger stamp.

He left a hairy purse o' shag,
  O' Highland goat-skin leather,
Likewise a clyster-pipe an' bag,
  Made o' a grumphy's blather.

He left to them a colley-dog,
  That aften catch'd a hare,
A pet-ewe, market on the lug,
  Worth ten pound Scots an' mair.

He left to them a routin' horn,
  A pair o' brods an' bank,
A durk, ance by her nanesell worn,
  A table foot an' stalk.

Twa beds, an am'ry, an' a press,
  Made o' the best o' oak,
And an auld crackit looking-glass,
  A bittle, an' a knock.

A Holland gravit for his neck,
  A grape, a fork, a hoe,
A forpit-dish, a tatie-peck,
  A firlot, an' a row.

Twa cogs, a luggie, an' a cap,
  A pair o' cloutet shoon,
A parratch-stick, a mouse's trap,
  Sax cutties, an' a spoon.

O' blankets he had twa'r three pair,
  A' gayly worn wei daffin',
Twa tykes o' bed, sae thin an' bare,
  They scarce wad he'd the caff in.

A razor for to scrape his beard,
  A mell for knockin' bear,
A sturdy spade to delve the yard,
  A bridle for his mare.

Three pair o' buckles, twa o' brass,
  The third was made o' capper,
A 'bacco-box, that maist wad pass
  To've been a miller's happer.

He also had a knife and fork,
  Made o' the best o' steel,
A bottle-screw, to draw the cork,
  (That trade he liked weel.)

An' last o' a', a hecklin' kame,
  A pair o' gude tow-cards,
A mustard-pat I soudna name,
  Some said it was the laird's.
          [Thomson 1819:108-14]

When I first read the poetic inventory above, I thought immediately of Warren Roberts and his infectious and abiding interest in the "old traditional way of life." And I thought as well of literature as a source of data for reconstructing the past—"Willy Weir's Legacy" being the poetic equivalent of household inventories, probate records so often mined for knowledge of lives no longer lived. The author of this and other insightful pieces was a Scottish local poet, part of a literary tradition which emerged as a widespread phenomenon after literacy had become the norm, when print had become an accessible and cheap commodity—that is, mid- to late-eighteenth century. Building on earlier and simultaneous forms of literary expression—canonical, oral and local—the content of the poetry is, at least overtly, significantly local and limited, appealing to and written for a particular audience whose values and concerns shape the poetry. Thus, the local poet is a chronicler, often a barometer, of the community's events, concerns, values; and through poetry and song plays an integral role in the life of a locale or region. The local poet then is witness to and recorder of the round of life—hence the value of the poet and poetry to the study of folklife, as data for cultural history.

The local poet is a leisure-time poet, an artist by avocation. Often referred to as the poet of a locale such as "Methven poet" or "Paisley bard," the local poet is in some ways an unofficial poet laureate, the group's artistic voice. It follows that the local poet's work is usually conservative, adhering to the accepted and expected in form and content. James VI's interesting advice, "Ze man also bewarre with composing onything in the same manner as hes been ower oft vsit of before" (Henderson 1910:334), contradicts the implied aesthetic sensibility of the local poet and his poetic aims. The local poet suffers little if any "anxiety of influence" (Bloom 1973). Much of the poetry, whether narrative or lyric, deals with local events, places, characters, and attitudes known to and representative of the poet's loose-knit constituency.

Poet and audience share both physical and perceptual worlds: the poet and his artistry depend on the community. The poet's primary audience is local and known and the poet addresses it specifically. When removed from place and audience, the poetic voice may fail as it did for Robert Tannahill during his absence from Paisley and for William Thom, the Inverurie poet, when he went to London. While the local poet tradition is primarily a literate tradition, many songs and poems are communicated verbally and aurally rather than by silent reading, that is, they are recited from memory or read aloud from manuscript or print, performed in formal and informal groups for family or friends at home; in clubs, pubs, and bothies; at weddings and on other convivial occasions. Many works, no doubt, languish at this point; some few are picked up and widely circulated orally. Others reach print and sometimes wider audiences through magazines, newspapers, chap publications, anthologies, and editions of individual poets. The latter were often facilitated in the eighteenth and nineteenth centuries by a subscription taken prior to publication from among one's friends and family, in other words the local audience. A poet's work might then circulate orally, scribally, and typographically, and today, electronically.

Although a participatory, local, ephemeral movement flourishing in the nineteenth century, the local poet tradition was not *sui generis*. Rather the local poet took themes, content, form and style and borrowed compositional and socialization techniques as well as audiences from oral tradition. Literacy enabled the local poet to know and be influenced by the written literary tradition, to adapt forms, reflective compositional techniques, and, above all, to utilize an additional means of dissemination—print. The local poets then might be called the genuine heritors of what T. C. Smout has designated "a magnificent double heritage"—the ballad makers and the "markaris" of the court circle who gave "the Scottish tongue a literary force and sweetness" (Smout 1970:188). Taking aspects from both, the local poet tradition is a combination, perhaps a synthesis, precipitated by the age of print.   Beginning in the eighteenth century, thriving in the nineteenth, the tradition continues in attenuated form today.

The author of "Willy Weir's Legacy" was a typical local poet. Once compared to Burns, James Thomson the man and poet is today—unlike The National Poet of Scotland—largely forgotten. Born 10 September 1763 (died 6 May 1832), his appeal was confined to a place and a specific time largely because of the nature of his poetic endeavors: many of his poems refer to local characters, specific events, or were written as letters to friends and acquaintances. The audience was very local.   Currie Village and the surrounding area were suburbs of Edinburgh and during Thomson's life saw many changes—a move from an agricultural and cottage industry economy to a more industrialized economy with the establishment of several paper mills.[1]   Thomson himself stayed with the old ways, a cottage industry—as weaver; his occupational preference reflects a personal conservatism which also informed his poems and no doubt accounted for at least some of their success.   He was known and recognized as bard, the Kenleith Bard.

Thomson was born in 1763 in Edinburgh but shortly thereafter was sent to Currie to live with his grandparents, who really became the only parents he ever knew.   He attended the local school but a severe case of smallpox when he was seven kept him home for an extended period of time and effectively ended his formal education. His grandmother and an aunt filled the gap, teaching him what they knew.   During his early years, between seven and thirteen, Thomson was responsible for herding his grandfather's cows; with him he often took a book of songs or ballads—perhaps by Allan Ramsay or Robert Burns. The other herders sought him out for a poem or song.   But such pastoral pursuits ended when he was thirteen and was apprenticed to his grandfather, a weaver.   He really had no choice and began at that age his intended lifetime occupation.   He may well have attended school early in this period; accounts suggest, however, that if he did he was more concerned with making rhymes on his classmates than learning to spell.   Some time after the conclusion of his apprentice-ship, he moved to nearby Colinton, taking Elizabeth Burns as wife in 1787.   When his grandfather died, he returned to Currie; it was then that he came to the attention of Thomas Scott from the local Malleny estate. Perhaps Scott was taken, as some accounts suggest, with the poem Thomson had carved on a beam above his loom:

> A simple weaver at his loom,
> Wi' duddy coat and pooches toom,
> May hae as guid and honest hert
> As ony Laird in a' the pert. [Bertram n.d:2]

and persuaded the poet to part with it. At any rate, Scott more or less became Thomson's patron and provided him with a cottage and land in return for Thomson's taking on a supervisory role on the estate—keeping a general eye on things and letting farms; this freed Thomson from the economic necessity of weaving. Thomson paid tribute to Scott's role by dedicating one edition of his poetry to him. Weaver, steward—he was also bloodletter, barber, butcher; no doubt these various roles enabled him to know in considerable detail what was being done, by whom, and why—ideal information for a successful local poet. He and Elizabeth Burns had a large family: seven daughters, one named Fergusson after the poet Robert Fergusson, and one son who was killed—at fifteen—when he fell off a horse.

As local poet Thomson took advantage of his numerous roles, official and unofficial. In his Malleny Estate job he versified the rules governing hunting or coursing on General Thomas Scott's property:

> A' ye wha liberty hae got
> To course the lands o' General Scott,
> The following rules observe ilk ane,
> Or faith ye'll ne'er get leave again.
> I'm authorised, gentlemen,
> By my good laird, to let you ken.[2]

ending with the 7th:

> Three deaths we grant, nae mair, a-day,
> These are our laws, you must obey;
> And tho' ye think them rather hard,
> Ye manna gang to blame the Bard.[ibid]

As barber, he had occasion to sharpen the local minister's razors, returning them with a verse which led Reverend James Dick to encourage Thomson to publish his work:

> Your razors, man, were baugh indeed,
> An' they o' sharpin' had great need;
> But now, I think, they will come speed,
>   An' glegly rin,
> Sae, redd ye, billie, tak gude heed,
>   They slipna in.[3]

Early supporters of Thomson made clear that he did not shirk his other duties to write poetry—he wrote after work. Nonetheless, what he wrote was often congruent with his work and with other facets of his life. Many poems were specifically written as letters or notes: in a letter "To The Rev. Mr. D—" he complains about the substitute minister who *read* his sermon. "To a Confectioner" describes his daughter and asks the confectioner's aid in finding her a job. Clearly his poems served him well, specifically and generally. Visitors from the locality flocked to his house for evenings of tunes (he played the fiddle), recitations of his poems, songs, stories, and refreshments of whiskey and oat cakes.

Thomson's poetry is markedly free of overt allusion to literary works; he mentions Gray, Aesop's Fables, the Bible, Dr. Blair, Allan Ramsay and wrote one poem "On Meeting a Gentleman at the Gravestone of Mr. Robert Fergusson" and another "To the Memory of the Late Mr. Robert Burns." The poetic forms he employed, however, offer implicit evidence of the primary influences on his work, for the bulk of his poetry utilizes one or the other of two widely known poetic forms, Standard Habbie and the ballad stanza or modifications thereon, illustrating the dual influences of written and oral vernacular literary traditions.

Thomson's work may best be read as local history, as poetry recording aspects not only of the round of life but of the values and concerns shared by weavers and farmers/farm workers at the turn of the nineteenth century. Numerous poems are imbedded with maxims which no doubt reflect community views. In "On the Approach of Winter, Addressed to Mr. J. Comb," he says:

> There's ae thing sure, that die we must,
> All flesh is grass, and comes to dust;
> The hardest mettle will by rust
>   Consume away;
> The rocks are mouldering, crust by crust,
>   Into decay.[1819:39]

In another poem "Lines Addressed to a Miller, on seeing him torturing a rat," Thomson asserts:

> Our neighbor's fau'ts are often shewn
> Without attending to our own,
> Which if we did wi' candid e'e,
> Far less censorious would we be.[1819:42]

In a poem of advice to a young man choosing a wife, the lines below offer time-worn advice:

> Look whare ye'll light before ye loup,
> An' tyne not certainty for hope;
> For if ye do, like Aesop's colley,
> Too late ye will repent your folly.[4]

And in a poem urging shearers to do a good job at their work and masters to recognize that shearers are only human, he says:

> The gowden rule keep i your ee,
> "What ye wad ithers to you be,
> The very same to them do ye."[5]

He had the knack, then, of encapsulating in verse widely accepted views. Two other poems deserve mention because of their timeless reference. In a brief epigram Thomson suggests what many believed then and now:

> Ye Doctors, use your greatest care,
> Your patients' lives a while to spare;
> On this alone depends your wealth,—
> To keep alive, though not in health.[6]

And the lines written "On the Times, in 1799" might well have been written only yesterday:

> What will poor bodies do ava,
> For ev'ry thing's grown prices twa',
> The like o' this we never saw,
>   Or ever kent,
> They'll tak our very life awa'
>   Or e'er they stent.[1801:23]

The appeal of his works was undoubtedly based in part on their pithy articulation of a shared worldview. Other poems were well received because they described aspects of life—some local and some widespread—in delightful specificity. Whatever his subject, overt description played a part as in "Truth Rewarded" whose central character's literal and figurative undoing was at the hands of a woman:

> Undress's themsells, to bed they jumpit,

> And in a sea of pleasure plumpit,
> Too delicate, ye'll a' allow,
> To be describ'd in words to you;[1801:61]

but goes on, later adding a description of the couple's awakening and leave-taking:

> But first he snatch'd a morsel more,
> Then slipp'd her canny to the door.[ibid:62]

Several of his most appealing poems are catalogues, extended descriptions, as in "Willy Weir's Legacy." Thomson describes a local barmaid Marion Cunningham, now deceased. "On Raising and Selling the Dead" is virtually a journalistic account of an actual occurrence—the capture of body snatchers who had exhumed two bodies in Lanark and were on their way to Edinburgh to seek financial gain for their nocturnal activity. Other descriptions are less concrete: several poems are based on local beliefs—in witches and ghosts—and often mock those very beliefs while taking the gullible reader or hearer in by asserting the "truth" of the account as:

> There's mony lies an' stories tauld
> O' hares an' witches slee an' bauld
> But this I'm gaun to tell to you,
> As I'm alive, it's very true.[7]

In addition to the poems whose appeal lay in the maxims or truisms they contained or in their joyful descriptive play, other works no doubt appealed because of their surprise endings. "Willy Weir's Legacy" ends a descriptive catalogue of Willy's possessions by hinting that his tobacco box was really the miller's container, by alluding to Willy's love of drink, and by suggesting that the mustard pot be excluded: though among Willy's possessions, it belonged to the laird! Thomson adds a postscript to his poem lamenting the death of the barmaid Marion Cunningham, which advises against depression: a new Marion, every bit as good as the old one, has now taken her place. His short poem "To Mr. A—R R—E, A Friend of the Author" illustrates his penchant for twist conclusions:

> Sir, please receive thir twa three switches,
> They'll keep awa frae ye the witches,
> An' ither de'ils that may ye fright,
> Whan ye come dand'rin' hame ae night.
> Sic things my gude-dam tauld to me,
> How that a switch o' rowan tree,

Gars a' the de'ils and witches fyke;
But O I think it's befin like!
But should they fail in this, I say,
O' drivin' de'ils an' ghaists away,
You'll find them usefu' ay at least,
Apply them to a lazy beast. [1801:133]

Thomson communicated his work orally, in manuscript, and in pamphlet and book. The first and primary way was, undoubtedly, oral. George Maclaurin, the presumed author of the prefatory statement to the 1801 edition of his work, describes Thomson's compositional and socializing techniques: "As naebody could read what he wrote, he seldom was at the trouble to use the pen, but committed the effusions of his Muse to the tablets of his memory, which were never allowed to rust; for his companions, delighted with his simple strains, tired him with their importunities, and forced him to repeat them" (1801:v-vi). Later in the same piece, Maclaurin recounts Thomson's method of reciting his own works: "his pieces receive no little embellishment from the manner in which he repeats them, [as] he interests, as well as amuses, the hearer. He never refuses to rehearse his compositions when he is asked; he delivers them with that steady and unaltered voice which marks the honest simplicity of an independent mind" (ibid:ix). But Thomson was not limited to the oral means of communication. He certainly communicated in handwritten manuscripts: the letters and notes he wrote to friends, acquaintances, and business associates offer evidence. Other poems were passed from hand to hand, especially those which dealt with a timely event or described a local figure. Certain poems on topics with potential interest beyond the very immediate locality were printed in pamphlet form; two of these exist: "On Raising and Selling the Dead" and "Elegy to the Memory of the Reverend Mr. James Dick, Minister of Currie."

Publishing of books came after Thomson had established an audience and received encouragement from individuals above his own social, economic, and educational background and position. Two volumes, in 1801 and in 1819, were published by subscription; and both subscription lists, printed as per tradition in the volumes, contain names of persons from many social classes and include some of the worthies of the day. The 1801 volume contains over 600 names, the 1819 over 500.

Thomson reached his audience then orally, in manuscript, and in print: these three means of communicating enabled an expanding circle of potential audiences. The subscription lists represent the fullest extent of his audience, located in the greater Edinburgh area, and include individuals from various class and social divisions. The closer one lived to Thomson and the nearer in social status, the greater the chance of face-to-face encounter; the farther away, the greater the likelihood of printed communication. There is evidence that Thomson had a *very* vocal, very local fan club which visited him periodically, certainly yearly on his birthday. Called the Kent Club after the Kent or shepherd's crook they each carried in imitation of Thomson, they processed to his house behind a piper. Many other individuals came as well, both to show their esteem for his work and to hear him recite. He kept a Visitor's Book, signed by 1,500 persons by 1827, five years before his death. Thomson, then, had a following, was known and visited as poet.

He was obviously aware, too, that an audience mattered—whether he communicated orally or in writing. He could and did adjust his language depending on the subject of his poem or the social position of the intended addressee or audience: the higher up the class ladder an individual was, the more likely was Thomson to use English rather than Scots. His "Elegy" for Rev. Dick is in English, befitting a piece intended to recall a deceased minister to his fellow clergymen. A more couthy Scots vernacular dominates in letters to friends, in descriptions of farms. The force of oral communication and its demand for an audience undoubtedly influenced Thomson: he needed one too. The Dedication of the 1801 volume to the Merchants of Leith recognizes the role of the audience as necessary co-participants in artistic communication:

> Come, tell me, lads when you let slip
> Frae out your port a dainty ship,
> Dinna ye get a pilot stout,
> To guide her right, and steer her out?
> Sae should an author 'bout him look,
> For patrons to protect his book.[1801:xxi]

He got them; and for a span of twenty years or so at the beginning of the nineteenth century, Jamie Tamson—as he was familiarly known—had an audience. Perhaps he and his work have not been well-remembered beyond that time and place—despite the published editions—because his real audience was a primary one, based on face-to-face oral communication, a contemporary primary audience who could share both poetry and its reflection of local life as in the poem "To a Confectioner in Edinburgh, Requesting Him to Find a Place for one of The Author's Daughters"—a real letter, albeit in verse:

I'm taul'd you can, whene'er you please,
Find places wi' the greatest ease,
For servant-maids o' ilka station,
Wi' the brawest gentry in the nation.
A friend of mine requests your aid,
To find a lady wants a maid,
To mak' her duds, an' busk her braw,
Or lift her scissars when they fa';
To deck the head, an' plait the hair,
And every faded charm repair;
Or dext'rously supply with art,
That bloom which Nature failed t' impart;
Whiles smuggle a letter from her jo',
An many other things you know,
That wad be tedious here to mention;
Indeed, they're past my comprehension.

   Gif sic a place cannot be had,
Her neist resort's a chambermaid;
An' for the rest—eight pound's her fee,
An ither twa to find her tea;
For a' our lasses now-a-days,
They are bred up in siccan ways,
They maun hae tea, you neena doubt it,
Altho' their sarks be torn an' cloutit:
Should it be requisite for thee
To ken her eild, an' what she's wi'—
The Lassie's nearly twenty-one,
Nae doubt she's looking for a man;
Ilk maid that sees her time o' life,
Has ay a wish to be a wife,—
With Maxwell Gordon she's residing,
Four years wi' him she has been biding;
And that should help to recommend her,
To bodies wha hae never kend her.

   Now gif in this you'll favour me,
Your humble debtor I shall be;
And gif I e'er should hae to buy
A berry tart or apple-pie,
Or at the new-year, cake o' bread,
That's clad wi' sweeties on the head,
I'll come to you, ye needna fear,
I'll neither grudge nor ca' them dear;
But frankly put into your hand,
Whate'er in reason you demand:
But Oh! do try to serve my lasses!
          Your's,
                    Jamie Thomson,
                    At Parnassus.[1819:50-52]

His published works, of course, survive on library shelves[8] as data for reconstructing the life and art of his time and place. But there is another more public and persisting record of James Thomson, Bard of Kenleith, in place names: the standard Geographic Plan of Edinburgh shows five names in Currie which recall the Kenleith (now spelled Kinleith) Bard, although few people today know their significance. The name Kenleith was undoubtedly derived from the Kinleith Burn and the two adjacent farms (Easter Kinleith and Middle Kinleith). The map shows a Thomson Crescent, a Thomson Road, a Thomson Drive; more significantly, it marks his cottage with the name he gave it, Mt. Parnassus; and the portion of the burn behind and below his house is marked, "Poet's Glen." (See Fig. 2)   Today the Glen is overgrown and minimally accessible. While no fan clubs watch over the relics of the poet—his glen or cottage still inhabited *and* bearing over the main door its Thomson given name—there is a current local tradition which identifies a field enclosed with a dry stane dyke somewhat south and to the side of his cottage as the "Poet's Home," one place he went to write. Few remember his poetry because it was so tied to time and place, qualities which make the work of Thomson and other local poets ideal sources of data for folklife specialists—an artistic change of pace—Jamie Tamson's legacy to Warren and his ilk!

NOTES

[1]   I am particularly indebted to John Tweedie, Currie, for references to Thomson and for useful historical information.

[2]   From "Rules: To be observed by those who hunt or course on the property of General Thomas Scott of Malleny" (Thomson 1819:162-64).

[3]   From "To the Rev. Mr. J.D–K of Currie, on the Author's being employed by him to set his Razors" (Thomson 1801:137).

[4]   From "Advice to Young Men" (Thomson 1801:10).

[5]   From "To the Masters" (Thomson 1801:13).

[6]   From "Epigram" (Thomson 1801:45).

[7]   From "The Hare" (Thomson 1819:173).

[8]   In addition to Thomson's publications, their prefatory material, and an edition *Poems of James Thomson Weaver of Kenleith* (Langwill 1894), I have had the benefit of several other sources of information on Thomson, including Bertram *Currie Chronicle: Journal of the Currie District History Society* (March 1976); John Geddie (1896); the General

Register Office for Scotland; W.J.I. (1813); Catherine G. Peutherer (n.d.); James U. Thomson (1963, 1979); and John Tweedie and Cyril Jones (1975).

Research on Thomson and other local poets was made possible by the American Council of Learned Societies and the Institute for Advanced Studies in the Humanities, University of Edinburgh; I am grateful for their support.

REFERENCES CITED

Bertram, Tom
 n.d. James Thomson: The Weaver Poet of the Glen. Unpublished manuscript.
Bloom, Harold
 1973 *The Anxiety of Influence: A Theory of Poetry.* New York: Oxford.
Geddie, John
 1896 *The Water of Leith from Source to Sea.* Edinburgh: W.H. White.
Henderson, T.F.
 1910 *Scottish Vernacular Literature.* Edinburgh: John Grant.
Langwill, R.B. ed.
 1894 *Poems of James Thomson Weaver of Kenleith.* London: Archibald Constable.
Peutherer, Catherine G. ed.
 n.d. *History of Currie Village.* Currie: Scottish Women's Rural Institute.
The Scots Magazine
 1813 Biographical Sketch of Thomson, the Poet of Kenleith, with a desultory
    description of his celebrated Parnassus. 75: 645-48. (Signed by W.J.I.).
Smout, T.C.
 1970 *A History of the Scottish People 1560-1830.* (2nd Edition) London: Collins.
Thomson, James
 1801 *Poems, in the Scottish Dialect.* Edinburgh: J. Pillans; Leith: W. Reid.
 1819 *Poems, Chiefly in the Scottish Dialect.* Leith: William Reid.
Thomson, James U.
 1963 Pentland Poet. *Scotland's Magazine and Scottish Country Life* September:
    24-27.
 1979 Weaving with Words—the Village Poet. The *Evening News* 3 February:7.
Tweedie, John and Cyril Jones
 1975 *Our District: The Historical Background of Currie and Ratho Parishes.* Currie:
    District Council.

Figure 1. James Thomson.

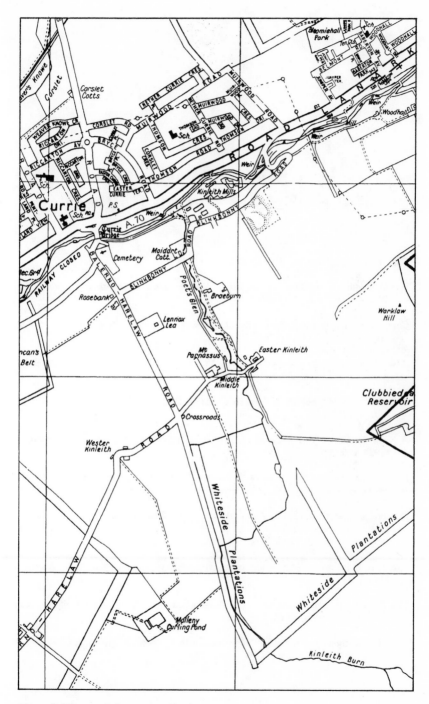

Figure 2. Thomson's home near Currie.

A Select Bibliography
of the Works of Warren E. Roberts

Children's Game Rhymes. *Hoosier Folklore* 8 (1949).

Spenser's Fable of the Oak and the Briar. *Southern Folklore Quarterly* 16 (1950): 150-54.

Comic Elements in the English Traditional Ballad. *Journal of the International Folk Music Council* 3 (1951): 76-80.

Addenda to *Studies in Cheremis Folklore*. Vol. 1 with Thomas A. Sebeok, Jonas Balys, and Archer Taylor. *Journal of American Folklore* 65 (1952): 167-77.

Some Folksong References in Kennedy's *Swallow Barn. Southern Folklore Quarterly* 17 (1953): 249-54.

A Norwegian Fairy Tale in Jamaica. *Arv, Tidskrift for Nordisk Folkminnesforskning* 10 (1954): 109-13.

Ballad Themes in the Fair Maid of the West. *Journal of American Folklore* 68 (1955): 19-23.

Folklore in the Novels of Thomas Deloney. In *Studies in Folklore in Honor of Distinguished Service Professor Stith Thompson*. Ed. W.E. Richmond. Bloomington: Indiana University Press, 1957, pp. 119-29.

The Special Forms of Aarne-Thompson Type 480 and Their Distribution. *Fabula* 1 (1957): 119-29.

The Folktale: A Symposium, with R.M.Dorson and H. Halpert. *Journal of American Folklore* 70 (1957): 49-65.

Die Märchenforschung seit dem Jahre 1945, with L. Röhrich and others. *Deutsches Jahrbuch für Volkskunde* 3 (1957): 494-514.

The Tale of the Kind and the Unkind Girls. Berlin: de Gruyter, 1958.

A Spaniolic-Jewish Version of 'Frau Holle'. In *Studies in Jewish and Biblical Folklore* Bloomington: Indiana University Folklore Series and Memoirs of the American Folklore Society, 1960, pp. 177-82.

Types of Indic Oral Tales: India, Pakistan, and Ceylon. With Stith Thompson, FFC 180, Helsinki, 1960.

Folklore in Norway: Addendum. *Journal of American Folklore* 74 (1961): 321-24. Reprinted in *Folklore Research Around the World.* Ed. by R.M.Dorson, Port Washington, N.Y.: Kennikat Press, 1973, pp. 35-38.

A Tale Type Index for India and Pakistan. In *Internationaler Kongress der Volkserzahlungsforscher in Kiel und Kopenhagen* Ed. by K. Ranke. Berlin: Vortrage und Referatte, 1961, pp. 338-40.

Two Welsh Gypsy and Norwegian Folktales. *Fabula* 4 (1961): 264-66.

Aarne-Thompson Type 577, 'The King's Tasks,' in Scandinavia. *Norveg* (Oslo), 9 (1962): 79-88.

Norwegian Folktale Studies: Some Aspects of Distribution. Studia Norvegica No. 13. Oslo, 1964.

Verrier Elwin (1902-1964). *Asian Folklore Studies* 23 (1964): 212-14.

Translation of G. Henningsen, 'The Art of Perpendicular Lying'. *Journal of the Folklore Institute* 2 (1965): 180-219.

'The Black and the White Bride,' Aa-Th 403, in Scandinavia. *Fabula* 8 (1965): 64-92.

Holbek on the Type Index: A Rejoinder. *Journal of the Folklore Institute* 3 (1965): 229-35.

Stith Thompson: His Major Works and a Bibliography. *Arv* 21 (1965): 5-20.

Translation of G. Henningsen, 'The Great Ship' and 'The Great Farmhouse,' AT 1960 H and E. *Journal of the Folklore Institute* 3 (1966): 50-69.

International Folktales Among the North American Indians. *Acta Ethnographia* 15 (1966): 161-66.

The Sheep Herder and the Rabbits. *Journal of the Folklore Institute* 3 (1966): 43-49.

The Making Modesty Pay Motif: Some Folktale Analogs of a Ballad. In *Volksüberlieferung: Festschrift für Kurt Ranke* F.Harkort et al, eds., Göttingen: Verlag Otto Schwarz, 1968, pp. 469-72.

The Waggoner Log House Near Paragon, Indiana. In *Forms Upon the Frontier* Ed. by Austin Fife, Alta Fife, and Henry Glassie. Utah State University Monograph Series, 16:2 (April 1969), pp. 28-30.

Fieldwork: Recording Material Culture. In *Folklore and Folklife: An Introduction* Ed. Richard M. Dorson. Chicago: University of Chicago Press, 1971, pp. 431-44.

Folk Architecture. In *Ibid*. pp. 281-94.

Folk Crafts. In *Ibid*. pp. 233-52.

Function in Folk Architecture. *Folklore Forum* Bibliographic and Special Series, No. 8 (1971), pp. 10-14.

Folk Architecture in Context: The Folk Museum. *Proceedings of the Pioneer America Society* 1 (1972):34-50.

Some Comments on Log Construction in Scandinavia and the United States. In *Folklore Today: A Festschrift for Richard Dorson*. Ed. by L. Dégh, F. Oinas, H. Glassie. Bloomington: Indiana University, 1976, pp. 437-50.

The Whitaker-Waggoner Log House from Morgan County, Indiana. In *American Folklife* Ed. Don Yoder. Austin: University of Texas Press, 1976, pp. 185-207.

Social Customs and Crafts: A Note. *Kentucky Folklore Record* 23 (1977):72-79.

The Tools Used in Building Log Houses in Indiana. *Pioneer America* 9 (1977):32-61. Reprinted in *Common Places: Readings in American Vernacular Architecture*. Ed. by Dell Upton and John M. Vlach. Athens: University of Georgia Press, 1986, pp. 182-203.

The Folklife Research Approach to Textiles, Indiana University Textile Conference, May 15-17, 1978. *The Preservation of Historic Textile and Costumes, Selected Papers*, pp. 1-9.

Tools on Tombstones: Some Indiana Examples. *Pioneer America* 10 (1978):106-11.

Wood Screws as an Aid to Dating Wooden Artifacts. *Chronicle of the Early American Industries Association* 31 (March 1978):14-16.

Were Tomatoes Considered Poisonous?. *Pioneer America* 11 (1979):112-13.

Word Origins and Tools. *Chronicle of the Early American Industries Association* 32 (Sept. 1979):46-47.

Drawer Joints and Forstner Bits. *Chronicle of the Early American Industries Association* 33 (March 1980):9.

Traditional Tools as Symbols: Some Examples from Indiana Tombstones. *Pioneer America* 12 (Feb. 1980):54-63.

Dieb und Tiger (AA-TH 177). *Enzyklopädie des Märchens* 3 (1981):644-46.

Hoosier, Yankee, and Yoho: Some Comments on Family Names in Indiana. *Kansas Quarterly* 13 (1981):73-82.

Turpin Chairs and the Turpin Family: Chairmaking in Southern Indiana. *Midwestern Journal of Language and Folklore* 7 (1981):57-106.

Ananias Hensel and his Furniture: Cabinetmaking in Southern Indiana. *Midwestern Journal of Language and Folklore* 9 (1983):67-122.

The Green Tree Hotel: A Problem in the Study of Ethnic Architecture. *Pioneer America* 15 (1983):105-12.

Indiana Plane Makers. *Ohio Toolbox* Issues 3 and 4, 1984.

Investigating the Tree-Stump Tombstone in Indiana. In *American Material Culture and Folklife* Ed. by Simon Bronner. Ann Arbor: UMI Research Press, 1984, pp. 135-45.

Log Buildings of Southern Indiana. Bloomington: Trickster Press, 1984.

Folklife and Traditional Material Culture: A Credo. *Material Culture* 17 (1985):89-95.

Tombstones in Scotland and Indiana. *Folk Life* 23 (1985):97-105.

Another American Example of a Turner's Tool. *Chronicle of the Early American Industries Association* 39 (June 1986):28.

Early Tool Inventories: Opportunities and Challenges. *Chronicle of the Early American Industries Association* 39 (Sept. 1986):40-44.

German American Log Buildings of Dubois County, Indiana. *Winterthur Portfolio* 21 (Winter 1986):265-75.

Planemaking in the United States: The Cartography of a Craft. *Material Culture* 18 (Fall 1986):167-85.

Viewpoints on Folklife: Looking at the Overlooked. Ann Arbor: UMI Research Press, 1988.

CONTRIBUTORS

Richard Bauman is Professor of Folklore and Chair of the Folklore Institute, Indiana University. He is a past editor of the *Journal of American Folklore*, and is internationally recognized for his work in folklore and semiotics, and linguistic and sociolinguistic approaches to verbal art. His book *Story, Performance, and Event: Contextual Studies of Oral Narrative* was awarded Second Prize for the 1987 Chicago Folklore Prize.

Olav Bø is a recently retired Professor of Folklore at Oslo University where he was Director of the Institute for Folklore Research. He has published numerous articles and books over the past 35 years, focusing primarily on Norwegian and Scandinavian folk tradition.

Christopher Bobbitt is a Ph.D. Candidate in the Folklore Institute, Indiana University. He is currently working on his dissertation, which is an examination of double-pen houses in Harrison County, Indiana.

Simon J. Bronner is Professor of Folklore and American Studies, and Coordinator of the American Studies Program at the Pennsylvania State University at Harrisburg. A past editor of *Material Culture*, he has published extensively on American folklore topics, including *American Folklore Studies: An Intellectual History*, a Centennial Publication of the American Folklore Society. He received his Ph.D. in Folklore in 1981 from Indiana University.

Mary Ellen Brown is Professor of Folklore in the Folklore Institute, and Director of the Women's Studies Program at Indiana University. She has written extensively on ballads, British folklore, folklore and women, and the relationship of folklore and literature, including the book *Burns and Tradition*.

Jan H. Brunvand is Professor of Folklore in the Department of English at the University of Utah. He received his Ph.D. in Folklore from Indiana University in 1961, and has since published widely on a variety of folklore topics, including a textbook now in its third edition, and numerous books, articles, and a nationally syndicated newspaper column on urban legends.

Thomas Carter is an architectural historian with the Utah Division of State History and teaches in the Graduate School of Architecture, University of Utah. He received his Ph.D. in Folklore from Indiana University in 1984. He has written a number of articles on folk architecture in the West, and has recently co-authored two books: one on vernacular architecture in Utah, and the other a cultural resource survey of a small Mormon cattle ranching region in the same state.

Linda Dégh is Distinguished Professor of Folklore at the Folklore Institute, Indiana University. She is an internationally recognized authority on folk narrative, European and Euro-American folk tradition, and is the author of numerous books and articles, including *Folktales and Society: Story-telling in a Hungarian Peasant Community*.

Harry Gammerdinger is a Folklorist at the Center for Southern Folklore in Memphis, Tennessee. He received his Ph.D. in Folklore in 1988 from the Folklore Institute, Indiana University, and has published widely on material culture and folklife topics, and the use of film and video in folklore studies.

Robert Georges is Professor of English and Folklore in the Folklore and Mythology Program at the University of California, Los Angeles. After receiving his Ph.D. in Folklore from Indiana University in 1964, he has gone on to publish widely in the field of folklore, writing about ethnic and immigrant folk tradition, the nature of storytelling and narrative, and problems involved in the fieldwork process.

Janet C. Gilmore received her Ph.D. in 1981 from the Folklore Institute, Indiana University. She currently works out of Mount Horeb, Wisconsin, as a free-lance folklorist and has recently published a book, *The World of the Oregon Fishboat*. Over the years she has been engaged in numerous maritime folklife projects, working on the Great Lakes, the Mississippi River, the Oregon Coast, and Puget Sound.

Henry Glassie is College Professor of Folklore at the Folklore Institute, Indiana University. Throughout his distinguished career he has published voluminously on a broad range of topics, most notably on material culture studies and Irish and American folk culture. He is currently President of the American Folklore Society.

Christine Goldberg received her Ph.D. in 1981 from the Folklore Institute, Indiana University. Currently residing in Los Angeles, she specializes in folk narrative, and has recently published an article in the *Journal of Folklore Research* on "The Construction of Folktales."

Phyllis Harrison is Director of the Puget Celebration Project, conducted through the Institute of the NorthAmerican West. In 1983 she received her Ph.D. from the Folklore Institute, Indiana University, and has since worked on various public sector folklife projects. She has written on such diverse topics as Brazilian social behavior and country auctions as symbolic interaction.

John Wm. Johnson is Associate Professor of Folklore in the Folklore Institute, Indiana University. In 1978 he received his Ph.D. in Folklore from Indiana University, and has since written extensively on African folklore, folklore and popular culture, and especially the folk epic, including the recent book *The Epic of Son-Jara: A West African Tradition*.

Deborah Phillips King is the Cartographic Supervisor and a faculty member in the Department of Geography at The University of Akron. She is currently pursuing a Ph.D. in education at The University of Akron, and is focusing upon geographic education issues.

Jens Lund is State Folklorist and Director of Folklife Programs for the Washington State Folklife Council. In 1983 he received his Ph.D. from the Folklore Institute, Indiana University. He has been involved in numerous public sector folklife projects throughout the United States, taught classes at both Indiana University and the University of Washington, and published widely on folk music, occupational folklife, and regional culture.

W.K. McNeil is Folklorist at the Ozark Folk Center, Mountain View, Arkansas. He received his Ph.D. in 1980 from the Folklore Institute, Indiana University, and has since published extensively on the regional folk culture of the American South, folk music, and folklore historiography. He is editor of the forthcoming *Appalachian Images in Folk and Popular Culture.*

Howard W. Marshall is Director and Associate Professor of Art History in the Missouri Cultural Heritage Center, the University of Missouri. He received his Ph.D. in 1976 from the Folklore Institute, Indiana University. While his publication credits include works on cowboy life in Northern Nevada, he has long specialized in the material and regional folk culture of the American South and Midwest, and has written the book *Folk Architecture in Little Dixie: A Regional Culture in Missouri.*

Lynwood Montell is Professor of Folk Studies and Coordinator of Programs in Folk Studies at Western Kentucky University. He received his Ph.D. from the Folklore Institute, Indiana University, in 1964. His interests in the relationship between history and folk tradition, and the regional culture of Kentucky have led to numerous publications, including *The Saga of Coe Ridge* and *Killings: Folk Justice in the Upper South.*

Alice M. Mordoh received her Ph.D. in 1986 from the Folklore Institute, Indiana University. Her dissertation was a folklife study of a displaced community in South-Central Indiana, and she has published articles in *Indiana Folklore* and *The Children's Literature Association Quarterly.*

Allen G. Noble is Professor of Geography and Chair of the Geography Department at the University of Akron, Ohio. He is a prominent figure in American cultural geography studies today, and has published extensively, including the monumental *Wood, Brick and Stone: The North American Settlement Landscape.*

W. Edson Richmond is Professor Emeritus of English and Folklore at Indiana University. Over the course of his long and distinguished career he has served on numerous editorial boards, received many honors and awards, and achieved international recognition for his work on medieval and comparative literature, with a particular emphasis on ballads and Scandinavia.

J. Sanford Rikoon is a Research Associate in Rural Sociology at the University of Missouri. In 1986 he received his Ph.D. from the Folklore Institute, Indiana University. He has written or co-edited numerous articles and books on folklore and history, ethnicity, and American material culture, including *Threshing in the Midwest, 1820-1940: A Study of Traditional Culture and Technological Change.*

George H. Schoemaker is a Ph.D. Student at the Folklore Institute, Indiana University. He is currently co-editor of *Folklore Forum*, and has published in *Material Culture* and *Northwest Folklore.*

Sandra K. Dolby Stahl is Associate Professor of Folklore in the Folklore Institute, Indiana University, where she received her Ph.D. in 1975. Her interests in American folklore, folklore and literary theory, and the personal experience narrative have led to numerous publications including the recently published book *Literary Folkloristics and the Personal Narrative.*

Beverly J. Stoeltje is Associate Professor of Folklore in the Folklore Institute, Indiana University. After receiving her Ph.D. from the University of Texas-Austin, she has gone on to publish widely in such journals as *Western Folklore, Journal of Folklore Research,* and *Journal of American Folklore.* Her work focuses on such topics as ritual and festival, women and folklore, semiotics, and African and American folklore.

John Michael Vlach is Professor and Director of the Folklife Program at The George Washington University. In 1975 he received his Ph.D. from the Folklore Institute, Indiana University, and since that time has become a prominent scholar in American folklife studies. He has published extensively, with a particular emphasis on African and Afro-American folk tradition. He is the author of the recently published *Plain Painters.*

Robert E. Walls is a a Ph.D. student in the Folklore Institute, Indiana University. He is a past editor of *Folklore Forum*, and has written a book, *Bibliography of Washington State Folklore and Folklife.*

William H. Wiggins is Associate Professor of Afro-American Studies and a Fellow of the Folklore Institute at Indiana University. He received his Ph.D. in 1974 from the Folklore Institute, and has gone on to publish extensively on Afro-American folk tradition. His book *O Freedom! Afro-American Emancipation Celebrations* was recently awarded Honorable Mention for the Chicago Folklore Prize.